Norm Research in International Relations

Series Editor

Antje Wiener, Institut für Politikwissenschaft, University of Hamburg, Hamburg, Germany

This book series offers an outlet for interdisciplinary research on norms in the context of international relations and global governance. It features scientific and scholarly studies which examine the way norms are created and re-created through interactions between actors at the international level, taking into account the reflexive nature of governance relationships and their impact on state behaviour through the re-constitution of norms.

Norms in international relations are defined as ideas of varying degrees of abstraction and specification that concern fundamental values, organising principles or standardised procedures. They resonate across states and global actors in the form of official policies, laws, treaties and agreements, while their meaning may be stable or contested.

Norm Research in International Relations (NRIR) welcomes proposals for research monographs, edited volumes and handbooks from a variety of disciplines that seek to advance theories and applied research in international relations and to arrive at a better understanding of the role and impact of norms. Relevant topics include, but are not limited to, issues of international justice, research on contestation, human rights, international treaties in areas such as energy, environment or security, and constructivist norm research in international relations theory, recognition theory and international law.

More information about this series at http://www.springer.com/series/15646

Carmen Wunderlich

Rogue States as Norm Entrepreneurs

Black Sheep or Sheep in Wolves' Clothing?

Springer

Carmen Wunderlich
Institute of Political Science
University of Duisburg-Essen
Duisburg, Germany

ISSN 2522-8676 ISSN 2522-8684 (electronic)
Norm Research in International Relations
ISBN 978-3-030-27989-9 ISBN 978-3-030-27990-5 (eBook)
https://doi.org/10.1007/978-3-030-27990-5

This Springer imprint is published by the registered company Springer Nature Switzerland AG
The registered company address is: Gewerbestrasse 11, 6330 Cham, Switzerland

Foreword

This book is refreshing because its approach is counterintuitive. It looks at the despised group of international outlaws or "rogue states" as they are called with their US label from an unusual perspective: What do we see when the lens through which we look presents the "rogue" as a norm entrepreneur that aims not at chaos and disorder, but at a different form of order (maybe one which we would like distinctly, but order anyway). This approach (that must by no means be confused with propagating sympathy with the "rogue") aims at an enhancement of the debate on norms in the study of international relations. Taking a critical view at the partially silent, partially open ethical basis of most norm research (norms are "good," and norm entrepreneurs must be "good guys"), she proposes to look at "rogues" as "norm revisionists." Based on a careful and meticulous research design and much empirical effort, the book investigates whether Iran behaves like a norm entrepreneur of sorts. Thus, it tackles a "hard case," looking at the archetype of a US-designated "rogue" for forty years, which is fully back in this role those days after a brief interim thaw between 2015—when the nuclear agreement was adopted —and the start of the Trump presidency.

Based on her solid empirical work, she answers her research question in a quite surprising manner: Yes, Iran acts in many respects like a norm entrepreneur, and the Islamic Republic does not even site at the most radical wing of oppositional norm entrepreneurship. Rather, it ranges between the type "reformer" and "revolutionary." Our knowledge about norms and norm entrepreneurs in international relations has been considerably enriched by this study. Moreover, Carmen Wunderlich develops operational criteria for indicating "norm entrepreneurship," a typology of modes of behavior toward norms, and an operational distinction between "reformist" and "revolutionary" norm entrepreneurs that are of great utility as instruments for future empirical norm research.

The book contains many details worth to be known about one of the most disputed and at the same time most active members of the world of states, the Islamic Republic of Iran. The author deals with this tricky subject with a sovereign neutrality, but never uncritically, observing a reasonable distance between herself and the object of her study. This makes her results and the knowledge she transfers on her readers all the more reliable.

Carmen Wunderlich is one of the rising younger members of Germany's International Relations community and already well established in the international research community dealing with norms at the conceptual–theoretical and the proliferation of mass destruction weapons at the empirical and political level. Her first monography in English language, based on her Ph.D. thesis, makes a significant contribution, theoretically, empirically, and for political–practical purposes.

Frankfurt, Germany Harald Müller

Acknowledgements

Writing a book is always a challenge, and translating and updating it are even more so. I was blissfully unaware of this, when Antje Wiener encouraged me to publish an English version of my dissertation in her promising series "Norm Research in International Relations," published with Springer International. In fact, I felt flattered that she perceived my argument to hold innovative strength and I thought this a good opportunity to present it in all its details to an English-speaking audience. This book is the revised version of my dissertation that has been published in German in 2017. I am grateful to Springer VS for granting the English translation rights.

Along the journey of writing the dissertation, turning it into a book and working out an English translation, I was lucky to having received the support of several individuals and institutions. It is thanks to Tanja Brühl that I got introduced into the research on norm dynamics during my studies in Frankfurt, and it was Harald Müller who led me the way into academia. Harald was to become not only my mentor, sharing his time and wisdom and opening up invaluable networks, but also one of my dissertation supervisors. To the other, Nicole Deitelhoff, I owe no less gratitude for it was her encouragement and support that guided me through the last, troublesome meters.

While working on my Ph.D. thesis, I have benefitted from the generosity of several institutions that provided institutional and financial support, and of colleagues who shared their critical thoughts and offered helpful comments on drafts. The Peace Research Institute Frankfurt (PRIF) was to become my intellectual breeding ground that sparked my scientific interest in counterintuitive and unorthodox questions related to the research on global norm dynamics and norms pertaining to the control of weapons of mass destruction. The project group on "international dissidence" made it possible to further act out my liking for analyzing global troublemakers, and in this context I benefitted enormously from the intellectual charisma of Klaus-Dieter Wolf. Numerous other colleagues at PRIF were a source of great support, be it through providing invaluable comments to drafts of the manuscripts, sharing the "sorrows" of a Ph.D. student's life or by becoming dear friends over the years.

In addition, I was fortunate to having had the opportunity to further expand my academic focus through research stays at the Vienna Center for Disarmament and Non-Proliferation (VCDNP) in 2012 and the Berlin Social Science Center (WZB) in 2014. The Anna Lindh Library at the Swedish National Defense College and the Swedish Government Offices archive provided temporary shelter (and scanning devices!) during field research in Sweden. Numerous interview partners and witnesses of the past were willing to share their knowledge and memories, thus enabling me to validate and assess the information obtained through "mere" documentary analysis. I am most thankful for their support.

In January 2018, I joined the Peace Research Center Prague and profited enormously from the vibrant intellectual environment and interdisciplinary focus of the participating scholars. I am indebted to Charles University Research Centre program UNCE/HUM/028 (Peace Research Center Prague/Faculty of Social Sciences) for providing me with financial support.

During the time I worked on my thesis, I was given the chance to present parts of this work at various conferences. I am grateful for the helpful comments I received at these events and during personal conversations with colleagues. Besides those that have already been mentioned, these include Evgeniya Bakalova, Ann-Kristin Beinlich, Alan Bloomfield, Clifford Bob, Lyndon Burford, Marco Fey, Sassan Gholiagha, Regina Heller, Stefanie Herr, Andreas Jacobs, Konstanze Jüngling, Gregor Hofmann, Jeffrey S. Lantis, Daniel Müller, Michal Onderco, Carsten Rauch, Scott Sagan, Richard Price, Maria Rost Rublee, Michal Smetana, Elena Sokova, Nikolai Sokov, Nina Tannenwald, Alexandros Tokhi, Wolfgang Wagner, Irene Weipert-Fenner, Rachel Whitlark, Antje Wiener, Simone Wisotzki, members of the DVPW Thematic Group "Norms in International Relations," and the members of PRIF's colloquium of doctoral students. Katharina Hemming, Hiwa Rostami, Steffen Schiklenk, Matthias Schulze, and Manjana Sold provided valuable research assistance. For invaluable, interdisciplinary mental support, I would like to thank my SciMento group, Simone Claar, Melanie Sachs, Claudia Schreider, and Ursula Birsl. Without the meticulous work and tireless effort of Nadine Benedix, this book would never have taken shape. I am much obliged to her for her support in translating and editing the final manuscript. My thanks also go to Anna Güttel-Bellert for language editing the whole manuscript and for providing words of encouragement and support. Finally, I owe special thanks to Johannes Glaeser, Publishing Editor from Springer-Verlag, for his unwavering patience and assistance in publishing this book.

Last but not least, I would like to thank my family and friends: my parents and my sister for their unswerving belief in me, my husband Florian for his unwavering support and for keeping me sane, and my son Joshua for taming my perfectionism and involving me in welcome distractions.

While numerous people have been involved in the writing of this book, any remaining errors are, of course, my own responsibility.

Bonn, Germany
May 2019

Carmen Wunderlich

Contents

Chapter 1
Introduction: Norm Breakers as Norm Makers?

> The 'bad guys' [...] also know quite a lot about norm creation. Human-rights advocates and scholars who study norms are fond of using the term 'norm entrepreneurs' to describe people such as Gandhi, Nelson Mandela, and Mother Teresa. The term is not ill-used; all of these people managed to persuade quite a lot of other people to alter some of their most deeply held beliefs. But if Mandela is a norm entrepreneur, so is Osama bin Laden, and so are the planners of Palestinian suicide bombings. So was Slobodan Milosevic, and so were the Hutu leaders [...] who succeeded in dramatically shifting the normative commitments of several million Rwandan Hutus [...]. Hitler, too, was a norm entrepreneur, a chillingly successful one. (Ehrenreich Brooks 2003: 2326–2327)

The above quote may at first cause discomfort, incomprehension or even dismay among readers: Isn't the concept of "norm entrepreneur" usually used to describe do-gooders and principled actors who have devoted themselves to working for the civilization of humanity? Such an understanding is at least conveyed by mainstream liberal-constructivist research on norm dynamics in International Relations (IR). Constructivist explanations on the diffusion and change of norms draw as much on structural level explanations as they emphasize agency-related factors. In these models, transnational and local actors—so-called norm entrepreneurs—proactively advocate new ideas or norms which they deem necessary to solve current problems and thus to further develop the current normative order (e.g., Florini 1996; Finnemore and Sikkink 1998; Keck and Sikkink 1998).

So far, norm scholars have used the concept of norm entrepreneurship in a rather unsystematic and one-sided way. For a long time, empirical norm studies were confined to analyzing the norm entrepreneurial activities of prototypical liberal and Western norm entrepreneurs dedicated to the genesis and diffusion of (in their view) supposedly "positive"[1] or morally desirable norms. These were usually derived from the same cultural contexts and aimed to reproduce or to gradually reform the prevailing normative order in the direction of improvement.

[1] Due to its implicit normative connotation, the attribution as "positive" or "negative" is always subjective and is thus closely connected with the perspective of the beholder. This fact will be taken into account in the further course of the work.

C. Wunderlich, *Rogue States as Norm Entrepreneurs*,
Norm Research in International Relations,
https://doi.org/10.1007/978-3-030-27990-5_1

This liberal bias has been challenged and overcome by more recent—critical constructivist—approaches to norms which highlight the contested nature and dual quality of norms as both structuring and constructed through social interaction (seminal Wiener 2004, 2007). Rather than analyzing how fixed norms are diffused to normalize the behavior of deviant actors, such approaches are interested in bottom-up processes of norm construction and negotiation taking into account non-Western, non-state centric perspectives (e.g., Acharya 2004, 2011; Wiener 2004, 2018a, b; Adamson 2005; Bettiza and Dionigi 2014; Hofius et al. 2014). Others have pointed toward the existence of "bad norm dynamics" (Heller et al. 2012) and the role of norm challengers (Heller and Kahl 2013) or antipreneurs (Bloomfield 2016) in undermining normative structures through opposing behavior and/or discursive contestation.

Still, and quite puzzling, many liberal-constructivist norm researchers stick with a rather positivist understanding of norm diffusion and norm entrepreneurship (compare, e.g., the literature on norm robustness, Deitelhoff and Zimmermann 2019). This has not gone unnoticed within the camp of liberal norm scholars themselves. In 2012, Jeffrey Checkel complained about "a tendency to view norm entrepreneurs as heroes, always out to make the world a better place" and concluded "the failure to address norm entrepreneurship of a less feel-good sort is worrying" (Checkel 2012: 3). In fact, such a limited view not only equates norm diffusion with the universal spread of Western liberal ideas about what a normative order should ideally look like. The selection bias also entails further analytical constraints, particularly with regard to the identified instruments used by norm entrepreneurs to achieve their objectives. As Checkel critically observes:

> The typical answer in the literature is that entrepreneurs promote new norms by cajoling, persuading, or by the force of their own moral legitimacy. Is norm creation really always and only such a nice affair? (Checkel 2012: 3)

Critical constructivist and poststructuralist works on norm dynamics have demonstrated that normative structures of meaning-in-use rely on interactive bottom-up processes of social construction rather than unidirectional top-down directives (Wiener 2004, 2008; Towns 2012; Widmaier and Park 2012). In fact, scholars argue that norm contestation is the engine driving norm dynamics (Wiener 2014; Müller and Wunderlich 2018) and that actors are always involved in disputes over normative meaning with rival norm entrepreneurs or try to counteract their efforts (e.g., Bob 2012; Heller et al. 2012; Bloomfield 2016).

To sum up, despite some notable effort of critical norm scholars, the liberal-constructivist literature on norms still applies a narrow approach to norm diffusion within the wider liberal world order focusing on Western liberal actors and dismissing a more nuanced and flexible understanding of norms as contested by nature. As a corollary, norm entrepreneurs are stylized as "forces for the good" spreading Western liberal norms universally. Moreover, there is a tendency to dismiss opposition to and contestation of the current (normative) order as mere hostility to norms. This can be clearly seen in the case of so-called "rogue states"[2]—a heterogeneous group of states

[2] I use quotation marks to illustrate the constructed character of the label.

that is perceived as a threat to world peace and international security and therefore stigmatized by reference to this term. The labeling as a "rogue" does not constitute an objective category to identify states that have committed violations of certain international norms (Nincic 2005: 18). Rather, the "rogue state" label constitutes an ascription (mainly used by the USA) (Wunderlich 2017), a tag that became popular in the second half of the 1990s, and that primarily helped the USA to make certain policies acceptable and to maintain the current status quo (Klare 1995; Hoyt 2000: 307–309).

If we take a closer look at the statements of the stigmatized actors, we can see that they primarily challenge the hegemony of a few states and the liberal structure of the international system as shaped by them. Stigmatization assigns "rogue states" the role of outsiders in the international system of states. They are not recognized as legitimate promoters of alternative concepts of order (e.g., Lake 1994: 45; Litwak 2012: Chap. 1) and thus denied agency. Scholarly accounts on the "rogue state" concept mostly focus on its selective and inconsistent usage (e.g., George 1993; Litwak 2000; Caprioli and Trumbore 2005) and are empirically limited to tracing the deviant behavior of such states (e.g., Litwak 2000; Geldenhuys 2004; Nincic 2005). This view of presumed "rogue states" as being merely norm breakers is also shared by liberal-constructivist norm researchers (e.g., Wendt 1998: 113; Flockhart 2004: 367) who either view them as objects of normative education, addressees of socializing campaigns or norm enforcement and thus as counterparts or even antagonists of norm entrepreneurs (Müller 2011: 72–73). The extent to which "rogue states" act in a manner that is driven by normative considerations and which normative visions of order they advocate, has rarely been the subject of research (for exceptions, see Pirseyedi 2013; Wunderlich et al. 2013, Wunderlich 2014, 2017; Jacobi et al. 2014). As a top-down construction, the concept primarily serves to stabilize a narrative contrasting a Global North following reputable liberal norms with a Global South which is increasingly characterized by "rogues" or "failed states" seeking to destroy the liberal world order.

1.1 The Argument: "Rogue States" as Norm Entrepreneurs

This book applies a critical constructivist approach to norms and seeks to critically engage with the narrow perspective on norm diffusion taken by liberal norm scholars. It does so by drawing on recent approaches which emphasize norm construction processes that take as a starting point the contestedness of norms and the diversity of stakeholders included in norm negotiation and diffusion processes. In practice, I seek to overcome two biases: The narrow focus of liberal norm studies on Western liberal norm entrepreneurs on the one hand as well as the tendency to dismiss criticism directed toward the current (liberal) normative order as hostility, e.g., by labeling said actors as "rogue states," on the other. While the notion of "rogue states" does not fit well with a critical constructivist approach, I use the pejorative label for case selection only—as will become clear in the remainder of this book, I propose to refuse the usage of this and similar stigmatizing concepts as top-down constructions serving to stabilize dichotomous identities and discourses.

Against the background of and thus challenging liberal norm studies, in this book I examine countries labeled as "rogue states" and seek to critically explore their strategies of norm advocacy. Can their practices also be considered as norm entrepreneurship? How are these different from the activities of prototypical Western liberal norm entrepreneurs? What are the implications? Do the norms propagated by countries stigmatized as "rogue states" essentially differ from those promoted by Western liberal actors?[3] Are these alternatives to prevailing normative scripts or are presumed "rogue states" also concerned with promoting norms that support the current normative order?

The empirical analysis therefore begins with reconstructing the normative concepts of order advocated by a country that has been labeled "rogue state" with quite some fervor by the USA and with an assessment of how these notions relate to the ruling order. Subsequently, I will investigate whether the policy of the state in question includes elements of norm entrepreneurship. Naturally, it is not my intention to exculpate states that are guilty of fundamental human rights violations and other (internal) political and international law abuses. Nevertheless, I contend that norm scholars miss important insights if they ignore alternative normative meanings as well as the actors propagating them. The assumption that supposed "rogue states" primarily aim to destroy international norms seems worth to be investigated empirically. It might be possible that behind the hostile attitude there is a serious attempt to establish (alternative) norms or to promote normative meanings that fundamentally deviate from the prevailing liberal perspective.

With such a change of view I would like to gain the following insights:

Firstly, by taking an analytical view of "rogue states" as norm entrepreneurs, it is possible to show the limitations that liberal-constructivist norm research accepts due to its restricted case selection. In addition, this change of perspective contributes to further theoretical and conceptual developments as the findings show that the exclusive focus on Western liberal norm entrepreneurs obscures insights into the contested nature of norm dynamics, such as the role of so-called norm challengers in norm construction and norm diffusion processes, the particular practices of contestation that they employ as well as causes of the success or failure of norm advocacy.

Secondly, addressing the norm entrepreneurial potential of presumed "rogue states" makes it possible to once again reveal the constructed nature of this category and to overcome the usual representation of states labeled so as objects of hegemonic intervention. Rather, the question can be raised as to whether they really are pure norm breakers, as postulated by the concept. Or is authentic norm entrepreneurship obscured by their obstructive behavior? Such a counterintuitive approach calls into question not only the use of the "rogue" label itself. It also allows the analytical

[3] In accordance with the prevailing definition of norm entrepreneurs other "unorthodox" non-state norm advocates are conceivable, such as the Mafia or transnational terrorist networks like al-Qaeda. In this book, I focus on states whose norm entrepreneurial potential has become a focus of research over recent years.

inclusion of possible counter-hegemonic notions of how the normative order should look like. The knowledge gained in this work can thus be fruitful even beyond norm research.

Thirdly, the findings of this work also contribute to the emerging constructivist-inspired research on deviance (Smetana 2020, forthcoming; Wagner et al. 2014; Wunderlich 2017) and dissidence in international relations (Daase and Deitelhoff 2014; Gertheiss et al. 2017) as well as on the "dynamics of dissent" (see the special issue edited by Stimmer and Wisken 2019).

1.2 Terms and Definitions

This study takes a critical constructivist approach and sees itself in the tradition of studies that refer to agency-based explanations of normative change (e.g., Risse 2000; Finnemore and Sikkink 2001; Sikkink 2011; or most recently the contributions to a special issue edited by Draude 2017). Directing the focus of empirical research on the practices of individual actors seems to be particularly useful in this regard "because focusing on the propagation, contestation, adaption, adoption, or rejection of norms puts into focus that changes in the distribution of norms are tied to politics" (Bucher 2014: 14).

Since some of the basic concepts used in this work are not clearly defined in IR, they will be briefly conceptualized in the following as far as they are relevant to the empirical analysis.

In liberal-constructivist norm research, according to the standard definition of Katzenstein (1996: 5), norms are usually described as collective, intersubjectively shared expectations of appropriate behavior for actors with a given identity (for a critique of this liberal community-based approach to norms see Wiener 2008, 2014). They provide binding rules of action for members of a social group—in the case of international norms, for the global community of states (Checkel 2012: 1). They determine which actions are considered to be socially appropriate and thus permitted and which ones are considered to be inadequate and thus prohibited. By defining standards of appropriate behavior for recurring situations, they produce expectable behavior. As a result of these functions, norms enable orientation in a complex social environment (Elster 1989). In addition, they have a constitutive effect on the self-concept of the actors (March and Olsen 1998: 951–952).

However, despite their stabilizing function, norms are not static. As various (critical constructivist) works have shown, the practices arising from them and vis-á-vis them are highly interpretative and constantly transform themselves through interactive processes of negotiation and contestation (seminal Wiener 2004, 2008; Sandholtz 2007). In this study, I therefore follow authors who propose a discursive understanding of norms as processes (e.g., Wiener 2008: 41, 2014; Krook and True 2012: 106). As a result, norms can be interpreted as historically contingent, intersubjectively shared and situation-specific standards of appropriate behavior. They influence the interests and identities of actors just as they are influenced by them. As such, norms can be understood as "works-in-progress" (Stimmer and Wisken 2019: 517).

Although a large number of empirical studies have traced the role of different norm entrepreneurs in processes of norm diffusion, a uniform usage and operationalization of the term is still lacking. The present work is based on the definition proposed by Björkdahl (2002) in her seminal study on Sweden's role as a norm entrepreneur in international conflict prevention. In this context, Björkdahl emphasizes in particular the purposive behavior of actors: "By identifying or creating opportunities, actors committed to a particular idea set out to change the existing normative context and alter the behavior of others in the direction of the new norm" (Björkdahl 2002: 46).

She refers in particular to the initiating function of norm entrepreneurs of proposing completely new "norm candidates" for solving existing problems or providing existing norms with new meanings. Other authors use the term "norm entrepreneurs" more generally in the sense of norm advocates for actors who are involved in promoting, institutionalizing or implementing, maintaining, and strengthening norms (Finnemore and Sikkink 2001: 401; Johnston 2007: 127; for a further operationalization see Chap. 5).

In referring to the "rogue state" concept, this study follows the (linguistic) usage and political practice of the USA for countries that are alleged to have transgressed universally accepted standards of behavior. Developed by the first Clinton administration, the label was to become one of the defining features of the US security narrative for the past decades (Homolar 2011). As a socially constructed category, the "rogue" label demarcates the designated countries as outsiders and attributes a special responsibility to the USA, as the only remaining superpower, to transform these states into constructive members of the international community (Lake 1994: 45–46). In particular, Iraq, Iran, Libya, Cuba, and North Korea have been labeled "rogue states" on a regular basis (Hoyt 2000; O'Reilly 2007).

While the US administration justified the labeling with reference to four core normative transgressions, namely engaging in hostile activities, violating human rights at home and abroad, supporting international terrorism, and seeking to acquire weapons of mass destruction (WMD) (White House 2002), the concept does not represent an impartial, objective classification of a group of states (e.g., George 1993; Litwak 2000; Caprioli and Trumbore 2005). Rather, it is a top-down construction that serves the demarcation between presumed outsiders and "decent" members of the international community. In this way, it is used to strategically shape the space for political action.

1.3 Research Design

The case selection takes a reverse perspective compared to the mainstream liberal research on norm entrepreneurs and applies a "most counterintuitive" or "least likely case" design (Goertz and Mahoney 2012: 84). While all types of different norm challenger are conceivable, I apply the concept of norm entrepreneurship to so-called "rogue states." According to the dominant scholarly perspective (which is oriented toward a US American political understanding), these states are to be understood primarily as norm-averse or norm-violating actors. Their actions and rhetoric are aimed at undermining and destroying the normative order. A radical opposition to and rejection of the (basic tenets) of the ruling liberal world order lead these states to a willingness to use radical strategies. This serves to overthrow the existing system and establish a new order that clearly defines boundaries that separate it from the overthrown order. Based on these assumptions, two alternative explanations for the behavior of "rogue states" toward norms can be distilled drawing on liberal research on norms. According to the literature, countries labeled as "rogue states" either adopt a hostile attitude toward and are thus supposed to be more reluctant to accept international norms, or they respond to global norm diffusion processes in a purely reactive way. Norm compliance and norm entrepreneurship—as formulated in the critical constructivist based hypothesis guiding the research—is not to be expected.

Whether my hypothesis of supposed "rogue states" acting as potential norm entrepreneurs can be plausibilized or whether the alternative hypotheses develop greater explanatory power will be central to the empirical investigation of the present study. In order to test the hypotheses, I apply the concept of norm entrepreneurship to a country that has been perceived as prototypical "rogue state": The Islamic Republic of Iran (IRI) has long been a permanent member of the group of alleged "rogue states," which have been described by the USA as members of an "axis of evil."[4]

The research is structured as follows: In a first step, Iran's foreign policy and notions of world order are empirically traced. This will be done in the form of a "within case analysis" (Goertz and Mahoney 2012: 71) that takes into account three levels:

First, I will explore Iran's normative world order concepts,[5] which are assumed to be the guiding principles for Iran's foreign and security policy decisions. The aim is to create a normative profile that will provide information on the extent to which Iran's politics can be described as counter-hegemonic in the sense of fundamentally attacking the ruling order as such. This will also reveal whether Iran's actions are geared toward destroying or promoting norms. It is possible that Iran's propagation of the revolutionary ideology could already be seen as norm entrepreneurship. However, whether this is the case will only become apparent in the empirical analysis. The analysis draws on secondary literature and primary documents, such as programmatic speeches given annually by the Heads of Government and Foreign Ministers at the United Nations General Assembly. From the text corpus, a weighted random sample was drawn which was then analyzed by means of inductive qualitative content analysis. In addition, the data was triangulated with the help of expert interviews.

---

[4]For a representation of Iran as a "rogue" par excellence, see Geldenhuys (2004).

[5]In accordance with the terminology of the Frankfurt Cluster of Excellence "The Formation of Normative Orders," normative orders are conceived here as justification orders. They are understood as a complex of norms and values that legitimize the basic structure of a society (or the structure of inter-, supra- or transnational relations), namely the exercise of political authority and the distribution of elementary living or basic goods (Forst and Günther 2011: 15). Normative orders are characterized by their dynamic, never-ending and process-like as well as conflictuous nature.

For the analysis of Iran's potential to act as a norm entrepreneur, I turned to a specific policy field: the multilateral control of weapons of mass destruction. This policy sector represents a central building block in the international security policy architecture (Müller 2013: 3–4). With regard to the stigmatization of "rogue states," it is concepts of order in the realm of security policy in particular that are perceived as threats and intentional counterproposals by the supporters of the ruling order. The analysis takes into account the three relevant regimes for the control of weapons of mass destruction: The Biological and Toxin Weapons Convention (BTWC), the Chemical Weapons Convention (CWC), and the Nuclear Non-Proliferation Treaty (NPT). Within this context, I will search for the focal points of Iranian engagement in arms control policy, the assumption being that this may provide clues regarding instances of Iranian norm entrepreneurship. The analysis takes into account the positions toward and interpretations of the relevant regime norms advocated in each case. For these aims, the analysis draws on a qualitative content analysis of speeches given by Iranian delegates at the regular review conferences of the treaty regimes, the International Atomic Energy Agency (IAEA), and the relevant United Nations (UN) forums. As in step one, the data is triangulated by an analysis of secondary literature and expert interviews.

The arms control policy profile obtained enables the identification of potential norm entrepreneurial activities by Iran. If available, in a third step, such "instances of norm entrepreneurship" are studied in detail and analyzed with the help of a catalog of criteria which summarizes the central characteristics of prototype norm entrepreneurship as used in the liberal norms literature (see Sect. 5.2.1). In so doing, the type of norm entrepreneurship shown by Iran can be mapped, "[in order to] capture the nuance, dynamism, sense of process, and mechanisms at work in any given instance of entrepreneurship" (Checkel 2012: 4).

In a final step, in order to be able to draw further conclusions about the nature of Iranian norm entrepreneurship and with regard to implications for the concept as such, a comparison with the prototypical norm entrepreneur Sweden and the Democratic People's Republic of North Korea—known as a notorious norm breaker—is conducted. The latter comparison will reveal whether norm entrepreneurship is arbitrary and whether every state can ultimately qualify as a norm entrepreneur. In addition, the contrasting cases also allow an exploration of the explanatory power of the alternative explanations derived from liberal norms literature.

1.4 Outline of the Book

In the chapters following the introduction, I present the state of the art of norms research and the theoretical framework of the study (Chaps. 2–4). The main focus is on the concept of norm entrepreneurship as developed in the context of liberal-constructivist research on norms.

The presentation of the state of the art unfolds in three steps: First, the shortcomings identified in the respective approaches are presented—the normative bias of liberal-constructivist norms research (Chap. 2) and the stigmatization of so-called "rogue states" as norm breakers (Chap. 3). These two analytical limitations are then contrasted with the hypothesis that countries labeled as "rogue states" can also act as norm entrepreneurs (Chap. 4).

In detail, Chap. 2 starts with an overview of the research on norm dynamics in IR and traces the normative bias inherent in liberal-constructivist norm studies. The chapter further reconstructs how the concept of norm entrepreneurship has been applied in various empirical norm studies and discusses the consequences of its selective and arbitrary usage. Subsequently, gaps in research that are inherent to the concept will be discussed.

Chapter 3 deals with the "rogue states" concept and traces its evolution both in the US foreign and security policy discourse as well as its role in scholarly debate. It concludes with an account of the relationship between "rogue states" and international norms as portrayed in the literature.

In Chap. 4, I develop the hypothesis guiding this study that "rogue states" can also act as norm entrepreneurs. The chapter ties in with a few innovative works that have already applied the concept of norm entrepreneurship to non-Western and non-liberal actors and takes into account insights from critical constructivist research on norm contestation and resistance toward norms. The chapter concludes with alternative explanations put forward in liberal-constructivist literature on norms, which could serve as an alternative explanation for Iran's behavior toward norms.

The research design is presented in Chap. 5. I explain the case selection, operationalize the central concepts and hypotheses and introduce the methods of data collection and analysis. The following chapters represent the empirical analysis underlying this study (Chaps. 6–8).

Chapter 6 begins with an overview of the institutional and ideological foundations of Iranian foreign and security policy. I assess and discuss Iran's world order concepts based on an analysis of primary documents and interviews. Above all, the display of an antagonistic attitude toward the Western liberal world order and the strategic propagation of a normative alternative can be interpreted as challenging international norms. Teheran's career as "rogue no. 1" and the normative misconduct attributed to Iran are also discussed.

Chapter 7 comprises the empirical core of this study tracing three instances of Iranian norm entrepreneurship in a selected policy field. The chapter begins with a brief description of Iran's rhetorical and practical behavior regarding the control of weapons of mass destruction, in particular its policies within the three regimes on biological, chemical, and nuclear weapons. This overview reveals three focal points of Iranian engagement which are further studied by means of a detailed process tracing in the subsequent sections. Drawing on the blueprint of the concept of norm entrepreneurship as was derived from norm literature, and the three instances of norm entrepreneurship are thoroughly reconstructed and traced by means of qualitative content analysis (Sects. 7.2–7.4). The last section evaluates the strategies and means through which Iranian norm entrepreneurship unfolds.

Chapter 8 begins with a summary and discussion of the findings of the empirical investigation in light of the hypothesis guiding the research, as well as the alternative explanations. Before I turn to a discussion of the consequences of the findings of this study in the last chapter, Sects. 8.2 and 8.3 present the results of a comparison of the peculiarities of Iranian norm entrepreneurship with two contrasting cases. The comparison with the prototypical norm entrepreneur, Sweden, in Sect. 8.2, serves to reveal differences between the applied normative strategies. The comparison with North Korea (Sect. 8.3) helps answer whether other countries labeled as "rogue states" also act as norm entrepreneurs and under what circumstances resistance to the ruling order might transform into activism or isolation.

Based on the empirical results, in the concluding chapter, the concept of norm entrepreneurship is revisited. In Chap. 9, I reflect upon the implications of "rogue states" being norm entrepreneurs for both critical constructivist scholarship on norms and for research on "rogue states." I further discuss practical implications for dealing with Iran. I end with an outlook on further research.

References

Acharya, A. (2004). How ideas spread: Whose norms matter? norm localization and institutional change in asian regionalism. *International Organization, 58*(2), 239–275.

Acharya, A. (2011). Norm subsidiarity and regional orders: Sovereignty, regionalism, and rule-making in the third world. *International Studies Quarterly, 55*(1), 95–123.

Adamson, F. B. (2005). Global liberalism versus political islam: Competing ideological frameworks in international politics. *International Studies Review, 7*(4), 547–569.

Bettiza, G., & Dionigi, F. (2014). Beyond Constructivism's liberal bias: Islamic norm entrepreneurs in a post-secular world society. EUI Working Paper MWP 2014/10. https://cadmus.eui.eu/bitstream/handle/1814/31692/MWP_WP_Bettiza_Dionigi_2014_10.pdf?sequence=1. Accessed April 28, 2017.

Björkdahl, A. (2002). *From idea to norm: Promoting conflict prevention*. Lund: Lund University.

Bloomfield, A. (2016). Norm antipreneurs and theorizing resistance to normative change. *Review of International Studies, 42*(2), 310–333.

Bob, C. (2012). *The global right wing and the clash of world politics*. New York, NY: Cambridge University Press.

Bucher, B. (2014). Acting abstractions: Metaphors, narrative structures, and the eclipse of agency. *European Journal of International Relations, 20*(3), 742–765.

Caprioli, M., & Trumbore, P. (2005). Rhetoric versus reality: Rogue states in interstate conflict. *Journal of Conflict Resolution, 49*(5), 770–791.

Checkel, J. (2012). Norm entrepreneurship—Theoretical and methodological challenges. Memo prepared for a workshop on *"The Evolution of International Norms and 'Norm Entrepreneurship": The Council of Europe in Comparative Perspective*. Oxford: Wolfson College, Oxford University.

Daase, C., & Deitelhoff, N. (2014). *Reconstructing global rule by analyzing resistance* (Internationale Dissidenz Working Paper 1/2014). Resource Document. Internationale Dissidenz Working Paper. http://dissidenz.net/wp-content/uploads/2013/03/wp1-2014-daase-deitelhoff-en.pdf. Accessed April 28, 2017.

Deitelhoff, N., & Zimmermann, L. (2019). Norms under challenge: Unpacking the dynamics of norm robustness. *Journal of Global Security Studies, 4*(1), 2–17.

Draude, A. (2017). The agency of the governed. Norm diffusion and institutional transfer in the global south [special issue]. *Third World Thematics—A TWQ Journal, 2* (5).

Ehrenreich Brooks, R. (2003). The new imperialism: Violence, norms, and the "rule of law". *Michigan Law Review, 101*(7), 2275–2340.
Elster, J. (1989). *The cement of society: A study of social order*. New York, NY: Cambridge University Press.
Finnemore, M., & Sikkink, K. (1998). International norm dynamics and political change. *International Organization, 52*(4), 887–917.
Finnemore, M., & Sikkink, K. (2001). Taking stock: The constructivist research program in international relations and comparative politics. *Annual Review of Political Science, 4,* 391–416.
Flockhart, T. (2004). "Masters and Novices": Socialization and social learning through the NATO Parliamentary Assembly. *International Relations, 18*(3), 361–380.
Florini, A. (1996). The evolution of international norms. *International Studies Quarterly, 40*(3), 363–389.
Forst, R., & Günther, K. (2011). Die Herausbildung normativer Ordnungen. Zur Idee eines interdisziplinären Forschungsprogramms. In R. Forst & K. Günther (Hrsg.). Die Herausbildung normativer Ordnungen: Interdisziplinäre Perspektiven. Frankfurt: Campus Verlag.
Geldenhuys, D. (2004). *Deviant conduct in world politics*. Houndmills: Palgrave Macmillan.
George, A. (1993). *Bridging the gap. Theory and practice in foreign policy*. Washington, DC: United States Institute of Peace Press.
Gertheiss, S., Herr, S., Wolf, K., & Wunderlich, C. (Eds.). (2017). *Resistance and change in world politics: International dissidence*. Cham: Palgrave Macmillan.
Goertz, G., & Mahoney, J. (2012). *A tale of two cultures: Qualitative and quantitative research in the social sciences*. Princeton, NJ: Princeton University Press.
Heller, R., & Kahl, M. (2013). Tracing and understanding 'bad' norm dynamics in counterterrorism. The current debates in IR research. *Critical Studies on Terrorism, 6*(3), 414–428.
Heller, R., Kahl, M., & Pisoiu, D. (2012). The "dark" side of normative argumentation—The case of counterterrorism policy. *Global Constitutionalism, 1*(2), 278–312.
Homolar, A. (2011). Rebels without a conscience: The evolution of the rogue states narrative in US Security Policy. *European Journal of International Relations, 17*(4), 705–727.
Hofius, M., Wilkens, J., Hansen-Magnusson, H., & Gholiagha, S. (2014). Den Schleier lichten? Kritische Normenforschung, Freiheit und Gleichberechtigung im Kontext des »Arabischen Frühlings«. Eine Replik auf Engelkamp/Glaab/Renner, Ulbert und Deitelhoff/Zimmermann. *Zeitschrift für Internationale Beziehungen, 2,* 85–105.
Hoyt, P. (2000). The "Rogue State" image in American Foreign Policy. *Global Society, 14*(2), 297–310.
Jacobi, D., Weber, C., & Hellmann, G. (2014). Dissident foreign policy and the (re-)production of international orders. In W. Wagner, W. Werner, & M. Onderco (Eds.), *Deviance in international relations: "Rogue States" and international security* (pp. 106–131). Basingstoke: Palgrave Macmillan.
Johnston, I. (2007). The secretary-general as norm entrepreneur. In S. Chesterman (Ed.), *Secretary or general? The UN secretary-general in world politics* (pp. 123–138). Cambridge: Cambridge University Press.
Katzenstein, P. (1996). Introduction: Alternative perspectives on national security. In P. Katzenstein (Ed), *The culture of national security: Norms and identity in world politics* (pp. 1–32). New York, NY: Columbia University Press.
Keck, M., & Sikkink, K. (1998). *Activists beyond borders: Advocacy networks in international politics*. Ithaca, NY: Cornell University Press.
Klare, M. (1995). *Rogue States and nuclear outlaws: America's search for a new foreign policy*. New York, NY: Hill and Wang.
Krook, M., & True, J. (2012). Rethinking the life cycles of international norms: The United Nations and the global promotion of gender equality. *European Journal of International Relations, 18*(1), 103–127.
Lake, A. (1994). Confronting backlash states. *Foreign Affairs, 73*(2), 45–55.

Litwak, R. (2000). *Rogue states and U.S. foreign policy: Containment after the cold war*. Washington, DC: Woodrow Wilson Center Press with Johns Hopkins University Press.

Litwak, R. (2012). *Outlier states: American strategies to change, contain, or engage regimes*. Washington, DC: Woodrow Wilson Center Press with Johns Hopkins University Press.

March, J., & Olsen, J. (1998). The institutional dynamics of international political orders. *International Organization, 52*(4), 943–969.

Müller, H. (2011). Habermas meets role theory. Communicative action as role playing? In S. Harnisch, C. Frank, & H. Maull (Eds.), *Role theory in international relations. Approaches and analyses* (pp. 55–73). London: Routledge.

Müller, H. (2013). Introduction: Where it all began. In H. Müller & C. Wunderlich (Eds.), *Norm dynamics in multilateral arms control, interests, conflicts, and justice* (pp. 1–19). Athens, GA: University of Georgia Press.

Müller, H., & Wunderlich, C. (2018). Not lost in contestation. How norm entrepreneurs frame norm development in the nuclear nonproliferation regime. *Contemporary Security Policy, 39*(3), 341–366.

Nincic, M. (2005). *Renegade regimes: Confronting deviant behavior in world politics*. New York, NY: Columbia University Press.

O'Reilly, K. (2007). Perceiving rogue states: The Use of the "rogue state" concept by U.S. foreign policy elites. *Foreign Policy Analysis, 3*(4), 295–315.

Pirseyedi, B. (2013). *Arms control and Iranian Foreign Policy: Diplomacy of discontent*. New York, NY: Routledge.

Risse, T. (2000). Let's argue! Communicative action in world politics. *International Organization, 54*(1), 1–39.

Sandholtz, W. (2007). *Prohibiting plunder: How norms change*. New York, NY: Oxford University Press.

Sikkink, K. (2011). Beyond the justice cascade: How agentic constructivism could help explain change in international politics. Revised paper from a keynote address at *Millenium Annual Conference, "Out of the Ivory Tower. Weaving the Theories and Practice of International Relations"*. London: London School of Economics. https://www.princeton.edu/politics/about/file-repository/public/Agentic-Constructivism-paper-sent-to-the-Princeton-IR-Colloquium.pdf. Accessed April 28, 2017.

Smetana, M. (2020). *Nuclear deviance stigma politics and the rules of the nonproliferation game*. Basingstoke: Palgrave Macmillan (forthcoming).

Stimmer, A., & Wisken, L. (2019). The dynamics of dissent: When actions are louder than words. *International Affairs*, 9583, 515–533.

Towns, A. (2012). Norms and social hierarchies: Understanding international policy diffusion "from below". *International Organization, 66*(2), 179–209.

Wagner, W., Werner, W., & Onderco, M. (Eds.). (2014). *Deviance in international relations: "Rogue States" and international security*. Basingstoke: Palgrave Macmillan.

Wendt, A. (1998). On constitution and causation in international relations. *Review of International Studies, 24*(5), 101–118.

White House. (2002). *The national security strategy of the United States of America*. Resource Document. White House. http://www.state.gov/documents/organization/63562.pdf. Accessed 28 April 2017.

Widmaier, W., & Park, S. (2012). Differences beyond theory. Structural, strategic, and sentimental approaches to normative change. *International Studies Perspectives, 13*(2), 123–134.

Wiener, A. (2004). Contested compliance: Interventions on the normative structure of world politics. *European Journal of International Relations, 10*(2), 189–234.

Wiener, A. (2007). The dual quality of norms and governance beyond the state: Sociological and normative approaches to interaction. *Critical Review of International Social and Political Philosophy, 10*(1), 47–69.

Wiener, A. (2008). *The invisible constitution of politics: Contested norms and international encounters*. Cambridge, NY: Cambridge University Press.

Wiener, A. (2014). *A theory of contestation*. Heidelberg: Springer.

Wiener, A. (2018a). Agency of the governed in global international relations: Access to norm validation. *Third World Thematics: A TWQ Journal, 2*(5), 709–725.

Wiener, A. (2018b). *Contestation and constitution of norms in global international relations*. Cambridge, NY: Cambridge University Press.

Wunderlich, C. (2014). A "Rogue" gone norm entrepreneurial? Iran within the nuclear nonproliferation regime. In W. Wagner, W. Werner, & M. Onderco (Eds.), *Deviance in international relations: "Rogue States" and international security* (pp. 83–104). Basingstoke: Palgrave Macmillan.

Wunderlich, C. (2017). Delegitimisation à la Carte: The "Rogue State" label as a means of stabilising order in the nuclear non-proliferation regime. In S. Gertheiss, S. Herr, K. Wolf, & C. Wunderlich (Eds.), *Resistance and change in world politics: International dissidence* (pp. 143–189). Cham: Palgrave Macmillan.

Wunderlich, C., Hellmann, A., Müller, D., Reuter, J., & Schmidt, H.-J. (2013). Non-aligned reformers and revolutionaries. Egypt, South Africa, Iran, and North Korea. In H. Müller & C. Wunderlich (Eds.), *Norm dynamics in multilateral arms control, interests, conflicts, and justice* (pp. 246–295). Athens, GA: University of Georgia Press.

Chapter 2
Dedicated to the Good: Norm Entrepreneurs in International Relations

Social constructivist research on norms was established in the late 1980s in the course of the so-called "constructivist turn in IR" (Checkel 1998), according to which ideational factors, such as ideas, norms, or world views, have a constitutive impact on the behavior of collective actors. Offering a social perspective on international politics, constructivism holds that actors are shaping the international system as much as they are shaped by its normative structure. While on the one hand, structures constitute actors' interests and preferences, on the other, agents are actively shaping and changing the structures within which they act. Structures and agency are thus mutually constitutive (seminal: Wendt 1992).

Nowadays, a huge constructivist research program on norm dynamics has been established (Wunderlich 2013: 20), exploring the construction, dissemination, change, and most recently also the decay and contestation of norms. The concept of "norm entrepreneurship" has played an important role in providing explanations for the successful formation and diffusion of international norms (e.g., Florini 1996: 375; Finnemore and Sikkink 1998: 893).

The forthcoming chapter introduces the conceptualization of international norms underlying the study and gives an overview of how the scholarly discussion on norms has evolved over time. The main focus is on actor-centered models and the concept of norm entrepreneurship as developed in *liberal* constructivist research on norms. The aim of this chapter is to provide an overview of the current state of the art in research on the role of norm entrepreneurs in the process of norm dynamics. Therefore, the concept of norm entrepreneurship will be reconstructed and made analytically comprehensible on the basis of its use in empirical (liberal-constructivist) norm research. The questions guiding the literature review are: How has the concept of norm entrepreneurship been used so far? Which actors are commonly referred to as norm entrepreneurs and which characteristics are attributed to them? How do norm entrepreneurs act and what motives drive their actions? How does "successful" norm entrepreneurship manifest itself and what are the conditions for it? And above all: How can we identify norm entrepreneurs? In concluding, I will also point out

C. Wunderlich, *Rogue States as Norm Entrepreneurs*,
Norm Research in International Relations,
https://doi.org/10.1007/978-3-030-27990-5_2

analytical biases and research gaps in agency-based norm research, which are caused by the one-sided use of the concept by liberal-constructivist norm scholars. Taking a critical constructivist view, in this book I aim to overcome such a limited view (see Chap. 4).

2.1 Conceptualizing International Norms

What exactly do social scientists mean when they talk about (international) norms?[1] As alluded to in the introductory chapter, in liberal-constructivist norms research, norms are conventionally defined as collective, intersubjectively shared expectations of behavior (Katzenstein 1996: 5). In IR, the concept of norms is often used in an extremely heterogeneous way. As a result, the concept has been criticized several times for lacking clarity (e.g., Thomson 1993: 67; Hurrell 2001: 143; Reich 2005: 215). Social constructivist scholars, however, agree on three central characteristics of norms.

Firstly, norms differ from individual idealistic concepts such as ideas or beliefs due to their *intersubjective* and collective character. They provide standards of behavior for a group of actors who share a common identity (e.g., Klotz 1995a: 14; Jepperson et al. 1996: 54; Finnemore and Sikkink 1998: 37, 89). Actors comply with norms because they want to belong to a certain social group. In order to be accepted, they have to adhere to specific behavioral patterns (Nadelmann 1990: 524; Klotz 1995a: 166). Global norms define which behaviors are expected by members of the international community and which ones are prohibited.

Secondly, on this basis, norms form *regular patterns* of behavior for the reference group they are related to (e.g., Goertz and Diehl 1992: 636–637; Finnemore 1996: 23; Florini 1996: 164). This in turn allows the actors to establish mutual expectations. In the words of Jon Elster, norms are the "cement of society" (Elster 1989). In fact, they shape the actors' scopes of action by defining what constitutes and what can be expected of an actor in a particular situation (Raymond 1997: 214; March and Olsen 1998: 951–52).

Thirdly, norms formulate "'oughtness' claims" (Finnemore and Sikkink 1998: 916) in the form of prescriptions and proscriptions for behavior. In doing so, they distinguish between what is permitted or desirable and what is forbidden. Furthermore, they are able to (de)legitimate certain actions and practices.[2] Accordingly, actors follow norms because they believe they are doing the right thing (Raymond 1997: 217; March and Olsen 1998: 951–952).

There is disagreement regarding further characteristics of norms, such as whether they have an inherently moral content (e.g., Nadelmann 1990: 481–482; Goertz and Diehl 1992: 638–639; Price 2008: 3) or can also merely be functional (e.g., Bull

[1] Parts of this and the following section are based on Wunderlich (2013).

[2] Appropriateness can refer to different dimensions of moral and functionalist argumentation, e.g. good/bad, right/unjust, right/false, or purposive/unpurposive.

1977: 53; Elster 1989: 89–90). It is also up to controversy whether norms have to be reinforced through sanctions in order to have an effect (e.g., Axelrod 1986; Goertz and Diehl 1992: 638) or not (Katzenstein 1996: 21).

While these two characteristics are of less relevance to the present study,[3] the relationship between norms and interests (see Goertz and Diehl 1992: 637) is of importance, particularly with regard to the question of why actors follow norms or even promote them. Quite often, adherence to a norm that is geared toward satisfying a collective interest (and which thus follows a "logic of appropriateness") may collide with the pursuit of one's own interests. Nevertheless, there can also be situations in which norm compliance corresponds to rational considerations. In practice, actions are usually based on a complex combination of motives that are both norm-guided and aimed at the free pursuit of interests (Klotz 1995a: 13; Finnemore 1996: 30–31).[4]

While scholars often portray the relationship between norms and interest as conflicting, I follow scholars who argue that what actors define as their interests is socially constructed and as such always embedded in a normative context and can follow a "logic of appropriateness"—or conversely, that appropriate behavior may at times and under certain circumstances mean following rationalist–utilitarian considerations (Müller 2013: 7–8). Norms and interests should not be understood as clearly distinguishable categories to be analyzed as if they belonged to separate realms. Rather, they are inextricably interwoven and mutually dependent: Norms not only represent institutionalized interests; these interests are also shaped by the prevailing normative context. Following this logic, even rational utility maximizers are always embedded in social structures and depend on normative argumentation (Jepperson et al. 1996: 54; Müller 2004). Norms can therefore be both: An expression of the authentic belief in doing the right thing and the legitimate pursuit of rational interests (Müller 2013: 9).[5] If in the following I use both terms separately, this is not meant as an ontological statement, but serves exclusively analytical purposes. Ultimately, I do not intend to determine whether and when actors act primarily in accordance with norms or interests, but I rather want to show interwoven motifs.

Some other conceptual remarks are also useful when dealing with norms. On a metatheoretical level, different types of norms can be distinguished by the scope (social, legal, moral, etc.) and range (local, national, regional, and global) of their application as well as by their degree of abstraction. In contrast to these horizontal typologies, vertical typologies classify norms according to the importance attributed to them (for an overview: Raymond 1997: 223–279). These models are based on the assumption that there are basic or fundamental norms from which all other norms

[3] I agree with Deitelhoff (2006: 43–44) that norms always have an implicit moral component, albeit a weak one. Even assumed purely functional norms are always embedded in normative structures. Norm acceptance or deviant behavior is always morally charged because any potential violation of the norm can be understood as a challenge to the normative order as such.

[4] Constructivist studies on the effects of norms assume that actors follow different logics of action depending on the situation (e.g., Finnemore and Sikkink 1998: 888; Checkel 1999b).

[5] Authors also argue that it is hardly possible to methodically ascertain whether an action is based on self-interest or on norm-induced motivation, e.g., when self-interest is justified by alleged moral motives (Nadelman 1990: 480; Müller 2013: 7–9).

derive their validity (e.g., Kelsen 1967; Fastenrath 1993). To give a recent example, Antje Wiener distinguishes fundamental norms located at the metalevel from organizing principles and standardized procedures (Wiener 2008: 66–67). Fundamental norms, such as the principle of non-intervention, human rights or the rule of law, entail universal moral claims and high levels of abstraction. Defined as superordinate principles, such "meta or umbrella norms" apply across political fields and are to be separated from ordinary norms (Müller 2013: 5–6). As such, they are of major importance for the functioning of social order (Sandholtz and Stiles 2009: 17). In arms control, reciprocity (Keohane 1986) or, more recently, justice have been identified as examples for such fundamental norms (Müller 2013: 5). To what extent norm entrepreneurs also refer to superordinate norms in the course of their advocacy is dealt with in the course of the study.

2.2 A Brief Overview of Norms Research

In the last two decades, an extensive (social constructivist) research program on international norm dynamics has been established in IR (for an overview see Widmaier and Park 2012; Wunderlich 2013). While a first "wave" (Cortell and Davis 2000: 66; Hoffmann 2010: 5412) of scholarship was occupied with empirically tracing the effectiveness of norms and thus with proving its worth in relation to established (rationalist) approaches, a second "wave" of norms research was primarily interested in mechanisms and conditions for the diffusion, implementation, and change of norms. Current critical constructivist strands of research are focusing on dynamic aspects of norm change, such as interactive processes of norm contestation and interpretation as well as bottom-up processes of norm diffusion.

For pragmatic reasons, empirical works of the early 1990s had a tendency to treat norms as stable, static entities, "a relatively bounded set of appropriate behaviors […] that did not change" (Hoffmann 2010: 5413). Thus, despite the constructivist credo of the mutual constituency of actor and structure (Giddens 1984; Dessler 1989), during the initial stages, norm research remained stuck in a structuralist perspective that left little room for interaction in the process of norm construction and diffusion. Because of such a "freezing" (Hoffmann 2010: 5413) of norms, their influence was often simplistically represented as a linear process of progressive evolution (Finnemore and Sikkink 2001: 403). Scholars considered the acceptance and institutionalization of a global norm that was clear in its meaning and requirements on its addressees to be the result of successful socialization or persuasion (for an overview see Alderson 2001; Schimmelfennig 2003). In fact, empirical studies have often focused on a limited set of "successfully" diffused norms, e.g., on global prohibition regimes (Nadelmann 1990), on the fight against apartheid (Klotz 1995a), on the abolition of slavery (Keck and Sikkink 1998), on the power of human rights (Risse et al. 1999), or on the chemical and nuclear weapons taboo (Price and Tannenwald 1996; Price 1997; Tannenwald 1999).

For a long time, this "bias toward the norm that worked" (Kowert and Legro 1996: 485) led to a distorted view of the ambivalent impact of norms. The first generation of constructivist norm scholars was therefore criticized for not being able to offer a convincing explanation for normative change. They were also accused of favoring structural over agency-related factors in their explanations (Checkel 1998: 340–342; Elgström 2000; Shannon 2000: 311–312; Sending 2002).[6]

Agency-related factors as well as the dynamic and the unsteady nature of norms became the focus of research in the early 2000s. Within this second "wave" of norm research, scholars engaged in a number of intraconstructivist debates on concepts and models of norm diffusion and compliance. Norms were no longer treated as stable, fixed entities, but as products of strategic social construction (Widmaier and Park 2012). Agency-based analyses emphasize the role of norm entrepreneurs—mainly transnational networks and non-governmental organizations (NGOs)—who use both ideational and material resources to bring about normative change (e.g., Nadelmann 1990; Haas 1992; Finnemore and Sikkink 1998: 896–901; Keck and Sikkink 1998).

For example, norm-promoting actors are central in the life-cycle model of norm emergence and evolution that has been put forward by Finnemore and Sikkink (1998). Norm entrepreneurs are regarded as catalytic in order for norms to emerge. Dissatisfied with the normative state of affairs, these actors advocate what they deem to be ideas about appropriate behavior and seek to persuade other actors to change their preferences and thus their behavior in accordance with the advocated norm. As soon as a critical mass of states has accepted the (new) norm, a tipping point is reached, initiating a norm cascade. In the course of the socialization process thus initiated, more and more states are convinced of the legitimacy of the norm. The authors also speak of a "contagion effect" (Finnemore and Sikkink 1998: 902) and refer to mechanisms such as positive and negative incentives (praise and blame) as well as imitation processes. In the final phase, a norm has been internalized, i.e., it has become a standard of appropriate behavior that is no longer questioned.

The *boomerang model* developed by Keck and Sikkink (1998) also conceives of norm diffusion as being driven by the purposeful actions of so-called transnational advocacy networks (TANs). The aim of such groups of actors is to draw attention to the norm-breaking behavior of certain actors (e.g., states or multinational corporations) and to cause them to change their behavior. Networks do so in particular by providing information ("information politics"), engaging in praise and blame ("symbolic politics"), exerting material and social pressure ("leverage politics"), and by supervising the adherence to norms ("accountability politics"; Keck and Sikkink 1998: 16–24).

In their *spiral model*, a group of scholars (Risse et al. 1999) extended the boomerang model to a five-phase model examining the conditions under which international human rights norms can be successfully enforced at the domestic level.

---

[6]This one-sided view has partly been explained through the difficulty of adequately capturing the mutual constituency of agency and structure. Early norm studies therefore often used bracketing strategies: They focused their attention either on the structural effect of norms and consciously ignored agency, or vice versa (Finnemore 1996: 24–25).

Accordingly, norm diffusion processes are mainly initiated and sustained by "networks among domestic and transnational actors who manage to link up with international regimes, to alert Western public opinion and Western governments" (Risse and Sikkink 1999: 5) and as such put pressure on norm-violating governments to change their behavior. Confronted with public attention, the government in question will initially deny the violation of the norm or its validity, but will eventually make tactical concessions and thus fall into a discursive trap: By engaging in a normative discourse, the government recognizes the validity of the norm in principle. Over time, this leads to an argumentative self-entrapment (Risse and Sikkink 1999: 25–28) until the norm is finally officially recognized. Having acquired prescriptive status, the norm will be institutionalized into national law and eventually become internalized so that it achieves a "taken-for-granted" (Risse and Sikkink 1999: 17) quality.

Even though these approaches integrated agency into their analytical models, they remained attached to a linear understanding of norm diffusion. Norm entrepreneurs were primarily conceived of as transmitters of stable, given (Western liberal) norms in a sequential diffusion process (Bucher 2014). Subsequent studies increasingly shifted their focus away from the structuring effects of international norms to capturing the role of agency in norm dynamics and interaction processes, which ultimately led to a change in norms and their meaning. Scholars also began to take into account interpretation and translation processes originating from norm "takers," as well as interactions between domestic, national, and transnational levels in processes of norm diffusion (e.g., Gurowitz 1999, 2006; Cortell and Davis 2000, 2005; Acharya 2004, 2009; Zwingel 2012; Zimmermann 2017).

Acharya (2004), who pioneered norm localization research, argues that the socialization of international norms in domestic political contexts should not be seen as a process of passive norm adoption. Rather, he claimed, the manner in which norms are internalized ultimately hinges on how local actors interpret, appropriate and "localize" global norms into their domestic contexts, that is how they adapt these norms to fit their local (normative) structures and how they reformulate their original meaning. They could even develop counter-norms if they saw their autonomy endangered ("norm subsidiarity," Acharya 2011).

What is central to these approaches is that they no longer equated normative change with the replacement of a traditional (local) norm by a new (international) one. Instead, the diversity of normative change is emphasized and scholars are encouraged to "account for a range of responses to new norms, from constitutive compliance to outright rejection, and evolutionary and path-dependent forms of acceptance that fall in between" (Acharya 2004: 242). Top-down perspectives on norm diffusion cleared the way for an emphasis on bottom-up processes of norm construction and negotiation taking into account non-Western, non-state centric perspectives.

In this respect, critical constructivist studies are primarily concerned with the processes of (re-)interpretation and contestation of norms. While norms do regulate behavior and thus stabilize expectations, due to their inherent ambiguity and indeterminacy, they are contingent and therefore changeable, even after prior formal acceptance (Kersbergen and Verbeek 2007; Wiener 2008; Krook and True 2012; Sandholtz

2007). Due to the dynamic nature of norms, even actors within a normative community that shares the same norms may have different views as to what exact behavioral implications result from them (March and Olsen 2004: 8–9). These assumptions suggest a stronger consideration of agency. Finally, the universal, often ambiguous principles formulated in norms require active (re-)interpretation and transfer by actors in order to be translated into concrete behaviors. In this vein, various studies have shown that normative meanings change according to disputes about their practical application or particular meaning in certain contexts (for a cyclical model of norm change see Sandholtz 2007; Sandholtz and Stiles 2009; more recently Deitelhoff and Zimmermann 2013).

Critical constructivist or poststructuralist approaches within the field of norm research are increasingly dealing with the "dark side" of norms in a systematic way. In doing so, they are attempting to overcome the teleological bias that norm research has been accused of on various occasions (e.g., Finnemore and Sikkink 2001: 403; Epstein 2012b; Engelkamp et al. 2014a, b; most recently Rosert 2018b). In their view, norms should not only be perceived in the light of their problem-solving and cooperation-generating effect. Instead, norms may also generate competing and conflictual demands (e.g., Elgström 2000; Sandholtz 2007). Further, they could also be used to maintain and stabilize dominant power structures (e.g., Epstein 2012a, b; Towns 2012; Adler-Nissen 2014).

Other studies show that norms can also have unintended consequences, which could lead to undermining the prevailing normative order or, at the least, have negative effects that overshadow their apparently positive ones (e.g., Tannenwald 1999: 461; Carpenter 2007b; Heller et al. 2012; Rosert 2018a). Further studies show that even internalized norms are not protected from decay and can disappear into insignificance, and by so doing, also contradict assumptions of progressive norm evolution (Rosert and Schirmbeck 2007; McKeown 2009; Panke and Petersohn 2012).[7]

2.3 Norm Entrepreneurs: Definition and Genesis of a Concept

As mentioned in the previous section, in norms research, agency is considered to be central to the establishment and maintenance of norm dynamics, especially by the role model of norm entrepreneurs. The concept was introduced by proponents of "agentic constructivism" as this strand of research has recently been labeled by Sikkink (2011) as one factor accounting for norm construction and diffusion processes in liberal-constructivist norm research in the 1990s (e.g., Florini 1996: 375; Finnemore and Sikkink 1998: 893). Although the term has enjoyed some popularity since then and has been used in a large number of empirical studies, there is still a lack of uniformity in its use. In addition, many authors use the term, but neither explicitly define what they understand by it nor adequately operationalize the

[7] A more detailed discussion of critical constructivist approaches to norms can be found in Chap 4.

concept for empirical research. As a result, there is inconsistent use of terminology in the literature (for a cross-disciplinary overview see Pozen 2008: 310).

First attempts to systematically use the norm entrepreneurs' concept in political science were made by Björkdahl (2002a) in her study "From Idea to Norm: Promoting Conflict Prevention." In her study, she shows how Sweden acts as a norm entrepreneur advocating the establishment of a global norm of conflict prevention. The theoretical framework developed for this book builds on and complements Björkdahl's study.

The term *norm entrepreneur* has been coined by legal scholar Cass R. Sunstein who used it to refer to "people interested in changing norms" (Sunstein 1996: 909) and applied the term to domestic political actors.[8] In 1998, Harald Koh transferred the concept to an international context and spoke of "transnational norm entrepreneurs" (Koh 1998).

The normative connotation of the term stems from its use in criminology.[9] Howard Becker used the term "moral entrepreneur" (Becker 1963:147–176) to refer to individuals advocating the establishment and enforcement of rules to outlaw deviant behavior. Becker identified the "crusading reformer" (Becker 1963:147) as prototypical rule-setter, who driven by an "absolute ethic" is primarily concerned with combating a threatened social evil by all means at his disposal. Convinced that they are pursuing a "holy mission" (Becker 1963: 148) and are fighting for a good cause, moral entrepreneurs act with "fervent self-righteousness" (Muzzatti 2002). Such actors are often driven by humanitarian reasons, for example, in the case of the anti-slavery or prohibition movement in the USA: "Moral crusaders typically want to help those beneath them to achieve a better status. That those beneath them do not always like the means proposed for their salvation is another matter" (Becker 1963: 149).

While transnational moral entrepreneurs also found their way into political science vocabulary (e.g., Nadelman 1990), it is the term "norm entrepreneur" that has been taken up by Finnemore and Sikkink (1998: 897) and has by now become an established term in norms research. Generally speaking, the concept refers to individual and collective actors who eagerly strive to promote the establishment, diffusion, and institutionalization of norms (Finnemore and Sikkink 1998; Björkdahl 2002a: 44).

However, a closer look into the literature on norms reveals an almost excessive and inconsistent use of the term, which is further complicated by the term being paraphrased with various synonyms. There is a variety of terms ranging from "transnational moral entrepreneurs" (Nadelman 1990) to "norm advocates" (Björkdahl 2008:

---

[8]While Finnemore and Sikkink do not directly relate to Sunstein, they refer to central elements of his concept. According to Florini (1996: 375), the term "norm entrepreneur" was first used by John Mueller in a conference paper in 1993, yet in his further workings, he only spoke of "entrepreneurs […] to catalyse, create and crystallize ideas whose time they hope, has come" (Mueller 1996: 26).

[9]Note that the roots of the concept of entrepreneurship lie in economics. An entrepreneur in the capitalist sense is the founder and owner of a company who, according to Schumpeter (1912), is characterized by innovation and a willingness to take risks. In this way, he or she not only initiates socioeconomic changes on a long-term basis, but also acts as a driving force for social progress.

137), "norm-makers" (Checkel 1999a: 84; Björkdahl 2002a: 45), "norm leaders" (Finnemore and Sikkink 1998: 906; Coleman 2013), "norm transmitter" (Rublee 2008: 462–4628), "norm stewards" (Lantis 2011), or other entrepreneur types such as "meaning entrepreneurs" (Padamsee 2009: 424), "policy entrepreneurs" (Carpenter 2007a: 113), or "issue entrepreneurs" (Bob 2012: 21).

Although many of these synonyms highlight particular elements of the concept, all labels describe norm entrepreneurs as intentional "agents of normative change" (Risse and Sikkink 1999: 5): They are dedicated to a particular idea or cause and advocate its establishment and institutionalization in the sense of generally accepted standards of behavior (Björkdahl 2002a: 46; Hoffmann 2003: 44; Johnstone 2007: 126). The perception of a problem within the prevailing normative order or dissatisfaction with it are typically seen as causing norm entrepreneurs to take up a matter and put forward suggestions on how to solve these issues and to put them on the political agenda. For these purposes, norm entrepreneurs aim to raise public awareness for a particular problem and actively seek to persuade norm recipients to redefine their interests and preferences and thus to change their behavior. It is therefore the case that scholars describe norm entrepreneurs as "problem solvers" (Björkdahl 2002a: 45) and "meaning managers" who generate "new ways of talking about and understanding issues" (Finnemore and Sikkink 1998: 897).

If we take a closer look at Sunstein's seminal definition of norm entrepreneurs, we see that norm scholars have taken up central elements (without, however, giving proper credit to the origins of the concept). Sunstein particularly linked norm entrepreneurship with pursuing the common good and a certain moral sensitivity:

> [N]orm entrepreneurs can alert people to the existence of a shared complaint and can suggest a collective solution. Thus political actors, whether public or private, can exploit widespread dissatisfaction with existing norms by (a) signaling their own commitment to change, (b) creating coalitions, (c) making defiance of the norms seem or be less costly, and (d) making compliance with new norms seem or be more beneficial. (Sunstein 1996: 929)

Literature also notes that norm entrepreneurs must be ready to spend a considerable amount of time, energy, resources, and reputation fighting for their cause (Kingdon 1995: 122, 179; Björkdahl 2008: 137). Besides, these actors are supposed to have superior technical intelligence, social intelligence, and leadership skills (Ellickson 2001: 12). Purposeful and resolute action is another characteristic trait of norm entrepreneurs that is often mentioned (Finnemore and Sikkink 2001: 400). Relatedly, norm entrepreneurship requires the ability to perceive and use windows of opportunity or opportunity structures (Kingdon 1995: Chap. 8; Wunderlich 2013: 30) or, if necessary, to produce them themselves (Björkdahl 2002a: 46).

Often, the concept of norm entrepreneurship is linked to the notion of "innovation" and in fact, a great deal of norm advocacy aims at the establishment of new norms (or new interpretations of established norms) and a redefinition of preferences (Klotz 1995a, b; Finnemore 1996). Innovation may also occur in the form of the practices that norm entrepreneurs use to foster their aims. Emma Sjöström (2010: 180) describes norm entrepreneurs as actors, "who break away from the established" (Sjöström 2010: 180) by formulating alternative policies, taking unusual measures or transforming established normative understandings. Their actions are typically described as active rather than reactive (Pozen 2008: 301). Characterizations such as "proselytizing mission" (Johnstone 2007: 126), "moral proselytism" (Nadelman 1990: 481) or "moral crusades" (Becker 1963: 148) in turn point to the high degree of commitment and sense of obligation often attributed to norm entrepreneurs, as well as to the normative connotation of the term.

2.4 Types of Norm Entrepreneurs

Norm entrepreneurs are usually identified as such ex-post, in other words, after their activities have been "successful" and led to the establishment, diffusion or strengthening of a norm. As such, the identification of norm entrepreneurship is a social construction and can be understood as an external attribution by the scholar in question.

The concept of norm entrepreneurship was initially designed for philanthropic individuals and transnational activist networks. The fact that research has for a long time taken particular account of non-state actors has led to a fatal dichotomy: On the one hand, the "good" civil society, committed to normative progress, and on the other, states primarily interested in pursuing (material) self-interests. This will be discussed in greater detail later in Sect. 2.4.

Henry Dunant, the Founder of the International Committee of the Red Cross (ICRC), is considered a prototype of the philanthropic norm entrepreneur (Finnemore 1996: 73–85; Finnemore and Sikkink 1998: 896–897). Deeply moved by the suffering of wounded civilians and soldiers in the Battle of Solferino in 1859, Dunant campaigned for the appropriate treatment of medical personnel and injured soldiers in the war. He recorded his impressions in a book he printed at his own expense and sent it to decision-makers throughout Europe. At the same time, he sought the support of various philanthropic personalities who shared his concern for the establishment of national charities and launched a massive media campaign. Appealing to Christian charity and the responsibility of civilized nations, the network succeeded not only in establishing the ICRC but also in adopting the Geneva Convention for the Amelioration of the Conditions of the Wounded in Armies in the Field. Within a relatively short period of time, almost all European countries had signed the convention.

Other *charismatic individuals* who can be considered prototypical norm entrepreneurs are Martin Luther King in the fight for the abolition of racial segregation or Mother Teresa in her commitment to the poor (Sunstein 1996: 929; Posner 1999; Ellickson 2001: 15; Ehrenreich Brooks 2003). Frequently, public persons function as standard bearers. Activist networks rely on their publicity to promote international campaigns (Price 1998b: 623; Busby 2010: 272). Besides "celebrities" (Price 1998b: 623; Drezner 2007; Cooper 2008; Busby 2010: 272; Budabin 2015) also quite ordinary "cosmopolitan individuals" (Stein 2008) may become norm entrepreneurs and as such form the core of transnational activist networks.

Moreover, Nadelmann (1990: 484) considers cosmopolitan motivations of committed civil servants and their collaboration with national and transnational networks to have been decisive in the establishment of various international prohibition regimes. While jurisprudence and economics consider lawmakers to be implicit norm entrepreneurs (Carbonara et al. 2008), IR scholars draw attention to the staff of *international bureaucracies* or organizations acting as norm entrepreneurs. For example, they have studied the UN Secretary-General (Johnstone 2007; Rushton 2008), the Director-General of the IAEA (Müller 2011: 64), chairs of multilateral negotiations (Blavoukos and Bourantonis 2011) and the staff working within the International Monetary Fund (Chwieroth 2008) and the World Health Organization (Kamradt-Scott 2010).

Some authors also refer to the norm entrepreneurial role of *scientists* or "epistemic communities" (seminal: Haas 1992)[10] who contribute important information to (normative) debates through assumptions on cause-and-effect relationships and who often act norm-driven themselves (e.g., Alford 2008; Zwolski and Kanuert 2011).

Most of the norm diffusion literature deals with the persistent work of common-good-driven *transnational advocacy networks* (e.g., Klotz 1995a, b; Finnemore 1996; Keck and Sikkink 1998; Risse et al. 1999; Khagram et al. 2002).[11] In their seminal work, Keck and Sikkink (1998) give a comprehensive account on the emergence, development, and effectiveness of such networks in the field of environmental and human rights policy. They define transnational advocacy networks (synonymously "issue networks") as "actors working internationally on an issue, who are bound together by shared values, a common discourse, and dense exchanges of information and service" (Keck and Sikkink 1998: 2). These include associations of domestic or international NGOs, research and advocacy organizations, local movements, political foundations, trade unions, the churches, consumer organizations, intellectuals, the media, regional and international intergovernmental organizations, and employees of national bureaucracies and parliamentarians (Keck and Sikkink 1998: 9).

Scholars have studied the activities of transnational advocacy networks in a wide range of policy areas, including human rights policy (e.g., Sikkink 1993a, b; Klotz 1995a; Finnemore 1996; Risse et al. 1999; Powell 2004; Montaya 2013; Baisley 2016), the control of weapons of mass destruction (e.g., Fisher 1999; Johnson 2000; Feakes 2003; Knopf 2012; Müller et al. 2013), humanitarian arms control

---

[10]It was Haas (1992) who coined the term "epistemic communities," that is networks of knowledge-based experts who make available their shared causal beliefs and technical-scientific expertise to help decision-makers define and solve the problems they face. However, the distinction between activist networks that adhere to shared moral aspirations and epistemic communities that are primarily oriented toward knowledge generation (Sikkink 1993a, b: 440; Finnemore 1996: 86; Keck and Sikkink 1998: 30) can hardly be maintained empirically. Epistemic communities also share normative beliefs and act in a way that is driven by norms, and NGOs in turn also generate knowledge and are partly integrated into larger epistemic communities (Brühl 2003: 165). One might, however, concede that they are less actively involved in norm-generating processes.

[11]This literature shares key conceptual assumptions with social movement literature, such as the term "multiplication of voices" for transnational activist networks used by Keck and Sikkink (1998: x).

(e.g., Price 1998a; Atwood 2002; Rutherford et al. 2003; Wisotzki 2008; Carpenter 2011), environmental protection (e.g., Busby 2010; Hoffmann 2005), the fight against poverty (e.g., Busby 2007, 2010; Hulme and Fukuda-Parr 2011), or international criminal jurisdiction (e.g., Deitelhoff 2006; Kelley 2007; Sandholtz 2007).[12]

Research particularly emphasizes the mobilizing function of transnational networks. In particular civil society groups in authoritarian states, which are denied the use of communication channels in their home countries, join forces with transnational human rights organizations. Doing so enables them to internationalize their interests and place their home country under normative pressure (Nadelman 1990: 482; Keck and Sikkink 1998; Risse et al. 1999).

The literature on global governance describes NGOs as the "vanguards of an emerging global civil society" (Josselin and Wallace 2001a: 1). Providing public goods grants them considerable political influence. NGOs possess a certain moral authority, collect and disseminate knowledge about root causes, produce publicity, and—by being transparent about what they do and how they operate—seek to achieve a "democratization" of political decision-making (Keck and Sikkink 1998: 9–10).

For a long time, a dichotomy persisted between (non-state) norm entrepreneurship and the (interest-led) world of states (Colonomos 2001: 87; Cowles 2003) as a corollary of which research on norm advocacy was dominated by a focus on non-state actors. States typically used to be treated and analyzed as addressees rather than advocates of norms. If at all, normative engagement was at best attributed to the moral action of individuals working in the government. However, at the beginning of the 2000s, the focus shifted to states (Björkdahl 2002a, b; Ingebritsen 2002; Rutherford et al. 2003) and private sector actors such as shareholders (Sjöström 2010) or transnational corporations (Cowles 2003; Wrage and Wrage 2005; Flohr et al. 2010; Hofferberth et al. 2011; Dashwood 2012: 68–69).

However, when ascribing norm entrepreneurial potential to states, scholars often fell into the trap of focusing on the rhetoric and behavior of governmental elites in the global North (Björkdahl 2002a, b: 47) while neglecting the "agency of the governed."[13] Studies focus in particular on so-called small and medium-sized powers, which have committed themselves to promoting norms that lie in the public interest and thus serve the common good. Often, these are equated with liberal-democratic norms (Ingebritsen 2002, 2002; Rutherford et al. 2003; Becker-Jakob et al. 2013; Youde and Slagter 2013; Wallbott 2014). Their inclination to foster norms is often linked to their specific political culture and their intrinsic belief in the propagated values (Müller 2011: 67). It is the "moral greatness" (Neumann and Gstöhl 2006: 8) of these alleged *good international citizens* that helps them compensate for their comparative disadvantages resulting from the relative lack of resources. As research has shown, for smaller countries in particular, proactive engagement might serve as a foreign policy strategy geared toward "creat[ing] a niche for themselves in

---

[12]Busby (2010: 17–32) provides an overview of various TANs in different policy areas and the authors who deal with the respective networks.

[13]For a critique and first efforts to overcome this bias, see the contributions in the special issue edited by Risse and Draude (2018).

international politics" (Björkdahl 2002a: 48; Cooper 1997). Because of their lack of resources, small countries typically seek niches within which they can establish a "moral balance of power in the international system" (Ingebritsen 2006: 290) and develop a role as a "social laboratory of innovative solutions" (Ingebritsen 2006: 289).

It is striking that Australia, Japan, Canada, Canada, Sweden, and New Zealand lead the league of typical *good international citizens*.[14] The fact that they can hardly be presumed to have hegemonic aspirations (Ravenhill 1998: 313), that some of them even explicitly appear as critics of the great powers, and that they have a reputation as "honest brokers" (Garris 1973: 201) is regarded as a prerequisite for being given moral credibility by other actors (and scholars alike). Drawing on Andrew Cooper, Ronald M. Behringer describes those states as "'catalysts' in launching diplomatic initiatives, 'facilitators' in setting agendas and building coalition of support, and 'managers' in aiding the establishment of regulatory institutions" (Behringer 2012: 18). In their favored niches, these states demonstrate such a high level of influence that Gareth Evans even ascribes leadership qualities to them: "if not by force of authority, then at least by force of ideas" (Evans 2011).

Under the label "Global Good Samaritans" (but not that of the norm entrepreneur concept), Brysk (2005, 2009) analyzes not only medium-sized countries but also small states such as Costa Rica or the Netherlands, which exert normative influence in human rights policy far beyond their size. In her view, all these states share certain characteristics: They are democracies with a low to medium level of development and have a strong focus on human rights and a stable security situation. They also favor multilateral policies and are particularly active in development policy, peace building and refugee protection.[15] These attributes are also referred to in other works: *Good international citizens* are thus characterized not only by their size, but also a certain foreign-policy identity and the aspiration to externalize their domestic values (Björkdahl 2013: 325; Becker-Jakob et al. 2013: 208–209).

Small and medium-sized powers as norm entrepreneurs are also characterized by the fact that they form proactive coalitions with civil society actors, but also with other states (so-called *like-minded coalitions*; e.g., Cooper 2002; Ingebritsen 2002; Rutherford et al. 2003). More recently, scholars have taken greater account of state actors from the global South, e.g., in their effort to promote their version of the emerging norm of a responsibility to protect (Benner 2012; Acharya 2013; Herro 2015; Brosig and Zähringer 2015; Stuenkel 2015), as protagonists of human rights norms (Sikkink 2014) or advocates fighting climate change (Wallbott 2014).

Whereas the role of great powers is mostly reduced to enforcing norms by coercive means, some scholars have also analyzed their potential to act as norm entrepreneurs working for the genesis and maintenance of global norms by persuasive means (Kaufmann and Pape 1999; Job 2006; Saunders 2006; Fey et al. 2013; Garwood-Gowers

[14]See Björkdahl (2002a, b, 2008, 2013), Ingebritsen (2002), Capie (2008), Brysk (2009), Rublee (2009), Carr (2012), Becker-Jakob et al. (2013), Wunderlich (2013), Youde and Slagter (2013).

[15]This definition also reveals the danger of circular reasoning when norm entrepreneurs are identified only ex-post on the basis of certain behaviors.

2015: 25; Davies and True 2017; Jose 2018). Increasing attention is also being paid to the norm entrepreneurial potential of rising powers such as China or India (Fey et al. 2013; Kumar 2017; Lanteigne 2017).

While their potential to act as "agents of social structural change" (Finnemore 1996: 25) and as "teachers of norms" (Finnemore 1993) was already noticed in the 1990s, international organizations and transnational bureaucracies were mostly perceived as mediating agencies and rather passive transmitters of norms (Barnett and Finnemore 1999). However, with the turn of the millennium, this perception changed. Not only national agencies such as the US Federal Trade Commission on data protection (Hetcher 2000), but also transnational bureaucracies and *intergovernmental organizations* (IGOs) or regional organizations are now considered to be norm entrepreneurs, including several UN organizations (Månsson 2008; Capie 2008; Müller et al. 2013; Aginam 2014; Orchard 2014), the Association of Southeast Asian Nations (ASEAN; Allison-Reumann 2017), the European Union (EU; Smith 2004; Zwolski and Kaunert 2011; Müller et al. 2013; Vadura 2015),[16] and the African Union (AU; Souaré 2014; Murithi 2016).[17]

The question still remains largely unanswered as to what extent the various institutional arrangements themselves can be regarded as breeding grounds for norm entrepreneurship, or whether it requires committed individuals to take up and use institutional, norm entrepreneur friendly structures. Müller et al. (2013: 326) conclude that the norm entrepreneurial potential ultimately depends on the respective organizational structure, the instruments available, the mandate and the homogeneity/heterogeneity of the membership of an I(G)O (Müller et al. 2013: 325–326). Indeed, being a high-ranked official in an international organization equips committed actors with discursive resources such as symbolic power, authority (credibility/legitimacy) as well as availability and access to expertise—privileges that non-state norm entrepreneurs often lack. The mentioned resources can facilitate agenda setting and mediation services.

2.5 Motives for Norm Entrepreneurial Action

The neglect of states and private sector actors as norm entrepreneurs may have something to do with a biased and oversimplified view on the motives driving norm advocacy. In fact, research tends to adopt a dichotomous view: In stark contrast

---

[16]In other words, these institutions are increasingly being labeled as norm entrepreneurs. In general, a lot of the works on the EU's eastward enlargement or its consolidation politics can also be described as norm entrepreneurship (e.g., the work of Schimmelfennig 2003 or Checkel 1999a, 2000). The concept of "normative power Europe" developed by Manners (2002) corresponds to the norm entrepreneur concept, namely—abbreviated—the effort to promote and further develop norms proactively and intentionally.

[17]There are also studies that have examined the role of IGOs in norm diffusion processes on a more general level (e.g., Santa-Cruz 2005), yet to the extent that they do not operate with the concept of norm entrepreneurship, they are not considered in the literature review.

to interest-led states, (non-state) norm advocates are conceptualized as altruistic, principled actors who are not primarily guided by their own interests. Martha Finnemore and Kathryn Sikkink conclude:

> Ideational commitment is the main motivation when entrepreneurs promote norms because they believe in the ideas and values embodied in the norms, even though the pursuit of the norms may have no effect on their well-being. (Finnemore and Sikkink 1998: 898)

Following this line of reasoning, norm entrepreneurship is prompted not by mere utility maximization, but by the added value of the propagated norms for the community. As an example, Finnemore (1996: 87, Fn. 46) refers again to Henry Dunant, who invested most of his own assets in his company and eventually went bankrupt. Sikkink (1993a, b: 411–412) distinguishes transnational activist networks according to the source of their engagement in more interest-led actors and norm entrepreneurs led by principles.

Ever since, a tendency to view empathy, altruism, and ideational motivation as decisive characteristics of norm entrepreneurship has prevailed, in particular in the literature on global governance and on social movements. Characterizations of NGOs as the "conscience of the world" (Willetts 1996) and of state norm entrepreneurs as "moral superpowers" (Ingebritsen 2006: 2) illustrate this focus on altruistic motives and are reminiscent of Becker's concept of a "moral entrepreneur" (Becker 1963: 147–176), who, driven by "absolute ethics," crusades against social evil.

This study takes a different view in line with John Kurt Jacobsen, who warns: "entrepreneurs do not descend from Mount Olympus; they are usually interested actors who benefit when their ideas are adopted" (quoted after Björkdahl 2002a: 48). What has been noted above with regard to the relationship between norms and interests applies to the motivation of norms entrepreneurs as well: In reality, actors act in both an interest- and a norm-driven way (Klotz 1995a: 13). Both logics of action can coincide, as Björkdahl (2002a: 48; 2002b: 5) shows with the example of small and medium-sized powers acting as norm entrepreneurs. Predominantly driven by normative reasons, their norm entrepreneurship is also a diplomatic strategy that helps these actors to fill a certain "niche" in world politics and thus gain political weight beyond material resources. In addition, their commitment to international solidarity and the protection of international law is also due to their knowledge of their own vulnerability and is therefore not free from the pursuit of their own interests (Björkdahl 2013: 333). Other authors also point out that actors can certainly benefit from their normative entrepreneurship insofar as they expect to gain prestige and other social benefits (e.g., increased self-esteem, credibility, and trustworthiness) (Ellickson 2001: 12; Adut 2004: 548).[18]

Interesting in this regard are studies that investigate norm-promoting activities of transnational corporations—i.e., actors who are primarily presumed to follow a rational logic of action oriented toward profit maximization. Their findings show that corporate norm entrepreneurship is less geared toward changing the practices of

[18]However, Robert C. Ellickson rightly points out that this is only the case after successful norm entrepreneurship, i.e., "when group members widely accept a new norm" (Ellickson 2001: 12).

states. Instead, business actors begin to change their own behavior by adopting "best practices" and eventually get caught in their own logic: They are required to convince competing companies to adopt the norms as well, because otherwise they would have to fear competitive disadvantages (Deitelhoff and Wolf 2013: 232). That they become norm entrepreneurs is therefore due to tactical rather than moral reasons. Moreover, norms research assumes that it is beneficial for the acceptance of a propagated norm if norm entrepreneurs succeed in "framing" their advocacy as primarily norm-based and less driven by their own interests as this would give them moral authority and legitimacy (Nadelman 1990: 482; Deitelhoff 2006: 145; Pozen 2008: 328).

Since this study perceives of norms and interests as being inseparably interwoven (see Sect. 2.1), it would be shortsighted to adhere to a synonymous usage of the attributes rational and interest-led, utility-maximizing on the one hand and norm-driven and altruistic on the other. As David E. Pozen reminds us, norm entrepreneurs are strategic yet not primarily profit-maximizing actors who are

> not simply […] saints, activists, moralists, or busybodies but […] players in a kind of social game. The entrepreneur label suggests that these individuals will share a distinct set of skills and tactics as well as personality traits. It suggests a role not only for persuasion and quid pro quos but also for coalition-building, marketing, tipping points, bandwagon effects, and the like. It adds both a strategic dimension and a social psychological dimension to the account of policy and norm construction. (Pozen 2008: 335)

Understood in this sense, norm entrepreneurship might be perceived of as geared toward pursuing redefined (that is normative) interests, particularly as it is often aimed toward satisfying collective needs and serves the common good (Björkdahl 2002a: 48; Becker-Jakob et al. 2013).

2.6 Objectives and Stages of Norm Entrepreneurship

Rather than enforcing their own norm-(interpretation), norm entrepreneurs try to convince as many actors as possible of the moral validity and appropriateness of the propagated norm(s) (e.g., Nadelman 1990: 482; Checkel 2001: 562; Payne 2001: 42).[19] To achieve this goal, they use genuine processes of persuasion and try to build up social pressure (e.g., through criticism). As Alastair Ian Johnston sums up:

> most non-coercive diplomatic influence attempts by most actors most of the time are aimed at 'changing the minds' of others, of persuading, cajoling, or shaming them to accept, and hopefully internalize, new facts, figures, arguments, norms, and causal understandings about particular issues. (Johnston 2001: 489)

[19] In contrast, Nicole Deitelhoff suggests that (non-state) norm entrepreneurs should not be perceived primarily as agents of persuasion in norm construction processes (Deitelhoff 2009). In her view, norm entrepreneurs are rather concerned with changing the institutional and normative context so as to enable states to enter into meaningful deliberation aimed at persuasion.

In order to achieve their goals, norm entrepreneurs have to cope with various subtasks[20]: First of all, they engage in agenda setting: they raise public awareness for a certain political problem and promote the propagated norm as a possible solution to it. Moreover, they have to persuade actors to change their behavior, discursive positions and institutional procedures in light of the norm (Keck and Sikkink 1998: 25). Björkdahl summarizes this process under the generic term "norm advocacy" and understands it as a mixture of "agenda-shaping, norm-negotiation, and coalition-building" (Björkdahl 2013: 326).

Norm entrepreneurs apply these different actions in the different phases of norm dynamics. While the bulk of empirical studies trace the efforts of norm entrepreneurs in norm construction processes (e.g., Nadelman 1990; Florini 1996; Finnemore and Sikkink 1998; Risse et al. 1999), several authors argue that norm entrepreneurship does not end with the institutionalization of the propagated norm. Rather, norm entrepreneurs continue to work hard to keep the norm in the public's consciousness, protect it against disputes, and from weakening (Hoffmann 2007: 18; Rublee 2008: 426; Wunderlich 2013: 35–36). Ian Johnstone therefore assigns managerial functions to norm entrepreneurs (Johnstone 2007: 124) and highlights three effects of norm entrepreneurship in particular: (1) the *construction* of new norms, (2) the *institutionalization* of these norms into national law, international bureaucracies, or political processes, and (3) the *continuous interpretation* and thus *confirmation* of established norms.

Accordingly, norm entrepreneurship can occur in different phases of norm dynamics and takes place in different steps (Wunderlich 2013: 27–29).[21] In the first phase, norm entrepreneurs primarily try to establish a new norm or normative meaning. In the subsequent phase of consolidation and further development, they advocate the promotion and maintenance of that norm (interpretation), which involves efforts to institutionalize/implement it and to monitor compliance with the norm (Björkdahl 2013: 326–333).

2.6.1 First Phase: Norm Construction

Often, norm entrepreneurship is triggered by perceived problem scenarios. In a first step, which is aimed at the construction of the propagated "norm candidate,"[22] advocates therefore seek to frame the problem to be solved as such: The present state of

---

[20]These tasks do not need to follow a linear sequence, but may be carried out in parallel. Moreover, it is not necessary to go through all the steps to successfully establish a (new) norm.

[21]The phases are analytical categories; in practice, the boundaries are fluid. The individual processes described here as part of certain steps can be carried out across all phases. Actors may also assume different roles simultaneously (Hamilton 2008).

[22]Following Björkdahl (2002a: 59), the term "norm candidates" refers to ideas that are presented as norms to be established by norm advocates to a group of potential norm addressees. Unlike established norms, they do not yet have intersubjective validity or are shared across a wider populace. According to Björkdahl (2002a: 72), norm entrepreneurs select ideas (1) whose content addresses

affairs is described as untenable and in need of a solution—if necessary—existing normative practices are delegitimized as inappropriate, while the norm candidate or modified normative practices are presented as appropriate solutions (Kingdon 1995: 122–124; Finnemore and Sikkink 1998: 897–898; Björkdahl 2002a: 61; Rosert 2018b).

In providing information and framing their cause, norm advocates use both fact-based knowledge as well as emotionally charged reports from those affected to demonstrate the urgency of the problems they address, thus appealing to a sense of collective responsibility (Keck and Sikkink 1998: 19: 200–201). If a problem is defined as an inadequate practice or as a practice in need of regulation, the norm entrepreneurs seek to mobilize support for the proposed solution (Nadelman 1990: 481; Keck and Sikkink 1998: 19; Koh 1998: 648). After formulating the norm (interpretation) to be propagated and demonstrating the need for political action, they try to generate public attention, put the topic on the political agenda, and actively promote the norm against competing norms or normative narratives (Elgström 2000).

In the course of such lobbying, norm advocates need not only to engage in interpretative framing; they also need to strategically select an appropriate institutional setting or venue (and/or, if necessary, change it; Coleman 2013: 168). The selection of such an institutional framework or organizational platform can be seen as a decisive point of departure for further norm diffusion, e.g., the institutional setting of norm negotiation processes may influence the content of the norm (Coleman 2013: 181–182). Björkdahl notes:

> Norm entrepreneurs, therefore, shop around for a forum that can assist them in their norm promoting activity and where the norm can become institutionalized and settled. Like traveling salesmen, the norm entrepreneurs arrive at a designated organization, which provides them with an international arena on which to exchange ideas and advance norms. Norm entrepreneurs consciously circulate 'their' norm in these international settings and they build coalitions to wield more support for the ideas and norms they intend to 'sell.' (Björkdahl 2002a: 50)

Access to organizational platforms is particularly relevant for weak actors, as these platforms provide them with expertise and access to information and decision-making processes (Finnemore and Sikkink 1998: 900).[23] In addition, organizations provide resources such as money, bureaucratic structures, or sanctioning mechanisms that norm entrepreneurs need in order to put pressure on norm-violating actors. Non-state norm advocates also use campaigns or counter-summits and active cooperation with the media in order to produce public pressure (Brühl 2003: 77–79) and to criticize inappropriate practices. Furthermore, norm entrepreneurs can form alliances with like-minded partners and thus bundle their resources (Keck and Sikkink 1998; Cooper 2002; Rutherford et al. 2003; Björkdahl 2013).

---

the problem at hand; (2) that resemble their own values, practices and patterns of thought; and (3) that possess a certain moral and theoretical appeal.

[23]The term "organizational platforms" includes international organizations, regimes, conferences of State Parties, summits, and TANs. A common agenda and availability of shared resources are crucial (Finnemore and Sikkink 1998).

Ariel Colonomos summarizes that "[t]he formation of multiple alliances permits a better diffusion of their message through a variety of channels, especially when trying to achieve international impact" (Colonomos 2001: 81). Ethan Nadelman describes the range of measures available to such alliances of states and activist networks as follows:

> Their agitation takes many forms, ranging from the diplomatic pressures, economic inducements, military interventions, and propaganda campaigns of governments to the domestic and transnational lobbying, educational, organizational, and proselytizing efforts of individuals and nongovernmental organizations. (Nadelman 1990: 485)

2.6.2 Phase 2 and 3: Consolidation and Further Development

The process of norm diffusion is to be understood as an ongoing and dynamic negotiation process (Elgström 2000: 459; Wunderlich 2013: 29). As a result, norm advocates also play an important role in maintaining and consolidating, developing, and enforcing established norms (e.g., Finnemore and Sikkink 2001:40; Johnstone 2007: 124; Müller and Wunderlich 2013). Due to the dynamic nature of norms, norm entrepreneurs are constantly engaged in preserving controversial or endangered norms or defending them against challengers. They do this by making norm violations public, thus acting as "guardians of norms" (Hamilton 2008: 40) or as "implementation assistants" (Brühl 2003: 79; transl. CW) monitoring the implementation of agreements. Against the background of the inherently ambiguous and contested nature of normative meanings, norm entrepreneurs also engage in "activating" norms in situations in which multiple (sometimes incompatible) norms would be applicable, e.g., by drawing attention to a certain normative meaning through intensified public relations work or symbolic actions (such as the introduction of a UN resolution, placing advertisements, public events, etc.) (Rublee 2008: 426–428).

During this phase, organizational platforms are also helpful for the diffusion, implementation and institutionalization of a norm, and the monitoring of norm compliance. They are regarded as central to the consolidation and internalization of norms (Finnemore 1993: 595; Finnemore and Sikkink 1998: 899–900). In this context, Harold H. Koh points out that intergovernmental organizations may figure both as "instigators of interaction, but also as creators of new interpretative fora" (Koh 1998: 678) with the help of which norm entrepreneurs can expand the discourse community and, by means of communicative affirmation, consolidate the meaning and validity of a norm.

2.7 The Norm Entrepreneurial Toolbox

In order to convince norm addressees of the moral validity of the propagated norms and to win supporters, norm entrepreneurs resort to a broad variety of resources and instruments. Contrary to rationalist approaches, which link the enforcement of norms with the sanctioning power of powerful states in the international system and thus refer to traditional power resources, constructivist studies emphasize the importance of "soft power" (Nye 1990)[24]: diplomatic, rhetorical and pedagogical skills, (technical) expertise, and social intelligence (among others Klotz 1995a; Keck and Sikkink 1998: 18–25; Björkdahl 2008: 138). Scholars also refer to moral authority and legitimacy, attributes that are ascribed to actors due to their reputation "based on repeated interaction, meeting obligations and behaving consistently with the international community's norms" (Björkdahl 2002a: 48). A norm entrepreneur who does not let his/her words be followed by deeds or whose normative record raises questions, risks being dismissed as hypocritical and thus losing credibility (Nagatzaam 2009: 75).

Studies on non-state norm entrepreneurs or small and medium-sized powers acting as norm advocates argue that they are able to offset power imbalances through superior expertise and competences in the field of "soft power." Investment in intellectual and diplomatic capacity, as well as the development of technical and political expertise would allow them to offer mediation services or, in the case of state representatives, to fill posts in international organizations or regimes (conference chairmanship, chairmanship of special commissions) which would give them access to decision-makers and thus political influence (e.g., Becker-Jakob et al. 2013: 231–232).

In addition to a certain social "acuity" (Mintrom and Norman 2009: 651–652) and the ability to recognize opening windows of opportunity (Kingdon 1995), scholars attest norm entrepreneurs a certain willingness to release resources for purposes of norm propagation. Moreover—and in particular in the phase of norm construction—as norm advocates often take an oppositional stance toward the normative status quo or even come into conflict with existing normative standards, a certain degree of resilience would also be required (Finnemore and Sikkink 1998: 897). As Job notes: "'Bucking the system' is difficult: it requires resource, both ideational and material; a capacity to absorb the costs of nonconformity; and innovative and distinctive leadership" (Job 2006: 61).

The literature on norms has identified a number of strategies that norm entrepreneurs use in order to foster their aims. They mainly focus on processes of strategic social construction and "[the] strategic use of information, symbolic politics, leverage politics and accountability politics, issue framing and shaming" (Finnemore and Sikkink 2001: 401; similarly Keck and Sikkink 1998: 16; Price 1998b). The choice of the respective strategies depends on the identity of the actor as

---

[24]According to Nye (1990), "soft power" is to be distinguished from "hard power," that is the exercise of power with recourse to military and financial resources. In contrast, "soft power" is based on being a role model, which can be traced back to a specific value system or the culture of a country.

well as on the respective structural context and the associated political opportunity structures (Björkdahl 2002a: 49; Sell and Prakash 2004: 150).

As norm entrepreneurs often lack hard power resources, they mainly resort to non-coercive instruments of norm diffusion. The majority of constructivist studies therefore regard norm entrepreneurs as agents of persuasion in norm construction processes, who try to convince states of the validity of a norm by means of the better argument and to set positive incentives for norm-compliant behavior (Nadelman 1990; Finnemore and Sikkink 1998; Payne 2001). Martha Finnemore (1996: 12–13), for example, shows that norm entrepreneurs may act as "active teachers," as socializing agents that try to convey new standards of appropriateness to state actors through processes of argumentation and persuasion. Deitelhoff (2009) argues that norm entrepreneurs create conducive institutional conditions for persuasion and discourse by providing expertise, creating publicity and qua moral authority. They would therefore act as strategic discourse brokers throughout the whole process of negotiating norms.

Framing is perhaps the most frequently used (and analyzed) strategy of norm diffusion (e.g., Finnemore and Sikkink 1998: 908; Keck and Sikkink 1998: 17; Payne 2001).[25] In social movement theory, *collective action frames* are conceptualized as interpretative instruments to ascribe meaning, which is "intended to mobilize potential adherents and constituents, to garner by-stander support, and to demobilize antagonists" (Snow and Benford 1988: 199). As a rule, these collective action frameworks consist of three components: (1) the representation of the present (normative) state as unjust and therefore worthy of change, (2) the formulation of alternative actions, and (3) the construction of dichotomous identities to demarcate norm followers from other social groups (Gamson 1992; Klandermans 1997).

The construction of certain frames and the recourse to them enables actors to raise awareness of norm addressees for a certain problem perception. Through this, they are able to shape the normative discourse (Price 1998b: 628). Frames represent filters of reality or "mental shortcuts" (Busby 2010: 50) that allow activists to highlight certain aspects, while consciously pushing others into the background (Finnemore and Sikkink 1998: 896–897; Payne 2001: 43; Charnysh et al. 2015: 327). Framing is most strongly used in the phase of norm construction (problem identification or "diagnostic framing"; formulation of a solution or "prognostic framing" as well as taking specific measures or "motivational framing", Benford and Snow 2000: 617). The development of a narrative, in which the propagated norm is embedded, and which clearly identifies the responsibility for the problem to be solved, remains central ("adversarial framing," Keck and Sikkink 1998: 27; Benford and Snow 2000: 616). This can be achieved above all through creating emotional bonding. Richard A. Posner sees the main task of norm entrepreneurs in "changing the boundaries of altruism," with a special emphasis on:

---

[25]The concept was developed by sociologist Goffman (1974) and also found its way into the literature on social movements. In accordance with the subject of this study, I focus on how the concept has been used in norms research.

> mix[ing] appeals to self-interest with emotional appeals that bypass our rational calculating faculty and stir inarticulable feelings of oneness with or separateness from the people who are to constitute or to be rejected from the community that the moral entrepreneur is trying to create. They teach us to love or hate whom they love or hate. (Posner 1999: 1667)

In order to construct a norm candidate, norm entrepreneurs do not need to invent new frames. Instead, framing is often geared toward reformulating existing knowledge or presenting alternative frameworks that change how the existing normative order is perceived (Keck and Sikkink 1998: 17; Benford and Snow 2000: 615). Central to the diffusion of normative frames is both the language being used and the situational and historical embedding of the issue to be regulated (Charnysh et al. 2015: 328). "Frame resonance" (Benford and Snow 2000: 619–620), that is linking the new norms to already existing normative structures or the normative "frame of mind" (Björkdahl 2002a: 52) of the norm recipients, is considered a determining factor for norm acceptance (Florini 1996: 376; Finnemore and Sikkink 1998: 906; Keck and Sikkink 1998: 17; Payne 2001: 44).[26] A related yet specific case is the strategic and conscious "grafting" (Price 1998b: 628) of the propagated norm to an already established norm in the same political field, a tactic also known as "norm transplantation" (Farrell 2001: 63). Linking norms to symbolic actions that have an effect on the public can also serve to frame a situation in a normative way. This can be done, for example, by using emotionally charged images, organizing protest actions or awarding prizes (Keck and Sikkink 1998: 22).

Framing usually takes place in highly competitive normative contexts: Norm entrepreneurs engage in "frame contests" (Payne 2001: 44) or strategically use "counterframing" (Benford and Snow 2000: 616; 625–628; Finnemore and Sikkink 1998: 897; Keck and Sikkink 1998: 2) in order to thwart their opponents and push through "their" framing against competing normative claims. Ronald D. Krebs and Patrick Thaddeus Jackson speak of "rhetorical coercion" when actors succeed in rhetorically cornering opponents who then find themselves "publicly endorsing positions they may, or may not, find anathema" (Krebs and Jackson 2007: 42).

The question as to why some frames become accepted in the wake of "purposive moral struggle[s]" (Pozen 2008: 329) while others get dismissed has so far not been answered satisfactorily. However, it is believed that certain framings are more effective than others: Referring to normative precedents is just as much a success factor (Sandholtz 2007: 14) as referring to universally valid principles (Sandholtz 2007: 14, 21–23; Nagatzaam 2009: 75–76).[27] It may also be effective for norm advocates to link various (normative) issues or policy areas ("issue linkages", Keck and Sikkink 1998: 208). For instance, some studies refer to norms linked to the realm of international security (e.g., Charnysh et al. 2015: 344–345), international law

[26]Other synonyms are "issue linkage" (Koh 1998: 653), "cultural match" (Cortell and Davis 2000: 73), "normative fit" (Florini 1996: 376; Björkdahl 2002a, b: 52), "linking" (Rublee 2008: 44), or "nesting" (Müller 2013: 5).

[27]Whether or not an audience buys a certain frame is also influenced by the characteristics of the actors involved as well as by the content of the frame itself: by the simplicity and clarity of the message conveyed, by its resonance with the normative context of the addressees, and by its inherent consistency (Keck and Sikkink 1998: 73; Benford and Snow 2000: 619–621).

(Busby 2007; Johnstone 2007:125), the norms of physical integrity and equal opportunities (Finnemore and Sikkink 1998: 907), or linkages with metanorms, which are attributed higher importance in the hierarchy of norms (such as sovereignty or justice; Raymond 1997: 223; Wiener 2008: 66–67; Müller 2013: 5).[28] Others have found that norms that are consciously linked to the normative convictions of so-called "gatekeepers" (Busby 2010: 54; Carpenter 2011) are particularly influential. Likewise, studies dealing with diagnostic framing have pointed out the importance of so-called master frames that gain resonance independent of the issue they address and which are therefore taken up across different social movements, such as "rights frames" (Tarrow 2011) or "injustice frames" (Gamson et al. 1982; Cable and Shriver 1995; Carroll and Ratner 1996).

In addition to mobilizing supporters, framing also aims to build up social pressure. Summarized under the heading *naming, shaming, blaming*, scholars have found this strategy to be one of the most frequently used and most effective instruments in human rights policy (e.g., Sikkink 1993a, b; Keck and Sikkink 1998: 16; Risse et al. 1999; Liese 2006).[29] This refers in particular to verbal criticism,[30] accusations, and public exposure. The public "denouncing" aims to create pressure for justification and adaptation on the part of the norm violators (Liese 2006: 104). The classical targets of such strategies are usually state elites, who are considered to be vulnerable when social pressure is exerted on them in the form of public shaming and fearful of damage done to their reputation (Checkel 2001; Hafner-Burton 2008: 690). Because states fear a loss of reputation through public accusation and exposure, they are thought to initially enter into purely tactical behavioral concessions—e.g., because they want to preserve their identity as "decent" members of the international community. In the long run, however, they become entangled in the normative rhetoric to which they have become accustomed, and permanent behavioral changes occur (Keck and Sikkink 1998: 23–24; Risse et al. 1999; Liese 2006). By stigmatizing norm violators as outsiders to the community of civilized nations, norm advocates appeal to an actors' identity, a sense of belonging. Thomas Risse and Kathryn Sikkink sum up the underlying mechanisms as follows: "[S]haming then implies a process of persuasion, since it convinces leaders that their behavior is inconsistent with an identity to which they aspire." (Risse and Sikkink 1999: 15). Because it helps them build up social pressure, naming, shaming and blaming are particularly interesting for non-state actors such as transnational advocacy networks who lack more classical coercive means. The burden of proof is reversed, as norm-violating states are forced to justify

[28]Busby (2010: 53) argues that activists may consciously rely on ambiguous frames in order to generate greater resonance among different norm addressees.

[29]On the difference between strategies of framing and shaming, Busby notes: "Shaming is a close cousin of framing and is often implicitly referenced as a kind of framing. Where framing efforts […] can rely on appeals to actors' better angles and ideas about what is good and right, shaming efforts seek to punish and rhetorically bludgeon actors for failure to live up to their values. As a consequence, shaming has a more coercive feel" (Busby 2010: 16).

[30]Jüngling (2013: 51, fn. 12) defines verbal criticism as written or oral articulation of the disapproval of an action or a specific policy of one or more actors, which may not be followed by concrete actions on the part of the criticizing actor(s).

their adherence to normative practices which are challenged by norm entrepreneurs (Price 1998b: 517).

Other rhetorical techniques are also based on the exercise of social pressure, such as "shunning, exclusion, and demeaning, or dissonance derived from actions inconsistent with role and identity" (Johnston 2001: 499). In contrast to the instruments and techniques aimed at persuasion, naming, shaming, and blaming are categorized in the literature as "coercive means," which aim less to create a change of preference and rather to engender a revision of the cost-benefit calculation of the norm addressees (Price 2003: 590).[31] Often, these techniques are supplemented by sanctions ranging from trade boycotts and suspension of membership to symbolic sanctions such as entry bans (Risse and Sikkink 1999: 27).

In order to depict the existing normative order as obsolete and thus in need of regulation, norm entrepreneurs not only apply rhetorical strategies. In many cases, they also demonstrate their dissatisfaction with the prevailing normative order by deliberately seeking to undermine it and relying on provocation and scandals (Finnemore and Sikkink 1998: 904; Keck and Sikkink 1998: 22). Symbolic acts and deliberate violations of norms in the sense of inappropriate behavior (e.g., civil disobedience, rebelliousness) are particularly suitable means of attracting public attention for non-state actors that lack traditional power resources (Adut 2004: 532). Social movements in particular are increasingly relying on "shock tactics" (Sell and Prakash 2004: 169; Tarrow 2011) to generate media attention.

In summary, the instruments that norm entrepreneurs have at their disposal can be illustrated according to Busby's (2010: 39) *coercion-conversion* continuum[32] (Fig. 2.1).

coercion	negative incentive	positive benefit	attention shift	conversion
violent means (including civil disobedience, protests etc.)	sanctions, shaming	reward, praise	strategic framing (rhetorical action)	consensual dialogue (communicative action)

Fig. 2.1 Instruments of norm entrepreneurs. *Source* Adapted from Busby 2010: 39

[31]Genuine persuasion is geared toward actors changing their preferences and therefore requires that all actors involved are prepared to be convinced by the force of the better argument (Deitelhoff 2006: 76–77). Therefore, Björkdahl also raises the question, "whether norms established through coercive means, such as arm-twisting, shaming or moral sanctions which require constant monitoring to ensure compliance, can be considered as authentic norm adoption" (Björkdahl 2008: 136).

[32]While the literature on social (protest) movements illustrates the full spectrum of these techniques (Josselin and Wallace 2001b: 255), norm research has only recently begun to acknowledge norm advocates' usage of more confrontational, destructive means (e.g., Bob 2012).

2.8 Conditions for "Successful" Norm Entrepreneurship

Norm entrepreneurship becomes analytically comprehensible only after it has resulted in the (further) institutionalization, maintenance or strengthening of a propagated norm. As a corollary, scholars tend to focus on instances of "successful" norm entrepreneurship while ignoring cases in which advocates have failed in their efforts or in which their commitment has been deadlocked (for a critique, see Pozen 2008: 314–315). This is quite unfortunate because successful norm entrepreneurship is only *one* form of norm advocacy.[33] I thus suggest determining norm entrepreneurship based on the activities and normative argumentation that actors use in order to promote norms. Whether these result in the establishment, institutionalization or further strengthening of norms is of secondary importance.

The literature has different answers to the question of how to assess "successful" norm entrepreneurship. Some authors consider raising public awareness and assuming the role of a spokesperson as a sign for successful influence. As Björkdahl specifies: "norm entrepreneurs can be regarded as influential if they merely take the lead on a specific issue and gain support from only a few other actors" (Björkdahl 2002a: 49; similar Price 1998b: 638). The definition of "successful influence" used by Busby is more specific and ultimately hinges "on whether or not countries important for implementation have accepted the policy that advocates are pursuing through some domestic decision-making process" (Busby 2010: 37–38). Based on Finnemore and Sikkink, Deitelhoff (2006: 149) regards the explicit approval of a norm by about one-third of all norm addressees as an indicator of successful norm construction and refers for measurement purposes to the final votes in negotiations. Mere acceptance of a norm is thus supplemented here by a form of institutionalization (in the case of Busby in national decision-making procedures, in the case of Deitelhoff by codification in international documents). Such a form of institutionalization of the propagated norm can be seen as a relatively strong indicator of successful norm entrepreneurship (Finnemore and Sikkink 1998: 900). Although complete internalization has repeatedly been cited as an alleged endpoint of norm diffusion processes (e.g., Finnemore and Sikkink 1998), only a few authors equate "successful" norm advocacy with the internalization of the propagated norm. Whether the change in behavior occurred due to the insight into the moral validity of the norm or for tactical reasons is ultimately considered irrelevant for the success of norm entrepreneurship (Risse and Sikkink 2013: 284).

In approaching "successful" norm entrepreneurship, it might be useful to turn to Keck and Sikkink (1998: 201) who analyze the "effectiveness" of networks in various stages of the process of norm diffusion: (1) putting an issue on the political agenda and thus influencing public debates, (2) discursive commitments in light of the propagated norm, (3) normative changes at the domestic or international level, (4) policy changes, and (5) behavioral change on the part of norm addressees.

[33] Pozen (2008: 310) notes that some norm entrepreneurs may have been dismissed as "busybodies" or lunatics prior to norm institutionalization and sees the impossibility of ex-ante identification of norm entrepreneurs as the biggest difference to the entrepreneur concept used in economics.

It is not possible to predict with certainty whether norm entrepreneurship will ultimately follow one of the above-mentioned paths, whether it will get stuck, fail, or even have the opposite effect (Payne 2001: 44). However, the literature on norms and social movements has identified various conditions that are conducive for "successful" norm entrepreneurship. These relate to (1) external, structural factors;[34] (2) the characteristics of the normative context within which actors act (including properties of the propagated norm and the norm addressees), and (3) the characteristics and strategies of the norm entrepreneurs themselves. The last point is particularly interesting for this study and will therefore be highlighted in the following.

1. *External, structural factors* may create windows of opportunity for norm entrepreneurship (see also Wunderlich 2013: 29–30). Structural changes in the form of crises or political upheavals such as the end of the Cold War may lead to a change in political routines as a result of which norm entrepreneurs are able to inject alternative notions of how the normative order should look like into the public debate (e.g., Sandholtz and Syles 2009: 323–325; Florini 1996: 384–385). Such windows of opportunity may also be opened up by technological developments that provide actors with new instruments for enforcing norms or monitoring compliance (Price 2003: 596; Rosert et al. 2013).
2. Secondly, *characteristics of the normative context* might also impact the success of norm entrepreneurship. Rublee (2008: 429) concludes that uncertainty in a given situation increases the probability of success of norm advocacy. Political opportunity structures, such as already existing norms and the discursive and material structures in which actors are embedded, are also perceived as influencing norm entrepreneurship (Khagram et al. 2002: 18–20). While some studies identify ideological structures such as liberalism as being favorable for norm entrepreneurship (Keck and Sikkink 1998: 206; Adamson 2005), others point to certain "moments in 'world time'" (Risse et al. 1999: 21; Klotz 1995a: 17; Colonomos 2001: 87) that may be conducive to successful norm diffusion. In a similar vein, Coleman (2013) points to characteristics of the chosen institutional setting, such as the membership structure, mandate, formal, and informal decision-making procedures and legitimacy attributed to the respective institutional setting. Moreover, the possibilities for participation of civil society actors as well as procedural justice and the respective culture of deliberation have been found to play a role (Wiener 2008: 204–208).
   Whether advocacy leads actors to believe in the moral validity of the propagated norm or to change their behavior moreover depends on the characteristics of the norm addressees, such as to what extent these are vulnerable to social pressure (Keck and Sikkink 1998: 29; Risse and Sikkink 1999: 208). For state actors, the domestic political structure also plays a role (Checkel 1997; Cortell and Davis 1996: 454; Acharya 2004). Insights from social psychology seem to suggest that norm addressees are more likely to be influenced by "similar" actors when they

[34] It should be noted that the effect of these factors is not unidirectional, but can have beneficial and inhibitory effects on norm entrepreneurship. When I speak of conditions for success in the following, this is done for reasons of practicality.

seek recognition within a social community to which both actors feel they belong (Rublee 2008: 430).

The external factors presented above may impact the success or failure of norm entrepreneurship, yet norm entrepreneurs have only limited influence on their presence and shaping. This is not the case for the following factors, which can be directly influenced by norm advocates through the selection and framing of norms as well as the characteristics of the norm entrepreneurs themselves.

3. In fact, and thirdly, *characteristics of the propagated norm* may impact norm diffusion. Scholars disagree on whether clearly and precisely formulated norms are more likely to be accepted (e.g., Finnemore and Sikkink 1998: 906; Schimmelfennig 2003: 412–414) or whether the ambiguity of generally held norms can be regarded as conducive for norm diffusion (Krook and True 2012:105). Similarly, scholars have emphasized that whether advocacy is influential to a large extent depends on how norm entrepreneurs frame the norm and whether they are able to create linkages to already established norms or normative contexts (Finnemore and Sikkink 1998: 908; Keck and Sikkink 1998: 26–28, 204–205; Risse and Sikkink 1999: 2).[35]

Research on social movements and empirical norm studies have also identified a number of *actor characteristics* that can be beneficial to "successful" norm entrepreneurship. The ability of actors to organize is thus cited as an important prerequisite to feed their demands into political debates. The group size, the degree of social cohesion, a dense network structure, and clear membership criteria are regarded as decisive for the success of activist networks (Keck and Sikkink 1998: 28–29). In addition, certain types of actors are more likely to become active as norm entrepreneurs due to their institutional embeddedness (e.g., the UN Secretary-General).[36] The ability to articulate and the strategies used by the norm entrepreneurs are also considered decisive for the success or failure of their commitment (Busby 2010; Bob 2012: 27; Coleman 2013; Nagtzaam 2009:67). Scholars have also found that TANs in particular benefit from charismatic leaders with outstanding structural, communicative and strategic or intellectual skills and visionary goals (Brysk 2005: 462, 2009: 28). For state norm entrepreneurship, scholars refer to the existence of well-trained diplomats in addition to committed leaders (Björkdahl 2002a: 47, 2013: 330; Brysk 2005: 456; Müller 2011: 65) as influencing factors.

Many studies also show that a positive reputation, which goes beyond the respective policy area and thus the (perceived) status of an actor, can influence the success

[35] While norm entrepreneurs can increase the chances of "their" norm being diffused by respective framing, other content-related features of the propagated norm are only to a limited extent within the sphere of their influence, e.g., which political field it originates from or whether it refers to superordinate norms and principles such as sovereignty or justice. These factors could thus as well be assigned to the characteristics of the normative context.

[36] At the same time, such structures may constrain norm entrepreneurship: The UN Secretary-General, for example, acts on the basis of the UN Charter and relies on the normative consensus of the majority of member states.

of norm entrepreneurship[37]: If an actor is considered to be trustworthy, reliable and impartial, this increases the legitimacy attributed to it (Finnemore and Sikkink 1998: 906; Keck and Sikkink 1998: 14; Price 2003: 588–590; Charnysh et al. 2015: 6). The degree of such "moral authority" (Björkdahl 2002a: 48) ultimately hinges on the extent to which normative entrepreneurship is perceived as being oriented toward the common good and thus detached from self-interest (Finnemore and Sikkink 1998: 896–899). Moreover, the actors' expertise in the relevant field and his or her willingness to make it available to others plays a role (Kingdon 1995: 180–181; Halliday 2001: 36).

There is a link between the credibility of actors and the perception of consistency in behavior (Benford and Snow 2000: 619). Obviously, norm entrepreneurs are more influential if their words match their deeds across time and various audiences (particularly consistency between international obligations and domestic behavior, Risse et al. 1999; Björkdahl 2008: 137; Rublee 2008: 426–428).

2.9 A Bias Toward "Feel-Good" Norm Entrepreneurship

A vast literature deals with the emergence, diffusion, enforcement, and contestation of norms and analyzes how norm entrepreneurs of different types actively seek to persuade others of the moral validity of their normative visions. Yet, notwithstanding a comprehensive research program on norms, some gaps remain (for a (German) overview see Rosert 2012): There is still a lack of clear, consensual definitions which leads to ambiguous use of central terms such as "norm" or "norm entrepreneur." Moreover, norm researchers have been accused of being tied to an inherent belief in progress (Rosert and Schirmbeck 2007: 253) and of focusing in their empirical accounts on success stories of normative evolution, often with a bias on Western liberal norms (e.g., Epstein 2012b: 121).[38]

As has already been pointed out, the first generation of norm researchers was aware of the analytical limitations of their approach. They did acknowledge that norms always remain controversial, "competing values and understandings of what is good, desirable, and appropriate in our collective, communal life" (Finnemore 1996: 135). As early as 1996, Martha Finnemore emphasized: "there is nothing inherently 'good' about social norms" and consequently described her case selection (humanitarian protection standards and poverty alleviation) as "a comment on the paradigms I am engaging, not on my approach" (Finnemore 1996: 32). In order to show "how the 'ought' becomes the 'is'" (Finnemore and Sikkink 1998: 916), scholars needed to

[37]Some authors argue that it is easier for powerful states to become norm entrepreneurs because of the wealth of resources at their disposal, i.e., because they have higher communication resources, access to decision-making fora or coercive power (Florini 1996: 375; Reich 2005: 13–14).

[38]This normative bias has repeatedly been attributed to a liberal bias of constructivism itself (Sterling-Folker 2000; Barkin 2003; Adamson 2005). See also the recent debate on the limits and possibilities of critical norm research (Engelkamp et al. 2014a, b; Deitelhoff and Zimmermann 2014; Hofius et al. 2014).

focus on "successful" cases of norm diffusion, and that has often translated into assuming an—undertheorized—normative attitude toward their objects of inquiry.[39]

In their seminal study on transnational human rights networks, Keck and Sikkink (1998: 77) did acknowledge the existence of groups whose work was not per se aimed at the dissemination of "good" norms. Thomas Risse et al. point out that their spiral model of human rights diffusion is not based on a "belief in civilizing progress" (Risse et al. 1999), but that this model can explain both progressive normative development and stagnation or norm decay. Barnett and Finnemore take a "normative bias" (1999: ix), which they define in their own work, as a starting point for analyzing pathologies and dysfunctional or ineffective behavior of international organizations. Likewise, Tannenwald (1999: 437,461) emphasizes that norms may produce multiple and often unintended effects. For example, she points out that due to the emergence and consolidation of the "nuclear taboo," technological developments have shifted to conventional weapons and that these have become more legitimate. Many of the early works on successful norm diffusion processes also reveal negative or ambiguous effects of norms and point out that phenomena such as slavery, nationalism or heroism are also norm-based social constructions (Kowert and Legro 1996: 485, Fn. 81, Checkel 1998: 339; Finnemore and Sikkink 2001: 404; Barnett 2009: 207). During the initial stages of norm research, it was already true that "there are no bad norms from the vantage point of those who promote the norm" (Finnemore and Sikkink 1998: 892). Nevertheless, this was not reflected in empirical research designs. Martha Finnemore and Kathryn Sikkink concede that

> [t]he bias toward 'nice' norms has persisted, however, even after constructivism established itself as a legitimate analytic approach in IR [International Relations; CW]. Constructivists in IR have tended not to investigate the construction of xenophobic and violent nationalisms, for example, and the focus on social structures most of us admire has continued (Finnemore and Sikkink 2001: 404).

Although recent work has begun to address the "dark side of normative argumentation" (Heller et al. 2012), alternative norms deriving from non-liberal contexts have remained largely unconsidered in liberal norms research. Supposedly "bad" norms have so far only been given attention to the extent that their ostracism or ban, but not their construction, have been analyzed (for a review see Kowert and Legro 1996: 485; Checkel 1998: 339; Cowles 2003: 110–11). This is surprising given that as early as 1998 Jeffrey Checkel asked his colleagues to "give equal attention to the

[39]Consequently, Price (2008) confronts the criticism of a progressive bias inherent in norm research with an invitation to his constructivist colleagues to make their normative attitudes explicit. They should not shy away from facing difficult moral dilemmas that could arise as the downside of moral progress. According to Price, the explicit revelation of a normative standpoint would allow constructivists "to identify some of the morally undesirable implications of erstwhile progressive developments. This includes identification of complicity of the progressive with the oppressive" (Price 2008: 35). However, Matthew J. Hoffmann makes the following restrictions: "constructivism cannot provide guidance on whether socially constructed values are good or not, but it can expose the social constructedness of ideas that have come to count as moral values. This is valuable whether or not one analyzes normative structures widely understood (from perspectives other than constructivism) to be morally 'bad', ambiguous, or 'good'" (Hoffmann 2009: 242).

bad things in world politics that are socially constructed." In his view, this would "not only protect these scholars from getting caricatured as peaceniks by theoretical opponents, but it will also direct their attention to important unexplored issues such as the role of social construction in ethnic conflict and war" (Checkel 1998: 339).

The "good norms problem" (Kowert and Legro 1996: 385, Fn. 81) also affects other concepts of norm research. As already mentioned in the introductory chapter, another research gap that inspired this study is the tendency of liberal-constructivist norm research to focus on ideal-type norm entrepreneurs: In most cases, norm advocates are perceived of and conceptualized primarily as advocates of cosmopolitan and Western liberal norms. Often, they are considered "ethically good" (Cowles 2003: 111) and "typically respect-worthy actors pressing for salutary or at least reasonable changes" (Pozen 2008: 303).

The previous overview of how the concept of norm entrepreneurship has been used confirms this analytical bias: Norm entrepreneurs are typically considered to be morally oriented personalities or transnationally organized non-state actors committed to spreading Western liberal values. If attention has been put on states, researchers focused mainly on types of states that meet these criteria, namely small and medium-sized countries with an ostentatious orientation toward the common good—i.e., countries whose history, foreign policy, or political culture qualify them to act as advocates of "ethically good" or liberal-democratic norms.

The extent to which actors other than the transnational activist networks or good international citizens are committed to the construction and diffusion of norms and the nature of these norms has so far been largely ignored by liberal-constructivist norm scholars. Other gaps follow from this biased case selection: Not only do scholars ignore cases of failed norm entrepreneurship (for a critique see Carpenter 2007a: 114; Checkel 2012: 5; Pozen 2008: 332). As shown in this chapter, the selection bias also leads to a distorted view on the motives of and instruments used by norm advocates—often the effects of norm entrepreneurship are explained with persuasion and social influence by moral authority (see also Checkel 2012: 3). This not only contradicts recent critical constructivist work on the contestation of norms (Wiener 2008; Deitelhoff and Zimmermann 2014), it also fails to address the plurality of normative orders (and notions of order). Consequently, despite all conceptual diversity, only a few models of norm diffusion are able to analytically capture resistant practices and criticism of the prevailing normative order in the process of norm dynamics.

Moreover, it often remains inadequately theorized that norm diffusion processes are a decidedly political endeavor (but see Bucher 2014). While norm research has to be credited for having left a dichotomous view of norm-driven advocates on the one hand and interest-based states on the other, there is still a tendency to romanticize the activities of norm entrepreneurs as "do-gooders" (see e.g., Blakeley 2013; for a critique see Bob 2012: 4–5; Klotz and Lynch 2007:62).

For this reason, some scholars have pointed to the activities of conservative NGOs (Bob 2012) or "conflict entrepreneurs" (Ehrenreich Brooks 2003: 2326–27; Checkel 2012: 4) who specifically use violence and other "unpleasant techniques" (Checkel

2012: 4) to achieve their goals.[40] While still lacking systematic theorizing, these studies were able to demonstrate that the normative bias toward Western liberal, supposedly "progressive" norm entrepreneurs, has obscured important insights into the process of norm dynamics. Rather, they show that the application of the concept beyond prototypical cases can be promising. I will discuss these studies as well as critical constructivist approaches of norm construction and negotiation in Chap. 4. Before I do so, the following chapter addresses another unorthodox candidate whose eligibility as norm entrepreneur seems rather counterintuitive. It turns to those countries that are regarded as pariahs of the international community of states, which are neither willing nor able to abide by the basic norms and rules of the global order and who have thus been labeled "rogue states" by the USA.

References

Acharya, A. (2004). How ideas spread: Whose norms matter? Norm localization and institutional change in Asian regionalism. *International Organization, 58*(2), 239–275.

Acharya, A. (2009). *Whose ideas matter? Agency and power in Asian regionalism*. Ithaca, NY: Cornell University Library.

Acharya, A. (2011). Norm subsidiarity and regional orders. Sovereignty, regionalism, and rule-making in the third world. *International Studies Quarterly, 55*(1), 95–123.

Acharya, A. (2013). The R2P and norm diffusion. Towards a framework of norm circulation. *Global Responsibility to Protect, 5*(4), 466–479.

Adamson, F. (2005). Global liberalism versus political Islam: Competing ideological frameworks in international politics. *International Studies Review, 7*(4), 547–569.

Adler-Nissen, R. (2014). Stigma management in international relations: Transgressive identities, norms, and order in international society. *International Organization, 68*(1), 143–176.

Adut, A. (2004). Scandal as norm entrepreneurship strategy: Corruption and the french investigating magistrates. *Theory and Society, 33*(5), 529–578.

Aginam, O. (2014). The role of international organizations in promoting legal norms. In J. Yann & B. Knoppers (Eds.), *Routledge handbook of medical law and ethics* (pp. 390–400). New York: Routledge.

Alderson, K. (2001). Making sense of state socialization. *Review of International Studies, 27*(3), 415–433.

Alford, R. (2008). The nobel effect: Nobel peace prize laureates as international norm entrepreneurs. *Virginia Journal of International Law, 49*(1), 61–153.

Allison-Reumann, L. (2017). The norm-diffusion capacity of ASEAN: Evidence and challenges. *Pacific Focus, 32*(1), 5–29.

Atwood, D. (2002). NGOs and disarmament: Views from the coal face. *Disarmament Forum, 1*, 5–14.

Axelrod, R. (1986). An evolutionary approach to norms. *American Political Science Review, 80*(4), 1095–1111.

Baisley, E. (2016). Reaching the tipping point? Emerging international human rights norms pertaining to sexual orientation and gender identity. *Human Rights Quarterly, 38*(1), 134–163.

Barkin, J. (2003). Realist constructivism. *International Studies Review, 5*(3), 325–342.

[40] As examples of such techniques, Checkel cites rape and hazing as admission rituals in socialization processes of groups (Checkel 2012: 4). Even if for normative reasons it is doubtful as to what extent violent norm entrepreneurship is possible by definition, such an extension would make it possible to search for conditions of violent or non-violent norm construction or enforcement (see Chap. 10).

Barnett, M. (2009). *The international humanitarian order*. Abingdon: Routledge.
Barnett, M., & Finnemore, M. (1999). The politics, power, and pathologis of international organizations. *International Organization, 53*(4), 699–732.
Becker, H. (1963). *The outsiders. Studies in the sociology of deviance*. New York, NY: The Free Press.
Becker-Jakob, U., Hofmann, G., Müller, H., & Wunderlich, C. (2013) Good international citizens: Canada, Germany and Sweden. In H. Müller & C. Wunderlich (Eds.), *Norm dynamics in multilateral arms control, interests, conflicts, and justice* (pp. 207–245). Athens, GA: University of Georgia Press.
Behringer, R. (2012). The human security agenda: How middle power leadership defied us hegemony. New York, NY: Continuum.
Benford, R., & Snow, D. (2000). Framing processes and social movements: An overview and assessment. *Annual Review of Sociology, 26*(1), 611–639.
Benner, T. (2012). Brasilien als Normunternehmer: Die "Responsibility While Protecting". *Vereinte Nationen, 6*, 251–256.
Björkdahl, A. (2002a). *From idea to norm: Promoting conflict prevention*. Lund: Lund University.
Björkdahl, A. (2002b). Norms in international relations: Some conceptual and methodological reflections. *Cambridge Review of International Affairs, 15*(1), 9–23.
Björkdahl, A. (2008). Norm advocacy: A small state strategy to influence the EU. *Journal of European Public Policy, 15*(1), 135–154.
Björkdahl, A. (2013). Ideas and norms in Swedish peace policy. *Swiss Political Science Review, 19*(3), 322–337.
Blakeley, R. (2013). Human rights, state wrongs, and social change: The theory and practice of emancipation. *Review of International Studies, 39*(3), 599–619.
Blavoukos, S., & Bourantonis, D. (2011). Chairs as policy entrepreneurs in multilateral negotiations. *Review of International Studies, 37*(2), 653–672.
Bob, C. (2012). *The global right wing and the clash of world politics*. New York, NY: Cambridge University Press.
Brosig, M., & Zähringer, N. (2015). Norm evolution a matter of conformity and contestedness: South Africa and the responsibility to protect. *Global Responsibility to Protect, 7*(3–4), 350–375.
Brühl, T. (2003). *Nichtregierungsorganisationen als Akteure internationaler Umweltverhandlungen. Ein Erklärungsmodell auf der Basis der situationsspezifischen Ressourcennachfrage*. Frankfurt a. M.: Campus Verlag.
Brysk, A. (2005). Global good samaritans? Human rights foreign policy in Costa Rica. *Global Governance, 11*(4), 445–466.
Brysk, A. (2009). *Global good Samaritans: Human rights as foreign policy*. Oxford, NY: Oxford University Press.
Bucher, B. (2014). Acting abstractions: Metaphors, narrative structures, and the eclipse of agency. *European Journal of International Relations, 20*(3), 742–765.
Budabin, A. C. (2015). Celebrities as norm entrepreneurs in international politics: Mia Farrow and the 'Genocide Olympics' campaign. *Celebrity Studies, 6*(4), 399–413.
Bull, H. (1977). *The anarchical society: A study of order in world politics*. London: Basingstoke.
Busby, J. (2007). Bono Made Jesse Helms Cry: Jubilee 2000, Debt relief, and moral action in international politics. *International Studies Quarterly, 51*(2), 247–275.
Busby, J. (2010). *Moral movements and foreign policy*. New York, NY: Cambridge University Press.
Cable, S., & Shriver, T. (1995). Production and extrapolation of meaning in the environmental justice movement. *Sociological Spectrum, 15*(4), 419–442.
Capie, D. (2008). Localization as resistance: The contested diffusion of small arms norms in Southeast Asia. *Security Dialogue, 39*(6), 637–658.
Carbonara, E., Parisi, F., & Wangenheim, G. (2008). Lawmakers as norm entrepreneurs. *Review of Law and Economics, 4*(3), 779–799.
Carpenter, C. (2007a). Setting the advocacy agenda: Theorizing issue emergence and nonemergence in transnational advocacy networks. *International Studies Quarterly, 51*(1), 99–120.

Carpenter, C. (2007b). Studying issue non-adoption in transnational advocacy networks. *International Organization, 61*(3), 643–667.

Carpenter, C. (2011). Vetting the advocacy agenda: Network centrality and the paradox of weapons norms. *International Organization, 65*(1), 69–102.

Carr, A. (2012). *Australia as a middle power norm entrepreneur in the Asia-Pacific 1983–2010*. Canberra: University of Canberra.

Carroll, W., & Ratner, R. (1996). Master frames and counter-hegemony: Political sensibilities in contemporary social movements. *Canadian Review of Sociology, 33*(4), 407–435.

Charnysh, V., Lloyd, P., & Simmons, B. (2015). Frames and consensus formation in international relations: The case of trafficking in persons. *European Journal of International Relations, 21*(2), 323–351.

Checkel, J. (1997). International norms and domestic politics: Bridging the rationalist-constructivist divide. *European Journal of International Relations, 3*(4), 473–495.

Checkel, J. (1998). The constructivist turn in international relations theory. *World Politics, 50*(2), 324–348.

Checkel, J. (1999a). Norms, institution, and national identity in contemporary Europe. *International Studies Quarterly, 43*(1), 83–114.

Checkel, J. (1999b). *Regional norms and domestic social mobilization: Citizenship politics in post maastricht, Post-Cold War Germany*. ARENA Working Papers WP, 99(3), Oslo.

Checkel, J. (2000). Book review: The power of human rights. *Comparative Political Studies, 33*(10), 1337–1341.

Checkel, J. (2001). Why comply? Social learning and European identity change. *International Organization, 55*(3), 553–588.

Checkel, J. (2012). Norm entrepreneurship—Theoretical and methodological challenges. In *Memo prepared for a workshop on "The Evolution of International Norms and 'Norm Entrepreneurship". The Council of Europe in Comparative Perspective*. Oxford: Wolfson College, Oxford University.

Chwieroth, J. (2008). Normative change from within. The international monetary fund's approach to capital account liberalization. *International Studies Quarterly*, *52*(1), 129–158.

Coleman, K. (2013). Locating norm diplomacy: Venue change in international norm negotiations. *European Journal of International Relations, 19*(1), 163–186.

Colonomos, A. (2001). Non-state actors as moral entrepreneurs: A transnational perspective on ethics networks. In D. Josselin & W. Wallace (Eds.), *Non-state actors in world politics* (pp. 76–89). New York, NY: Palgrave.

Cooper, A. (1997). *Niche diplomacy: Middle powers after the cold war*. New York, NY: Palgrave Macmillan.

Cooper, A. (2002). Like-minded nations, NGOS, and the changing pattern of diplomacy within the UN system: An introductory perspective. In A. Cooper, J. English, & R. Thakur (Eds.), *Enhancing global governance: Towards a new diplomacy?* (pp. 1–18). Tokyo: United Nations University Press.

Cooper, A. (2008). *Celebrity diplomacy*. Boulder: Paradigm Publishers.

Cortell, A., & Davis, J. (1996). How do international institutions matter? The domestic impact of international rules and norms. *International Studies Quarterly, 40*(4), 451–478.

Cortell, A., & Davis, J. (2000). Understanding the domestic impact of international norms: A research agenda. *International Studies Review, 2*(1), 65–87.

Cortell, A., & Davis, J. (2005). When norms clash: International norms, domestic practices, and Japan's internalisation of the GATT/WTO. *Review of International Studies, 31*(1), 3–25.

Cowles, M. (2003). Non-state actors and false dichotomies: Reviewing IR/IPE approaches to European integration. *Journal of European Public Policy, 10*(1), 102–120.

Dashwood, H. (2012). CSR norms and organizational learning in the mining sector. *Corporate governance: The international journal of business in society, 12*(1), 118–138.

Davies, S. E., & True, J. (2017). Norm entrepreneurship in foreign policy: William Hague and the prevention of sexual violence in conflict. *Foreign Policy Analysis, 13*(3), 701–721.

Deitelhoff, N. (2006). *Überzeugung in der Politik: Grundzüge einer Diskurstheorie internationalen Regierens*. Frankfurt am Main: Suhrkamp taschenbuch wissenschaft.

Deitelhoff, N. (2009). The discursive process of legalization. Charting islands of persuasion in the ICC Case. *International Organization*, *63*(1), 33–66.

Deitelhoff, N., & Wolf, K. (2013). Business and human rights: How corporate norm violators become norm entrepreneurs. In T. Risse, S.C. Ropp, & K. Sikkink (Eds.), *The persistent power of human rights: From commitment to compliance* (pp. 222–238). Cambridge: Cambridge University Press.

Deitelhoff, N., & Zimmermann, L. (2013). Things we lost in the fire: How different types of contestation affect the robustness of international norms. *International Studies Review, viy080*. https://doi.org/10.1093/isr/viy080.

Deitelhoff, N., & Zimmermann, L. (2014). From the heart of darkness. Critical reading and genuine listening in constructivist norm research. A reply to Stephan Engelkamp, Katharina Glaab, and Judith Renner. *World Political Science Review*, *10*(1), 17–31.

Dessler, D. (1989). What's at stake in the agent-structure debate? *International Organization, 43*(3), 441–473.

Drezner, D. (2007). Foreign policy glam. *The National Interest, 92,* 22–28.

Ehrenreich Brooks, R. (2003). The new imperialism: Violence, norms, and the "rule of law". *Michigan Law Review, 101*(7), 2275–2340.

Elgström, O. (2000). Norm negotiations: The construction of new norms regarding gender and development in Eu foreign aid policy. *Journal of European Public Policy, 7*(3), 457–476.

Ellickson, R. (2001). The market for social norms. *American Law and Economics Association, 3*(1), 1–49.

Elster, J. (1989). *The cement of society: A study of social order*. New York, NY: Cambridge University Press.

Engelkamp, S., Glaab, K., & Renner, J. (2014a). Office hours: How (critical) norm research can regain its voice. *World Political Science Review, 10*(1), 33–61.

Engelkamp, S., Glaab, K., & Renner, J. (2014b). One step forward, two steps back. A reply to Nicole Deitelhoff and Lisbeth Zimmermann. *World Political Science Review*, *10*(1), 1–16.

Epstein, C. (2012a). Stop telling us how to behave: Socialization or infantilization? *International Studies Perspectives, 13*(2), 135–145.

Epstein, C. (2012b). Symposium: Interrogating the use of norms in international relations. An Introduction. *International Studies Perspectives, 13*(2), 121–122.

Evans, G. (2011). *Middle power diplomacy*. Lecture by Professor the Hon Gareth Evans, Chancellor of The Australian National University, President Emeritus of the International Crisis Group and former Foreign Minister of Australia. Santiago: Chile Pacific Foundation Santiago. Resource Document. http://www.gevans.org/speeches/speech441.html. Accessed 28 April 2017.

Farrell, T. (2001). Transnational norms and military development: Constructing Ireland's professional army. *European Journal of International Relations, 7*(1), 63–102.

Fastenrath, U. (1993). Relative normativity in international law. *European Journal of International Law, 4*(3), 305–340.

Feakes, D. (2003). Global society and biological and chemical weapons. In M. Kaldor, H. Anheier, & M. Glasius (Eds.), *Global Civil society yearbook* (pp. 87–117). Oxford: Oxford University Press.

Fey, M., Hellmann, A., Klinke, F., Plümmer, F., & Rauch, C. (2013). Established and rising great powers: The United States, Russia, China, and India. In H. Müller & C. Wunderlich (Eds.), *Norm dynamics in multilateral arms control: Interests, conflicts, and justice* (pp. 163–206). Athens, GA: University of Georgia Press.

Finnemore, M. (1993). International organizations as teachers of norms: The United Nations educational, scientific, and cultural organization and science policy. *International Organization, 47*(4), 565–597.

Finnemore, M. (1996). *National interests in international society*. Ithaca, NY: Cornell University Press.

Finnemore, M., & Sikkink, K. (1998). International norm dynamics and political change. *International Organization, 52*(4), 887–917.
Finnemore, M., & Sikkink, K. (2001). Taking stock: The constructivist research program in international relations and comparative politics. *Annual Review of Political Science, 4,* 391–416.
Fisher, C. S. (1999). *Reformation and resistance: Nongovernmental organizations and the future of nuclear weapons* (Report No. 29). Washington, DC: Henry L. Stimson Center.
Flohr, A., Rieth, L., Schwindenhammer, S., & Wolf, K. (2010). *The role of business in global governance: Corporations as norm-entrepreneurs*. Basingstoke: Palgrave Macmillan.
Florini, A. (1996). The evolution of international norms. *International Studies Quarterly, 40*(3), 363–389.
Gamson, W. (1992). The social psychology of collective action. In A. Morris, C. Mc Clurg Mueller (Eds.), *Frontiers in social movement theory* (pp. 3–76). New Haven, CT: Yale University Press.
Gamson, W., Fireman, B., & Rytina, S. (1982). *Encounters with unjust authority*. Homewood: Dorsey.
Garris, J. (1973). Sweden's debate on the proliferation of nuclear weapons. *Cooperation and Conflict, 8*(4), 189–208.
Garwood-Gowers, A. (2015). China's "responsible protection" concept: Re-interpreting the Responsibility to Protect (R2P) and military intervention for humanitarian purposes. *Asian Journal of International Law, 6*(1), 1–30.
Giddens, A. (1984). *The constitution of society*. Berkley, CA: University of California Press.
Goertz, G., & Diehl, P. (1992). Toward a theory of international norms: Some conceptual and measurement issues. *The Journal of Conflict Resolution, 36*(4), 634–664.
Goffman, Erving. (1974). *Frame analysis*. Cambridge: Harvard University Press.
Gurowitz, A. (1999). Mobilizing international norms: Domestic actors, immigrants, and the Japanese state. *World Politics, 51*(03), 413–445.
Gurowitz, A. (2006). The diffusion of international norms: Why identity matters. *International Politics, 43*(3), 305–341.
Haas, P. M. (1992). Introduction: Epistemic communities and international policy coordination. *International Organization, 46*(1), 1–35.
Hafner-Burton, E. M. (2008). Sticks and stones: Naming and shaming the human rights enforcement problem. *International Organization, 62*(04), 689.
Halliday, Fred. (2001). The romance of non-state actors. In D. Josselin & W. Wallace (Eds.), *Non-state actors in world politics* (pp. 21–36). Houndmills: Palgrave Macmillan.
Hamilton, D. (2008). *The United States: A normative power?* Working Document 291/2008. Centre for European Policy Studies CEPS. http://aei.pitt.edu/9320/2/9320.pdf. Accessed 28 April 2017.
Heller, R., Kahl, M., & Pisoiu, D. (2012). The "dark" side of normative argumentation—The case of counterterrorism policy. *Global Constitutionalism, 1*(2), 278–312.
Herro, A. (2015). The responsibility to protect, the use of force and a permanent United Nations Peace service. *International Journal of Human Rights, 19*(8), 1148–1162.
Hetcher, S. (2000). The FTC as internet privacy norm entrepreneur. *Vanderbilt Law Review, 53*(6), 2041–2062.
Hofferberth, M., Brühl, T., Burkart, E., Fey, M., & Peltner, A. (2011). Multinational enterprises as "social actors"—Constructivist explanations for corporate social responsibility. *Global Society, 25*(2), 205–226.
Hoffmann, M. (2003). Constructing a complex world: The frontiers of international relations theory and foreign policy-making. *Asian Journal of Political Science, 11*(2), 37–57.
Hoffmann, M. (2005). *Ozone depletion and climate change: Constructing a global response*. Albany, NY: State University of New York Press.
Hoffmann, M. (2007). *My norm is better than your norm: Contestation and norm dynamics*. Paper prepared for presentation at the annual meeting of the International Studies Association, Chicago, IL.
Hoffmann, M. (2009). Is constructivist ethics an oxymoron? *International Studies Review, 11*(2), 231–252.

Hoffmann, M. (2010). Norms and social constructivism in international relations. In Denemark, R. (Ed.) *The international studies encyclopedia* (pp. 5410–5426). Oxford: Blackwell Publishing.

Hofius, M., Wilkens, J., Hansen-Magnusson, H., & Gholiagha, S. (2014). Den Schleier lichten? Kritische Normenforschung, Freiheit und Gleichberechtigung im Kontext des «Arabischen Frühlings». Eine Replik auf Engelkamp/Glaab/Renner, Ulbert und Deitelhoff/Zimmermann. *Zeitschrift für Internationale Beziehungen, 21*(2), 85–105.

Hulme, D., & Fukuda-Parr, S. (2011). International norm dynamics and "the end of poverty": understanding the millennium development goals. *Global Governance: A Review of Multilateralism and International Organizations, 17*(1), 17–36.

Hurrell, A. (2001). Norms and ethics in international relations. In W. Carlsnaes, T. Risse, & B. Simmons (Eds.), *Handbook of international relations* (pp. 137–154). London: Sage.

Ingebritsen, C. (2002). Norm entrepreneurs: Scandinavia's role in world politics. *Cooperation and Conflict, 37*(1), 11–23.

Ingebritsen, C. (2006). *Scandinavia in world politics*. Oxford: Rowman & Littlefield.

Jepperson, R., Wendt, A., & Katzenstein, P. (1996). Norms, identity, and culture in national security. In P. Katzenstein (Ed.), *The culture of national security: Norms and identity in world politics* (pp. 33–75). New York, NY: Columbia University Press.

Job, B. (2006). International peace and security and state sovereignty: Contesting norms and norm entrepreneur. In R. Thakur & W. Sidhu (Eds.), *The Iraq crisis and world order: Structural, institutional and normative challenges* (pp. 55–74). Tokyo: United Nations University Press.

Johnson, R. (2000). Advocates and activists: Conflicting approaches on nonproliferation and the test ban treaty. In A. Florini (Ed.), T*he third force: The rise of transnational civil society* (pp. 49–82). Tokyo, Washington D.C.: Carnegie Endowment for International Peace.

Johnston, A. (2001). Treating international institutions as social environments. *International Studies Quarterly, 45*(4), 487–515.

Johnstone, I. (2007). The secretary-general as norm entrepreneur. In S. Chesterman (Ed.), *Secretary or general? The UN secretary-general in world politics* (pp. 123–138). Cambridge: Cambridge University Press.

Jose, B. (2018). *Norm contestation: Insights into non-conformity with armed conflict norms*. SpringerBriefs in political science. Cham: Springer International Publishing.

Josselin, D., & Wallace, W. (2001a). Non-state actors in world politics. A framework. In D. Josselin & W. Wallace (Eds.), *Non-state actors in world politics* (pp. 1–20). Houndmills: Palgrave Macmillan.

Josselin, D., & Wallace, W. (2001b). Non-state actors in world politics. The lessons. In: D. Josselin, & W. Wallace (Eds.), *Non-state actors in world politics* (pp. 251–260). Houndmills: Palgrave Macmillan.

Jüngling, K. (2013). Großmächtige Worte? Zur Wirkung verbaler Menschenrechtskritik auf Russland im Falle des Grosny-Ultimatums. *Zeitschrift für Internationale Beziehungen, 20*(2), 35–63.

Kamradt-Scott, A. (2010). Making sense of global health governance: A policy perspective. *Global Public Health, 5*(5), 556–557.

Katzenstein, P. (1996). Introduction: Alternative perspectives on national security. In P. Katzenstein (Ed.), *The culture of national security: Norms and identity in world politics* (pp. 1–32). New York, NY: Columbia University Press.

Kaufmann, C., & Pape, R. (1999). Explaining costly international moral action: Britain's sixty-year campaign against the Atlantic Slave Trade. *International Organization, 53*(4), 631–668.

Keck, M., & Sikkink, K. (1998). *Activists beyond borders: Advocacy networks in international politics*. Ithaca, NY: Cornell University Press.

Kelley, J. (2007). Who keeps international commitments and why? The international criminal court and bilateral nonsurrender agreements. *American Political Science Review, 101*(3), 573–589.

Kelsen, H. (1967). *The pure theory of law*. Berkeley: University of California Press.

Keohane, R. (1986). Reciprocity in international relations. *International Organization, 40*(1), 1–27.

Kersbergen, C. J., & Verbeek, B. (2007). The politics of international norms: Subsidiarity and the imperfect competence regime of the Europenean Union. *European Journal of International Relations, 13*(2), 217–238.

Khagram, S., Riker, J., & Sikkink, K. (2002). From Santiago to Seattle: Transnational advocacy groups restructuring world politics. In S. Khagram, J. Riker, & K. Sikkink (Eds.), *Restructuring world politics: Transnational social movements, networks, and norms* (pp. 3–23). Minneapolis, MN: University of Minnesota Press.

Kingdon, J. (1995). *Agendas, alternatives and public policies*. New York, NY: HarperCollins.

Klandermans, B. (1997). *The social psychology of protest*. Oxford: Blackwell.

Klotz, A. (1995a). *Norms in international relations: The struggle against Apartheid*. Ithaca, NY: Cornell University Press.

Klotz, A. (1995b). Norms reconstituting interests: Global racial equality and U.S. sanctions against South Africa. *International Organization, 49*(3), 451–478.

Klotz, A., & Lynch, C. (2007). *Strategies for research in constructivist international relations*. Armonk, NY: M.E. Sharpe.

Knopf, J. (2012). NGOS, social movements and arms control. In R. Williams & P. Viotti (Eds.), *Arms control: History, theory, and policy* (pp. 169–194). Santa Barbara, CA: ABC-CLIO.

Koh, H. (1998). The 1998 Frankel lecture. Bringing international law home. *Houston Law Review, 623*, 646–655.

Kowert, P., & Legro, J. (1996). Norms, identity, and their limits: a theoretical reprise. In P. Katzenstein (Ed.), *The culture of national security: Norms and identity in world politics* (pp. 451–497). New York, NY: Columbia University Press.

Krebs, R. R., & Jackson, P. T. (2007). Twisting tongues and twisting arms: The power of political rhetoric. *European Journal of International Relations, 13*(1), 35–66.

Krook, M., & True, J. (2012). Rethinking the life cycles of international norms: The United Nations and the global promotion of gender equality. *European Journal of International Relations, 18*(1), 103–127.

Kumar, A. V. (2017). Norm entrepreneur, catalyst or challenger? India in the nuclear non-proliferation narrative. *South Asian Survey, 21*(1–2), 90–111.

Lanteigne, M. (2017). 'Have you entered the storehouses of the snow?' China as a norm entrepreneur in the Arctic. *Polar Record, 53*(2), 117–130.

Lantis, J. (2011). Redefining the nonproliferation norm? Australian Uranium, the NPT, and the Global Nuclear Revival. *Australian Journal of Politics and History, 57*(4), 543–561.

Liese, A. (2006). *Staaten am Pranger. Zur Wirkung Internationaler Regime auf Innerstaatliche Menschenrechtspolitik*. Wiesbaden: VS Verlag für Sozialwissenschaften.

Manners, I. (2002) Normative power Europe: A contradiction in terms? *JCMS: Journal of Common Market Studies, 40*(2), 235–258

Månsson, K. (2008). UN Peace operations as norm entrepreneurs: The challenge of achieving communicative action on human rights. In A. Swain, R. Amer, & J. Öjendal (Eds.), *Globalization and challenges to building peace* (pp. 121–144). London: Anthem Press.

March, J., & Olsen, J. (1998). The institutional dynamics of international political orders. *International Organization, 52*(4), 943–969.

March, J., & Olsen, J. (2004). *The logic of appropriateness*. Arena Working Paper 9/2004. http://www.arena.uio.no/publications/wp04_9.pdf. Accessed 28 April 2017.

McKeown, R. (2009). Norm regress: US Revisionism and the slow death of the torture norm. *International Relations, 23*(1), 5–25.

Mintrom, M., & Norman, M. (2009). Policy entrepreneurship and policy change. *The Policy Studies Journal, 37*(4), 649–667.

Montoya, C. (2013). *From global to grassroots: The European Union, transnational advocacy, and combating violence against women*. Oxford: Oxford University Press.

Mueller, J. (1996). Changing attitudes towards war: The impact of the First World War. *British Journal of Political Science, 21*(1), 1–28.

Müller, H. (2004). Arguing, bargaining and all that. Communicative action, rationalist theory and the logic of appropriateness in international relations. *European Journal of International Relations, 10*(3), 395–435.

Müller, H. (2011). Habermas meets role theory. Communicative action as role playing? In S. Harnisch, C. Frank, & H. Maull (Eds.), *Role theory in international relations. Approaches and analyses* (pp. 55–73). London: Routledge.

Müller, H. (2013). Introduction: Where it all began. In H. Müller & C. Wunderlich (Eds.), *Norm dynamics in multilateral arms control, interests, conflicts, and justice* (pp. 1–19). Athens, GA: University of Georgia Press.

Müller, H., & Wunderlich, C. (2013). *Norm dynamics in multilateral arms control, interests, conflicts, and justice*. Athens, GA: University of Georgia Press.

Müller, H., Below, A., & Wisotzki, S. (2013). Beyond the state: Nongovernmental organizations, the European Union, and the United Nations. In H. Müller & C. Wunderlich (Eds.), *Norm dynamics in multilateral arms control, interests, conflicts, and justice* (pp. 296–336). Athens, GA: University of Georgia Press.

Murithi, T. (2016). The African Union as a norm entrepreneur: The limits of human protection and mass atrocities prevention. *Global Responsibility to Protect, 8*(2–3), 227–248.

Muzzatti, S. (2002). Moral Panic. In D. Levinson (Ed.), *Encyclopedia of crime and punishment* (pp. 1076–1079). London: Sage.

Nadelmann, E. (1990). Global prohibition regimes: The evolution of norms in international society. *International Organization, 44*(4), 479–526.

Nagtzaam, G. (2009). *The making of international environmental treaties: Neoliberal and constructivist analyses of normative evolution*. Cheltenham: Edward Elgar Publishing.

Neumann, I., & Gstöhl, S. (2006). Introduction: Lilliputians in Gulliver's world? In C. Ingebritsen & I. Neumann (Eds.), *Small states in international relations* (pp. 3–36). Seattle, WA: University of Washington Press.

Nye, J. (1990). Soft power. *Foreign Policy, 80,* 153–171.

Orchard, P. (2014). *A right to flee*. Cambridge: Cambridge University Press.

Padamsee, T. (2009). Culture in connection: Re-contextualizing ideational processes in the analysis of policy development. *Social Politics, 16*(4), 413–445.

Panke, D., & Petersohn, U. (2012). Why international norms disappear sometimes. *European Journal of International Relations, 18*(4), 719–742.

Payne, R. (2001). Persuasion, frames and norm construction. *European Journal of International Relations, 7*(1), 37–61.

Posner, R. (1997). Social norms and the law: An economic approach. *The American Economic Review, 87*(2), 365–369.

Posner, R. (1999). *The problematics of moral and legal theory*. Cambridge, MA: Harvard University Press.

Powell, C. (2004). The role of transnational norm entrepreneurs in the U.S. "War on terrorism". *Theoretical Inquiries in Law*, *5*(1), 47–80.

Pozen, D. (2008). We are all entrepreneurs now. *Wake Forest Law Review, 43,* 282–340.

Price, R. (1997). *The chemical weapons Taboo*. Ithaca, NY: Cornell University Press.

Price, R. (1998a). International norms and the mines Taboo: Pulls toward compliance. *Canadian Foreign Policy Journal, 5*(3), 105–123.

Price, R. (1998b). Reversing the gun sights: Transnational civil society targets land mines. *International Organization, 52*(3), 613–644.

Price, R. (2003). Transnational civil society and advocacy in world politics. *World Politics, 55*(4), 579–606.

Price, R. (2008). Moral limit and possibility in world politics. In R. Price (Ed.), *Moral limit and possibility in world politics* (pp. 1–52). Cambridge: Cambridge University Press.

Price, R., & Tannenwald, N. (1996). Norms and deterrence: The nuclear and chemical weapons taboos. In Katzenstein, P. (Ed.), *The culture of national security. Norms and identity in world politics* (pp. 114–152), New York, NY: Columbia University Press.

Ravenhill, J. (1998). Cycles of middle power activism: Constraint and choice in Australian and Canadian foreign policies. *Australian Journal of International Affairs, 52*(3), 309–327.

Raymond, G. (1997). Problems and prospects in the study of international norms. *Mershon International Studies Review, 41*(2), 205–245.

Reich, S. (2005). *Global versus national norms: Are codes of conduct converging across regions?*. Pittsburgh, PA: Ford Institute for Human Security.

Risse, T., & Draude, A. (2018). Special issue: The agency of the governed. *Third World Quaterly, 2*(5).

Risse, T., Ropp, S., & Sikkink, K. (1999). *The power of human rights, international norms and domestic change*. New York, NY: Cambridge University Press.

Risse, T., & Sikkink, K. (1999). The socialization of international human rights norms into domestic practices: Introduction. In T. Risse, S. Ropp, & K. Sikkink (Eds.), *The power of human rights, international norms and domestic change* (pp. 1–38). New York, NY: Cambridge University Press.

Risse, T., & Sikkink, K. (2013). Conclusion. In T. Risse, S. Ropp, & K. Sikkink (Eds.), *The persistent power of human rights: From commitment to compliance* (pp. 275–295). Cambridge: Cambridge University Press.

Rosert, E. (2012). Fest etabliert und weiterhin lebendig. Normenforschung in den Internationalen Beziehungen. *Zeitschrift für Politikwissenschaft, 22*(4), 599–623.

Rosert, E. (2018a). Salience and the emergence of international norms: Napalm and cluster munitions in the inhumane weapons convention. *Review of International Studies, 45*(1), 77–99.

Rosert, E. (2018b). Norm emergence as agenda diffusion: Failure and success in the regulation of cluster munitions. *European Journal of International Relations* (open access). https://doi.org/10.1177/1354066119842644.

Rosert, E., Becker-Jakob, U., Franceschini, G., & Schaper, A. (2013). Arms control norms and technology. In H. Müller & C. Wunderlich (Eds.), *Norm dynamics in multilateral arms control: Interests, conflicts, and justice* (pp. 109–140). Athens, GA: University of Georgia Press.

Rosert, E., & Schirmbeck, S. (2007). Zur Erosion internationaler Normen. Folterverbot und nukleares Tabu in der Diskussion. *Zeitschrift für Internationale Beziehungen, 14*(2), 253–288.

Rublee, M. (2008). Taking stock of the nuclear nonproliferation regime: Using social psychology to understand regime effectiveness. *International Studies Review, 10*(3), 420–450.

Rublee, M. (2009). *Nonproliferation norms: Why states choose nuclear restraint*. Athens, GA: University of Georgia Press.

Rushton, S. (2008). The UN Secretary-General and norm entrepreneurship: Boutros Boutros-Ghali and democracy promotion. *Global governance: A review of multilateralism and international organizations, 14*(1), 95–110.

Rutherford, K., Brem, S., & Matthew, R. (2003). *Reframing the agenda: The impact of NGO and middle power cooperation in international security policy*. Westport, CT: Praeger.

Sandholtz, W. (2007). *Prohibiting plunder: How norms change*. New York, NY: Oxford University Press.

Sandholtz, W., & Stiles, K. (2009). *International norms and cycles of change*. Oxford, NY: Oxford University Press.

Santa-Cruz, A. (2005). Constitutional structures, sovereignty, and die emergence of norms: The case of international election monitoring. *International Organization, 59*(3), 663–693.

Saunders, E. (2006). Setting boundaries: Can international society exclude "rogue states"? *International Studies Review, 8*(1), 23–53.

Schimmelfennig, F. (2003). Internationale Sozialisation. Von einem "erschöpften" zu einem produktiven Forschungsprogramm? In G. Hellmann, K. Wolf, & M. Zürn (Ed.), *Die neuen internationalen Beziehungen. Forschungsstand und Perspektiven in Deutschland* (pp. 401–427). Baden-Baden: Nomos.

Schumpeter, J. (1912). *Theorie der wirtshaftlichen Entwicklung*. Leipzig: Duncker & Humblot.

Sell, S., & Prakash, A. (2004). Using ideas strategically: The contest between business and NGO networks in intellectual property rights. *International Studies Quarterly, 48*(1), 143–175.

Sending, O. (2002). Constitution, choice and change: Problems with the "logic of appropriateness" and its use in constructivist theory. *European Journal of International Relations, 8*(4), 443–470.
Shannon, V. (2000). Norms are what states make of them: The political psychology of norm violation. *International Studies Quarterly, 44*(2), 293–316.
Sikkink, K. (1993a). Human rights, principled issue-networks, and sovereignty in Latin America. *International Organization, 47*(2), 411–441.
Sikkink, K. (1993b). Transnational politics, international relations theory, and human rights. *PS: Political Science and Politics*, 31(3), 516–523.
Sikkink, K. (2011). *Beyond the justice cascade: How agentic constructivism could help explain change in international politics*. Revised paper from a keynote address. Millenium Annual Conference, "Out of the Ivory Tower. Weaving the Theories and Practice of International Relations", London School of Economics. https://www.princeton.edu/politics/about/file-repository/public/Agentic-Constructivism-paper-sent-to-the-Princeton-IR-Colloquium.pdf. Accessed 28 April 2017.
Sikkink, K. (2014). Latin American countries as norm protagonists of the idea of international human rights. *Global Governance, 20*(3), 389–404.
Sjöström, E. (2010). Shareholders as norm entrepreneurs for corporate social responsibility. *Journal of Business Ethics, 94*(2), 177–191.
Smith, K. (2004). The European Parliament and human rights: Norm entrepreneurs or ineffective talking shop? *Dossier El Parlamento Europeo en la Política Exterior, 11(2004).*
Snow, D., & Benford, R. (1988). Ideology, frame resonance, and participant mobilization. *International Social Movement Research, 1*(1), 197–217.
Souaré, I. (2014). The African Union as a norm entrepreneur on Military Coups d'Etat in Africa 1952–2012. An empirical assessment. *Journal of Modern African Studies, 52*(1), 69–94.
Stein, T. (2008). *Global social and civil entrepreneurs: An answer to the poor performance of global governance?* Discussion Paper SP IV 2008-304, Wissenschaftszentrum Berlin für Sozialforschung.
Sterling-Folker, J. (2000). Competing paradigms or birds of a feather? Constructivism and neoliberal institutionalism compared. *International Studies Quarterly, 44*(1), 97–119.
Stuenkel, O. (2015). *The BRICS and the future of global order*. Lanham, MD: Lexington Books.
Sunstein, C. (1996). Social norms and social roles. *Columbia Law Review, 96*(4), 903–968.
Tannenwald, N. (1999). The nuclear taboo: The United States and the normative basis of nuclear non-use. *International Organization, 53*(3), 433–468.
Tarrow, S. (2011). *Power in movement: Social movements and contentious politics*. New York, NY: Cambridge University Press.
Thomson, J. (1993). Norms in international relations: A conceptual analysis. *International Journal of Group Tensions, 23*(1), 67–83.
Towns, A. (2012). Norms and social hierarchies: Understanding international policy diffusion "from below". *International Organization, 66*(2), 179–209.
Vadura, K. (2015). The EU as 'norm entrepreneur' in the Asian region: Exploring the digital diplomacy aspect of the human rights toolbox. *Asia Europe Journal, 13*(3), 349–360.
Wallbott, L. (2014). Keeping discourses separate: Explaining the non-alignment of climate politics and human rights norms by small island states in United Nations climate negotiations. *Cambridge Review of International Affairs, 27*(4), 736–760.
Wendt, A. (1992). Anarchy is what states make of it. The social construction of power politics. *International Organization*, *46*(2), 391–425.
Widmaier, W. W., & Park, S. (2012). Differences beyond theory: Structural, strategic, and sentimental approaches to normative change. *International Studies Perspectives, 13*(2), 123–134.
Wiener, A. (2008). *The invisible constitution of politics: Contested norms and international encounters*. Cambridge, NY: Cambridge University Press.
Willetts, P. (1996). *"The conscience of the world": The influence of nongovernmental organizations in the UN system*. Washington, DC: Brookings Institution.

Wisotzki, S. (2008). Negotiating human security at the UN: Transnational civil society, arms control and disarmament. In J. Joachim, & B. Locher (Ed.), *Transnational Activism in the UN and the EU. A Comparative Study* (pp. 74–89). Abington: Routledge.

Wrage, S., & Wrage, A. (2005). Multinational enterprises as "moral entrepreneurs" in a global prohibition regime against corruption. *International Studies Perspectives, 6*(3), 316–324.

Wunderlich, C. (2013). Theoretical approaches in the study of norms. In H. Müller & C. Wunderlich (Eds.), *Norm dynamics in multilateral arms control, interests, conflicts, and justice* (pp. 20–47). Athens, GA: University of Georgia Press.

Youde, J., & Slagter, T. (2013). Creating "good international citizens", middle powers and domestic political institutions. *Seton Hall Journal of Diplomacy and International Relations, 14*(2), 123–133.

Zimmermann, L. (2017). *Global norms with a local face? Rule-of-law promotion and norm translation*. New York: Cambridge University Press.

Zwingel, S. (2012). How do norms travel? Theorizing international women's rights in transnational perspective. *International Studies Quarterly, 56*(1), 115–129.

Zwolski, K., & Kaunert, C. (2011). The EU and climate security: a case of successful norm entrepreneurship? *European Security, 20*(1), 21–43.

Chapter 3
Against the Norms of International Society: Rogues, Outlaws, and Pariahs

As has been pointed out in the previous chapter, liberal norm research can be criticized for focusing on those kinds of norm entrepreneurs working for the progressive diffusion of Western liberal norms. At the same time, opposition and resistance to the current normative order are usually stigmatized as hostility to prevailing norms. This becomes obvious when looking at the concept of so-called "rogue states", a social construct that gained prominence in the US security policy discourse in the 1990s. The following chapter firstly discusses the coinage and meaning of the term in the context of US foreign and security policy. I start by tracing the central elements of the so-called "rogue state" doctrine, go on to discuss the selective and seemingly arbitrary usage of the term, particularly with regard to policy making, and take a look into the academic approach to the "rogue state" concept. The concluding section is of central importance for the focus of this study as it evaluates how "rogue states" are judged in terms of their attitude toward international norms by both academic and policy circles.

3.1 "Rogue States" as a Construct of American Security Policy

The concept of "rogue states" only became an inherent part of the US foreign and security policy narrative during the first half of the 1990s (Klare 1995; Litwak 2000, 2007; Homolar 2011). While precursors of the demonizing term, such as "nuclear outlaw,"[1] had already been used in the 1970s, prior to 1980, the term "rogue states" or equivalents were rarely used to designate regimes such as Idi Amin's Uganda,

[1] Countries suspected of considering a nuclear option, such as Israel, South Africa, South Korea or Taiwan were repeatedly been labeled as outlaws or pariahs during that period (Quester 1975; Betts 1977; Harkavy 1981). Some authors claim that this paved the way for a change of perspective on the external misconduct of alleged "rogue states" (Litwak 2007: 28).

C. Wunderlich, *Rogue States as Norm Entrepreneurs*,
Norm Research in International Relations,
https://doi.org/10.1007/978-3-030-27990-5_3

Pol Pot's Cambodia under the Khmer Rouge or South Africa during apartheid (Litwak 2000: 50, 2007: 27–28). Stigmatization was primarily based on objectionable *domestic policy* practices of states against their own population. Their behavior in the international system was of lesser importance.

In 1979, the focus shifted for the first time to foreign policy misconduct (often accompanied by aggression toward neighboring countries). At that time, the State Department under US President Jimmy Carter began publishing an annual list of states suspected of supporting international terrorism.[2] In 1985, President Ronald Reagan spoke of "outlaw states" and as such can be regarded as having pioneered the "rogue states" concept. He referred to countries such as Cuba, Iran, Nicaragua, and North Korea, which, as leaders of a "confederation of terrorist states," were suspected of undermining the US foreign policy objectives (quoted from Klare 1995: 26). At the end of the 1980s, terms such as "rogue," "renegade," and "outlaw" had become an integral part of the US foreign and security policy vocabulary (Klare 1995: 27). Subsequently, the label was also applied to other countries such as Iraq and Libya. The alleged charges, which included support for international terrorism, possession of weapons of mass destruction (WMD), and ballistic delivery vehicles, or the pursuit of them, served to stigmatize the states as "rogues." From the US point of view, these countries threatened the basic principles of the global (nuclear) order (Klare 1995; Litwak 2000; Henriksen 2001).

However, it was the first Clinton administration that comprehensively coined and shaped the concept which, as Klare (1995) claims, mainly served to replace the previous enemy image of the "evil empire" (Reagan 1983) of the USSR and—in the long run—to preserve bureaucratic structures in the US Department of Defense (for a critical assessment, see Litwak 2000: 7).

The best-known definition of the concept was probably formulated by Anthony Lake, President Clinton's national security advisor, in 1994. He warned against "recalcitrant, outlaw and backlash states" (Lake 1994: 45) which he saw as being on the wrong side of history and which therefore had to be contained. According to Lake, the USA, being the only remaining superpower, was responsible for transforming such "backward" states into constructive members of the international community. In detail, Lake summarized the definition of "rogue states" used by the Clinton administration as follows:

> Our policy must face the reality of recalcitrant and outlaw states that not only choose to remain outside the family [of nations; CW] but also assault its basic values. There are few "backlash states": Cuba, North Korea, Iran, Iraq, and Libya. For now, they lack the resources of a superpower, which would enable them to seriously threaten the democratic order being created around them. Nevertheless, their behavior is often aggressive and defiant. […] These backlash states have some common characteristics. Ruled by cliques that control power through coercion, they suppress human rights and promote radical ideologies. While their political

[2]This list was created in 1979 by the State Department under the Export Administration Act. Since then, it has been published annually by the Coordinator for Counterterrorism of the State Department. Until 2003, it was entitled "Patterns of Global Terrorism" and since 2004, it has been named "Country Reports on Terrorism." All documents are available at https://www.state.gov/j/ct/rls/crt/; 28.04.2017.

> systems vary, their leaders share a common antipathy toward popular participation that might undermine the existing regimes. These nations exhibit a chronic inability to engage constructively with the outside world. [...] They are often on the defensive, increasingly criticized and targeted with sanctions in international forums. Finally, they share a siege mentality. Accordingly, they are embarked on ambitious and costly military programs—especially in weapons of mass destruction (WMD) and missile delivery systems—in a misguided quest for a great equalizer to protect their regimes or advance their purposes abroad. (Lake 1994: 45–46)

Typically, "rogue states" were henceforth characterized as despotic dictatorships (Tanter 1999), whose behavior was unpredictable (and thus incalculable). In 1998, Foreign Minister Madeleine Albright declared: "they [rogue states; CW] not only have no stake in the system but, on the contrary, [...] their very being revolves around the fact that they want to undo the system, literally throw hand grenades into it to destroy it" (Albright 1998).

The combination of perceived aggressive external behavior and the possession of weapons of mass destruction or the quest for them produced a threat perception in the USA that went far beyond that associated with the Soviet Union, which—in comparison—was considered militarily stronger, but ultimately more rational (Senn 2008: 14). "Rogue States," however, were seen not only as irrational and destructive but also as being culturally inferior opponents and disadvantaged by power asymmetries (Hoyt 2000: 307–309). Therefore, pure containment strategies were considered unreliable. Instead, President Clinton favored a more confrontational containment strategy based on coercive means such as economic sanctions, subversion, and diplomatic isolation, and—if all else failed—the use of force. In the words of Lake, the USA as the only remaining superpower had a "special responsibility [...] to neutralize, contain and, through selective pressure, perhaps eventually transform these backlash states into constructive members of the international community" (Lake 1994: 46).

However, in his last year in office (1999/2000), US President Clinton changed his approach toward supposed "rogue states" to a more moderate and differentiated policy that was also reflected in a change of wording. The provocative term "rogue states" was supplemented with the less pithy expression "states of concern." This shift not only resulted from the recognition that "a single description, one size fits all" (Litwak 2000: 9) was of little benefit in approaching and dealing with the heterogeneous world of "rogues." Purportedly, it was also a reaction to vehement criticism of the American "rogue states" doctrine that had been voiced by European states as well as Canada and Japan (Saunders 2006; Stritzel and Schmittchen 2011). Correspondingly, strategies of containment were replaced by a policy of "constructive engagement" that followed the premise that regime change could rather be initiated through cooperation and economic incentives than through the threat of force (Senn 2008: 172).

However, this change in strategy was abruptly brought to an end when George W. Bush Jr. took office. Following the terrorist attacks of 9/11, the "rogue state" concept returned to the US policy toolbox. It became a metaphor for a whole bunch of "new" threats. In his first State of the Union address on January 29, 2002, President Bush identified an "axis of evil" between Iraq, Iran, and North Korea.[3] In so doing, he linked the stigmatizing label with the concept of "evil," known to be more likely to appeal to the general public (Geis and Wunderlich 2014; on the "evilization" of "rogue States" see Müller 2014).[4] According to Bush, "states like these [Iran, Iraq, North Korea; CW], and their terrorist allies, constitute an axis of evil, arming to threaten the peace of the world." And he concluded that "the price of indifference would be catastrophic" (Bush 2002).

According to the US national security strategy of 2002, "rogue states" were characterized by five criteria:

> [They] brutalize their own people and squander their national resources for the personal gain of the rulers; display no regard for international law, threaten their neighbors, and callously violate international treaties to which they are party; are determined to acquire weapons of mass destruction, along with other advanced military technology, to be used as threats or offensively to achieve the aggressive designs of these regimes; sponsor terrorism around the globe; and reject basic human values and hate the USA and everything for which it stands. (White House 2002: 14)

Due to their support for terrorism and their possible recourse to weapons of mass destruction, "rogue states" were seen as representing an imminent threat. Consequently, preemptive military strikes against these states and their terrorist allies were legitimate (Bush 2002: 14–15).

Later, Secretary of State John R. Bolton added Libya, Syria, and Cuba to what he termed "beyond the axis of evil" (Bolton 2002). While Operation Iraqi Freedom led to regime change in Iraq in 2003 and thus to the disappearance of the country from the rogue roster, in 2005, Secretary of State Condoleezza Rice described Iran and North Korea (together with Cuba, Belarus, Zimbabwe, and Myanmar) as "outposts of tyranny" (Rice 2005).

Like the terminology of the Reagan administration, the Bush administration's definition of "rogue states" was primarily based on domestic political conditions and human rights violations (Geis and Wunderlich 2014: 10). The US administration insisted on severe countermeasures against perceived "rogue states," favoring a strategy of regime change. This behavior was reinforced by the drastic events of 9/11, which left a feeling of vulnerability in the country. As Robert Litwak aptly summarizes: "Regime change was depicted as the only way to bring about durable change in rogue states because their threatening behavior derived from their very nature and they were deemed incapable of evolving" (Litwak 2012: 2).

---

[3]The term was coined by Bush's speechwriter at the time, David Frum. Originally, he had suggested an "axis of hatred," which Bush changed to the "axis of evil" (Frum 2003: Chap. 12).

[4]Contrary to the idea of evil, the term "rogue state" opens up courses of action other than preemption and regime change. These include containment, coexistence, or even the prospect of punishing the perceived "rogue," but ultimately leading him back on the right track and reintegrating him into the international community (Geis and Wunderlich 2014).

When Barack Obama took office in 2009,[5] the golden years of the "rogue states" concept seemed to be over. Shortly, after his inauguration, he announced a change of policy similar to that of the Clinton administration. Obama promised to the states, now called outliers, "to extend a hand if you are willing to unclench your fist" (Obama 2009). The policy toward these states was to be based on a two-tiered political strategy of rapprochement and "coercive diplomacy" (diplomatic engagement paired with pressure, on the concept, see George 1991). Obama's announcement and the shift in strategy were also interpreted as an attempt to counter the accusation of inconsistent "rogue" labeling (Litwak 2012: 15–19; Wagner 2014: 152–153). From that time on, the USA used the term "outlier states" to refer to states that did not meet their obligations as legitimate members of the international community and who therefore positioned themselves outside the community of "decent" states. The resulting policy toward them was based on the following offer: Those who showed willingness to adhere to internationally agreed rules and norms could count on being reintegrated into the circle of legitimate members of the international community. The norms on which the US administration focused and which they considered to be ignored by the outsiders were, in particular, the obligations arising from the nuclear non-proliferation regime. The main recipients of the label were therefore Iran and North Korea.

However, the change of terminology did not alter the inconsistent and selective usage of the label. Even though the fear that a state might seek to possess WMD capabilities seemed to be one of the decisive criteria of roguishness, how the label has been applied does not reflect the reality of the international system. At present, there are only five states outside the NPT: Security concerns and/or skepticism about the discriminatory nature of the treaty have motivated India, Pakistan, and Israel to refrain from signing the treaty and subsequently initiate their own nuclear weapon programs. In addition, in 2003, North Korea declared its withdrawal from the regime. In contrast to South Sudan, which has yet to sign the treaty, India, Pakistan, and North Korea clearly possess military nuclear programs.[6] Israel is pursuing a policy of "nuclear opacity" and refrains from officially declaring itself a nuclear weapon state

[5]This study does not take into account the current U.S. administration under Donald Trump as forty-fifth president of the USA, because the period of investigation for the empirical analysis ended in spring 2015. While it is noteworthy that President Trump reintroduced the "rogue state" label into the foreign and security policy discourse, this fact is not crucial for the question guiding the research interest here, namely whether Iran acts as a norm entrepreneur. It is suffice to note here that President Trump has clearly distanced himself from his predecessor's policies and political style, particularly in the area of foreign and security policy, and has made ample use of rhetorical provocations and threatening gestures. He has repeatedly labeled Iran, North Korea, and Venezuela as "rogue states" and he has promised to use "maximum pressure" (Trump 2018) in order to prevent these states from threatening vital interests.

[6]India conducted its first "peaceful" nuclear test in 1974. The second test was carried out in 1998 immediately after the indefinite extension of the NPT. Pakistan followed shortly in May of the same year. North Korea conducted underground nuclear tests in 2006, 2009, 2013, 2016, and, most recently, 2017.

(Cohen 1999).[7] Strictly speaking, the countries concerned do not violate internationally certified non-proliferation obligations through their possession of nuclear weapons, since they are not members of the NPT.[8] However, Israel, North Korea, and Pakistan in particular have been repeatedly accused of related norm violations in the past. These include Israel's attacks against the Osirak Iraqi nuclear reactor in 1981 (Joyner 2009: Chaps. 6–9; Spector and Cohen 2008) or the role of the Pakistani government in the smuggling network around the Pakistani nuclear physicist Abdul Qadeer Khan. Therefore, it is beyond controversy that these states are also "nuclear outlier states" (Lodgaard 2008; Johnson 2010) or "nuclear dissidents" (Sakar 2013), which pose a challenge—if not a threat—to the stability of the non-proliferation regime. Yet neither Israel, nor India and Pakistan, nor South Sudan was labeled a "rogue" or "outlier" state by the Obama administration.

The selective and sometimes arbitrary classification of different states as "rogue states" by the US administration has been a cause for vast criticism (e.g., Saunders 2006; Stritzel and Schmittchen 2011). Examples abound: Syria, which met the two key features defined by the USA (possession or pursuit of WMD and support for international terrorism), has never consistently been called a "rogue state," because of its role in the Middle East peace process. The fact that Cuba, which did not have a WMD program or ever aspired to do so, nor represented a serious threat to American interests, received the "rogue" label, has on several occasions been explained with reference to the fact that the Cuban exile population had considerable political influence on American politics (Litwak 2000: 380, 2007: 32). This inconsistent usage of the term by the US administration indicates that the "rogue states" concept does not represent an impartial, objective classification of a group of states. To a far greater extent, it is a foreign policy construct whose strategic benefit lies in shaping political options for action.[9] According to Litwak (2000: 202), the USA itself ultimately determines who is stigmatized as a "rogue state." Statistical analyses on the use of the label across different administration levels and different periods of time also support this conclusion. Hoyt (2000: 301–302) explains the frequent usage of the label in 1997 and 1999 with reference to President Clinton's efforts to persuade the Senate to ratify the CWC and adopt the national missile defense program.[10]

Therefore, the changing composition of the "gallery of rogues" can also be seen in terms of instrumental usage (Wunderlich 2017). Quantitative analyses of public statements by various American politicians show that the "rogue" label was mainly

[7]Israel supposedly initiated its military nuclear weapons program in 1968, the same year that the NPT was submitted for signature. Israel's tolerated nuclear weapons status has led to conflicts, particularly in the Middle East region. The perceived injustice and unequal treatment have repeatedly led to expressions of displeasure on the part of some Arab states, Iran, and members of the Non-Aligned Movement. Experts have expressed concern that dealing with Israel's nuclear status has given other countries in the region a pretext to develop their own programs.

[8]However, the legality and validity of North Korea's withdrawal from the NPT are controversial (Bunn and Timerbaev 2005).

[9]In this context, the lack of definition of the term in international law and in international legal language is also criticized (George 1993: 49; Litwak 2000: 47–48; Caprioli and Trumbore 2005).

[10]O'Reilly (2007) and Senn (2009: 138–140) come to similar conclusions.

used during the 1990s for Iraq, Iran, North Korea, and Libya (in decreasing frequency) and less for Syria, Cuba, and Zimbabwe or Sudan (Hoyt 2000; O'Reilly 2007). Since 1984, Iran has been continuously on the list of states suspected of supporting terrorism. North Korea, on the other hand, was removed from this list in 2008, only to be relisted in 2017. Libya, which abandoned all its WMD programs in 2003, can be regarded as a "transformed" rogue state (at least in terms of supporting terrorist groups and the pursuit of weapons of mass destruction). In 2011, the rehabilitated "ex-villain" Muhammar al-Gaddafi fell back into disgrace internationally as a result of civil war. However, Libya was not officially designated as being a rogue or outlier state again (Müller 2007: 94; Onderco 2014).

3.2 The Scholarly Discourse on "Rogue States"

The rapid career of the "rogue states" concept in American security policy has also affected the scientific landscape. The majority of scholarly accounts of the term takes a policy-oriented perspective and examines how to deal with presumed "rogue states" (e.g., Litwak 2000, 2007: Chap. 3; Malici and Walker 2014; Rubin 2014). Only a few scholars agree with the US practice of using the term as an objective category of deviant states (although with varying indicators of their characteristics; Henriksen 2001; Caprioli and Trumbore 2003; Geldenhuys 2004; Nincic 2005; Rotberg 2007). Instead, most of the academic literature on "rogue states" emphasizes the concept's constructedness and examines its instrumental use as a (US foreign and security policy (mobilization) strategy (for a seminal assessment, see Litwak 2000: 63).

Herring (2000; see also Senn 2009: 17–23) distinguishes between a conservative, liberal, left-wing, and interpretivist perspective. Advocates of a *conservative* perspective propagate the analytical usefulness of the term. Consequently, they regard the threat emanating from these states as being objective and perceive the "rogue" label to be an adequate expression to propagate this view (e.g., Tanter 1999; Henriksen 2001; Rotberg 2007).[11] While they share the assumption that certain states pose a threat to international security, supporters of a *liberal* perspective on "rogue states" claim, however, to be aware of the subjective connotation associated with labeling. They admit that the label is primarily an instrument for political mobilization (e.g., Klare 1995; Litwak 2000; Caprioli and Trumbore 2005). In doing so, they criticize the fact that the stigmatization of highly heterogeneous actors represents a generalization that makes it impossible to formulate differentiated policies vis-à-vis those states (e.g., Hoyt 2000: 308–309; Litwak 2000: 241; O'Reilly 2007). Authors associated with the *left*-wing camp point out that the "rogue" label—if consistently interpreted—would also apply to the USA itself and its allies (Blum 2002; Derrida 2006) if one were to take the used definition "states that do not regard themselves as bound by international norms" (Chomsky 2000: 1) seriously.

[11] Some of these authors refrain from using the term "rogue state" and refer more generally to "deviant states" (e.g., Geldenhuys 2004; Nincic 2005).

Scholars who take an *interpretative* perspective are less concerned with whether the "rogue" label represents an objective or subjective category. Rather, they understand the labeling practice as part of the conceptual structure of the international system. In their view, the concept represents a strategic social construct serving to maintain the current power structure (Herring 2000; de Graaff and van Apeldoorn 2011). Many of these authors follow a social constructivist or critical constructivist paradigm (e.g., Senn 2009; Homolar 2011; Stritzel and Schmittchen 2011; Wagner et al. 2014; Wunderlich 2017).

Some of these studies seek to explain the "rogue states" concept by making use of research on "enemy images" (Herrmann and Fischerkeller 1995: 432–436; Hoyt 2000: 307–309). They show that the use of strong enemy images not only increases the willingness to take interventionist measures but also that the act of labeling itself puts actors in a position of confrontation that hinders alternative courses of action (Herrmann and Fischerkeller 1995: 432–436; Hoyt 2000: 307–9). Martin Senn (2009: 25) emphasizes the constitutive role of *mutual* threat perceptions for the stigmatization of a state as a "rogue state": Crucial for the labeling is the undemocratic and irrational nature of the state in question, as well as its fundamental opposition to the current world order and the pursuit of a revisionist foreign policy (Senn 2009: 143–147; similar O'Reilly 2007: 298).

Such an understanding of "rogue states" as retrograde and irrational suggests that their primary goal is the destruction of the current world order. In this vein, the "rogue" concept resembles Kant's "unjust enemy" (Müller 2014). Applying the label then serves to justify exceptional measures against the countries concerned in order to prevent a threat to international security and peace (Geis and Wunderlich 2014).

Some authors point out that the behavior of the stigmatized "rogue states" themselves may be influenced by threat perceptions and that the interaction between presumed "rogues" and labeling actors ought to be seen as a result of mutually perpetuating hostile attitudes (Beeman 2005; Senn 2009). Similarly, Malici (2009) warns that the term "rogue state" could become a self-fulfilling prophecy and cites exaggerated threat perceptions and concerns about the resurgence of communism that had prompted the USA to adopt a hostile attitude toward countries such as Cuba, Iran, and North Korea, even though some of these countries actually sought friendly relations with the USA. By framing these states as "rogues" and at the same time using preemptive military strategies against them, the USA has intensified the designated "perceived threat by the rogue states" and has ultimately led them to seek WMDs as deterrent.

3.3 On the Relationship Between "Rogue States" and International Norms

The majority of studies rather uncritically identifies "rogue states" by their relationship to international norms. "Rogue states" are by definition not considered legitimate members of the international community and are characterized as outsiders in relation to the group of "respectable states" (Rawls 2002: 79–80), who are neither willing nor able to comply with the rules of the prevailing normative order (Lake 1994; Klare 1995; Litwak 2000, 2007, 2012; Henriksen 2001; Caprioli and Trumbore 2003).[12]

Both in the academic literature and in the political discourse, "rogue states" are primarily conceived of as violators of basic norms of international conduct. For example, the Clinton administration characterized them as outsiders who consciously position themselves in opposition to the international community and its fundamental values (Lake 1994: 45). While the Bush administration was preoccupied with the "nature" of presumed "rogue states," President Obama's shift in terminology once again made the reference to norms very clear: "Outlier states" were to be regarded as such because of their disrespect for central rules and norms of the international community. The national security strategy of 2010 states that "[I]f nations challenge or undermine an international order that is based upon rights and responsibilities, they must find themselves isolated" (The White House 2010).

Other scholars refrain from using the term "rogue states." Yet norm deviance again becomes the defining element. Speaking of "renegade states," Miroslav Nincic sees "norm-breaking [as] their key defining feature" (Nincic 2005: 18) when it comes to domestic constitution, policy objectives, and means. In particular, "renegade states" deviate from international standards of appropriateness by violating human rights, supporting international terrorism, seeking WMD, and engaging in territorial aggression (Nincic 2005: 48–53).

Deon Geldenhuys sees "rogue states" as being a subgroup of "deviant" states, "that behaved badly and deserved to be shunned by other respectable members of international society" (Geldenhuys 2004: 11).[13] In 1998, Alexander Wendt characterized "rogue states" by their "rejectionist attitude toward the norms of the international community" (Wendt 1998: 113). By that, they are ultimately perceived and described as "outlaw states" (see also Klare 1995: 26; Hoyt 2000: 303; Schmittchen 2006: 4; O'Reilly 2007: 307; Senn 2009: 13).[14] The (perceived or attributed) transgression of international norms turns "rogue states" into bad international citizens (Kustermans

[12]It is not argued here that the governments designated as "rogue states" are usually not among the most norm-compliant members of the international community. In fact, they have often been found guilty of norm-breaking behavior, particularly when it comes to human rights or security policy. Yet this does not change the fact that similar norm violations have been and still are committed by "legitimate" members of the international community, whose membership in the circle of "respected" states—for whatever reasons—is officially not questioned.

[13]In sociology, deviance is characterized by the fact that anomalous behavior is primarily attributed to an actor by its respective social reference group. Rather than being an actor quality, deviance is a social construct used for exclusory purposes. Geldenhuys lists eleven "sins" commited by deviant international actors: (a) the threat to world peace and international security, including the pursuit of weapons of mass destruction, (b) support for international terrorism, (c) conventional armament, (d) regional (territorial) aggression, (e) an autocratic system and domestic human rights violations, (f) crimes against humanity, (g) war crimes, (h) export of the revolution, (i) anti-Americanism/ "anti-Westernism", (j) "international assertiveness," and (k) drug trafficking (Geldenhuys 2004: 23–37).

[14]The states usually considered as "rogue states" by the USA are not necessarily the same states designated as such in the scholarly literature. However, both attributions stigmatize certain states and deprive them of their right to have a say because of perceived deviations from prevailing norms.

2014: 19), which as a consequence are denied membership of the “decent” community of states. They are accused of wanting to destabilize or destroy the current normative order, which in the eyes of the members of the international community turns them into threats to international security and peace (Henriksen 2001; Klare 1995; Lake 1994). Consequently, presumed “rogue states” are often described as revisionist states whose misconduct has its origin in the rejection of a current normative order perceived as deeply unjust (Claes 2012; Geldenhuys 2004: 23; Litwak 2012: 25).

The states in question are furthermore suspected of not complying with the “rules of rationality” (Malici 2009: 39). Their behavior is thus regarded as being unpredictable, and preemptive measures are therefore justified.[15] Some authors even go as far as to call the states concerned “*anomic*, unsavory, and troublesome places” (Rotberg 2007: 8; emphasis added). This corresponds to a tendency in the literature as well as in the political discourse to assume that “rogue states” do not act in a normative manner.[16] In this vein, Michael Rubin notes: “The problem with rogues is that they don’t subscribe to diplomatic norms” (quoted from the National Review 2014; for a similar assessment, see Koh 1998: 676).

However, as has been aptly demonstrated by norms research, the meaning of norms is generally contested. Their content and the objectives resulting from them are ambiguous and therefore subject to constant negotiation processes (among others: Wiener 2008). Müller concedes at best “a thin layer of a normative international framework” (Müller 2011: 60). Accordingly, studies that deal with the constructed nature of the “rogue states” concept argue that the usage of the “rogue” label can also be seen as an expression of power. As Nincic aptly summarizes, “deviant behavior is not identified by wholly objective criteria since, even if abstract norms are widely agreed upon, considerable scope remains for subjective assignment of the label “deviant” to specific sorts of conduct” (Nincic 2005: 21).

According to Kustermans (2014: 17), the “rogue states” concept, as perceived and constructed by the US administration, represents certain features that are primarily aimed at stabilizing the construction of an international community based on universal values and common interests (Kustermans 2014: 17). Saunders (2006) even assumes that the invention and application of the term itself have made the USA a norm entrepreneur, demarcating the borders of the international community. In her reflection on Iran’s and North Korea’s nuclear “deviance,” Ogilvie-White (2007, 2010) explains the opposition of both states to the norms of the global nonproliferation regime by the fact that they have been denied full integration into the international community.

---

[15] Nevertheless, many authors stress the intentionality of deviant behavior of so-called “rogue states” (Senn 2009: 24–25; Ogilvie-White 2010). Indeed, the intentional, strategic deviation from international norms might serve to maintain or expand domestic political power, albeit driven by ideological motives (ethno-nationalist, religious, political-ideological) which justify deviations from international norms—particularly so if these are in opposition to national normative structures (Nincic 2005: 14, 24).

[16] See for example, the common accusation that Iran is governed by “mad mullahs.” In the academic field, Dror (1971) uses the term “crazy states.”

The present study perceives itself as being part of the tradition of critical approaches that emphasize the social constructedness of the "rogue state" concept and that question its usefulness as an analytical category. Above all, the label serves to maintain the current normative order and to delineate identities. The instrumentalizing function of the label is also reflected in the fact that most of the literature fails to take into account the perspectives of the designated "rogues"—even in cases that acknowledge the socially constructed relationship between "rogue states" and labeling actors (for a few exceptions, see Heradstveit and Bonham 2007; Jacobi et al. 2014; Wunderlich 2014, 2017). Among scholars—particularly those coming from a Western liberal context—there seems to be agreement that so-called "rogue states" are defined by their norm deviance and that they are to be treated as objects of normative intervention rather than agents shaping the normative order of which they are an integral part of. However, deviance from international norms is very often merely presumed and lacks clear proof. The question remains as to which normative order concepts these countries represent. Also, no exploration has been made as to what extent the states stigmatizing others as "rogue states" merely try to avoid potential norm conflicts instead of recognizing the stigmatized states' contribution to the evolution of norms.

References

Albright, M. (1998). *Remarks by Secretary of State*. Resource document. Madeleine K. Albright at Howard University, Washington, DC, 14.04.1998. http://www.fas.org/news/usa/1998/04/98041503_tpo.html. Accessed April 28, 2017.

Beeman, W. O. (2005). *The "Great Satan" vs. the "Mad Mullahs: How the United States and Iran demonize each other*. Chicago, IL: University of Chicago Press.

Betts, R. (1977). Paranoids, pygmies, pariahs & nonproliferation. *Foreign Policy, 26,* 157–183.

Blum, W. (2002). *Rogue state: A guide to the world's only superpower*. London: Zed Books.

Bolton, J. R. (2002, May 6). *Beyond the axis of evil: Additional threats from weapons of mass destruction*. http://www.heritage.org/research/lecture/beyond-the-axis-of-evil. August 28, 2015.

Bunn, G., & Timerbaev, R. (2005). The right to withdraw from the nuclear non-proliferation treaty (NPT): The views of two NPT negotiators. *Yaderny Kontrol, 10*(1–2), 20–29.

Bush, G. W. (2002). *State of the Union Address, The White House, Washington, DC, 29.01.2002*. Resource document. http://georgewbush-whitehouse.archives.gov/news/releases/2002/01/20020129-11.html. Accessed April 28, 2017.

Caprioli, M., & Trumbore, P. (2005). Rhetoric versus reality: Rogue states in interstate conflict. *Journal of Conflict Resolution, 49*(5), 770–791.

Caprioli, M., & Trumbore, P. F. (2003). Identifying "Rogue" states and testing their interstate conflict behavior. *European Journal of International Relations, 9*(3), 377–406.

Chomsky, N. (2000). *Rogue States: The rule of force in world affairs*. Cambridge, MA: South End Press.

Claes, J. (2012). Protecting civilians from mass atrocities: Meeting the challenge of R2P rejectionism. *Global Responsibility to Protect, 4*(1), 67–97.

Cohen, A. (1999). *Israel and the bomb*. New York, NY: Columbia University Press.

De Graaff, N., & van Apeldoorn, B. (2011). Varieties of US post-cold war imperialism: Anatomy of a failed hegemonic project and the future of US geopolitics. *Critical Sociology, 37*(4), 403–427.

Derrida, J. (2006). *Schurken. Zwei Essays über die Vernunft*. Frankfurt am Main: Suhrkamp.

Dror, Y. (1971). *Crazy states: A counterconventional strategic problem*. Lexington, MA: Heath Lexington Books.
Frum, D. (2003). *The right man: The surprise presidency of George W. Bush*. New York: Random House.
Geis, A., & Wunderlich, C. (2014). The good, the bad, and the ugly. Comparing the notions of "Rogue" and "Evil" in international politics. *International Politics, 51*(4), 458–474.
Geldenhuys, D. (2004). *Deviant conduct in world politics*. Houndmills: Palgrave Macmillan.
George, A. (1991). *Forceful persuasion: Diplomacy as an alternative to war*. Washington, DC: United States Institute of Peace Press.
George, A. (1993). *Bridging the gap. Theory and practice in foreign policy*. Washington, DC: United States Institute of Peace Press.
Harkavy, R. E. (1981). Pariah states and nuclear proliferation. *International Organization, 35*(1), 135–163.
Henriksen, T. H. (2001). The rise and decline of rogue states. *Journal of International Affairs, 54*(2), 349–371.
Heradstveit, D., & Bonham, M. (2007). What the axis of evil metaphor did to Iran. *Middle East Journal, 61*(3), 421–440.
Herring, E. (2000). Rogue rage: Can we prevent mass destruction? *Journal of Strategic Studies, 23*(1), 188–212.
Herrmann, R., & Fischerkeller, M. (1995). Beyond the enemy image and spiral model: Cognitive-strategic research after the cold war. *International Organization, 49*(3), 415–450.
Homolar, A. (2011). Rebels without a conscience: The evolution of the rogue states narrative in US Security Policy. *European Journal of International Relations, 17*(4), 705–727.
Hoyt, P. (2000). The "Rogue State" image in American Foreign Policy. *Global Society, 14*(2), 297–310.
Jacobi, D., Weber, C., & Hellmann, G. (2014). Dissident foreign policy and the (re-)production of international orders. In W. Wagner, W. Werner, & M. Onderco (Eds.), *Deviance in international relations: "Rogue States" and international security* (pp. 106–131). Basingstoke: Palgrave Macmillan.
Johnson, T. (2010). *The four nuclear outlier states, council on foreign relations*. Resource document. http://www.cfr.org/proliferation/four-nuclear-outlier-states/p22164. Accessed April 28, 2017.
Joyner, D. H. (2008). *International law and the proliferation of weapons of mass destruction*. Oxford: Oxford University Press.
Joyner, D. (2009). *International law and the proliferation of weapons of mass destruction*. Oxford: Oxford University Press.
Klare, M. (1995). *Rogue states and nuclear outlaws: America's Search for a new foreign policy*. New York, NY: Hill and Wang.
Koh, H. (1998). The 1998 Frankel lecture. Bringing international law home. *Houston Law Review, 623,* 646–655.
Kustermans, J. (2014). "Roguery" and citizenship. In W. Wagner, W. Werner, & M. Onderco (Eds.), *Deviance in international relations: "Rogue States" and international security* (pp. 15–35). Basingstoke: Palgrave Macmillan.
Lake, A. (1994). Confronting backlash states. *Foreign Affairs, 73*(2), 45–55.
Litwak, R. (2000). *Rogue states and U.S. foreign policy: Containment after the cold war.* Washington, DC: Woodrow Wilson Center Press with Johns Hopkins University Press.
Litwak, R. (2007). *Regime change: U.S. strategy through the prism of 9/11*. Washington, DC: Woodrow Wilson Center Press with Johns Hopkins University Press.
Litwak, R. (2012). *Outlier states: American Strategies to change, contain, or engage regimes*. Washington, DC: Woodrow Wilson Center Press with Johns Hopkins University Press.
Lodgaard, S. (2008). Dealing with the outliers. In J. du Preez (Ed.), *Nuclear challenges and policy options for the next U.S. Administration*. Monterey, CA: James Martin Center for Nonproliferation Studies.
Malici, A. (2009). Rogue states: Enemies of our own making? *Psicología Política, 39,* 39–54.

Malici, A., & Walker, S. G. (2014). Role theory and "Rogue States". In W. Wagner, W. Werner, & M. Onderco (Eds.), *Deviance in international relations: "Rogue States" and international security* (pp. 132–151). Basingstoke: Palgrave Macmillan.

Müller H. (2007). The exceptional end to the extraordinary libyan nuclear quest. In M. Bremer & S. Lodgaard (Eds.), Nuclear proliferation and international security (pp. 73–95). New York, NY: Routledge.

Müller, H. (2011). Habermas meets role theory. Communicative action as role playing? In S. Harnisch, C. Frank, & H. Maull (Eds.), *Role theory in international relations. Approaches and analyses* (pp. 55–73). London: Routledge.

Müller, H. (2014). Evilization in liberal discourse. From Kant's "Unjust Enemy" to today's "Rogue State". *International Politics, 51*(4), 475–491.

National Review. (2014). *Diplomatic dangers and cautions, NR Interview, 20.02.2014.* Resource document. http://www.nationalreview.com/article/371525/damned-if-you-do-interview. Accessed April 28, 2017.

Nincic, M. (2005). *Renegade regimes: Confronting deviant behavior in world politics.* New York, NY: Columbia University Press.

O'Reilly, K. (2007). Perceiving rogue states: The use of the "Rogue State" concept by U.S. Foreign Policy elites. *Foreign Policy Analysis, 3*(4), 295–315.

Obama, B. (2009). *Inaugural address, 21.01.2009.* Resource document. https://www.whitehouse.gov/blog/inaugural-address. Accessed April 28, 2017.

Ogilvie-White, T. (2007). International responses to Iranian Nuclear Defiance: The non-aligned movement and the issue of non-compliance. *European Journal of International Law, 18*(3), 453–476.

Ogilvie-White, T. (2010). The defiant states: The nuclear diplomacy of North Korea and Iran. *The Nonproliferation Review, 17*(1), 117–138.

Onderco, M. (2014). From a "Rogue" to a parolee: Analyzing Libya's "De-roguing". In W. Wagner, W. Werner, & M. Onderco (Eds.), *Deviance in international relations: "Rogue States" and international security* (pp. 171–192). Basingstoke: Palgrave Macmillan.

Quester, G. (1975). *What's new on nuclear non-proliferation.* Aspen: Aspen Institute for Humanistic Studies.

Rawls, J. (2002). *Das Recht der Völker.* Berlin: Walter de Gruyter.

Reagan, R. (1983). *Evil empire speech, Transcript, 08.03.1983.* Resource document. http://millercenter.org/president/speeches/speech-3409. Accessed April 28, 2017.

Rice, C. (2005). *Opening remarks by secretary of state-designate Dr. Condoleezza Rice, Senate Foreign Relations Committee, Washington DC, 18.01.2005.* Resource document. http://2001-2009.state.gov/secretary/rm/2005/40991.ht. Accessed August 28, 2015.

Rotberg, R. (2007). *Worst of the worst: Dealing with repressive and rogue nations.* Cambridge, MA: World Peace Foundation.

Rubin, M. (2014). *Dancing with the devil: The perils of engaging rogue regimes.* New York, NY: Encounter Books.

Sakar, J. (2013). *The nuclear non-proliferation regime and its dissidents: A conflict of paradigms?* Resource document. Yale Journal of International Affairs. http://yalejournal.org/op-ed_post/the-nuclear-non-proliferation-regime-and-its-dissidents-a-conflict-of-paradigms/. Accessed April 28, 2017.

Saunders, E. (2006). Setting boundaries: Can International Society exclude "Rogue States"? *International Studies Review, 8*(1), 23–53.

Schmittchen, D. (2006). *"Rogue States"—"Schurkenstaaten". Ein stringentes US-Konzept im Kampf gegen Terrorismus und Proliferation von ABC-Waffen?* Resource document. Forschungsgruppe Sicherheitspolitik. Berlin.

Senn, M. (2008). *Rogue No More!? Die iranische Bedrohung in der Wahrnehmung der USA.* Resource document. IPG 3/2008. http://library.fes.de/pdf-files/ipg/ipg-2008-3/05_a_senn_d.pdf. Accessed April 28, 2017.

Senn, M. (2009). *Wolves in the woods: The rogue state concept from a constructivist perspective*. Baden-Baden: Nomos.

Spector, L., & Cohen, A. (2008). *Israel's airstrike on syria's reactor. Implications for the non-proliferation regime*. Arms Control Association, 07.08.2008. Resource document. http://www.armscontrol.org/act/2008_07-08/SpectorCohen. Accessed April 28, 2017.

Stritzel, H., & Schmittchen, D. (2011). Securitization, culture and power: Rogue states in US and German discourse. In T. Balzacq (Ed.), *Securitization theory. How security problems emerge and dissolve* (pp. 170–85). New York, NY: Routledge.

Tanter, R. (1999). *Rogue regimes: Terrorism and proliferation*. New York, NY: St. Martin's Griffin.

The White House. (2010). *National Security Strategy, Washington, 01.05.2010*. Resource document. https://www.whitehouse.gov/sites/default/files/rss_viewer/national_security_strategy.pdf. Accessed April 28, 2017.

Trump, D. (2018). *State of the union speech, 30. January 2018*. Resource document. The White House. https://www.whitehouse.gov/briefings-statements/president-donald-j-trumps-state-union-address/. Accessed September 18, 2018.

Wagner, W., Werner, W., & Onderco, M. (Eds.). (2014). *Deviance in international relations: "Rogue States" and international security*. Basingstoke: Palgrave Macmillan.

Wagner, W. (2014). Rehabilitation or exclusion? A criminological perspective on policies towards "Rogue States". In W. Wagner, W. Werner, & M. Onderco (Eds.), *Deviance in international relations: "Rogue States" and international security* (pp. 152–170). Basingstoke: Palgrave Macmillan.

Wendt, A. (1998). On constitution and causation in international relations. *Review of International Studies, 24*(5), 101–118.

White House. (2002). *The national security strategy of the United States of America*. Resource document. http://www.state.gov/documents/organization/63562.pdf. Accessed April 28, 2017.

Wiener, A. (2008). *The invisible constitution of politics: Contested norms and international encounters*. Cambridge, NY: Cambridge University Press.

Wunderlich, C. (2014). A "Rogue" gone norm entrepreneurial? Iran within the nuclear nonproliferation regime. In W. Wagner, W. Werner, & M. Onderco (Eds.), *Deviance in international relations: "Rogue States" and international security* (pp. 83–104). Basingstoke: Palgrave Macmillan.

Wunderlich, C. (2017). Delegitimisation à la Carte: The "Rogue State" label as a means of stabilising order in the nuclear non-proliferation regime. In S. Gertheiss, S. Herr, K. Wolf, & C. Wunderlich (Eds.), *Resistance and change in world politics: International dissidence* (pp. 143–189). Cham: Palgrave Macmillan.

Chapter 4
The Ugly? Rogue States as Norm Entrepreneurs

As outlined in the previous chapter, "rogue states" are seen in large parts of the political and academic discourse as transgressors of universally accepted standards of behavior. They are perceived as norm breakers who display their opposing attitude vis-á-vis the current normative order by disregarding and transgressing basic rules and duties. Consequently, empirical studies usually focus on tracing their alleged non-compliance with norms.

This perspective is also shared by (liberal-constructivist) norms research, which at the best considers the countries concerned as objects of normative education, the norm-violating behavior of which must be prevented and which—if possible—should be reintegrated into the overarching normative order. Scholars focusing on the diffusion and enforcement of norms tend to conceptualize norm-violating states as antagonists to liberal-democratic states (e.g. Risse and Sikkink 1999: 9), usually focusing on authoritarian states found guilty of human rights violations. Along these lines, Trine Flockhart considers "rogue states" to be

> actors that completely reject the social norms of a socializing agent, who know that they have very little to gain from compliance with those norms, and who know they have no chance of gaining group membership anyway, [and thus] have no incentive to follow an agreed code of conduct. (Flockhart 2004: 367)

Conceptualized in such a way, "rogue states" cannot easily be socialized, since mechanisms based on social pressure are built on the assumption that the target of socialization efforts identifies in principle with the social reference group of the socializing agent to which it wants to belong. It is usually assumed that "rogue states" lack such a sense of identification. Found guilty of norm breaches, they are dismissed as "civilized" members of the international community and delegitimized (Risse 2002: 1). Notorious norm breakers and troublemakers as they are perceived to be, they are primarily conceptualized with regard to their resistance to prevailing norms. Their stigma as antagonists of prototypical moral entrepreneurs thus becomes manifest (e.g. Müller 2011: 72–73) and their potential for transformative change is theoretically and empirically dismissed as well.

C. Wunderlich, *Rogue States as Norm Entrepreneurs*,
Norm Research in International Relations,
https://doi.org/10.1007/978-3-030-27990-5_4

Contrary to this stance, this book adopts a counter-intuitive and unconventional approach. I argue that the assumption that "rogue states" only aim at destroying established international norms needs to be verified empirically. Their hostile attitude may be based on an attempt to establish alternative norms which radically deviate from the prevailing Western liberal concept of normative order. "Rogue states", as I will argue, can thus also take on the role of norm entrepreneurs.

In the following section, I will first link my argument to recent works that share a critical constructivist stance and which try to overcome the narrow perspective of liberal norm research by applying the concept of norm entrepreneurship to unconventional types of actors. I will then discuss research on norm contestation and resistance toward international norms and link the two perspectives. I conclude this chapter by formulating two alternative hypotheses which—following liberal-constructivist research on norms—could also explain the behavior of "rogue states" toward norms. In the empirical part of this study, these alternative explanations will be tested against the assumption that "rogue states" might act as norm entrepreneurs.

4.1 Research on Unconventional Norm Entrepreneurs and Resistance to Norms

Already in 1997, legal scholar Richard A. Posner referred to the existence of "bad-norm entrepreneurs" besides "moral entrepreneurs", citing as examples "aggressive panhandlers, vandals, drunks, junkies, prostitutes, gang members, loiterers, and other visibly antisocial persons" (Posner 1997: 42). While he did not provide a systematic empirical analysis, Posner identified a missionary eagerness as a unifying element for both types of entrepreneur: "Moral entrepreneurs typically try to change the boundaries of altruism, whether by broadening them, as in the case of Jesus Christ and Jeremy Bentham, or by narrowing them, as in the case of Hitler" (Posner 1998: 1667). In a similar vein, Rosa Ehrenreich Brooks argued that "bad guys [...] also know quite a lot about norm creation" (Ehrenreich Brooks 2003: 2326–7). To substantiate her argument, she referred to Palestinian suicide bombers, Slobodan Milosevic, Hutu fighters and Adolf Hitler, who had succeeded in shattering the existing normative order through advocating fundamentally different concepts of order.

While these studies did not go beyond the mere identification of such entrepreneur types, in the 2000s, political scientists began to empirically trace the applicability of the concept to actors other than the prototypical Western liberal actors.

Based on the observation that norm entrepreneurship is embedded in discursive, institutional and geopolitical opportunity structures, Adamson (2005) analyzes the attempts of two competing norm entrepreneurs—namely democracy assistance networks based largely in Western liberal democracies and Islamist networks—to advocate their respective normative agendas in post-Soviet Central Asia. To her, the biased focus on Western liberal norm entrepreneurs is due to the dominance of global liberalism, which she also regards as the breeding ground of today's established research community. As a consequence, concepts originating from political Islam have largely been neglected.

Bettiza and Dionigi (2014) also turn their attention to non-Western norm entrepreneurship. Focusing on international organizations that are dominated by liberal actors, the authors analyze the advocacy of the Organization of Islamic Cooperation (OIC) within the United Nations in promoting a "dialogue of civilizations" and a ban on defaming religion. They argue that the success of non-Western religious norm entrepreneurs largely depends on the extent to which they manage to translate Islamic concepts into secular liberal discursive structures. The authors ascribe the success of the initiative for a "dialogue of civilizations" initiated by Iranian President Mohammad Khatami to the fact that the norm advocates had refrained from explicitly referring to Islam in their campaign. Instead, they had produced an "open hermeneutic margin in the norm's meaning" (Bettiza and Dionigi 2014: 16). Rather than translating references to Islam into the UN's institutional grammar, the Islamic norm entrepreneurs made use of established secular principles such as self-determination, peace, equality, tolerance, and human rights. Their advocacy for a ban on the defamation of religion, in contrast, failed because the main focus was on preventing criticism of Islam and thus followed a particularistic concern. The propagated norm collided with basic liberal norms (such as equality, protection of the individual, and right to freedom of expression) and could not be translated to fit a secular order. The fact that the resolution eventually adopted by the UN Human Rights Council in 2011 did not contain any references to Islam is seen by the authors as a failure of the efforts of the OIC to establish a ban on defaming religion.

The non-Western norm entrepreneurs analyzed in these studies mainly rely on "classical" norm entrepreneurial instruments identified in the literature, such as argumentative persuasion and framing strategies. Other studies transcend this focus by examining the norm advocacy of violent actors. Lynch (2006) uses the term norm "entrepreneur" to describe Osama bin Laden's efforts to convince a critical mass of Arab and Muslim states of the superiority of a radical Islamic identity and corresponding norms. To this end, he contends, al-Qaeda has deliberately stylized world politics as a "clash of civilizations" in which religious extremism can be justified on moral grounds. Although Lynch describes al-Qaeda as a norm entrepreneur, he does not systematically apply the concept, and as a result, does not generate theoretical insights into its nature. Most recently, studies have explored Russian and Chinese efforts to challenge and—occasionally—undermine liberal norms as a form of norm entrepreneurship, e.g., Russia's attempt to justify the invasion of Crimea as a humanitarian intervention (Jose and Stefes 2018, or Carpenter 2014 who describes the same effort as an example of norm antipreneurship; on China see Alden and Large 2015).

Resistance to established norms has for long been ignored by norms research and dismissed as illegitimate hostility to norms (Acharya 2004: 242). Only in the course of the second wave of norms research have scholars shifted their attention to agency from below, i.e., processes of bottom-up norm diffusion. In this vein, scholars have analyzed processes in which local actors challenge global norms. Studies on norm appropriation and translation (e.g. Acharya 2004, 2009; Zwingel 2012; Großklaus 2015; Zimmermann 2017) emphasize that local actors should no longer be conceptualized as passive norm takers. Instead, these studies began to incorporate notions of criticism of global norms into their analytical models. Yet the focus was not on radical resistance to norms. Rather, criticism was perceived to be sparked by the effort to embrace and adapt basically desirable global norms to better fit local contexts.

In contrast, authors taking a poststructuralist and critical constructivist perspective focus on the active resistance against global norms which often turns into a reinterpretation of global normative meanings (Hirata 2004; Acharya 2011; Epstein 2012; Inayatullah and Blaney 2012; Towns 2012; Widmaier and Park 2012; Hofius et al. 2014; Jabri 2014; Steinhilper 2015). As these studies show, supposedly universal norms are often rejected by non-Western norm addressees who regard them as Western liberal constructs and instruments of hegemonic imposition. In contrast to the top-down perspectives inherent to liberal-constructivist accounts on norm diffusion, these works emphasize the variety of bottom-up norm construction and negotiation processes by focusing on "all involved stakeholders" (Wiener 2018: 3) who are often denied agency in scholarly accounts, ranging from "post-colonial agency" (Jabri 2014) by affected populations such as the Indigenous Movement in the Global South (Steinhilper 2015; Hasenclever and Narr 2019) to letting the subalterns speak (Hofius et al. 2014). For the purposes of this study, I will focus on Amitav Acharya's concept of norm localization and subsidiarity.

In this context, Amitav Acharya extended his concept of norm localization with the notion of norm subsidiarity, which he defines as a "[p]rocess whereby local actors create rules with a view to preserve their autonomy from dominance, neglect, violation, or abuse by more powerful actors" (Acharya 2011: 97).

Rather than adapting morally desirable norms to local contexts, subsidiarity describes an activity whereby local actors reject global norms by promoting normative alternatives (Acharya 2011: 98).[1] Acharya applies the concept mainly to post-colonial states and countries of the Global South and contends that the propagation of alternative norms has to be seen against the countries' historical background and experiences of marginalization, discrimination, and unfair treatment in an—in their view—Eurocentric international system that takes only insufficient account of the interests of former colonial states. Consequently, Acharya considers the promotion of subsidiary norms to be a merely reactive expression of resistance to hegemonic structures. While he describes the actors as "norm maker" (Acharya 2011: 98), he neither uses the term "norm entrepreneur", nor does his conception refer to the prototypical use of the concept as described in Chap. 2. For Acharya, the advocacy of norms arises from a purely reactive impulse. Accordingly, actors in post-colonial states formulate subsidiary norms when they regard the norm-promoting efforts of Western liberal norm entrepreneurs as potentially harmful to their autonomy and reject them.

Practices of resistance toward norms have also been taken up in work on norm erosion dynamics. Authors have pointed to the role of so-called "norm revision-

[1] As examples of subsidiary norms, Acharya cites sovereignty, territorial integrity, formal equality, non-intervention, and regional autonomy.

ists", "agents of moral regress" (McKeown 2009: 6; Dunne 2007: 270) or "norm challengers" (Rosert and Schirmbeck 2007: 269; Heller et al. 2012: 285), who are conceptualized as antagonists to prototypical norm entrepreneurs. Their actions are seen as aiming to challenge and ultimately undermine those norms that are considered obsolete, or which run counter to their own normative ideas and/or interests, through opposing behavior and/or discursive contestation (for an overview see Heller and Kahl 2013). Mainly, these studies focus on attempts by state actors (often the US Government) to legitimize counter-terrorism policies as "necessary" norm transgressions serving a higher common good (e.g., the antitorture norm or the guarantee of civil liberties) (e.g. Rosert and Schirmbeck 2007; Liese 2009; McKeown 2009; Panke and Petersohn 2012; Jetschke and Liese 2013). Instead of actively propagating alternative norms, these actors are primarily concerned with questioning established norms, shifting their significance, and thus delegitimizing them in the long term (Heller et al. 2012: 286; Heller and Kahl 2013: 415). Lantis (2011) examines the redefinition and shift in the meaning of the norm of non-proliferation of nuclear weapons by the USA. Once a strict advocate of restraint in the area of civilian nuclear cooperation with non-NPT member states, he shows how the USA has changed its argumentation in the mid-2000s by distinguishing between "responsible" technology recipients and norm-breaking pariahs. This rhetorical reinterpretation was cemented in 2008 by a nuclear deal with India, a non-NPT state, even though the US administration subsequently insisted that this had been an exceptional case.

In 2016, Alan Bloomfield coined the term "norm antipreneur" (Bloomfield 2016) for actors who aim to prevent the establishment of new norms (e.g., the Responsibility to Protect, R2P) by defending status quo norms (e.g., national sovereignty). Charli Carpenter (2014) took up this notion by arguing that especially powerful actors could try to sabotage emerging norms by reinterpreting them if they saw their interests endangered. As an example, she cites Russia's military intervention in Georgia and Ukraine: Perhaps Putin intended to demonstrate Russia's interpretation of the norm by referring to the norm of the Responsibility to Protect (R2P). But it was more likely that Russia had deliberately tried to weaken the emergent norm by applying it to a bad example from a Western point of view. Jochen Prantl and Ryoko Nakano (Prantl and Nakano 2011: 214) also refer to the R2P in what they term China's attempt to contain the norm's meaning and scope. Regardless of the conceptual differences, all of these actors are primarily concerned with counteracting—possibly also blocking or blighting—the efforts of norm entrepreneurs.[2]

Clifford Bob (Bob 2012: Chap. 2) investigates such sabotage tactics in his analysis of conflicts between rival activist networks: In order to achieve their goals, they not only exert typical "affirmative" strategies such as persuasion or framing aimed at establishing or supporting the propagated norm (Bob speaks of "policy making";

[2]In practice, however, such efforts might have the opposite effect of strengthening the efforts of norm entrepreneurs, who see themselves obliged to defend the norm (interpretation) that they propagate (Carpenter 2014).

Bob 2012: 16).[3] In addition, advocates also use destructive tactics ("unmaking") to advance their agendas and counteract their rivals and their goals.[4] This includes the following attempts: deconstructing the problem definition put forward by the adversary, i.e., denouncing the urgency of the situation, denying the existence of the problem altogether ("unframing", Bob 2012: 29) or reinterpreting their opponent's frames ("framejacking", Bob 2012: 30). Moreover, advocates try to discredit competing networks or institutional platforms chosen by them through staged accusations or scandals: "They [contending groups; CW] despise their adversaries as misguided, self-interested, deceitful, or downright evil" (Bob 2012: 7). In addition to rhetorical interferences such as protest actions or disruption of debates, counter-analysis or counter-initiatives are frequently used tools of activist networks. Rival groups are less interested in reaching political compromises than in "outdoing" their opponents. Such obstructionist policies are also analyzed by other authors: e.g., the tactic of "filibustering", meaning prolonged speaking, or procedural procrastination/delaying tactics such as excessive debates on the rules of procedure, discussion of voting rules, or deliberately produced lack of quorum by sending unauthorized negotiators in order to lengthen negotiations (Glozman et al. 2014; Junk 2014).

To sum up, while efforts have been made to apply the concept of norm entrepreneurship to non-liberal and illiberal actors, most of these studies still do not operate with a systematic conceptualization. In contrast to the literature on social movements, with the exception of Bob (2012) studies of norm entrepreneurship have not yet systematically analyzed such destructive strategies employed by norm advocates. Research on norm contestation and resistance toward norms focuses on the agency that is directed against attempts by prototypical norm entrepreneurs to establish (Western liberal) norms or to maintain or strengthen already established ones. Common to all of these works is the lack of a theoretically founded and systematic comparison of alleged norm antipreneurs and norm entrepreneurs.

4.1.1 Shift of Perspective: "Rogue States"—Norm Breakers or Norm Makers?

According to the literature, "rogue states" are mainly to be considered as norm breakers who reject the established normative order by all means. Compliance with norms and in particular norm entrepreneurship of supposedly norm-averse "rogue states", is, by contrast, regarded as rather unlikely.

Against this background, the following alternative explanations for their behavior seem more plausible (from the perspective of liberal norms research): "Rogue states" will try to assert their rejection of the current normative order by resistance in words

[3]Consequently, he compares affirmative and negative strategies: constructing/deconstructing problems; network building/unbuilding; activating/deactivating institutions; agenda setting/unsetting; persuasion/dissuasion; promoting/demoting outcomes (Bob 2012: 21–33).

[4]While Bob uses the term "negative" strategies, I feel destructive is the more appropriate term.

and deeds. At best, they will act as antagonists of norm entrepreneurs and try to undermine established norms, or try to block their diffusion. Being outsiders to the international community, their strategies are not be characterized by restraint, but by resorting to destructive practices designed to undermine existing norms and/or negotiation processes. This type of actor is hereinafter referred to as *norm destroyer.*

It is, however, quite conceivable that "rogue states" may advance subsidiary norms as conceptualized by Acharya (2011): They reject established norms because they perceive them as a threat to their autonomy and counteract them with normative alternatives.

In summary, the following (alternative) explanations (AE) for the behavior of "rogue states" in relation to norms can be derived from the literature on norms and "rogue states":

AE 1: "Rogue states" are primarily to be understood as norm breakers. Their actions and rhetoric are aimed at undermining and, if necessary, even destroying the normative order. This includes attempts to block or sabotage efforts of norm diffusion ("rogue states" as destructive forces or antipreneurs). Active norm entrepreneurship by "rogue states" is not to be expected.

AE 2: As an expression of their rejection of Western liberal norms, which they perceive as hegemonic interventions in their autonomy, "rogue states" may formulate subsidiary norms. These are conceived as mere counter-proposals to global norms and do not have their own normative impetus.

In the empirical part of this book, these alternative explanations are contrasted with the hypothesis that "rogue states" can also be prototypical norm entrepreneurs. AE 1 is an antithesis—should it prove to be valid, my hypothesis must be rejected. The possibility that "rogue states" propagate subsidiary norms in the sense of Acharya does not completely contradict my hypothesis—norm subsidiarity could rather be understood as a type of norm entrepreneurial activity. Which of these assumptions holds true will be verified in the empirical chapters of this book. In the following chapter, I shall introduce the research design, which, among other things, will further distinguish the alternative explanations from the hypothesis and present the criteria that guide the research.

References

Acharya, A. (2004). How ideas spread: Whose norms matter? Norm localization and institutional change in Asian regionalism. *International Organization, 58*(2), 239–275.

Acharya, A. (2009). *Whose ideas matter? Agency and power in Asian regionalism*. Ithaca, NY: Cornell University Library.

Acharya, A. (2011). Norm subsidiarity and regional orders. Sovereignty, regionalism, and rule-making in the Third World. *International Studies Quarterly, 55*(1), 95–123.

Adamson, F. (2005). Global liberalism versus political Islam: Competing ideological frameworks in international politics. *International Studies Review, 7*(4), 547–569.

Alden, C., & Large, D. (2015). On becoming a norms maker: Chinese foreign policy, norms evolution and the challenges of security in Africa. *The China Quarterly, 221,* 123–142.

Bettiza, G., & Dionigi, F. (2014). *Beyond constructivism's liberal bias: Islamic norm entrepreneurs in a post-secular world society*. EUI Working Paper MWP 2014/10. http://cadmus.eui.eu/bitstream/handle/1814/31692/MWP_WP_Bettiza_Dionigi_2014_10.pdf?sequence=1. Accessed 28 April 2017.

Bloomfield, A. (2016). Norm antipreneurs and theorizing resistance to normative change. *Review of International Studies, 42*(2), 310–333.

Bob, C. (2012). *The global right wing and the clash of world politics*. New York, NY: Cambridge University Press.

Carpenter, C. (2014). *"Norm antipreneurship" and Russia's [Reported] Use of autonomous weapons*. Resource Document. Duck of Minerva. http://duckofminerva.com/2014/04/norm-antipreneurship-and-russian-use-of-autonomous-weapons.html. Accessed 28 April 2017.

Dunne, Tim. (2007). "The rules of the game are changing": Fundamental human rights in crisis after 9/11. *International Politics, 44*(2–3), 269–286.

Ehrenreich Brooks, R. (2003). The new imperialism: Violence, norms, and the "rule of law". *Michigan Law Review, 101*(7), 2275–2340.

Epstein, C. (2012). Symposium: Interrogating the use of norms in international relations. An introduction. *International Studies Perspectives, 13*(2), 121–122.

Flockhart, T. (2004). "Masters and novices": Socialization and social learning through the NATO parliamentary assembly. *International Relations, 18*(3), 361–380.

Glozman, E., Barak-Corren, N., & Yaniv, I. (2014). False negotiations: The art and science of not reaching an agreement. *Journal of Conflict Resolution, 59*(4), 671–697.

Großklaus, M. (2015). Appropriation and the dualism of human rights: Understanding the contradictory impact of gender norms in Nigeria. *Third World Quarterly, 36*(6), 1253–1267.

Hasenclever, A., & Narr, H. (2019). The dark side of the affectedness-paradigm: Lessons from the indigenous peoples' movement at the United Nations. *Third World Thematics: A TWQ Journal*. https://doi.org/10.1080/23802014.2018.1553505.

Heller, R., & Kahl, M. (2013). Tracing and understanding 'bad' norm dynamics in counterterrorism. The current debates in IR research. *Critical Studies on Terrorism, 6*(3), 414–428.

Heller, R., Kahl, M., & Pisoiu, D. (2012). The "dark" side of normative argumentation—The case of counterterrorism policy. *Global Constitutionalism, 1*(2), 278–312.

Hirata, K. (2004). Beached whales. Examining Japan's rejection of an international norm. *Social Science Japan Journal, 7*(2), 177–197.

Hofius, M., Wilkens, J., Hansen-Magnusson, H., & Gholiagha, S. (2014). Den Schleier lichten? Kritische Normenforschung, Freiheit und Gleichberechtigung im Kontext des «Arabischen Frühlings». Eine Replik auf Engelkamp/Glaab/Renner, Ulbert und Deitelhoff/Zimmermann. *Zeitschrift für Internationale Beziehungen*, *2*, 85–105.

Inayatullah, N., & Blaney, D. (2012). The dark heart of kindness: The social construction of deflection. *International Studies Perspectives, 13*(2), 164–175.

Jabri, V. (2014). Disarming norms: Postcolonial agency and the constitution of the international. *International Theory, 6*(2), 372–390.

Jetschke, A., & Liese, A. (2013). The power of human rights a decade after: From Euphoria to contestation. In T. Risse, S. Ropp, & K. Sikkink (Eds.), *The persistent power of human rights: From commitment to compliance* (pp. 26–42). Cambridge: Cambridge University Press.

Jose, B., & Stefes, C. H. (2018). *Russian norm entrepreneurship in Crimea: Serious contestation or cheap talk?*. Hamburg: German Institute of Global and Area Studies.

Junk, J. (2014). Internal dynamics and dysfunctions of international organizations: An introduction to the special issue. *Journal of International Organization Studies, 5*(1), 8–11.

Lantis, J. (2011). Redefining the nonproliferation norm? Australian Uranium, the NPT, and the global nuclear revival. *Australian Journal of Politics and History, 57*(4), 543–561.

Liese, A. (2009). Exceptional necessity—How liberal democracies contest the prohibition of torture and Ill-Treatment when countering terrorism. *Journal of International Law and International Relations, 5*(1), 17–47.

Lynch, M. (2006). *Al-Qaeda's constructivist turn*. Resource Document. Praeger Security International. http://www.marclynch.com/wp-content/uploads/2011/03/Al-Qaedas-Constructivism.pdf. Accessed 28 April 2017.

McKeown, R. (2009). Norm regress: US revisionism and the slow death of the torture norm. *International Relations, 23*(1), 5–25.

Müller, H. (2011). Habermas meets role theory. Communicative action as role playing? In S. Harnisch, C. Frank, & H. Maull (Eds.), *Role theory in international relations. Approaches and analyses* (pp. 55–73). London: Routledge.

Panke, D., & Petersohn, U. (2012). Why international norms disappear sometimes. *European Journal of International Relations, 18*(4), 719–742.

Posner, R. (1997). Social norms and the law: An economic approach. *The American Economic Review, 87*(2), 365–369.

Posner, R. (1998). The problematics of moral and legal theory. *Harvard Law Review, 111*(7), 1637–1717.

Prantl, J., & Nakano, R. (2011). Global norm diffusion in East Asia: How China and Japan implement the responsibility to protect. *International Relations, 25*(2), 204–223.

Risse, T. (2002). Transnational actors and world politics. In W. Carlsnaes, T. Risse, & B. Simmons (Eds.), *Handbook of international relations*. Thousand Oaks, CA: Sage.

Risse, T., & Sikkink, K. (1999). The socialization of international human rights norms into domestic practices: Introduction. In T. Risse, S. Ropp, & K. Sikkink (Eds.), *The power of human rights, international norms and domestic change* (pp. 1–38). New York, NY: Cambridge University Press.

Rosert, E., & Schirmbeck, S. (2007). Zur Erosion internationaler Normen. Folterverbot und nukleares Tabu in der Diskussion. *Zeitschrift für Internationale Beziehungen, 14*(2), 253–288.

Steinhilper, E. (2015). From "the rest" to "the west"? rights of indigenous peoples and the western bias in norm diffusion research. *International Studies Review, 17*(4), 536–555.

Towns, A. (2012). Norms and social hierarchies: Understanding international policy diffusion "from below". *International Organization, 66*(2), 179–209.

Widmaier, W., & Park, S. (2012). Differences beyond theory. Structural, strategic, and sentimental approaches to normative change. *International Studies Perspectives, 13*(2), 123–134.

Wiener, A. (2018). Agency of the governed in global international relations: Access to norm validation. *Third World Thematics: A TWQ Journal, 2*(5), 709–725.

Zimmermann, L. (2017). *Global norms with a local face? Rule-of-law promotion and norm translation*. New York: Cambridge University Press.

Zwingel, S. (2012). How do norms travel? Theorizing international women's rights in transnational perspective. *International Studies Quarterly, 56*(1), 115–129.

Chapter 5
Researching and Operationalizing Prototypical and Unconventional Norm Entrepreneurship

This book departs from the observation that liberal-constructivist research on norms is analytically biased: analyses of "successful" norm diffusion usually focus on the institutionalization of liberal norms and trace these processes back to norm entrepreneurship of Western liberal actors. This study takes a different perspective grounded in a critical constructivist framing by arguing that "rogue states"—presumed norm breakers—can also be norm entrepreneurs. If this conjecture can be confirmed, the question arises as to what extent "roguish" norm entrepreneurship differs from the prototypes described in the literature on norms.

Rather than being guided by a classic "puzzle," this study aims to critically examine the limits of an analytical concept and thus to contribute to the further development of norm theory[1]: The literature review conducted in Chap. 2 revealed that the concept of norm entrepreneurship has hitherto been applied unsystematically and in a one-sided manner. Accordingly, in the empirical part of this study, the concept will be applied to a counterintuitive case (as seen from the perspective of mainstream, liberal-constructivist norms research) in order to demonstrate that the concept's current usage is far from convincing and needs to be specified more thoroughly.

I draw on a single-case study design which has been found to be a suitable method for such explorative research endeavors (George and Bennett 2004: 20–21). As Jack S. Levy notes, this is even more so for "cases that do not fit an existing theory" as it makes it possible "to explain why the case violates theoretical predictions and to refine or replace an existing hypothesis or perhaps specify its scope conditions" (Levy 2008: 5). Moreover, single-case studies are one of the most frequently used methods to analyze the genesis and diffusion of norms "as case studies capture the nuance, dynamism, sense of process, and mechanisms at work in any given instance of entrepreneurship" (Checkel 2012: 4). Empirical accounts of norm entrepreneurship usually proceed backward: Starting from the notion of a "successfully" diffused

[1] As such, the study is located at the interface between "theory-testing" and "literature-assessing" (George and Bennett 2004: 75, 121; van Evera 1997: 90).

C. Wunderlich, *Rogue States as Norm Entrepreneurs*,
Norm Research in International Relations,
https://doi.org/10.1007/978-3-030-27990-5_5

norm, scholars trace backward the role and impact of norm entrepreneurs for the establishment of the norm in question.[2]

This study also uses process tracing. Yet it is not located in a positivist framework that aims to demonstrate a causal mechanism between the presumed cause and the phenomenon to be explained (for different variants of process tracings, see George and Bennett 2004: 210–12). Rather, I conduct a theoretically driven exploratory analysis of Iranian engagement, in the course of which I examine whether the observed process meets the criteria of norm entrepreneurship. In the following sections, I will explain the case selection and explicate how the empirical analysis was structured, including the period of investigation as well as methods of data collection. Thereafter, I elaborate how I understand the concepts that are relevant for the study at hand. Lastly, the methods of process tracing and content analysis will be briefly introduced, and the technical details such as coding schemes and coding procedures will be presented.

5.1 Case Selection and Analytical Approach

5.1.1 "Rogue States" as Least-Likely Candidate for Norm Entrepreneurship

Since the study examines whether the concept of norm entrepreneurship can also be applied to actors other than the standard liberal norm entrepreneurs, the case selection is based on existing (liberal-constructivist) norm literature. By applying the concept of norm entrepreneurship to designated norm breakers, case selection follows a "most counter-intuitive" or "least-likely case" logic (Gerring 2007a: 116–20). For such cases, the validity of the applied theory is extremely unlikely (Blatter et al. 2007: 149)—according to the prevailing view in the literature, norm entrepreneurship by designated norm breakers is hardly to be expected.

In general, the successful application of a theoretical concept to a least-likely case is considered to confirm the explanatory power of the theory (Gerring 2007b: 116). Yet, here, some caveats are to be made:

First, the concept of norm entrepreneurship is not a theory in the strict sense, but a normatively charged analytical term. Authors use it in a biased and—as has been shown in the literature review—unsystematic way. So far, scholars have not come up with "scope conditions" or further systematic qualifications of the concept. The selective application is rather based on empirical and practical considerations. For these reasons, the successful transfer of the concept to proven norm breakers would not have to be regarded as confirmation of the concept. Yet it would further illustrate

---

[2]Checkel criticizes this bias and calls on scholars to also analyze failed cases, "where an entrepreneur works his/her magic and nothing happens" (Checkel 2012: 5). In addition, he complains that most scholars are rather intransparent about their methodological approach and often fail to make it clear that they use process tracing.

the need to specify the concept and reveal first glimpses into the scope conditions and possibilities for drawing more causal inferences.

From the universe of presumed norm breakers, I chose states that have been labeled "rogue states" by the USA. These constitute least-likely cases for norm entrepreneurship because most existing norm studies presume norm entrepreneurs to be liberal actors. Even though there are several official criteria that are used to justify labeling a country a "rogue state" (see Chap. 3), the label is generally used in an arbitrary manner. Hoyt (2000) and O'Reilly (2007) identify particularly Iraq, Iran, Libya, Cuba, and North Korea as repeatedly having been designated "rogues" over longer periods of time. While Cuba's place in the rogues' gallery has primarily been attributed to Cuban exiles' influence on the American decision-making process (Litwak 2000: 202),[3] Iraq disappeared from the list of terrorism-supporting states and thus from the "rogue radar" of the US government after the Bush administration forced regime change in 2003. Libya followed Iraq in 2006 when it voluntarily abandoned its WMD program. North Korea was removed from the list of state sponsors of terrorism in 2008 in exchange for its readiness to enter negotiations on its nuclear program, only to be redesignated in late 2017. While President Obama changed policy course and officially dropped the "rogue" rhetoric, he referred to Iran and North Korea as "nuclear outlier states." Since the period of investigation for this study ended in spring 2015, the recent revival of the "rogue state" rhetoric in the discourse by the Trump administration is not taken into account here. Thus, at the time of writing, Iran was the only consistent (and remaining) "rogue state" on the list of state sponsors of terrorism.

5.1.2 A Multilevel Analysis

The study follows a multistage research design:

In a *first* step, the thesis that guides this study ("rogue states can be norm entrepreneurs") is contrasted with two alternative explanations derived from the literature on norms and "rogues" (see Sect. 4.2). According to the latter, the behavior of "rogue states" as presumed norm breakers is directed toward undermining or completely destroying the existing normative order (AE1). Norm entrepreneurship is not expected of them. If anything, as an act of opposition to Western liberal norm entrepreneurship, they come up with their own subsidiary norms in order to resist what they perceive to be norm imposition and thus threats to their autonomy (AE2).

In order to evaluate the proposition guiding this research and the alternative explanations, I draw on a single-case study of the prototypical "rogue state" of Iran and conduct a "within case analysis" (Goertz and Mahoney 2012: 71) on three levels:

(1) I compile a profile of Iranian foreign policy identity and its notion of how the normative order should look. This may already provide some initial indications

[3] Cuba was removed from the list of state sponsors of terrorism and no longer referred to as a "rogue" when the USA restarted diplomatic relations with the Cuban government in 2015.

as to whether Iran—as suggested by the "rogue states" concept—intends to destroy or undermine the current normative order.

(2) Next, Iran's norm entrepreneurial potential is analyzed in practice, turning to the policy field of the control of weapons of mass destruction as an example. The aim is to provide an overview of Iran's arms control priorities, which might indicate potential areas for norm entrepreneurship.

(3) Such "instances of norm entrepreneurship" (i.e., Iran's norm entrepreneurial practices) are then traced in detail in three subcases (see Chap. 7). This is done by drawing on a set of criteria for prototypical norm entrepreneurship distilled from the literature, which is presented in the next section. If Iran's behavior corresponds to the elements identified to be prototypical norm entrepreneurial traits, my thesis would be plausibilized.

In a *second* step, the findings will be contrasted with other cases in order to specify the nature and peculiarities of Iranian norm entrepreneurship in more detail. In addition, insights drawn from cross-comparisons indicate to what extent the findings are generalizable. As George and Bennett conclude, "the strongest means of drawing inference from case studies is the use of a combination of within case analysis and cross-case comparisons within a single study of research program" (George and Bennet 2004: 18). Here, Iran's norm entrepreneurship is compared with Sweden, which has a reputation as a norm champion in multilateral arms control. Moreover, instances of Iranian norm entrepreneurship are compared with the activities of the long-standing "rogue state" North Korea.

5.1.3 Period of Investigation

The period for investigation differs according to the respective analytical stage:

For a survey of Iran's notions of world order, I drew on speeches held by Iranian delegates on the occasion of the annual UN general debate since the founding of the United Nations in 1945. I drew a full data sample for the period starting from the Islamic Republic in 1979. Pre-revolutionary documents (1945–1978) were taken into account along with salient historical events.[4] These statements were triangulated by a randomly generated sample of various speeches given by the revolutionary leaders Khomeini and Khamenei. The period of investigation ended in early 2015.

The analysis of Iranian arms control behavior was based on documentation of the negotiation processes of the respective treaty regimes within the Conference on

[4]In addition to the first-ever Iranian speech to the United Nations (1946), these were: The nationalization of the Anglo-Iranian Oil Company (1951), the coup against Prime Minister Mohammed Mossadegh (1953), and the year before the revolution (1978). If the salient events did occur after the general debate for the respective year, the speeches of the following year or the next participation were also taken into account. The general debates of 1987 (Khamenei), 2001 (Khatami), 2007 and 2012 (Ahmadinejad), 2014 (Rouhani) with presidential representation are particularly referred to in the text.

Disarmament (CD) and its respective predecessor organizations: The Biological and Toxin Weapons Convention (BWC) was negotiated from 1969 to 1971. In 1972, the BWC was submitted for signature. A prohibition on chemical weapons had been on the agenda of the CD since 1968, yet negotiations were concluded only in 1992. The Convention on the Prohibition of the Development, Production, Stockpiling and Use of Chemical Weapons (the Chemical Weapons Convention or CWC) was submitted for signature in 1993. Negotiations on the Threaty on the Non-Proliferation of Nuclear Weapons (NPT) began in the 1960s and ended in 1968 (for an overview of the negotiation history of the respective regimes, see Goldblat 2002). Besides the negotiation processes, the analysis also covered the discourse on the respective treaty regimes in established arms control forums, with the period of investigation ending in early 2015. The investigation period thus covered the entire period from the negotiation phase to subsequent debates about the respective treaty norms. Doing so allows to assess the continuity of Iranian commitment as well as to ensure that the norm entrepreneurship is not only due to the outstanding personal commitment of individual governmental representatives.[5]

For the instances of norm entrepreneurship (that is the individual subcases), the period of investigation varied in accordance with the duration of activities conducted by Iran in order to foster the respective norms. In some cases, the advocacy already started during the prenegotiation phase. This procedure has also been chosen for the analysis of the comparative case studies. For pragmatic reasons, the comparative case studies focus on the nuclear non-proliferation regime. For Sweden in particular, it would be beyond the scope of this study to fully cover the countries' extensive activities in the area of WMD arms control. For North Korea, this decision is justified by the fact that the country is not a member of the CWC and remains overly passive in the BWC. Table 5.1 provides an overview of the treaty memberships of the countries analyzed in this book.

Table 5.1 Overview of treaty memberships of the analyzed countries in the area of multilateral arms control policy

	NPT		BWC		CWC	
	Signature	Ratification/ entry into force	Signature	Ratification/ entry into force	Signature	Ratification/ entry into force
IRI	1.7.1968	2.2.1970	10.4.1972	22.8.1973	13.1.1993	3.11.1997
SWE	19.8.1968	9.1.1970	27.2.1974	5.2.1976	13.1.1993	17.6.1993
DPRK		12.12.1985 withdrawal: 1.1.2003		13.3.1987	–	–

[5]Iran was admitted to the then conference on the Committee on Disarmament, as the CD was called back in 1975. For the period from 1968 to 1975, I therefore drew on Iranian speeches given in the First Committee of the UN General Assembly.

5.1.4 Data Collection

The relevant data was collected from different sources: Secondary literature was supplemented by primary sources, gray literature, and expert interviews.

Primary data was collected from both international and national forums. It differs according to the stage of the analysis (see Sect. 5.1). The analysis of Iran's world order concepts was based on speeches given by Iranian representatives at the annual general debate of the UN General Assembly and national speeches given by the revolutionary leaders.[6] Reporting on the review conferences of the BWC, CWC, and the NPT is documented by a large number of NGOs and think tanks.[7] In addition to conference reports, some of these platforms also provide speeches and working papers held by government representatives during the review conferences. Primary resources were mainly derived from the respective UN bodies concerned with arms control issues, i.e., the First Committee of the UN General Assembly, the Conference on Disarmament and its predecessor organizations and the general debates of the IAEA.[8] Besides statements, I also relied on conference documentation (e.g., working papers) submitted by the analyzed countries during the review conferences.[9] Statements reflect the country's official policy, since they are authorized texts used to present and justify national positions and interpretations to other regime member states.[10] In the case of the review conferences, all documents submitted by Iran were analyzed in the respective period. In other UN arms control policy forums, however, I selected documents taking into account certain time intervals during "salient events" or relevant for the individual norm entrepreneurial subcases. The analysis of com-

---

[6]All speeches given within UN bodies were collected from relevant UN websites. See http://research.un.org/en/docs/ga/quick and http://unbisnet.un.org:8080/ipac20/ipac.jsp?profile=speech&menu=search. National statements by Khamenei can be found on his homepage: http://www.leader.ir/langs/en/index.php?page=2&p=bayanatArchive&year=2015; 28.04.2017 and http://english.khamenei.ir//index.php?option=com_content&task=archivesection&id=2&Itemid=31; 28.04.2017. Collected speeches by Khomeini are compiled in Algar (1981) and the International Affairs Department (1995).

[7]Among others, these included Acronym Institute (http://www.acronym.org.uk; 28.04.2017), Reaching Critical Will (http://www.reachingcriticalwill.org) and the journals Arms Control Reporter and Disarmament Diplomacy.

[8]The Conference on Disarmament dates back to the Eighteen Nation Disarmament Committee (ENDC), founded in 1962, which was expanded to 30 members in 1969 and renamed the Conference on the Committee on Disarmament. In 1975, it added a further five members (including Iran). In 1979, it was restructured and renamed Conference on Disarmament (CD). Today, the CD has 65 members.

[9]IAEA debates can be found at https://www.iaea.org/About/Policy/GC/GC59/Documents/; BWC and CWC documents at http://www.opbw.org/ and https://www.opcw.org/documents-reports/conference-states-parties/; for the NPT at http://unbisnet.un.org; reachingcriticalwill.org; or http://www.un.org/disarmament/WMD/Nuclear/NPT_Review_Conferences.shtml. Documents older than 1993 were not available online and were therefore obtained from the UN Depositary Library in Heidelberg. Relevant Swedish documents were collected during a field research stay in autumn 2010 in the library of the Foreign Ministry and the Anna Lindh Library.

[10]See interview with Klaus Scharioth, a former German diplomat with long-standing expertise in the field of arms control, July 16, 2012, Berlin.

parative cases was based mainly on secondary literature, but also included national statements from Sweden and North Korea in the relevant arms control forums. All sources used in the text are listed in the bibliography under primary documents.

Besides primary sources, I also drew on academic literature on the foreign and security policy as well as on the arms control policy of the countries in question. Yet academic coverage of Iran's arms control policy is scarce (see Sect. 7.1). While there is a multitude of policy-related research on Iran's nuclear weapons program and the conflict surrounding its nuclear ambitions, few authors have analyzed Iran's position within the respective arms control regimes (but see Ali 1996; Jones 1998; Pirseyedi 2013). The same holds true for North Korea's arms control diplomacy, while the availability of data for Sweden is excellent. For these reasons and in order to gain additional information and to answer open questions that arose from secondary and primary sources, I conducted additional expert interviews. If no direct conversation was possible, I sent written questionnaires.[11]

Interview partners included

- persons who were involved in the political decision-making processes relevant to this study or who had insight into these processes, i.e., former and acting government representatives (foreign ministry, delegation members, diplomats);
- employees of NGOs and think tanks dealing with disarmament issues; and
- scholars working on similar questions.

The interviews were usually conducted in the form of semistructured interviews, based on a questionnaire, but always left room for additional information. In addition, the interviewees were asked to comment on the research question. In most cases, it was possible to record the interviews. Nevertheless, I refrained from a comprehensive transcription of the interviews, as the interviews were not systematically evaluated by means of content analysis, but only served supplementary purposes. Access to decision-makers was sometimes difficult, especially because of the explosive nature of the conflict over Iran's nuclear program. In some cases, interlocutors were not authorized to give certain information.[12] Sometimes, they asked to be anonymized. In many cases, it was only possible to exchange emails and occasionally, no contact to the requested persons was possible.

---

[11]In total, I conducted about 30 personal interviews and three telephone conversations during field research stays in the Hague, Germany, Sweden, and the USA. In some cases, I received written answers to my questions (by email). Some persons agreed to the interview only on condition of anonymity, so that they are referred to only with a generalized description of their function (e.g., "member of the Non-Aligned Movement within the UN"). A detailed list of all interview partners is available on request.

[12]That the question concerned sensitive areas of Iranian national interest complicated issues further. It must also be born in mind that on both sides—Iran and the West, above all the USA—there is sometimes a mutual demonization, marked by propaganda and decades of misperception, which makes objective information more difficult. Especially at the beginning of field research, it was quite a challenge to maneuver through this "propaganda jungle."

5.2 Definitions and Concepts

5.2.1 Prototypical Norm Entrepreneurship

For the empirical analysis, prototypical norm entrepreneurship will be operationalized following the literature review in Chap. 2. The definition used for this study is based on the one suggested by Annika Björkdahl in 2002: "By identifying or creating opportunities, actors committed to a particular idea set out to change the existing normative context and alter the behavior of others in the direction of the new norm" (Björkdahl 2002: 46). Norm entrepreneurs are not only involved in processes of norm construction but also work for the further promotion, institutionalization or implementation, maintenance and strengthening of norms (Finnemore and Sikkink 2001: 401; Johnston 2007: 127; Björkdahl 2013: 325–6; Müller and Wunderlich 2013; Wunderlich 2017).

So what criteria must be given in order to identify a norm entrepreneur as such? Some features are consistently mentioned in the literature: Usually, norm entrepreneurs are conceived as actors who are committed to a particular idea or norm. Their effort of norm construction is often sparked by dissatisfaction with the prevailing normative order[13] and a desire to change it based on their normative convictions. This applies only to a limited extent to actors whose activities are directed toward affirming, implementing, or strengthening already established norms. Their norm entrepreneurship ties in with existing normative structures. If at all, they are dissatisfied with the inadequate implementation or the prevailing interpretation of the norm in question.

Norm entrepreneurs want to convince potential norm addressees of the factual validity and the normative as well as practical necessity of the propagated norm(s). Therefore, they engage in active lobbying: They promote their position among like-minded actors (states, regional, or intergovernmental organizations, civil society), seek organizational platforms to institutionalize the norm (agenda setting) and use a broad spectrum of strategies for this purpose (both affirmative and negative strategies aimed at undermining counter-positions; Bob 2012). Norm scholars particularly emphasize framing strategies, but they also mention the strategic use of a combination of material means (coercion, social pressure, bargaining) and non-material resources (persuasion/communicative action, deliberation, expertise; e.g., Finnemore and Sikkink 1998: 9010–11; Payne 2001).

The behavior of norm entrepreneurs is characterized by proactivity: Their actions are purposeful and intentional and show a high degree of consistency in speech and action (Becker et al. 2008: 820). As far as the construction of new normative mean-

[13]Norm entrepreneurship tends rather to be policy-specific than across the board. Often, activism centers on a special theme, yet it may well be motivated by a fundamental opposition to the current normative order. In addition, limited resources make cross-political norm entrepreneurship unlikely. However, some studies indicate that certain national identities and role models increase the probability that actors will become norm entrepreneurs (e.g., Björkdahl 2002; Becker et al. 2008; Müller and Wunderlich 2013).

ings is concerned, the strategies used are geared toward change, thus predominantly anticipatory, rather active than reactive and characterized by innovation (the latter may also apply to efforts of norm strengthening). Continuous, often altruistically motivated commitment to a certain norm does not preclude strategic action (Price 2003: 581).

Norm entrepreneurship manifests itself both in words and deeds, as Ian Johnstone notes: "[T]he process [of norm propagation; CW] is dynamic. It occurs partly through discourse and deliberation, in which actors promote, defend, explain, and justify their position [...]. But norm entrepreneurship also occurs through practices and institutionalization." (Johnstone 2007: 130). Practical activities aimed at promoting certain norms include the provision of knowledge and resources as well as the discursive "activation" (Rublee 2008) of the respective norm (interpretation).

Table 5.2 summarizes the main features of norm entrepreneurship. Some of the indicators can be extracted from primary sources originating from the assumed norm entrepreneur itself, such as the normative argumentation and framing of the "norm candidate" as well as references to practical activities geared toward norm promotion. In addition, archives of international organizations or documentation from international conferences (both primary sources as well as information material provided for by think tanks) might be of help. Yet other indicators are harder to obtain, such as references to the resilience of norm entrepreneurs or their moral credibility/legitimacy—for obviously these features are ascribed to the actors in question by outside observers (be they academics or the general public). An analysis of how the actor is portrayed in secondary literature and assessed by other actors might reveal interesting insights, but has to be treated carefully, as it might be biased.

While the operationalization is based on liberal-constructivist research on norms, my application of the concept deviates from the majority of empirical norm studies: So far, scholars have attributed norm entrepreneurship retrospectively, the "successful" construction or dissemination of a norm being a necessary condition (see Sect. 2.8). In contrast, cases of failed or ongoing norm entrepreneurship largely escaped empirical analysis. The present study includes cases in which norm entrepreneurship has not yet led to the establishment/strengthening of the respective norm. Thus, the analysis takes into account both cases in which Iranian activism led to the establishment or strengthening of a norm as well as cases in which the norm entrepreneurship is still ongoing.

I consider written codification of a norm (e.g., in treaty texts or in the final documents of the review conferences as well as in official documents of field-specific international organizations) as the strongest indicator for successful norm construction.[14] Norm propagation is considered to have been moderately successful if the norm is confirmed by other states (preferably in writing) or supported rhetorically. I regard the successful introduction of a norm candidate to the political agenda as

[14]Usually, the internalization of a norm—i.e., its being taken-for-grantedness—is regarded as the highest level of successful norm diffusion. However, this can hardly be proven empirically because an internalized norm is no longer reflected by the actors using it and thus leaves no empirical trail.

Table 5.2 Main features of norm entrepreneurship

(1) Normative argumentation/speech act	
Normative claim	
Framing (*diagnostic, prognostic, motivational*)	– Normative/historical precedents – Analogies – Reference to universal principles or construction of "collective action frames" (Gamson 1992; Klandermans 1997) – Linkages to other policy fields/norms – Relationship to the existing normative order (affirmative/negative/destructive; new frame/alternative interpretation; counter-frame) – Dramatizing or emotional language – Vested interest versus common good
Naming/shaming/blaming	– Verbal criticism – Naming, shaming, and blaming – Stigmatization/demonization
(2) Norm entrepreneurial practices and activities	
Selection of an organizational platform (venue)	
Strategic coalition-building	– Cooperation or alliance with like-minded actors (states, IOs, committed individuals, media, civil society actors) – Recruiting support from civil society
Symbolic actions	– Scandals – Protests – Symbolic norm deviation/civil disobedience
Resources	– Financial means – Practical support (capacity building) – Brokerage/mediating services/community services – Diplomacy – Provision of expertise and (technical and general) knowledge – Moral authority/reputation – Transparency

the weakest form of successful norm entrepreneurship, provided that the goal is the establishment of a new norm.

If a norm has already been adopted, norm entrepreneurs usually try to maintain or strengthen it.[15] This makes it more difficult to assess their "degree of success". First of all, it can be considered a success if norm entrepreneurs succeed in keeping a norm on the agenda and in activating and consolidating the propagated normative meaning

[15]This also corresponds to a logical chronological sequence, i.e., if an actor has succeeded in putting a topic on the political agenda; she will try to codify it and, if successful, will then work for its preservation.

in the discourse. I use the following indicators to assess measures aimed at confirming or strengthening an already established norm: Norm entrepreneurs may criticize other contracting parties for failing to implement the norm (e.g., by using naming, shaming, and blaming). A norm's meaning can also be confirmed through repeated verbal "activation" (Rublee 2008), e.g., in relevant debates of the respective treaty regimes or through various practical activities (organizing workshops, training, publishing information material, etc.). Efforts of norm strengthening are considered to be particularly successful if actors manage to formalize the relevance of the propagated norm in politically binding declarations or other official documents.

5.2.2 Alternative Explanations: "Rogue States" as Norm Breaker or Advocates of Subsidiary Norms

According to liberal-constructivist literature on norms and "rogues," it is extremely unlikely that the proposition guiding this study will prove true. Instead, it is more probable that "rogue states" act as opponents of prototypical norm entrepreneurs and try to undermine or even destroy the existing normative order in words and deeds (AE 1). Because of this and the fact that "rogue states" are considered to be radical actors (Wunderlich 2017), it seems plausible to assume that they use destructive strategies to undermine established normative structures and try to sabotage efforts of norm diffusion. While prototypical norm entrepreneurs aim toward changing a normative order which they deem to be in need of reform, but accept in principle, norm breakers aim at the collapse of the prevailing normative order. Therefore, their speech acts should entail indications of the rejection of established norms.

Table 5.3 illustrates the criteria used to verify AE 1.

Another alternative explanation for the relationship of "rogue states" toward norms arises from recent accounts on norm subsidiarity. According to Acharya (2011),

Table 5.3 Criteria for the verification of AE 1 ("rogue states" as mere norm breakers)

(1) Attitude toward the existing normative order	
See Table 5.5	
(2) Destructive strategies	
Words	Deeds
– Deconstruction of existing or opposing normative frames – Criticism of opponents or of norms propagated by them – Stigmatisation/demonisation	– Norm violations/non-compliance – Initiation of counter-events
Disruptive rhetorical actions such as – Filibuster – Procedural delaying tactics – Verbal provocations	Disruptive practical actions such as – Protest – Initiation of scandals

Table 5.4 Criteria for verification of AE 2 (norm subsidiarity)

Normative framing of subsidiary norms	
Framing	– Motive for action is not a perceived external problem, but a hegemonic norm interpretation – References to the fear that an established or promoted norm might lead to cuts in autonomy. Possible signal words:[a] autonomy, (counter-)hegemony, self-reliance, independence, self-sufficiency, discrimination, domination, dominance, colonialism, humiliation, dependency, power (politics), interference, double standards, hypocrisy – Indications that the norm (interpretation) proposed as a counterproposal is aimed against this perceived restriction of autonomy
Naming/shaming/blaming	– Verbal criticism – Naming, shaming, and blaming – Stigmatization/demonization

[a]Of course, the content analysis also takes into account other grammatical forms as well as descriptions of perceived hegemonic relationships

actors in the Global South who hold a post-colonial past may display resistance toward Western efforts of norm promotion out of fear that the norms propagated by them might interfere with their autonomy. As a result, they formulate normative counterproposals, so-called subsidiary norms. Their activism is therefore purely reactive and resembles the position of norm breakers described in AE1.

So, how to assess whether Iran merely formulates subsidiary counter-norms? Since this behavior can be seen as a very limited form of norm entrepreneurship, it might well be that some features fit the list of criteria for prototypical norm entrepreneurship. A great difference, however, is that with the formulation of subsidiary norms, an actor always reacts to norms or norm entrepreneurs perceived as hegemonic and a threat to its own autonomy. This should be reflected in the kind of normative framing. As illustrated in Table 5.4, the second alternative explanation can therefore be substantiated by reference to the following argumentative framing and corresponding naming, shaming, and blaming:

5.2.3 *Norms Pertaining to the Control of Weapons of Mass Destruction*

Arms control, disarmament, and non-proliferation are central components of the global norm structure governing the realm of security policy. Measures to control the proliferation and ultimately the elimination of weapons of mass destruction are embedded in a dense and highly contested norm cluster (Müller and Wunderlich 2018) and institutionalized in the form of multilateral regimes on the control of biological, chemical, and nuclear weapons. As governing tools embedded in cooperative security architecture, these measures primarily aim at creating stability, but they may also reinforce power structures. This is particularly evident in the case of the NPT, which is based on a distinction between nuclear weapon states and non-nuclear weapon states and establishes different rights and obligations accordingly (Albin 2001: Chap. 6; Müller 2010a; Tannenwald 2013). As a consequence, conflicts about the meaning and weighting of individual norms are pervasive and subject to ongoing negotiation processes (Müller et al. 2013).

In order to grasp the position of the analyzed states with regard to the basic regime norms, I draw on "norm catalogs" which were developed within the framework of a project conducted at the Peace Research Institute Frankfurt (PRIF) in which I was involved. These catalogs include the central regime norms and point out the lines of contestation within the respective regimes. A manual is available upon request.

5.3 Process Tracing and Content Analysis

The study is designed as an exploratory single-case study that examines instances of Iranian norm entrepreneurship in three subcases. Each of these subcases is based on a detailed process tracing intended to generate a comprehensive narrative that traces Iran's normative claims and framings as well as practical activities undertaken to promote the respective norms over a certain period of time. This makes it possible to assess whether the observed process meets the criteria of norm entrepreneurship derived from the literature.

My intention is not to conduct a causal process tracing geared toward explaining why X produces Y (for such an understanding, see King et al. 1994: 227). Whether Iranian norm entrepreneurship was essential for the emergence and/or strengthening of the respective norm is not decisive. The central question is whether Iran's commitment meets the criteria of norm entrepreneurship. The tracing of the process also makes it possible to capture the motives and circumstances that led to Iran's norm advocacy. Methodologically, it is hardly possible to determine the exact motivation of Iranian norm entrepreneurship without any doubts (Schörnig et al. 2013: 34). However, detailed process tracing, which triangulates information from different sources and checks the given motives for their consistency, at least presents an approximate indication of their authenticity.

As such, I am using process tracing mainly for tracing "final causality" (Müller 2010b: 6; Kurki 2006: 191–193) with the aim of "describing political and social phenomena, i.e. descriptive inference" (Collier 2011: 2). The insights gained from the process tracing can be used for further theorizing (Mahoney 2010: 125).

The analysis of the various subcases, as well as the comparison with the contrasting cases, follows the method of structured focused comparison (George and Bennett 2004: 67–72). In addition, they are analyzed against the background of the norm entrepreneurial concept in order to guarantee comparability of results.

The process tracing is supplemented by a qualitative content analysis which is a classical method for understanding textual data (e.g., transcribed interviews, protocols, and speeches, but also audio or video recordings). As such, it is grounded in the hermeneutic tradition but also integrates the strengths of quantitative approaches for proceeding in a rule-guided and systematic manner (Kohlenbacher 2006: 40).

In contrast to quantitative approaches, qualitative content analysis is not preoccupied with counting the frequency of textual information. Rather, the focus is on capturing substantial information which is filtered out of the texts by means of a predefined set of categories. Above all, qualitative content analysis is an "instrument for the collection of reality constructions" (Wagner 2006: 171, my translation). While changes over time can be captured via content analysis (ibid. 2006:186), it is difficult to infer whether the interests, motivations, or intentions expressed by an actor are authentic or purely strategic (Schörnig et al. 2013: 34–38). Evidence for the authenticity of statements can, however, be substantiated by drawing on additional sources (e.g., data or interviews obtained through process tracing) that indicate consistency over time or across audiences.

The present study applies a qualitative content analysis as developed by Mayring (2003: 42–99), in which certain informational aspects are extracted from the data according to predefined criteria based on the research question. At the heart of every qualitative content analysis is a predefined set of categories, which includes precise definitions of the units of analysis (coding scheme). Categories denote the dimensions and subdimensions contained in the research question and the proposition guiding the analysis. They serve as criteria for the assignment of text passages. In the present study, all text passages that contain statements relevant to the research question and that can therefore be assigned to one of the categories were regarded as units of analysis. In addition, a codebook was created that contained coding rules, explicit code definitions and examples. In developing the coding scheme, I used a combination of theory-led, deductive and empirically guided, inductive category formation and modified the codebook in the course of the analysis itself.

Although Mayring argues that the set of categories should be revised after a first trial run, other authors consider this to be technically too complex and suggest that it can be adapted to the characteristics of the material throughout the entire evaluation process (Gläser and Laudel 2009: 201). I adjusted the categories during the first coding procedure and abstained from a second run. To conduct the qualitative content analysis, I used the software MAXQDA.

In order to answer the research question guiding this study, two different category systems were developed (the codebook is available from the author on request).

The following set of categories (see Table 5.5) served to capture Iran's notions of how the normative order should look like. The analysis drew on selected national speeches by the supreme leaders of Iran as well as the annual statements given on the occasion of the opening of the UN General Assembly. Categories were added inductively during the coding.

For the contrasting cases, the notions of world order were not analyzed by means of a content analysis, but inferred from secondary literature. Since the contrast served to qualify Iran's norm entrepreneurship, this was not necessary and would have gone beyond the scope of the study.

Table 5.5 Category system for the identification of Iran's world order concepts

Self-description Iran
How does Iran perceive its current position within the prevailing normative order?
Are there recurring patterns of argumentation or "topoi" used to justify arguments, describe Iran's political culture, or to serve as principles guiding the country's foreign policy?
Prevailing normative order
How is the prevailing (normative) order perceived, i.e., described?
Who is designated as proponents of the current order?
Is the present order approved/accepted/rejected? If so, which elements of the prevailing order are rejected?
Quantitative amount of critique/blaming? What or who is criticized (for what/why)?
Vision of world order
What are important elements of the vision of world order articulated by Iran (peace, justice, sovereignty, multilateralism, etc.)? On which principles should an alternative world order be based? How are the individual elements defined? Are they in a certain hierarchy to each other? Is it possible to find connections to existing norms? Is a particular attitude toward WMD shown?
From the perspective of Iran, can a "new" world order be realized within the old structures (reform) or does it require a complete new beginning, based on the overthrow of old structures (revolution)?
Mode of contestation
Does Iran challenge the current world order as such? If so, does contestation take place mainly implicitly (negation, contempt, indifference, disregard of prevailing norms and rules) or explicitly (contradiction, resistance, questioning, alternative vision)?

For the subcases on instances of norm advocacy, the analysis was based on the set of categories outlined in Table 5.2, which summarized how the concept has been used in empirical norm studies. Aspects that were taken into account included Iran's position toward the propagated norm, how it framed its norm advocacy and the political activities undertaken to foster its dissemination.

For the analysis of the contrasting cases, I also used the coding scheme summarized in Table 5.6, although for pragmatic reasons, this was not done systematically but exemplary.

Data sources included both official national documents and pronouncements relating to multilateral arms control, as well as national or regional statements made within the United Nations, the review conferences of the treaty regimes or the International Atomic Energy Agency, respectively. Of course, the practical activities and resources used could not be inferred from speeches. For this, I had to rely on other data, especially interviews and secondary literature.

In a final step, the coded text passages were interpreted in line with the research question guiding the study. No further statistical analysis was conducted for the purposes of this paper. However, individual frequencies were taken into account if they provided insights into the nature of the norm entrepreneurship, e.g., the increase in the usage of certain normative framings over time, or if the steady occurrence of certain normative claims could be counted as indicators for consistency of the advocacy.

Table 5.6 Set of categories for the identification of norm entrepreneurship

Category	Subcategory	Definition
Argumentative/interpretative framing/construction of a narrative		
Normative claim		Text passages in which the normative claims are formulated. These can be directed toward the establishment of new norms or normative meanings, as well as toward maintaining or strengthening an already established norm, e.g., through repeated references which serve to "activate" it
Framing		Text passages that indicate a normative framing, both with regard to the perceived problem (diagnostic framing) and a preferred solution (prognostic framing). If necessary, the norm entrepreneur may have to prove his/her competence and credibility. The framing can be further specified into the following subquestions:
	Normative/historical precedents analogies Reference to universal principles or collective action frames	What kind of normative linkages are created and how is this done?
	Linkages to other policy areas Relation to the established normative order (affirmative/negative/destructive; new frame/alternative interpretation; counter-frame)	How is the propagated norm (interpretation) put in relation to the established order? Does the actor adopt an affirmative attitude to established norms or do they resort to destructive strategies aimed at challenging or undermining established structures? Does the actor possibly see his/her engagement as a propagation of subsidiary norms?
	Dramatisation/emotionalisation	Which rhetoric does the actor use? Does he/she rather resort to confrontational or accommodating language?
	Particular interest versus public interest	Indications of being part of a larger group and therefore representing a collective concern

(continued)

Table 5.6 (continued)

Category	Subcategory	Definition
Naming/shaming/ blaming	Verbal criticism Accusations of misconduct Stigmatization/demonization	Shaming and blaming serve as argumentative support for the actual claim. In contrast to framing, they are specifically aimed at criticising and punishing actors or their behaviour. Shaming refers mainly to public humiliation and "denouncing" of misconduct, while blaming serves to assign guilt to an actor
Norm entrepreneurial practices and activities		
Selection of an organizational platform (venue)		References to institutional forums or platforms through which the actor tries to advocate the propagated norm (interpretation)
Strategic coalition-building	Like-minded groups	Indications of reference group: Which actors are addressed as potential supporters or like-minded actors?
	Civil society	Indication of interaction with civil society actors (including the media)
Symbolic actions	Provocations Scandals Expressions of disapproval/protest Symbolic norm violations/civil disobedience	References to symbolic actions that serve mobilizational purposes and are primarily intended to attract public attention and that emphasize the urgency of normative change
Resources	Financial means Practical support (capacity building) Brokerage/mediating services/community services Diplomacy Provision of expertise and (technical and factual) knowledge Moral authority/reputation Transparency	Reference to resources that are provided in order to foster the propagated norm Power Knowledge Values

In order to ensure that the results are intersubjectively comprehensible and reproducible, qualitative content analysis procedures should ensure both intercoder reliability and intracoder reliability. While the first criterion ensures that identical text passages are not coded differently by different encoders, intracoder reliability means that the same text passage is coded by the same person in the same manner at different points in time.

However, for pragmatic reasons, the coding for this study was conducted by me alone. Yet reliability is ensured by making the process of data collection and analysis as transparent as possible in order to ensure the traceability of the findings/interpretations. With regard to validity, George and Bennet (2004: 19) attest qualitative studies a comparatively higher conceptual validity than quantitative studies. In addition, I triangulated data sources which also strengthened the validity of the findings. Moreover, I tried to ensure what Mayring has defined as "communicative validation" (2003: 112) by discussing my findings with interview partners.

The subject matter of this study—international norms—poses some methodological problems that should not be concealed here. As Ethan A. Nadelman points out,

> [i]t is difficult and often impossible to determine whether those who conform to a particular norm do so because they believe the norm is just and should be followed, or because adherence to the norm coincides with their other principal interests, or because they fear the consequence that flow from defying the norm, or simply because conforming to the norm has become a matter of habit or custom. Much the same holds true for those who deviate from the norm. Our understanding of the impact of norms on state and non-state behavior and of the processes by which norms evolve is thus limited by our inability to adequately penetrate the human consciousness. (Nadelmann 1990: 480)

This also applies for the motives driving norm entrepreneurship. Ultimately, even the most sophisticated data triangulation does not help to determine without any doubt whether the analyzed actor really believes in the norms he/she is propagating or whether he/she is doing so for purely interest-based reasons. As already discussed in the theoretical part of this study, I assume that norms and interests are interdependent and that it is not possible to come to safe conclusions regarding the underlying motivation from the outside. Methodologically, I try to approach this question by discussing to what extent the norms propagated by Iran are in contradiction to vital interests (or even beneficial to them). Indications as to whether the norm entrepreneurship is "genuine" or based on interests may also arise from examining whether the advocacy was continuous and consistent, in words and deeds, over time and across audiences.

References

Acharya, A. (2011). Norm subsidiarity and regional orders: Sovereignty, regionalism, and rule-making in the third world. *International Studies Quarterly, 55*(1), 95–123.

Albin, C. (2001). *Justice and fairness in international negotiation*. Cambridge: Cambridge University Press.

Ali, J. (1996). *Iran, a case study: Chemical and Biological Arms Control Institute*. Alexandria, VA: Chemical and Biological Arms Control Institute.

Becker, U., Müller, H., & Wisotzki, S. (2008). Democracy and nuclear arms control—Destiny or ambiguity? *Security Studies, 17*(4), 810–854.

Björkdahl, A. (2002). *From idea to norm: Promoting conflict prevention*. Lund: Lund University.

Björkdahl, A. (2013). Ideas and norms in Swedish Peace Policy. *Swiss Political Science Review, 19*(3), 322–337.

Blatter, J., Janning, F., & Wagemann, C. (2007). *Qualitative Politikanalyse*. Wiesbaden: VS Verlag für Sozialwissenschaften.

Bob, C. (2012). *The global right wing and the clash of world politics*. New York, NY: Cambridge University Press.

Checkel, J. (2012). Norm entrepreneurship—Theoretical and methodological challenges. Memo prepared for a Workshop on "*The Evolution of International Norms and 'Norm Entrepreneurship": The Council of Europe in Comparative Perspective*. Oxford: Wolfson College, Oxford University.

Collier, D. (2011). Understanding process tracing. *Political Science and Politics, 44*(4), 823–830.

Finnemore, M., & Sikkink, K. (1998). International norm dynamics and political change. *International Organization, 52*(4), 887–917.

Finnemore, M., & Sikkink, K. (2001). Taking stock: The constructivist research program in international relations and comparative politics. *Annual Review of Political Science, 4,* 391–416.

Gamson, W. (1992). The social psychology of collective action. In A. Morris & C. Mc Clurg Mueller (Eds.), *Frontiers in social movement theory* (pp. 3–76). New Haven, CT: Yale University Press.

George, A. L., & Bennett, A. (2004). *Case studies and theory development in the social sciences*. Cambridge, MA: MIT Press.

Gerring, J. (2007a). *Case study research: Principles and practices*. Cambridge, NY: Cambridge University Press.

Gerring, J. (2007b). Is there a (viable) crucial-case method? *Comparative Political Studies, 40*(3), 231–253.

Gläser, J., & Laudel, G. (2009). *Experteninterviews und qualitative Inhaltsanalyse als Instrumente rekonstruierender Untersuchungen*. Wiesbaden: VS Verlag für Sozialwissenschaften.

Goertz, G., & Mahoney, J. (2012). *A tale of two cultures: Qualitative and quantitative research in the social sciences*. Princeton, NJ: Princeton University Press.

Goldblat, J. (2002). *Arms control: The new guide to negotiations and agreements*. London: SAGE.

Hoyt, P. D. (2000). The 'Rogue State' image in american foreign policy. *Global Society, 14*(2), 297–310.

Johnstone, I. (2007). The Secretary-General as Norm Entrepreneur. In S. Chesterman (Ed.), *Secretary or general? The UN Secretary-General in world politics* (pp. 123–138). Cambridge: Cambridge University Press.

Jones, P. (1998). Iran's threat perceptions and arms control policies. *The Nonproliferation Review, 6*(1), 40–55.

King, G., Keohane, R., & Verba, S. (1994). *Designing Social Inquiry: Scientific inference in qualitative research*. Princeton, NJ: Princeton Univ. Press.

Klandermans, B. (1997). *The social psychology of protest*. Oxford: Blackwell.

Kohlenbacher, F. (2006). The use of qualitative content analysis in case study research. *Forum: Qualitative Social Research, 7*(1). Resource document. http://www.qualitative-research.net/index.php/fqs/article/view/75/153. Accessed April 28, 2017.

Kurki, M. (2006). Causes of a divided discipline: Rethinking the concept of cause in international relations theory. *Review of International Studies, 32*(2), 189–216.

Levy, J. S. (2008). Case studies: Types, designs, and logics of inference. *Conflict Management and Peace Science, 25*(1), 1–18.

Litwak, R. (2000). *Rogue states and U.S. Foreign Policy: Containment after the cold war.* Washington, DC: Woodrow Wilson Center Press with Johns Hopkins University Press.

Mahoney, J. (2010). After KKV: The new methodology of qualitative research. *World Politics, 62*(1), 120–147.

Mayring, P. (2003). *Qualitative Inhaltsanalyse. Grundlagen und Techniken*. Weinheim: Beltz UTB.

Müller, H. (2010a). Between power and justice. Current problems and perspectives of the NPT regime. *Strategic Analysis, 34*(2), 189–201.

Müller, H. (2010b). *Process-tracing*. Unpublished Manuscript. Frankfurt am Main.

Müller, H., & Wunderlich, C. (Eds.). (2013). *Norm dynamics in multilateral arms control: Interests, conflicts, and justice*. Athens, GA: University of Georgia Press.

Müller, H., & Wunderlich, C. (2018). Not lost in contestation: How norm entrepreneurs frame norm development in the nuclear nonproliferation regime. *Contemporary Security Policy, 39*(3), 341–366.

Müller, H., Below, A., & Wisotzki, S. (2013). Beyond the state: Nongovernmental Organizations, the European Union, and the United Nations. In H. Müller & C. Wunderlich (Eds.), *Norm dynamics in multilateral arms control, interests, conflicts, and justice* (pp. 296–336). Athens, GA: University of Georgia Press.

Nadelmann, E. (1990). Global prohibition regimes: The evolution of norms in International Society. *International Organization, 44*(4), 479–526.

O'Reilly, K. P. (2007). Perceiving rogue states: The use of the "Rogue State" concept by U.S. foreign policy elites. *Foreign Policy Analysis, 3*(4), 295–315.

Payne, R. (2001). Persuasion, frames and norm construction. *European Journal of International Relations, 7*(1), 37–61.

Pirseyedi, B. (2013). *Arms control and Iranian Foreign Policy: Diplomacy of discontent*. New York, NY: Routledge.

Price, R. (2003). Transnational civil society and advocacy in world politics. *World Politics, 55*(4), 579–606.

Rublee, M. (2008). Taking stock of the nuclear nonproliferation regime: Using social psychology to understand regime effectiveness. *International Studies Review, 10*(3), 420–450.

Schörnig, N., Geis, A., & Müller, H. (2013). The empirical study of "Democratic Wars": Methodology and methods. In A. Geis, H. Müller, & N. Schörnig (Eds.), *The militant face of democracy: Liberal forces for good* (pp. 34–38). New York, NY: Cambridge University Press.

Tannenwald, N. (2013). Justice and fairness in the nuclear nonproliferation regime. *Ethics & International Affairs, 27*(3), 299–317.

van Evera, S. (1997). *Guide to methods for students of political science*. Ithaca, NY: Cornell University Press.

Wagner, W. (2006). Qualitative Inhaltsanalyse. Die soziale Konstruktion sicherheitspolitischer Interessen in Deutschland und Großbritannien. In Siedschlag, A. (Ed.), *Methoden der sicherheitspolitischen Analyse. Eine Einführung* (pp. 169–188). Wiesbaden: VS Verlag.

Wunderlich, C. (2017). Delegitimisation à la Carte: The "Rogue State" label as a means of stabilising order in the nuclear non-proliferation regime. In S. Gertheiss, S. Herr, K. Wolf, & C. Wunderlich (Eds.), *Resistance and change in world politics: International dissidence* (pp. 143–189). Cham: Palgrave Macmillan.

Chapter 6
Iran and the International Community: A Counter-Hegemonic Norm Breaker?

Iran has been considered "a veteran of rule-breaking behavior within and beyond its borders" (Geldenhuys 2004: 112) even before the Islamic Revolution in 1979. In fact, Iran makes for an astonishingly persistent challenger to the international system. For a long time, Iran was regarded as the "gendarme of the West" in the Middle East. In 1977, US President Jimmy Carter had described the Shah regime as "island of stability in one of the most troubled areas of the world" (Carter 1977), deliberately ignoring the repressive-despotic style of Shah Mohammad Reza Pahlavi.

As the former Persian Empire, Iran is one of the oldest cultures in human history and generally considered to be the cradle of poetry and home of various famous philosophers. Due to this historical heritage, Iranians of all social classes express a strong national pride. The explosive geopolitical location between Asia, the Middle East and the Strait of Hormuz and its rich oil, and gas deposits has repeatedly made Iran a pawn of international politics. More than once, the country has suffered foreign rule. However, even after having been the object of Western imperialism for several decades, it never lost its formal sovereignty (for a historical overview see Axworthy 2008 or Takeyh 2009).

Any attempt to approach the world order conceptions of the Islamic Republic of Iran (IRI)[1] therefore have to acknowledge the institutional setting, the historical and geographical context in which the country is embedded and ideational traditions and identity constructions. The following sections thus give a short overview of the basic tenets of Iran's political culture, with regard to its institutional, historical, and ideational grounding. This builds the framework for the analysis of Iran's world order conceptions in Sect. 6.4.[2]

[1] For reasons of simplicity, in the following, I will use "Iran" when referring to the Islamic Republic of Iran after the revolution of 1979.

[2] I am thankful for research assistance by Jakob Bund and Hiwa Rostami who helped with data acquisition and analysis.

C. Wunderlich, *Rogue States as Norm Entrepreneurs*,
Norm Research in International Relations,
https://doi.org/10.1007/978-3-030-27990-5_6

6.1 Basic Tenets of Iran's Political System

Iran's political system poses some considerable challenges to the outside observer: Decision-making structures and the institutional system are quite complex and opaque. The Iranian system is composed of multiple institutions which sometimes seem to overlap in their areas of responsibility. It consists of coexisting elected and appointed posts, informal networks, and personal relationships, who all compete for resources and influence.[3] Since the Islamic Revolution in 1979, Iran's political system has combined elements of Islamic theocracy with albeit small shares of democracy—a unique balancing act that has often produced contradictions (Akbari 2006: 2–9). Non-elected authorities, clientelism, and widespread patronage make the political system vulnerable to blockades and stagnation and undermine institutions legitimated by the constitution. The ideological framework legitimating the revolution limits the political room for maneuver of the individual institutions considerably (Pirseyedi 2013: 14). Iran boasts about the institution of free elections, which it claims set it apart from most autocratic regimes in the Middle East. Yet Walter Posch rightly observes that "freedom of expression and the right to engage in political activities apply only to those who ideologically belong to the sphere of political Islam according to Khomeini's interpretation" (Posch 2008).

Various institutions are involved in the formulation and implementation of Iranian foreign and security policy: The forming of opinion mainly takes place within the formal institutions (i.e., the Office of the Supreme Leader, the President's Office, the Ministry of Foreign Affairs, the Supreme National Security Council, and the Iranian parliament). Figure 6.1 provides an overview of the most important of these (formal) institutions and their function in Iran's political system.

Since the revolution of 1979, the Iranian constitution has been based on the principle of the "guardianship of the jurist." Thus, as Iran's highest cleric, the **Supreme Leader**[4] has ultimate authority—he serves as head of state and enjoys supreme constitutional decision-making authority. Elected for life by the Assembly of Experts, he determines the guidelines of domestic and foreign policy and ensures that everyday political events conform to the values of the Islamic Revolution. No political decision is implemented without his consent—foreign policy initiatives also require his approval (Byman 2001: 22).[5]

The **Iranian president** is often considered to be the second most important political figure in the decision-making process. As the formal head of the executive, he heads the Council of Ministers and presides over the Supreme National Security Council of Iran. He implements the laws passed by parliament or by referendum, signs international treaties, and is responsible for the state budget and the appointment

[3]The following is based on Buchta (2000); Byman (2001); Posch (2008) and Thaler et al. (2010).

[4]The terms Supreme Leader and Revolutionary Leader are used synonymously.

[5]According to the constitution, the Assembly of Experts elected by the people can dismiss the Supreme Leader. However, since its members are chosen by the Guardian Council, this is extremely unlikely to happen (Akbari 2006: 5). As Posch (2008) notes, the political system of revolutionary Iran is above all based on loyalty to the revolutionary leader.

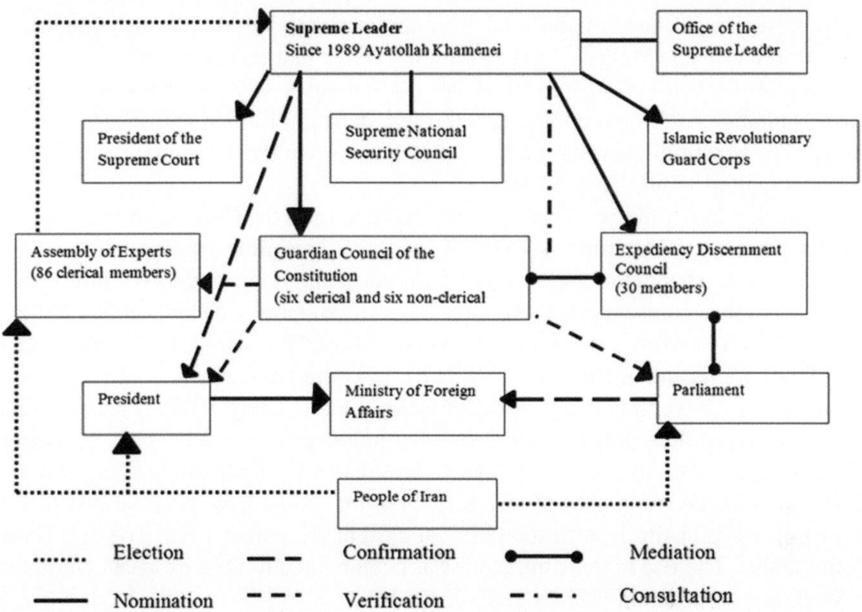

Fig. 6.1 Key institutions and their function in the political system of Iran. *Source* Adapted from http://www.nzz.ch/aktuell/international/uebersicht/iran-zwischen-militanz-und-aussoehnung-1.18098619,28.4.2017 (in German)

of his cabinet. He is only accountable to Parliament, the Supreme National Security Council and the Supreme Leader. The president's room for action is limited, but he can set priorities within the framework of the constitution and the ideological scope. The Foreign Ministry plays a much more important role in the forming of opinion and in implementing policy, rather than in the decision-making process (Ehteshami 2009).

The **Supreme National Security Council** (SNSC), founded during the course of the constitutional reform of 1989 and chaired by the president, is considered to be the "nerve center" (Ehteshami 2009) of political decision-making. It defines the political framework for action in consultation with the Chief Judicial Officer and is responsible for its coordination and resource management. Although the council functions primarily as a technical-administrative instrument, it often takes on the role of a clearinghouse (Posch 2013: 9). Decisions formulated in the SNSC and endorsed by the Supreme Leader become consensus decisions, i.e., "further discussion is proscribed, and the press is advised accordingly" (Thaler et al. 2010: 32).

The political system's consensus orientation is however often undermined by the strong influence of individuals striving to foster their particular religious, political, economic, or military interests, who often succeed in radicalizing political positions (Posch 2013: 8). As a consequence, political processes are often clouded with "factional maneuvering" (Thaler et al. 2010: 38) and political infighting (Ehteshami 2009).

Interest groups and the individual political fractions also try to exert influence in the **parliament** (the Majles)—an institutional venue that Posch describes as a place of fierce confrontation (2013: 8). However, parliament is only marginally involved in the formulation of foreign policy, e.g., through debating foreign and security policy issues. The constitution even prohibits the Majles from intervening in the executive's political matters (Ehteshami 2009).

While serving primarily domestic political functions, the **Council of Guardians**, the **Expediency Discernment Council,** and the **Assembly of Experts** are also involved in the shaping of foreign policy. In particular, they "balance political tendencies and thus contribute to foreign policy being supported by all political forces" (Posch 2013: 10). Most notably, long-term interests of the system and (foreign) policy guidelines are formulated in the Expediency Discernment Council.

Since the 1990s, the Islamic Revolutionary Guards Corps (IRGC) have significantly increased their political and economic influence, especially since Mahmoud Ahmadinejad took office in 2005.[6] Once established by Khomeini as the military-ideological backbone of the Islamic Republic, the IRGC have become one of the most important institutions in the political system (Katzman 1993: 165–68; Ehteshami 2009). The rise of their influence has been related to their involvement in the Iranian nuclear program (Thaler et al. 2010: 34).

To conclude, Iran's political system is based on a precarious balance between elected and unelected, formal and informal institutions whose stability ultimately depends on the support of the Supreme Leader. The more central a topic is to national security (e.g. the nuclear negotiations, see Sect. 7.4)—and thus to the survival of the regime—the greater the extent to which decision-making processes are restricted to the narrow circles of the Supreme Leader (Thaler et al. 2010: 46).

6.2 From "Gendarme of the Gulf" to the Center of the "Axis of Evil"

Analyses of Iranian foreign policy are usually organized around the following historical phases: (1) the pre-revolutionary phase; (2) the years of the revolutionary era from 1979 to 1989 centered on regime consolidation; (3) the era of Ali Akbar Hashemi Rafsanjani's presidency from 1989 to 1997, in which the regime took a more pragmatic political course, particularly as a result of the death of the revolutionary leader Ayatollah Ruhollah Khomeini and the Iran–Iraq war; (4) Mohammad Khatami's term of office from 1997 to 2005, which made history as era of the reform movement; (5) the period from 2005 to 2013 under the presidency of Mahmud Ahmadinejad, which

[6]The IRGC is a branch of the Iranian armed forces (besides the regular army), tasked with guaranteeing national security, both against internal and external threats. For an overview see Ward (2009) or Alfoneh (2013).

was marked by a radicalization of politics and an internal competition for power, and (6) another period of reform initiated with the entry of office of Hassan Rouhani in 2013.

6.2.1 Iran During the Shah's Rule

Interference in Iran's political and economic affairs dates back to the beginning of the twentieth century and culminated in the occupation of the country by British and Soviet troops during World War II and the removal of the Shah. As a result, Britain gained control of Iranian oil reserves—the Allies were to occupy Iran until the end of the war in 1945. Even though the USA had military personnel based in Iran in 1942, the US government was regarded as trustworthy and sympathetic to the Iranian people—probably also because both countries had by and large established a harmonious relationship built on the provision of economic advice to Iran since 1912 (Axworthy 2008: 227–234). Against this backdrop, the 1953 coup supported by British and American intelligence services and directed against the democratically elected Prime Minister Mohammad Mossadegh was a shock and the birth of an antagonistic relationship that grew into a fierce enmity following the 1979 revolution. The coup, which served to undermine Mossadegh's plan to nationalize Iranian oil reserves as well as to prevent Iran from drawing closer to the Soviet Union, once again confirmed Iran's perception that the country was merely a pawn in the hands of the superpowers.

With the support of the USA, Shah Mohammad Reza Pahlavi was able to consolidate his power. Domestically, the Shah sought to further Iran's international status—domestically, this translated into the initiation of a liberal modernization program and a recourse to the historical heritage of Persian culture. In terms of foreign policy, Iran sought above all to join forces with the West. In return for massive financial and military support, the USA hoped to gain important geostrategic advantages by building up Iran as client state. After Britain withdrew from the Gulf region, the USA consequently encouraged Iran's regional supremacy and did everything in their power to make the Shah regime the "deputy sheriff" of the USA. Ansari even contends that Nixon had given the Shah a "carte blanche" (Ansari 2006: 65) for conventional military build-up. The economic upturn and American financial aid allowed the Shah to heavily invest in the militarization of the country. The beginnings of Iran's ambitious nuclear energy program can also be traced back to this period (see Sect. 7.4).

6.2.2 The Early Years of the Islamic Republic of Iran 1979–1989

A few years later, a massive protest movement put an end to the Shah's dictatorship. For the people of Iran, the Shah had become a symbol of imperialist exploitation and a puppet of the West (Safiarian 2011: 83). Ayatollah Ruhollah Musavi Khomeini, who criticized the Shah's pro-Western course as a sell-out of Iran's national sovereignty, and who vehemently opposed American influence, declared himself the political leader of the movement.

The 1979 Revolution marked not only the birth of the Islamic Republic of Iran; it also became its defining element. Above all, the revolution aimed to overthrow the old political system under the reign of the Pahlavi dynasty (1925–1979). The Shah and his followers were considered slaves to the USA, as "friends of the dollar, they have no religion, no loyalty" (Khomeini 1963). Therefore, the Islamic Revolution was primarily concerned with abolishing the dependency structures (especially vis-à-vis the USA) which the Shah had established. The Supreme Leader declared resistance to the Shah's "regime of arrogance" (Khomeini 1978b) a revolutionary duty. Resistance to the "doctrine of domination" (Khamenei 1987a: 54–55) was declared as the first step in liberating humanity from the chains of Western hegemony. The ideological foundation of the revolution was framed as an alternative to the Western liberal world order (see Sect. 6.4). Suzanne Maloney describes the revolution as

> radical reinvention […] [which] dramatically transformed the nation's internal politics, economy, and society, and reconfigured the regional landscape, the geostrategic balance in the Middle East, and the discourse of political and economic development. (Maloney 2002: 88)

In the eyes of the USA and the rest of the Western world, however, Iran's Islamic revolution was perceived as running counter to the very idea of modernity and thus as being synonymous with a return to the Middle Ages (Akbari 2004: 10).

The occupation of the American embassy in Tehran in November 1979 and the subsequent 444-day hostage-taking of American embassy personnel cemented the break with the West. The incident left a deep scar in the historical memory of the USA.[7] Ansari compares the American feeling of betrayal with that of the Iranian people when the USA had removed Mossadegh:

> For hardline revolutionaries, the seizure of the embassy became the second revolution, the moment when the Islamic character of the revolution was consolidated. For the United States, emerging from the uncertainties of the 70s, it was a grave humiliation. For the revolutionaries, it marked a termination, an achievement. For the United States, it marked the beginning of an obsession with Iran, made all the more intense by the intimacy of the previous twenty-five years and the mutual sense of betrayal. (Ansari 2006: 90)

While during the first decade, post-revolutionary Iran was preoccupied with exporting the revolutionary ideology abroad, historical events—Khomeini's death

[7] Despite the formal breakdown of diplomatic relations in April 1980, informal cooperation between Iran and the USA, e.g., during the course of the so-called Iran–Contra affair, were repeatedly established. In this affair, the USA supplied weapons to Tehran and used the funds raised to support the Nicaraguan contra rebels.

as well as the war against Iraq (1980–1988)—set in motion a reorientation and a weakening of ideological elements. Iran saw itself increasingly isolated and, as a corollary, the economic situation of the country worsened (Juneau and Razavi 2013: 3). All of these elements contributed to ideological demobilization (Ansari 2006: 117). The Iran–Iraq war left a deep mark in the Iranian psyche and resulted in a pronounced anti-war attitude (Leverett and Leverett 2013: 38). At the same time, the war strengthened Iran's national identity and the feeling of solidarity, and further nourished an already deep notion of anti-Americanism. William R. Polk contends that "rather than horrifying and revolting the society [...] [the martyrdom of the youth, CW] gave the society an emotional stake in the revolutionary regime that went quite beyond mere nationalism. To criticize or oppose the regime became not only unpatriotic but also a sacrilege against the dead" (Polk 2011: 151).

The Iran–Iraq war was a dramatic experience for the country, also because Iran felt abandoned by the international community, which did not come to support Iran even when it became clear that the country had fallen victim to Iraqi chemical weapons (a fact that Iran claimed to be contrary to international law). The feeling of being left alone destroyed Iran's confidence in the international system. The question arising in Iran was whether the leading (Western) powers considered international law equally applicable to all states. That the West sided with Iraq was once again perceived as a strategic action by the major powers in order to destroy the Iranian Republic. This becomes evident in Khomeini's description of the war as "not a war between two countries, two armies; it was a war between an unwritten, global coalition against one nation" (quoted after Maloney 2002: 15). The conclusion was that in a Western-dominated international system, self-reliance in matters of security policy remained the only option (Leverett and Leverett 2013: 40).

At the end of the 1980s, Iran cemented its status as pariah state: The war had severely weakened the country, demoralized the public, and led to the international isolation of Iran. Therefore, Iranian leaders began to opt for a more pragmatic policy course with ideology being increasingly used merely "as a mask for realpolitik" (Byman 2001: 100).

6.2.3 *Iran's Turn to Pragmatism Under Rafsanjani 1989–1997*

During the period in office of presidents Ali Akbar Hashemi Rafsanjani (1989–1997) and Mohammad Khatami (1997–2005), Iran tried to normalize its relations with the West (Moshirzadeh 2007: 527). However, authors such as Posch (2013: 18) or Adebahr (2014: 18) argue that a weakening of Iran's ideological orientation should not be confused with a de-ideologization of foreign policy. Ultimately, they claim that Iran's political elite has been primarily concerned with maintaining the regime. Seen from a historical perspective, Iranian foreign policy could then be characterized as having steadily shifted between more pragmatic and more ideologically driven phases.

Domestically, Rafsanjani's presidency was marked by a "recurrent domestic struggle between Islamic radicals and more traditionalist clergy, which intensified in the wake of the controversial ceasefire and the battle over the succession decision" (Maloney 2002: 110). Inconsistency and stagnation characterized Iran's foreign policy at the time. Thus, the country often sent out contradictory signals to the world: Reform efforts and rapprochement ran parallel to continued support for terrorist groups such as Hezbollah in Lebanon and Hamas in Palestine. Iran sought to counter the expansion of US influence in the Persian Gulf as a result of the Iran–Iraq war by massive conventional armament and clandestine nuclear weapons activities. Posch concludes: "The foreign policy maxim now became expediency […], whereby the regime put the benefits for the nation (and itself) ahead of ideological orthodoxy" (Posch 2013: 17).

6.2.4 Reform Efforts Under Khatami 1997–2005

Mohammad Khatami (1997–2005) won the election mainly because he had promised a reform agenda which met the Iranian people's need for political participation, liberalization, and equality. Khatami's reform agenda was accompanied by de-ideologization and renationalization at home (Ansari 2006: 147–64). At the international level, he advocated a "dialogue of civilizations" based on intercultural understanding and active exchange. To the West, Khatami signaled a willingness to engage in dialogue, especially with the Clinton administration, which in its second term of office followed a policy of constructive engagement in its relations with "problem states" (Litwak 2007: 32–37).

In the USA, people reacted with skepticism and dismissed the Iranian willingness to talk as "window dressing" (Ansari 2006: 154). Commentators consider this wait-and-see attitude as a missed opportunity for dialogue. Moreover, the West's attitude may have weakened the reform movement in Iran (Ansari 2006). Two years later, when the USA signaled concessions, Khatami's domestic room for action had shrunk considerably. The conservative opposition and the revolutionary leader had dismissed or even arrested many reform-oriented cabinet members (Maloney 2008: 9). Ansari therefore concludes:

> By not engaging in dialogue with those who were willing to participate, they [the hawks in the West; CW] had facilitated a hardline backlash. For hard-liners, tough posturing rather than negotiation was the only way forward. It was a deteriorating, absurd, vicious cycle in which the rigid obstinacy of the hawks on both sides produced a self-fulfilling prophecy and its own justification. (Ansari 2006: 188–89)

Despite modest reform successes (e.g., regional policy of détente and improved relations with neighboring countries; a more moderate stance on the Israeli–Palestinian conflict; rapprochement with the USA, for example, through cooperation in the fight against terrorism or a willingness to suspend uranium mining), the foundations of the Iranian revolution remained untouched even in the 1990s. Domestically, conservative forces resisted Khatami's reform course and stoked fears of Western imperialism.

In the USA, the prospects of an American-Iranian rapprochement worsened with the entry into office of George W. Bush. Teheran strongly condemned the attacks of 9/11 and was one of the first states to show compassion both through official statements by the political elite and demonstrations on the streets. Even the slogan "Death to America", a ritual component of Friday prayers was suspended for a few weeks on presidential orders (Ansari 2006: 181). In the "fight against terrorism", Iran even provided support for the US led war against the Taliban in Afghanistan by granting overflight rights and by supporting the Northern Alliance. Paralleling President Bush's "war on terror", Khatami announced in 2001 a "jihad against this evil phenomenon [terrorism; CW]" (Khatami 2001). Following the 9/11 terrorist attacks, Khatami expressed a genuine interest in fighting (Sunni) terrorism beyond mere expressions of solidarity and condolence. In addition, the Iranian government deliberately distinguished itself from terrorist networks in Iraq: Khamenei described them as "misguided people" and emphasized that "they are brandishing their swords in the air, shedding the blood of the people. That method is not our method" (Khamenei 2006b). By contrast, President Bush, in his state of the union address in 2002, placed Tehran on an "axis of evil" thereby clearly signaling his intention to ground his future policy course toward Iran on the strategy of regime change (Takeyh 2009: 217–218). In doing so, he played into the hands of conservative radical forces in Iran and undermined Khatami's position (Ramazani 2013: 5).

Notwithstanding these developments, the two countries kept more secret communication channels open, particular in light of the evolving nuclear crisis. In May 2003, for example, Khatami indicated an offer for talks via Swiss ambassador Tim Guldimann with the aim of restarting diplomatic relations between the USA and Iran. Bush, however, supported by the neoconservative establishment in the USA and in Israel, preferred the strategy of regime change.

6.2.5 *Conservative Backslash Under Ahmadinejad 2005–2013*

While Rafsanjani and Khatami succeeded in weakening the ideological grounding of foreign policy, Ahmadinejad put them back at the center of his agenda. He launched a neoconservative agenda aimed primarily at reducing social injustice both internally and externally and strengthening Iran's role as a counter-balance to the West (Ansari 2007). His election victory is to be seen against the background of a "conservative re-Islamization" (Akbari 2006: 12, transl. CW), which had begun as a consequence of Khatami's reform discourse, as well as the increased influence of the Revolutionary Guards, whom Ahmadinejad himself was part of (Alfoneh 2013: 30–38). With his aggressive anti-American and anti-Zionist rhetoric, Ahmadinejad steered Iran toward a renewed course of confrontation with the West and Israel and strengthened the country's foreign policy isolation (Ansari 2006: 229; Maloney 2008: 69).

Efforts to find a diplomatic solution to the nuclear dispute went hand in hand with an intensification of the Iranian nuclear program, repeated violations of international rules and norms as well as the challenging of the authority of the UN Security Council (Senn 2009: 87–90). Sanctions led to a deterioration of the economic situation in Iran, although Ahmadinejad's foreign policy became more pragmatic toward the end of his first term of office (Posch 2010: 755). All in all, observers speak of an increasing militarization of the political and economic system during his term of office (e.g. Alfoneh 2013).

6.2.6 New Winds of Reform with the Entry into Office of Rouhani

After Hassan Rouhani's surprising election victory in June 2013, Iran resumed its rapprochement with the West. Striving to improve relations with the West and thus to fix Iran's broken economy, Rouhani put priority to solving the nuclear crisis—which will be described in more detail in Chap. 7. Meanwhile, the Obama administration also sought normalization of relations and had shifted US policy toward dialogue and diplomatic engagement. In fact, when the conflicting parties were able to reach a negotiated solution, the economic sanctions on Iran were lifted.

While Iran's economy received a boost with the lifting of nuclear-related USA and European sanctions, Rouhani's aspiration for reform and opening toward the world continued to meet domestic resistance from conservative forces. In fact, observers of Iranian (foreign policy) policy have emphasized that a more flexible approach is not to be equated with a fundamental change in policy direction. Adebahr (2014: 21), for example, shows that Anti-Americanism and (at least rhetorical) opposition to the West remains central elements of Iran's foreign policy.

Since Donald Trump took office, however, relations with Iran and the USA have considerably worsened. With the aim of setting himself clearly apart from the policy of his predecessor, already during the election campaign, Trump announced that the "disastrous" nuclear agreement needed to be renegotiated (Begley 2016). He criticized Iran massively for its destabilizing behavior in the Middle East and its support for terrorist organizations. At the time of writing, relations are at a new low point: In May 2018, the Trump administration unilaterally withdrew from the Iran nuclear accord and announced that it would re-impose economic sanctions. For now, Iran is abiding by the accord and together with the European signatories of the agreement tries to keep the deal alive without the USA. Yet Khamenei has repeatedly emphasized that Iran is not willing to renegotiate the deal and has ordered the resumption of uranium enrichment within the allowed framework. Rhetoric on both sides remains fierce, while domestically, a series of public protests indicate that the people in Iran are anything but content with their government's course.

6.3 Foreign Policy Identity and the Role of Iran

There are three main elements or "ideological pillars" (Posch 2010: 751) of Iran's foreign policy: Islam and Shiism (as interpreted by Khomeini), Persian nationalism and anti-imperialism/Third Worldism (Maloney 2002; Ehteshami 2009; Holliday 2011; Posch 2013). While being partly complementary, the three identity strands also contradict each other. Suzanne Maloney sees commonalities above all in a "Manichean dualism" (Maloney 2002: 102): The division of the world into "good" and "evil". However, they could conflict with each other as Islamism and Third Worldism are revolutionary ideologies with global reach, while Shiism and Persian nationalism are inherently self-centered and conservative (Posch 2010: 751).

According to Maloney, Article 154 of the Iranian constitution reveals a contradiction between anti-imperialist and Islamic elements of identity and at the same time exposes the "dueling conceptions of Iranian identity" (Maloney 2002: 103): Not only are the Muslim neighboring states called upon to follow Iran's example and to free themselves from the chains of foreign rule. The resistance against oppression should not stop at national borders. The state itself wants to support neighboring countries in their fight for freedom.

The three identity strands manifest themselves in different discourses (see Fig. 6.2) which will be discussed more thoroughly with relation to Iran's world order vision.Importantly, Moshirzadeh (2007) distinguishes three topical discourses on resistance, independence, and justice. In practice, individual identity elements are emphasized depending on the situation and context at hand and following a cautious balance of pragmatism and ideology (Posch 2008, 2013; Monshipouri 2013: 67; Ramazani 2013 [2010]: 197, 207).[8]

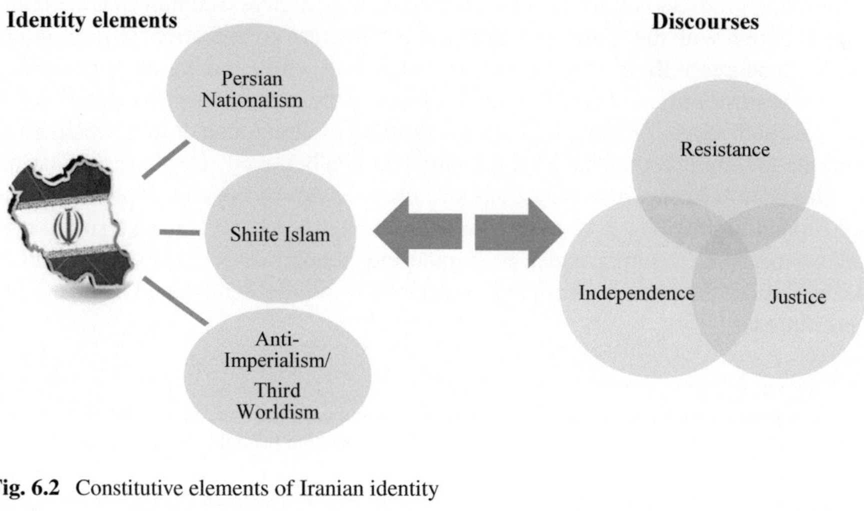

Fig. 6.2 Constitutive elements of Iranian identity

[8]For analytical purposes, the three identity strands and discourses are discussed separately. In practice, however, there are overlaps and mutual bonds, as shown in Fig. 6.2. For example, the

Regarding its religious underpinnings, Iran's political culture is based on the so-called Twelver Shia[9] in the tradition of quietist Islam. One of its central features is the rejection of all forms of dominance and a striving for a better, more just life based on equality and independence. The Twelver Shia has been stated religion in Iran since the sixteenth century and has been enshrined in the constitution. Until the revolution in 1979, Iranian Shiism was quietist, meaning that it was apolitical. In the course of the Islamic Revolution, Ayatollah Khomeini institutionalized his interpretation of the Shia and propagated a radical reinterpretation of the relationship between state and religion. In Khomeini's logic, Iran had to establish the "rule by the jurisprudent" in order to achieve universal justice. It would be only through his leadership that the deprived and oppressed could free themselves from the chains of tyranny (Adabi-Moghaddam 2012: 159). Religion served the revolutionary regime not only as a legitimating basis, but also provided a program of action: Khomeini declared resistance against all forms of tyranny and a quest for justice as a religious duty (Khomeini 1964b, in Algar 1981: 185). To this effect, the constitution in Article 154 (similarly Art. 3, para. 16) states that Iran "supports the just struggle of the mustad'afun (the oppressed, CW) against the mustakbirun (the oppressors, CW) in every corner of the world". Hence, the persistent denouncing of earthly injustice can be considered a central strategic component of Iranian politics that also influence Iran's role conceptions and world order vision (Ramazani 2013 [1990]: 133–134; Moshirzadeh 2007: 533).

While during the early years after the Islamic Revolution, Khomeini rejected Iranian nationalism in favor of a pan-Islamic vision directed towards the community of all Muslims (*ummah*), Ramazani's dictum that "the past is ever present in Iranian culture" (Ramazani 2013: 353) aptly describes the Iranian psyche: Nationalism in the sense of a return to pre-Islamic heritage nourishes national pride, which is firmly anchored in political culture. It is based both on experiences of unfair treatment and dissatisfaction with the status quo. Centuries of Western colonization, territorial loss and political and military dependency have left Iran with a feeling of vulnerability. The overthrow of Mossadegh in particular, but also the experiences during the Iran–Iraq war, symbolizes for many Iranians an enduring victimization of Iran, which gives them the feeling that they have been humiliated and betrayed. This "sense of unjust victimization" (Ansari 2006: 131) runs through speeches by both the Supreme Leader and Iranian dignitaries. It is used to call for compensation for injustice suffered as well as to justify the importance of Iranian independence (note also the slogan of the revolution "Independence, Freedom, Islamic Republic", embedded in the Iranian constitution).

---

pursuit of justice derives primarily from Shiism. At the same time, however, it is fed by historical experiences of injustice and can hardly be understood in isolation from the quest for independence and anti-imperialism.

[9]Twelver Shia Muslims believe in the existence of twelve Imams, the last of whom, (Muhammad al-Mahdi) did not die, but lives in secrecy and will return at the end of time to bring about righteousness, justice, and peace. As long as the hidden Imam has not returned, Shia scholars are responsible for the leadership of the community. See Sachedina (1981).

Resistance and independence are also deeply rooted in Persian culture. The fact that Iran was once a great empire of pre-Islamic times and one of the first civilizations of mankind nourishes national pride and a certain longing for great power status. A self-perception deeply shaped by anti-imperialist features is often accompanied by a "hegemonic" eagerness, which particularly came to the fore during the reign by the Shah (Holliday 2011: 50). Guided by what Maloney has described as a "sense of hegemonic destiny for Iran" (Maloney 2002: 96), he sought to secure Iran's status in the community of states—a striving that some have even labeled megalomania (c).

It is thus not surprising that the principle of independence is a central feature in the Iranian constitution (Posch 2013: 14–15). Article II rejects "all forms of oppression, both the infliction of and the submission to it, and of dominance, both its imposition and its acceptance".[10] In Article III, the government obligates itself to committing all its resources to "the complete elimination of imperialism and the prevention of foreign influence" and ensuring autonomy in the fields of science, technology, agriculture, military affairs, and culture. In the constitution, the principle of independence comes in the form of strict non-alignment, which was expressed by the revolutionary leadership with the slogan: "Neither East, nor West, only the Islamic Republic" (Khamenei 2008a). In fact, the Islamic Revolution sought to emancipate itself from both the West and the East and the materialistic ideologies of capitalism and communism. Yet, above all, the revolutionary regime's identity is based on a conscious strategic and ideological opposition to the USA—Mark N. Katz (2010) rightly observes that the Soviet Union was regarded as a "lesser Satan" as compared to the "Great Satan" of the USA. With the proclamation of the Islamic Republic in 1980, anti-Americanism has become the fundamental bedrock of the revolutionary ideology and is regarded as an important strategic element of foreign policy—occasional convergence of interests and pragmatic collaboration with the West notwithstanding (Posch 2013: 5; Adebahr 2014: 3).[11]

The discourse of independence and the Shia-based sensitivity for injustice led Iran on an anti-imperialist path influenced by both Persian nationalism and Shiite Islam (Maloney 2002: 95–96). That Iran seeks regional and international status is best shown by Khomeini's own chosen title "Prince of the Believers" (Posch 2013: 13; transl. CW) and Iran's self-proclaimed role as an "Islamic vanguard state" (Senn 2009: 91). The country sees itself as *primus inter pares* in its region and claims leadership of the entire Muslim world (see also Art. 11 of the Constitution). Walter Posch (2013: 15) rightly emphasizes that the constitution calls for equal treatment for all underprivileged Third World countries. Iran's Third World orientation is also grounded in the Shiite conception of justice. As Moshirzadeh points out:

---

[10] Article 153 describes similar principles in the field of foreign policy: "The foreign policy of the Islamic Republic of Iran is based on the rejection of all forms of hegemony and self-submission, as well as on the preservation of all-round independence and territorial integrity, the defense of the rights of all Muslims, the non-alignment with hegemonic powers and on mutual, peaceful relations with all peace-loving nations."

[11] Despite the official cutting of diplomatic relations following the hostage-taking of American embassy employees by a group of Iranian students, there have been repeated economic contacts or secret diplomatic talks between Washington and Teheran.

> In the Iranian version of Third Worldism, one may see how a systematic appeal to the concept of equality is used to delegitimize the idea of hierarchy in the system – hence the emphasis on the universality of the rules and norms of international society and the unjust nature of double standards, whether applied to a category of states or to particular groups of them. (Moshirzadeh 2007: 533)

6.4 Iran's Vision of World Order

In order to answer the question guiding this study—whether Iran's behavior is a symbol for the rejection of the current normative order geared toward its overthrow, or whether Iran's activities show some elements of norm entrepreneurship—it is essential to reconstruct and map Iran's vision of how the global order should look like. The fact that this vision is essentially based on the three identity elements described above also came to the fore in the qualitative content analysis on which the investigation of Iran's world order vision was based.[12] In a nutshell, and as will be described in greater detail below, Iran propagates and cultivates a discourse of resistance that focuses on (verbal) criticism of the prevailing normative order (essentially grounded in and shaped by Western liberal ideas), which is perceived as unjust and discriminatory and thus illegitimate. Iran's identity and the antagonistic position toward a Western liberal world order can also be found in the country's self-appointed role as "guardian of justice and equity for humankind" and "avenger of the dispossessed" (Wunderlich et al. 2013: 265–6). Particularly in its early years, the regime's foreign policy strategy aimed to universally spread an Iranian world order vision under the banner of "export of the revolution."

6.4.1 The Prevailing World Order as the "Order of Domination"

Iran's relationship to the current world order is primarily determined by antagonism. Iran often takes a verbal stance against the status quo and exposes its contradiction both implicitly and explicitly. It is concerned with exposing abuses and questioning and criticizing current structures, as well as expressing alternative proposals and reform ideas. Figure 6.3 summarizes Iran's central criticisms of the existing normative order.

Above all, Iran criticizes the discriminatory structure of the international system, in Khamenei's words, "the unfair balance of power in the world—in which the world

[12]Note that the references are used for illustrative purposes. In order to demonstrate continuity, I sought to refer to more recent as well as historical quotes.

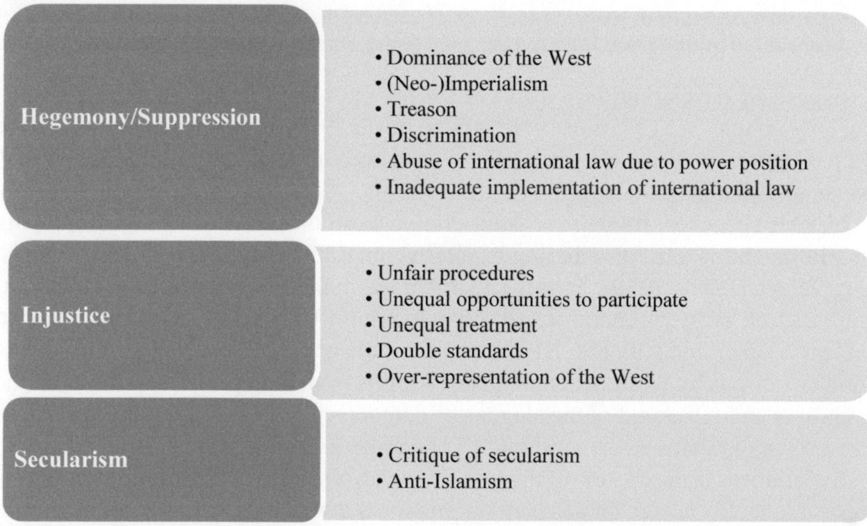

Fig. 6.3 Central features of Iran's criticism of the prevailing world order

is divided into the dominant and the dominated" (Khamenei 2009a, 1987b: 32).[13] The Manichaean division of the world into "good" and "evil", typical of the country's political culture, is a central element in the analyzed speeches, e.g., in the polar opposites of "oppressed" and "oppressors."

Time and again, Iranian leading figures draw attention to the omnipresent injustice, both globally as well as with reference to certain subfields of international relations, such as the world economic order that Iran has ever since sought to counter by establishing an "economy of resistance" (Khamenei 2010b: 4).

As early as 1987, Khomeini bemoaned a "defective geometry" (Khamenei 1987a: 43) of the international system caused by the overrepresentation of the West in many international bodies. He strongly urged that this structure of exploitation must not be tolerated and declared resistance to it to be a duty:

> We believe that the nations and Governments of the third world as well as the peoples of the dominator countries should not tolerate this evil order of things. The big Powers must be told to go back home and leave the affairs of the world to its peoples. We must tell them: you are not anybody's legal guardians! (Khamenei 1987a: 57)

In his view, the relationship of dominance had become even stronger after the end of the Cold War:

> [T]he political pyramid of the world has a vast base that leads to a tiny peak at an extremely sharp angle. And it is those who are at the peak who rule the world. This is the world of domination. After the collapse of the former Soviet Union, the world of domination became

[13]The data sample comprised a huge amount of statements uttered by revolutionary leaders and state representatives at various forums throughout the entire period of investigation. Reasons of space, however, allow for a selective reference to statements only.

> even more exclusive in scope. In one way or another, the peak of the pyramid has been monopolized by one government and one superpower, namely America. (Khamenei 2007a)

Instead of developing into a forum for the oppressed people (a hope that Iran had long upheld, see Entezam 1946: 908–9; Yazdi 1979: 444; Khamenei 1987a), the United Nations is seen as "a victim of the arrogance of the Imperial-minded Powers" (Velayati 1985: 300).

In their speeches, Iranian speakers often accuse the Western states of applying double standards and for adhering to international law only if it is in their interest (e.g. Velayati 1985, 1989). To this end, there are numerous references to collaboration between Western liberal states and autocratic (Arab-Sunni) dictatorships or to nuclear cooperation with non-NPT members India and Israel, as well as allusions to norm deviations by Western democracies. All this from their perspective reveals "the emptiness and falsehood of the slogans of democracy and equality in those systems [the existing systems in the world; CW]" (Khamenei 1987a: 26).

Experiences in the context of the Iran–Iraq war, when the international community seemed to tacitly accept breaches of international law, shattered Iran's confidence in the UN even further. The fact that the Security Council had condemned the attack by Iraq relatively late in the process left Iran with the feeling of having been deserted. It was for this reason that Khamenei 1987 described the Security Council in a speech to the United Nations as "a paper factory for issuing worthless and ineffective orders" (Khamenei 1987a: 57). He further concluded

> that the foundations of the security supported by such a [power-dominated; CW] Security Council is nothing but a nice-looking house of cards. The nations of the world, especially the peoples of the third world, who wish to remain independent of the super-Powers, may never have the security guaranteed by such a Security Council. (Khamenei 1987a: 48)

In their rhetoric, the supreme leaders often refer to conspiracy theoretical phrases (e.g., "agents and servants of imperialism"; Khomeini 1972, in Algar 1981: 211 or "imposing sanctions and hatching other plots"; Khamenei 2010b). In general, this has been geared to establishing and consolidating an enemy image as is the cultivation of the "U.S. Satan" (Velayati 1983: 26) ever since the founding of the Islamic Republic. Iranian delegates above all express continuous substantial criticism of the USA, repeatedly complaining about its military presence in the region, which is regarded as having created further tensions (Velayati 1990: 46). The term "Great Satan" is used synonymously with the USA and has mutated into an everyday phrase in the Iranian-American dialogue (accompanied with the label of "Mad Mullahs" in the USA). The USA is also described as "America, the global plunderer" (Khomeini 1980b, in Algar 1981: 286) and as the personification of evil and leader of the camp of "satanic powers" (Khamenei 1990), accused of "arrogance, interference, and transgression" (Khamenei 2006a). The global dissemination of American culture is perceived by Iranian politicians as "mental slavery" (Yazdi 1979: 448) and as an attack on both Islamic identity ("cultural invasion" (Khamenei 2006b) as well as on the entire world. As early as 1978, Khomeini stated: "America has created disasters for mankind" (Khomeini 1978a, in Algar 1981: 214). In 1990, his successor Khamenei lamented:

> [T]oday the satanic US government is interfering in the affairs of other nations more than ever before. They are interfering in all major affairs of other nations, and their interference is not limited to economic issues. They interfere in cultural and political affairs of other countries. They interfere in how other country should be run and in selecting the managers of other countries, (Khamenei 1990).

In Iran's eyes, Israel and allies of the USA also belong to the camp of "arrogant powers." The USA, its "agents", and "puppet governments" (Khomeini 1983) or "mercenaries" (Khamenei 1990) such as Israel or Sunni Arab governments cooperating with the USA are accused of working with unfair means ("treachery") and spreading negative propaganda against Iran. Moreover, they are accused of using psychological warfare in order to destroy Iran's spiritual "stronghold" (Khamenei 2009c). Like anti-Americanism, anti-Zionism is one of the cornerstones of Iran's revolutionary rhetoric. Shortly before Khomeini was sent into exile in 1964, he announced:

> All of our troubles today are caused by America and Israel. Israel itself derives from America; these deputies and ministers that have been imposed on us derive from America – they are all agents of America, for if they were not, they would rise up in protest. (Khomeini 1964b, in Algar 1981: 187)

In a letter to Iranian Prime Minister Amir Abbas Hoveyda in 1967, Khomeini, living in Iraqi exile at the time, described Israel as "pseudo-state" (Khomeini 1967, in Algar 1981: 191). Israel is seen as a product of the imperial powers: "Israel was born out of the collusion and agreement of the imperialist states of East and West. It was created in order to suppress and exploit the Muslim peoples, and it is being supported today by all the imperialists" (Khomeini 1971, in Algar 1981: 210). In 1971, he went further by describing the country as "stubborn enemy of Islam and the Qur'an" (Khomeini 1971, in Algar 1981: 201). In a speech to the UN General Assembly in 1983, then Foreign Minister of Iran Velayati noted: "[t]here is no cure for the cancerous growth of Zionism except surgery" (Velayati 1983: 187).[14] Under President Ahmadinejad, the aggressive anti-Israel rhetoric reached its peak. He called, for example, for the disappearance of the occupation regime during a conference called "The World without Zionism" in Tehran in 2005.[15] In his speech, he dismissed the Holocaust as a myth and organized a controversial Holocaust conference in December 2006 (Fathi 2006).

More moderate presidents such as Khatami or, more recently, Rouhani, distanced themselves from radical anti-Israeli rhetoric. But they left it up to the conserva-

---

[14] In the following sentence, however, peaceful means are mentioned first: "If the allies could have persuaded Hitler to withdraw and recognize the rights of other nations, then we could do the same with the Zionists today" (Velayati 1983: 187).

[15] The correct translation of the Farsi speech by Ahmadinejad was the subject of fierce controversy. The president's web page says: "O dear Imam (Khomeini)! You said the Zionist regime that is a usurper and illegitimate regime and a cancerous tumor should be wiped off the map" (quoted after IRNA 2008). However, this translation was criticized retrospectively as a misinterpretation and it was contended that Ahmadinejad had neither used the Persian words for "map" nor for "to wipe off", but that he had literally said that the occupation regime had to disappear from the pages of history (Amirpur 2010).

tive hardliners to use such slogans, since this clearly secured them some grains of sympathy in the Arab and Muslim world. Also, Khamenei adheres to the anti-Israeli rhetoric, speaking of "evil Zionists" (Khamenei 2009b) and referring to Israel in 2014 as "illegitimate", "fake regime", and "savage and wolfish regime" (Khamenei 2014). The current speeches of the revolutionary leader are also regularly accompanied by shouts of "Death to America, Death to Israel" from a heated crowd. On International Quds Day, which is celebrated annually, the state organizes rallies against Israel and for the liberation of Palestine. They are accompanied by more or less aggressive anti-Israeli rhetoric.[16]

In the literature on Iran, the opinion prevails that the Islamic Republic is on a collision course with the West and with the norms and rules of the international community.[17] Nevertheless, the content analysis revealed that Iran's criticism is not directed against the normative structure of the world order as such, even if individual bodies such as the UN Security Council are regarded as being in need of reform. In essence, Iranian speakers criticize the design and implementation of the hegemonic world order, above all the practices of the powerful countries, some of which, from Iran's point of view, run fundamentally counter to international law. This notwithstanding, this would ultimately have no consequences for the powers concerned. Similarly, Iran does not per se reject international law and the international organizations set up to implement it. Contrary to common wisdom, the Islamic Republic does not therefore stand in fundamental opposition to the system and its structures per se, but aims with its behavior to disclose their inadequate, i.e., unjust, implementation.

6.4.2 Iran's Self-stylization as the Anti-imperialist Spearhead of the Third World

As has been demonstrated, Iran sees itself primarily as a victim of oppression and exploitation by the West. Its socioeconomic, political, and scientific weaknesses

---

[16]When asked, Iranian officials often say directly that Iran does not want the extermination of the Israeli people. Rather, they claim the criticism to be directed against the unlawful regime and the occupation of Palestine (personal interview with Soltanieh, 25 April 2012). However, the following statement contradicts these claims. It shows that anti-Zionism, similar to anti-American rhetoric, serves primarily domestic purposes and that the regime does not speak with one voice on this issue: "The claim that there are friendly relations between our people and the Israeli people is false. This is a false and illogical remark. Who are the Israeli people? They are the ones who are being used as a tool by Israeli officials to encroach on the lands and properties of the Palestinian people. The Israeli people are a tool in the hands of the Israeli officials to achieve their goals. A Muslim nation—the Iranian nation—cannot adopt a passive stance towards these people who are acting as a tool in the hands of the enemies of the Muslim world" (Khamenei 2008c).

[17]To give but one example: "After thirty-four years of the Islamic Republic, Iran's position on the fundamental norms that make up today's international system is still unclear. Whether Tehran has accepted these norms and is trying to improve its position within this system or whether it still genuinely opposes the norms of contemporary international relations remains an open question" (Adebahr 2014: 12).

are perceived to be rooted in Western colonization and to be the results of political and military dependencies. The "world-killing superpowers", according to Khomeini (1989), had constantly tried to keep Iran—and basically all countries from the Global South—in a subordinate position.

This line of argumentation is also employed when the conflict over Iran's nuclear program is portrayed as a strategy of the West to prevent Iran from making technological progress and thus from catching up with modernization:

> Today they raise the issue of nuclear technology. Even if there was not such an issue, they would raise another issue: This is the enemy's tactic. Whatever helps a nation achieve progress is considered a threat for global powers. Nations should not make progress. If our nation had the capability to extract and refine its oil and if it had the capability to use its oil for different purposes, there would have been no need for the English to take over the responsibility for extracting and refining our oil. At that time, they took advantage of the incapability of our nation. Now our nation is capable and it wants to manage its own country. It wants to exploits [sic!] these resources on its own and it wants to use them for itself, but they are upset about this. The truth is that they are opposed to the progress of the Iranian nation, because this progress prevents them – forever – from pursuing their illegitimate interests in our country. That is why they are opposed to our progress. (Khamenei 2006a)

In Tehran's eyes, it is not only Iran that is being exploited and treated unfairly, but all so-called "third world countries" are affected. Describing relations between the USA and the Global South, Khamenei speaks of

> a master-subject relationship – the Americans being the master, and third world countries being their subjects. The Americans think they have the right to do whatever they want in third world countries. They think they can plunder third world countries' oil and gas resources, act against their interests, take away their wealth, promote American interests and humiliate their people. (Khamenei 2010d)

Khomeini's vision therefore does not stop at national borders. The "oppressed masses of the world" should see "the Islamic government in Iran and [...] Iran's struggling people" as examples (Khomeini 1983). Particularly in the first phase after the revolution, Iranian foreign policy was less geared toward pursuing *national* interests, but extended to representing the interests of all Muslim states. Support for the "deprived nations of the world" (Khomeini 1983) was already announced by the first delegate of the revolutionary Iranian regime in a speech to the UN General Assembly: "It is intrinsic to the Islamic Republic of Iran that our representative in the world Organization should always side with the victims of colonialism, imperialism, exploitation, racism, and Zionism" (Yazdi 1979: 443).

That Iran stylized itself as the spearhead of dissidence and propagated Islamic universalism as a counter-model to the Western liberal and communist path is also observed by other scholars (e.g. Fürtig 2003; Ramazani 2013 [1983]: 71–93). Iran presents itself above all as a protective power of the Shiites toward Muslim countries, as an anti-imperialist "avenger of the dispossessed" (Wunderlich et al. 2013: 266) and as "spearhead of the developing countries" (Posch 2013: 6). As leader of an anti-hegemonic coalition (Firooz-Abadi 2012: 48), Iran sees itself as responsible for actively spreading the contents of the Islamic Revolution (Khamenei 1987a). Henner Fürtig therefore speaks of "counter-globalization in the name of universal

Islam" in the course of which "all the questionable elements of Western globalization would be replaced by a genuine Islamic offer based on justice, contentedness, and egalitarianism" (Fürtig 2003: 48).

In this sense, and despite all political pragmatism that involves rapprochement with the West, the revolutionary regime sees itself as the leader of an "axis of resistance" (CNN 2012; Abdulrazaq 2015)[18] that also includes Hamas, Hezbollah, Islamic Jihad, and Syria—actors who are perceived to be aiming to undermine or even abolish international norms.

6.4.3 Elements of an Iranian World Order Vision

Unsurprisingly, the results of the content analysis reveal that Iran's world order vision is based on the three pillars of identity: Shia Islam, Persian nationalism and anti-Imperialism/Third Worldism. Since they have already been discussed in Sect. 6.3, I will only briefly elaborate which place they are assigned in Iran's world order vision and discuss in which forums Iran seeks to promote normative alternatives and how it would like to see them implemented.

Khomeini stipulated in his will that the aim of the Islamic revolution was "to rid the oppressed masses of contemporary history of the evil of oppressor" (Khomeini 1983). Revolutionary resistance was not only directed against the Pahlavi regime, but against all forms of dominance (Khamenei 2010a: 3–4). Even if Iran addresses the countries of the Global South in particular, it sees itself as the savior of all humanity, who has "come for the liberation of mankind both from the chains and cuffs of arrogant and oppressive systems pressure on different classes of people and thus establish a just government." (US Institute of Peace 2014). Iran's goal is thus to reform the international system and free it from all forms of rule and oppression, in accordance with the principles of independence, justice, and Islamic ideology that underlie Iran's identity.

The need for anti-imperialist and anti-Western opposition is justified religiously and thus legitimized transcendently. For Khomeini protest and opposition against all forms of tyranny were not only the religious duty of the clergy, but of the whole population. All Muslims in particular were urged "to awaken people, to expose sinister and destructive designs of imperialism" (Khomeini 1971, in Algar 1981: 204, 207).

From 1985 onwards, there are less religious references in the analyzed speeches, i.e., less recitations from the Quran or phrases such as "In the Name of God, the Compassionate, the Merciful". Nevertheless, someone who does not believe in the aims of the revolution is still considered "not morally healthy" (Khamenei 2007b). Often,

[18] As a reaction to Bush's "axis of evil", the term refers to an alliance between Iran, Syria, Hezbollah and Hamas, directed against American hegemony. IT has been used repeatedly by Iran's political elite in particular, but also by Syrian President Bashar al-Assad. It is said that Iran also counts North Korea as an "axis of resistance" (The Daily Beast 2014).

the recourse to religiously underpinned, justice-based and peace-orientated concepts of order seems to be mere labeling for they miss valid argumentations, e.g., why a secular foundation of values could not be equally effective. As already mentioned above, Iran criticizes the status quo as insufficient and links this untenable situation with the inadequacy of a purely secular value orientation. What exactly should make their religious foundation immune to double standards, however, remains unclear.

Iran regards justice as the central component of the new world order. In an interview in 1980, Khomeini described justice as "the very substance of Islam" (Khomeini 1980a, in Algar 1981: 338). Khamenei declared it the "pivot" of the revolution (Khamenei 2005). In 1989, Foreign Minister Velayati demanded: "[W]e must [...] alter unjust international relations and give them a basis of justice and respect for international law" (Velayati 1989: 91). Justice is regarded as the supreme principle on the basis of which all other values come to their full development:

> We shall rise to the challenge of distributing peace, security and development among all nations on the basis of justice and come to believe that in today's interconnected world, we cannot live in islands of prosperity and progress while the rest of the world are increasingly caught in poverty, illiteracy, disease and insecurity. The more we can distance our world's material progress from coercion, discrimination and inequality, and draw closer to equality, justice and fairness, the more likely it would be to prevent crisis, violence, and acts of terror. A stable and secure world is one based on spirituality, love and justice. (Khatami 2001)

The criticism of unipolar structures goes hand in hand with remarkably frequent pleas for willingness to compromise and for a fair coexistence of peoples based on a balance of interests. Iran not only claims these criteria for itself, but also wants them to be realized on a global level (Velayati 1996). An excerpt from Khamenei's speech to the UN General Assembly in 2006 indicates what "justice" means to Iran:

> What is justice? There might be differences of opinion regarding the meaning and interpretation of justice, but there are fixed and definite criteria: for example, reducing social distinctions, providing everybody with equal opportunities, encouraging honest and upright people and controlling those who try to steal from national sources of wealth, promoting justice in the structure of government. (Khamenei 2006b)

Iran's vision is based on a comprehensive concept of justice, including procedural justice (such as fair participation and equal rights), a fair distribution of rights and obligations as well as recognition in the form of respect and fair treatment. The international community should respect all countries regardless of their power and status and treat them equally in accordance with the principles of international law:

> Globalization will bear fruitful results when it is accompanied with a non-selective and non-discriminatory approach; when it provides equal opportunities for all within the framework of a global partnership. If the developed countries fail to fulfill their responsibilities, globalization can hardly be claimed as a success story. (Kharrazi 2002)

In a speech of 1987, Khamenei states that the value of justice is even more important than peace:

> Peace is without a doubt, a beautiful and attractive word. This is so true that even the biggest international warmongers and the producers of weapons for global destruction flirt with it and

> love it hypocritically. But, in our opinion, justice, a word that the powerful and the oppressors regard with fearful caution, is even more important and more beautiful. (Khamenei 1987a: 42)

In addition to a fundamental structure based on Islam and justice, the political leaders also mention the following principles that must be implemented: National sovereignty or non-interference in the internal affairs of states, independence and self-determination, and the unity of the *ummah*. Khomeini believed that the only means of overcoming hegemonic dependencies was the production of "Islamic independence" (Khomeini 1964a in International Affairs Department 1995: 163). However, this independence runs the risk of falling victim to a conspiracy against Islam—above all through Western support for the Zionist movement and the state of Israel. Khomeini considered the connection to one of the two superpowers to be doomed for the Muslim nations in 1972:

> If the Muslim states and peoples had relied on Islam instead of relying on the Eastern or Western bloc – had placed before their eyes the luminous and liberating teachings of the Nobel Qur'an, and then practiced those teachings – they would not be enslaved today by the Zionist aggressors, terrorized by American Phantoms, and at the mercy of the satanic cunning of the Soviet Union. (Khomeini 1971, in Algar 1981: 210)

Accordingly, Khomeini demanded: "Rid yourselves of the 'isms' of the East and the West; stand on your own feet and stop relying on foreigners" (Khomeini 1980b, in Algar 1981: 294). Even if antagonism to the East did not reach the identity-building function of anti-Americanism, Khomeini warned in principle that the countries of the South should no longer attempt to imitate the West or the Soviet Union: "We are at war with international communism no less than we are struggling against the global plunderers of the West, headed by America, Zionism, and Israel" (Khomeini 1980b, in Algar 1981: 288). This attitude is based on the assumption that the economic and technological dependence on the West, as pursued by the Shah regime, tended to slow progress and development in the long term.

In 1987, in a speech to the UN General Assembly, the former President of Iran Khamenei called on the countries of the Global South to unite to form a "Union" and to fight together against "the system of world domination" (Khamenei 1987a: 57, 56). In international forums, Iran is primarily seeking alliances with the Non-Aligned Movement (NAM),[19] with which it shares the historical experience of colonialism and the goal of establishing an alternative world order, based on the principles of anti-imperialism, national sovereignty, and non-interference in internal affairs (except for self-defense purposes) as well as multilateralism and equal decision-making structures (Wunderlich et al. 2013).

After the East-West conflict had ended, and thus after the dissolution of the bloc confrontation, then Foreign Minister Ali Akbar Velayati expressed Iran's hope that "a golden opportunity for a new world order" could result from the changed world political constellation, "a new order founded on the United Nations Charter and the principles of justice, peace, security, equality, and mutual respect for sovereignty and

---

[19]Iran officially joined the Non-Aligned Movement in 1979.

the territorial integrity of states, and for the cultural and moral values of all nations" (Velayati 1991: 48).

Iran perceived the UN General Assembly to be a suitable place for discussing the design and function of such an order, since only there would developing countries whose participation was regarded as essential for a just new world order, be sufficiently represented (Velayati 1995). As a corollary, proposals to reform the UN take up a great proportion in the analyzed statements. In Iran's view, the realization of a just international order requires independent, legitimate, fair, and "democratic" institutions that are beyond the control of the powerful states. To compensate for the unequal representation of the world population in the world organization, Iran therefore demanded a permanent seat on the Security Council for Islamic countries, including the right of veto (Ahmadinejad 2007: 7).

President Khatami's efforts to establish a "dialogue of cultures" at the end of the 1990s can also be seen as an attempt to promote Iran's ideas of world order at the international level. With the declared aim "[to] found a participatory global order based on dialogue, tolerance and synergy" (Khatami 2000: 8), the concept was meant to initiate a paradigm shift. It was based on the equal participation of peoples with the involvement of civil society, on the "democratization" of international structures, on pluralism, diversity, and cultural diversity, and on "inclusive justice" (Khatami 2000: 8). Interestingly, the share of blaming and shaming in the speeches decreases with Khatami's inauguration in 1997. Instead, the idea of joint conflict management under the auspices of the UN dominates. A phrase that is often used is, for example, that solving global problems requires joint efforts, whether in the fight against drugs or against terrorism (Kharrazi 1999: 12).

6.4.4 Means to an End: Export of the Revolution in Words and Deeds

That Iran's opposition to the prevailing world order goes beyond mere resistance is demonstrated by the fact that verbal criticism and the outlining of an alternative structure of order became essential elements guiding the policy of the country particularly in the early years of the Islamic Republic. The regime claimed universal validity for its own revolutionary ideology. Khomeini therefore framed the export of the revolution as intentional foreign policy strategy, a "sacred duty" (Mir-Khalili 2008), which found broad support domestically, notwithstanding some minor differences regarding the methods and means by which revolutionary export was to take place (Monshipouri 2013: 67).

Yet revolutionary export must not be seen solely as an expression of the spread of Islamic ideology. It also provided Iran an opportunity to consolidate the young regime and protect it against internal and external enemies. What Iran framed as constituting a means of advocating Islam, however, was in stark contradiction to the principle of non-interference in internal affairs, which also occupied a central position in the Iranian constitution. Especially in the 1980s, which are considered the heyday of revolutionary activism, the export of revolution was not limited to Islamic propaganda, but also included practical support for liberation movements. Thus, the (early) policy of revolutionary export can actually be seen as a practice of challenging the current world order and its normative underpinnings. This concerned above all the norm of national sovereignty and territorial integrity and the principle of non-interference.

With its revisionist "parallel foreign policy" (Posch 2013: 12, transl. CW), Iran initially aimed to secure influence in the region and to attract followers. These were found in other Islamic states such as Sudan, but above all in the various "liberation movements", whose religious or ideological objectives coincided with those of the Iranian revolution and which were therefore supported in word and deed, e.g., through financial aid, arms supplies and logistical support culminating in establishing a Revolutionary Liberation Movement Bureau in the Foreign Ministry (Fürtig 2003: 38). With the help of the Ministry of Intelligence and the Revolutionary Guards, political bodies were established in neighboring countries to support the liberation movements, for example, by organizing demonstrations or coups, to expose the injustices of the current order and to spread Islamic propaganda (Maloney 2008: 25–82). Moreover, religious, semigovernmental charities, and foundations were founded, e.g., the Imam Khomeini Relief Committee, which has also been active in neighboring countries; or the Foundation of the Martyrs supporting families of martyrs of the revolution and the Iran–Iraq war even outside Iran. Groups such as Hezbollah in Lebanon or the Palestinian Hamas were regarded as "vanguard of the Islamic Ummah against the Zionist aggressors" (Khamenei 2006c), in whose open support the revolutionary regime saw nothing reprehensible. As Shahram Chubin notes, "[t]errorism was easily accepted and even congenial to revolutionaries; at a time when the regime was still not consolidated, terrorism was an extension of revolutionary politics: clandestine, coercive, and nonattributable" (Chubin 2002: 89).[20]

This leads us to the question of non-violence, which is also a rhetorically propagated, central element of an Iranian world order. Article 152 of the Iranian constitution obliges the country to coexist peacefully with other states except in cases of self-defense.[21] Indeed, despite the omnipresent aggressive saber rattling, Iran has so far not been involved in any acts of war except for defensive purposes (Gohari

[20]Many of the Arab and Sunni Gulf states saw the export of the revolution as a threat to their national security and a threat to the regional balance. Saddam Hussein in particular feared that Iran could try to radically expand its influence, a reason that has been put forward as a motive for initiating the war against Iran (Akbari 2004: 20).

[21]Ramazani (2013 [1990]: 137–139) notes that Khomeini's view of the use of military force follows the Shia interpretation of law according to which the use of the holy war (jihad) for purely defensive purposes is the prerogative of the imam (and in his absence the revolutionary leader). The precise definition of self-defense is relatively complex in that Khomeini's vision of world order goes beyond the borders of the nation-state and aims at the unity of the *ummah*. The extension of the Iran–Iraq war to Iraqi territory was justified, for example, by the fact that supports of the Islamic revolution would extend far beyond Iran's territorial borders. Ramazani also points out that it is even more difficult to decide about the legitimacy to use force below the threshold of war, e.g., in connection with subversion or terrorism.

2012: 208). That the question of Iran's relation to violence is not easy to answer is demonstrated by the country's support for violent rebellion (Hamas, Hezbollah), but also by quotations such as the one from Khamenei in 2009:

> [T]he only way to achieve final victory is to keep treading the straight path of faith in God, in your capabilities, in national power, in national self-confidence, in all types of sincere efforts – such as scientific and practical efforts and military action whenever necessary – and in jihad. (Khamenei 2009a)

Despite the massive (material) support for liberation movements, Khomeini stressed from the very beginning that the export of the revolution must rely on peaceful means. Instead of openly admitting Iran's military support for liberation movements, the religious leaders cultivated a rhetorical narrative to the outside world according to which Iran rejected military intervention in other states and instead relied on cultural influence:[22] "It was the people who established the order of an Islamic Republic, and their weapons were their faith, their determination and their blood—and blood overcame the sword" (Khamenei 1987a: 29–30). In 1990, Khamenei explained exactly what Khomeini understood by revolutionary export:

> He did not mean that we will wage wars in different parts of the world and encourage the people to rise up against their governments. This was not what the Imam (r.a.), meant. Such a thing is not among our policies and principles. On the contrary, it is unacceptable. (Khamenei 1990)

This ambivalence comes also to the fore in speeches given before the United Nations: "Our position in international relations is clear. We do not interfere in the internal affairs of other countries. But morally and spiritually we are with the oppressed people everywhere for ideas and beliefs transcend national boundaries" (Ardakani 1980: 671). In 2008, Khamenei asserted that "the thought of invasion and occupation of other countries never crossed the minds of the Iranian people and their officials" (Khamenei 2008b)—a claim that stands in stark contrast to Khamenei's demand that the West Bank should arm itself in order to take action against the unlawful Israeli occupation (Khamenei 2014). The Quds Force, an elite unit of the Revolutionary Guards, was entrusted with the task of supporting forces close to Iran, among others through financial aid, training of fighters or the provision of arms, equipment, and operations on the ground. In addition to Palestinian liberation movements such as Hamas, the Islamic Jihad Movement in Palestine and the al-Aqsa group, the Quds Force support Hezbollah, Kurdish insurgents in Iraq, the Houthi rebels in Yemen, and the Syrian army. They are also said to have helped Islamic forces in Bosnia and the Afghan Northern Alliance in the fight against the Taliban. Purportedly, in 2005, Iran also founded a garrison named "Lovers of Martyrdom" to carry out systematic suicide attacks if necessary (Frick 2011: 6).

In addition to "hard" resources, Tehran also used "soft" resources to export the revolution. Thus, Shia minorities and opposition groups abroad could also count on

---

[22] However, some authors stress that the commitment to non-violence and the rejection of military aggression and subversion is merely theoretical. In practice, Iran has continuously been accused of supporting terrorist groups and has been found guilty of being involved in various terror attacks (Senn 2009: 91; Ramazani 2013 [1983]: 81).

Iranian support, for example, through infrastructure measures (through the construction of schools, hospitals, and streets) and through rhetorical support.

According to official rhetoric, despite this ambivalence, the current strategy of the Islamic Republic is above all to exercise leadership by example. Khomeini and his successor wanted to present Iran's path as a political alternative to the Arab governments in the region allied with the USA (Khamenei 1990). In 1979, Khomeini described the Iranian population as "exemplars for all the world's oppressed" (Khomeini 1979, in Algar 1981: 267) and—later—"pioneers" (Khamenei 2000). This view was still valid 28 years later, when in 2007 Khamenei praised the Islamic revolution as an "inspirational movement, it will stir the world of Islam and it will make nations think" (Khamenei 2007c). Similarly, in 2010 he explained:

> Fortunately our dear nation is a role model in this regard – it is an example. Our people are vigilant. Our people are united. Our nation is pursuing global issues in a caring and enthusiastic manner. Our nation is actively involved in the issues of the world of Islam and adopts clear positions on these issues. (Khamenei 2010c)

Khomeini installed a massive propaganda machine with the help of which he sent the populace, government officials, and a network of clergymen to advocate in the name of Islam (Maloney 2008: 68). He had already demonstrated his knowledge of public relations work in pre-revolutionary times, when from exile he skillfully disseminated his political views, e.g., via tape-recording. In addition, his revolutionary repertoire included regular public appearances and visits to Muslim pilgrimage sites as well as the distribution of information material, the sending of letters or of "spiritual commissioners" to the cultural departments of Iranian embassies (Buchta 2000: 48–51). Frequently, the revolutionary leaders address the people of Iran, e.g., through Friday prayers, instructions for the armed forces or diplomatic personnel, speeches to the "martyrs" of the revolution, and to the country's youth. In a speech to Iranian embassy personnel, Khomeini called on the "apostle of the revolution" as he used to call them (Ramazani 2013 [1983]: 81):

> It does not take swords to export this ideology. The export of ideas by force is not export. We shall have exported Islam only when we have helped Islam and Islamic ethics grow in those countries. This is your responsibility and it is a task which you must fulfill. You should promote this idea by adopting conduct conducive to the propagation of Islam and publishing the necessary publications in your countries of assignment. This is a must. (Khomeini 1981, in Ramazani 2013 [1983]: 81)

With the death of Khomeini and the following shift to a more pragmatist foreign policy course, the export of the revolution also changed from being an active strategy to secret support. As one of the most prominent Iranian foreign policy experts, Rouhollah K. Ramazani noted back then,

> [t]he notion of an Islamic world order began to wane. The idea of Islam in one country began to gain momentum. Iran was still viewed as the 'Islamic citadel' (umm-al qora), but it was viewed so as a model to emulate, not as one to export through incitement of political opposition in other Muslim states. (Ramazani 2013 [2001]: 165).

Rather than establishing a fully universal Islamic republic spanning all Muslim nations, the focus was henceforth put on securing a leading role and promoting

Muslim solidarity (Fürtig 2003: 46; Senn 2008: 48). The export of the revolution made room for a more diplomatic policy geared toward spreading Islamic values within the immediate vicinity. In this regard, observers often point to the fatwa that the Iranian clergy had uttered against British writer Salman Rushdie. It became a symbol of the Muslim fight against inequality and unfair treatment and provided Iran with an opportunity to stylize itself (once again) as the leader of a global Muslim movement (Fürtig 2003: 40; Ansari 2006: 127; Maloney 2008: 69). To this end, Iranian leaders addressed meetings of the leaders of Muslim states (e.g., within the framework of the Organization of Islamic Countries, OIC) or the Non-Aligned Movement as well as Muslim civil society. For example, in 2007, Khamenei explained to the Basij militia student organization that "[e]stablishing centers for thinking and theorizing is among the things you need" (Khamenei 2007a). Spreading the Islamic revolution necessitated a "scientific jihad", "a movement for production of knowledge in the country" (Khamenei 2006b).

Iran's efforts to spread its world order visions increased with the pace of technological development. "Export of the revolution 2.0" is increasingly taking place in social networks in the form of "Twitter diplomacy"—despite the fact that the majority of Iranians are still forbidden access to these media channels by means of strict Internet censorship. Some observers even speak of "propaganda war" (Adebahr 2014: 7) which the political leaders would use mainly for the strategic dissemination of those elements of order which are supposed to attract high global fit (i.e., justice and equality).

6.5 The "Rogue State" in the Dock

Together with North Korea, Iran can be counted among the most renowned members of the league of "rogue states" designated by the USA. Iran's "rogue career" was heralded with the Islamic Revolution, in the early phase of which Iran attracted particular attention through active and sometimes aggressive export of the revolution and attempts to destabilize the region (Senn 2008: 47). Indeed, Iran is to be found in every single paper dealing with alleged "rogue states." Observers of Iranian foreign policy usually claim that the country displays an oppositional stance to or at least a certain "unease" toward international norms (e.g. Adebahr 2014: 22). Ali M. Ansari aptly summarizes:

> Iran is not simply a problem, it's the problem. It's not just a member of the Axis of Evil, but the founding member, the chief sponsor of terrorism, or to use a more recent characterization, the central banker for terrorism. No rhetorical flourish, no level of hyperbole seems excessive in the ritual condemnation of Iran. (Ansari 2006: 3–4)

Because of its perceived confrontational behavior toward its neighboring states, the missionary enthusiasm of the early revolutionary phase, and identity-based anti-Americanism and anti-Zionism, Iran evolved from being a regional ally during the reign of the Shah to an arch enemy of the USA. With regard to the criteria listed in

Chap. 3, Iran was particularly accused of supporting international terrorism as well as striving for weapons of mass destruction and ballistic means of delivery (Nincic 2005: 64). Especially in the early phase of the revolution, the regime was perceived to be irrational and its actions were deemed unpredictable for Western countries. The view that Iran posed a massive threat to world peace and international security thus consolidated. The perception of Iran as a "destabilizing force" (Takeyh 2007: 19) persisted even when in the late 1990s the regime chose a more pragmatist foreign policy course (Senn 2008: 48).

In the following, I will briefly discuss each of the norm deviations that Iran was or is accused of in detail. The section is structured along the core norm deviations of "rogue states" as discussed by Nincic (2005: 48–53): support for international terrorism, striving for weapons of mass destruction and for ballistic means of delivery, territorial aggression and human rights violations within the country as a result of a repressive, autocratic system of government (see also Lake 1994: 45–46; Ansari 2006: 36).

6.5.1 Support for International Terrorism

The US State Department first added Iran to its list of state sponsors of terrorism in 1984 (US Department of State 1985). Iran remains there until today—the latest (2016) version states that "Iran's state sponsorship of terrorism worldwide remained undiminished" (US Department of States Publication 2016: 166).

In addition to direct support for terrorist groups, Iran has repeatedly been accused of wanting to undermine regional stability in the Middle East, for example, through directed appeals to Arab countries (e.g., Saudi Arabia or Iraq) to rebel against the ruling regimes (allied with the West) (Byman 2008: 170–172). In the 1980s and 1990s, Iran made headlines through the murder of Iranian dissidents abroad (e.g., the so-called Mykonos assassination in Berlin in 1992), through bomb attacks on US embassies (e.g., Beirut in 1983 and Kuwait in 1983) or through its involvement in the kidnapping of Westerners in Lebanon.

Even though Iran's revolutionary eagerness has diminished over the years and the policy of export of the revolution has declined, Nincic concludes that "few regimes have been as guilty as Iran" (Nincic 2005: 53). It might thus come as a surprise that Iran did support the "fight against terrorism" after the attacks of September 11. The Islamic Republic took an active role in the fight against the Taliban in Afghanistan and vehemently opposed (Sunni) terrorism.

Nevertheless, in the 2016 Country Report on Terrorism, the USA in particular accused Iran of supporting Palestinian groups and the Lebanese Hezbollah (US State Department 2016: 300). As has already been explained in Sect. 6.4.4, this assistance should be seen in the context of the export of the revolution. Moreover, Iran is accused of supporting Syria's Assad regime, the Houthi rebels in Yemen and Shiite opposition groups in Bahrain and Iraq—practices that also bear witness to aggressive external behavior. The Revolutionary Guards, in particular the Quds Force, are considered

Iran’s central organization for providing technical, logistical, financial, and personnel support to terrorist groups abroad.

6.5.2 *Iran’s Quest for Weapons of Mass Destruction*

As described in Sect. 7.4, Iran’s nuclear ambitions can be traced back to the times of the Shah, who sought control over the full fuel cycle. Shortly after the revolution, the Iranian nuclear program was abandoned and was only resumed after the Iran–Iraq war. In 2002, an Iranian opposition group revealed that Iran had been secretly working for decades on a uranium enrichment program under the guise of a peaceful nuclear energy program without informing the IAEA. This was the beginning of a decade of political conflict in the course of which Iran further developed its capabilities in enrichment and reprocessing technology.

Even though the IAEA and Western intelligence services concluded that actual weapons research was more or less halted by 2003 (Davenport 2019), some authors repeatedly express (ed) doubts about the peaceful intentions of Iran’s nuclear program. Indeed, for a long time, Iran failed to comply with IAEA and UN Security Council resolutions to cease its fuel cycle activities; it complicated cooperation with the IAEA by using diplomatic stalling tactics and intentionally lied about past activities; all of which further nourished the suspicion that Iran at least wanted to keep the option of nuclear armament open. This was also supported by the oversized scale of the civilian nuclear infrastructure, to which observers could only give meaning if military intentions were taken as a basis (e.g., Singh 2014). Also, the missile program that Iran had built up with increasing range and precision since the war against Iraq, and which could be equipped with both conventional and non-conventional ammunition, was seen as an indication that Iran might strive to obtain a nuclear deterrent capability.

In July 2015, after more than 12 years of negotiations, the West and Iran finally succeeded in reaching a comprehensive nuclear agreement. The agreement imposed clear restrictions on Iran’s nuclear capabilities. Moreover, it also obliged the country to take far-reaching transparency measures and to clarify past military activities for a period of up to 25 years (Müller 2015). While Israeli and US politicians described the agreement as a mistake, the overwhelming majority of arms control experts saw the deal as an opportunity to dispel any doubts about Iran’s peaceful intentions and to permanently block Tehran’s path to the bomb. While this calculation seems to have worked and the IAEA repeatedly confirmed that Iran had been abiding by the nuclear deal, the Trump administration unilaterally withdrew from the accord in May 2018. In response, Iran suspended parts of its commitments under the nuclear accord.

What is Iran’s record on biological and chemical weapons? At first, the revolutionary regime vehemently rejected all weapons of mass destruction. Due to the experiences during the Iran–Iraq war, when Iran repeatedly fell victim to Iraqi chemical weapons attacks and the international community remained inactive for quite some time, the country began to develop its own chemical weapons program. In ratifying the Chemical Weapons Convention, Iran admitted that it had produced (but not used) chemical warfare agents. Tehran declared that it had phased out the program in 1988 after the signing of the ceasefire agreement and destroyed existing stocks (Alborzi 1998; Cordesman and Kleiber 2007: 158). The USA, however, accused Iran of having used chemical warfare agents against Iraq (in violation of the Geneva Protocol) in 1988 and of having retained chemical warfare agents (Rice 2005).

The USA also showed a considerable degree of skepticism toward Iran's declared policy on biological weapons control: Iran's signature of the BWC in 1973 notwithstanding, the USA suspects that the country has worked on a biological weapons program against the background of the Iran–Iraq war and has retained the corresponding warfare agents (Rice 2005; Eisenstadt 1998; Cordesman and Seitz 2009: 2–3). However, experts doubt these allegations (Ali 2001: 51; Sands and Johnson 2001: 19).

6.5.3 Territorial Aggression

Iran, unlike Iraq, is not actually guilty of territorial aggression (Nincic 2005: 60). Rather, the perception of Iran as a threat stems from its aggressive anti-American and anti-Zionist rhetoric. Iran also vehemently opposed the Arab-Israeli peace process in the 1990s and froze all relations with Arab states that recognized Israel's right to exist (e.g., Egypt, Jordan, Morocco, and Tunisia). Even more than the aggressive rhetoric, the strategy of revolutionary export pursued in the 1980s and the support of violent (terrorist) rebel groups reinforced the fear felt by Iran's Arab neighbors. In addition, the status quest inherent in Persian culture and Iran's perceived ambition for power (among other things through conventional armament and repeated missile tests; Senn 2009: 92) contributed to the threat perception.

6.5.4 Autocratic Character/Human Rights Violations

Even though Iran's political system has democratic elements, its democratic character is doubtful. While boasting with a multiparty system, and the institution of free elections, the system shows clearly undemocratic elements: Unelected, informal political institutions exist; the most power remains in the hands of the Supreme Leader; there are repeated reports of censorship, repression of free press and freedom of assembly, as well as freedom of expression. Moreover, human rights violations are continuously being reported. Political repression was already common during the Shah's time—when Iran was not considered a "villain" but a gendarme of the West (Geldenhuys 2004: 125–126). Reports from UN human rights forums and international human rights organizations show that little has changed to date. These institutions repeatedly denounce Iran for harsh attacks by Iranian security forces, torture and other abuses, criminal arbitrariness, detention without trial, unfair trials, disappearances, or extrajudicial executions (Amnesty International 2015).

6.6 Preliminary Conclusion: Stay or Go? Iran's Position Within the Current World Order

The reconstruction of Iran's world order vision shows that the country's foreign policy is geared toward changing existing power structures. This finding is also confirmed by the secondary literature where authors have labeled Iran repeatedly a "revisionist state" (Alikhani 2012: 7; Firooz-Abadi 2012: 43).

Proponents of power transition theory see dissatisfaction with the respective status quo as the essence of revisionist foreign policy. Dissatisfaction would lead the revisionist states to try to weaken or change the current order in order to upgrade their own status (e.g. Schweller 1994; Claes 2012). According to the alternative hypothesis, AE 1 formulated in the theoretical part of this study (see Sect. 4.2), Iran would thus be understood as a mere norm breaker whose objective is to undermine and destroy the current normative order. Is this hypothesis accurate?

The question of whether Iran is trying to realize its world order vision within the given structures (reform) or is working toward overthrowing the existing order (revision or revolution) is however not as easy to answer as Iran's narrative of resistance suggests. There is no doubt that Iran's call for an alternative world order poses a challenge to the current system. Iran vehemently criticizes and delegitimizes current normative structures and their proponents. Sometimes, Iran's behavior is geared toward blocking norm diffusion processes or openly violates established norms. However, a policy aimed exclusively at destroying the prevailing normative order could not be observed.

Moreover, the line of argument shown by Iran is not free from contradictions. In the early years of the revolution, Iran's policy was focused on extreme resistance to the norms and rules of the international system (e.g., by taking hostages or by instigating upheavals in neighboring countries). Since the early 1990s however, Iran rather stuck to verbally opposing the system and pursued an increasingly pragmatic policy course. Nevertheless, Tehran continues to support terrorist organizations such as Hamas or Hezbollah. The imperative of the export of the revolution is still anchored in the constitution and stands in stark contrast to established global norms (e.g., the norms of national sovereignty and the principle of non-interference in foreign affairs). Iran itself, however, repeatedly refers to these established norms and claims that these be observed.

Despite all revolutionary rhetoric and repeated violations of international norms, Iran has remained within the order which it has rhetorically rejected and questioned since the proclamation of the Islamic Revolution. Some authors argue that Iran has not (yet) taken the last, consistent step of turning away from the current order, because Iran is ultimately dependent on supporters. In this vein, Cornelius

Adebahr writes: "Among audiences critical of American leadership, Tehran benefits from being regarded as an underdog rather than an outlaw" (Adebahr 2014: 16). Sadeghi (2008: 17) refers to Iran's imperative of expediency—and thus cites pragmatic reasons—to explain why Iran tolerates the existing Westphalian state system as a modus vivendi, although it would actually seek to destroy it. Farhang Rajaee describes Iranian foreign policy primarily as reactive and concludes that Tehran is ultimately reluctant to take ownership and act as an active agent of change (Rajaee 2013: 212).

However, this perspective implies a purely strategic maneuvering and ignores the fact that Iran's world order vision is based on the desire to be recognized as an equal member of the international community. Not only did the Islamic Republic defend the raison d'être of various international norms and institutions, whose unjust and discriminatory design by the major powers it criticized (e.g., the UN or multilateral arms control regimes). Iran also demands equal participation and membership in established organizations (e.g., the World Trade Organization, WTO), which the international community of states (led by the Western states) has denied so far. Moreover, a large part of the norms propagated by Iran or its interpretations of norms is perfectly compatible with the prevailing normative landscape. Often Iran merely puts forward merely alternative readings. It criticizes a misinterpretation or insufficient or false implementation of norms that the country approves of in substance. This also leads to the paradoxical situation that Iranian delegates criticize UN conventions that their country has signed.

Ultimately, Iran has chosen to remain within the existing normative order despite all criticism and rhetoric of resistance. The assumption that Iran is merely acting as a norm destroyer, as AE1 suggests, therefore proves to be untenable. Teheran is attempting to break the isolation associated with stigmatization as a "rogue state" by moving closer to the West (excluding Israel and the USA). Apparently, Iran sees itself as part of the international order, which it doesn't reject in its basic structure. Its criticism is directed at the interpretation and implementation of global norms which it considers to be in need of reform. In Iran's eyes, the international order which is in itself reasonably designed turns to an "order of domination" because of misinterpretation and misimplementation (Khamenei 1987a).

Does Iran's behavior thus validate AE2? Is it Tehran's aim to counter Western liberal norms with the provision of alternative norms? Indeed, Iran framed its alternative world order vision as a counter-project to the prevailing "unjust normative order", which according to Tehran is dysfunctional and illegitimate. The propagation of a "counter-hegemonic order of values" also points to an absolute claim to superiority and comes along with the strategies set out in Sect. 5.2.1: In the analyzed speeches, Iranian dignitaries and high-ranking politicians criticized the Western liberal order and its bearers (naming, shaming, and blaming) and framed the perceived grievances as unjust, hegemonic, and discriminatory. The alternative world order vision propagated by Iran is aimed at overcoming all these shortcomings, as illustrated in Fig. 6.4. However, Tehran wanted more than to merely show its resistance. The activities geared toward advocating the alternative world order vision exceed

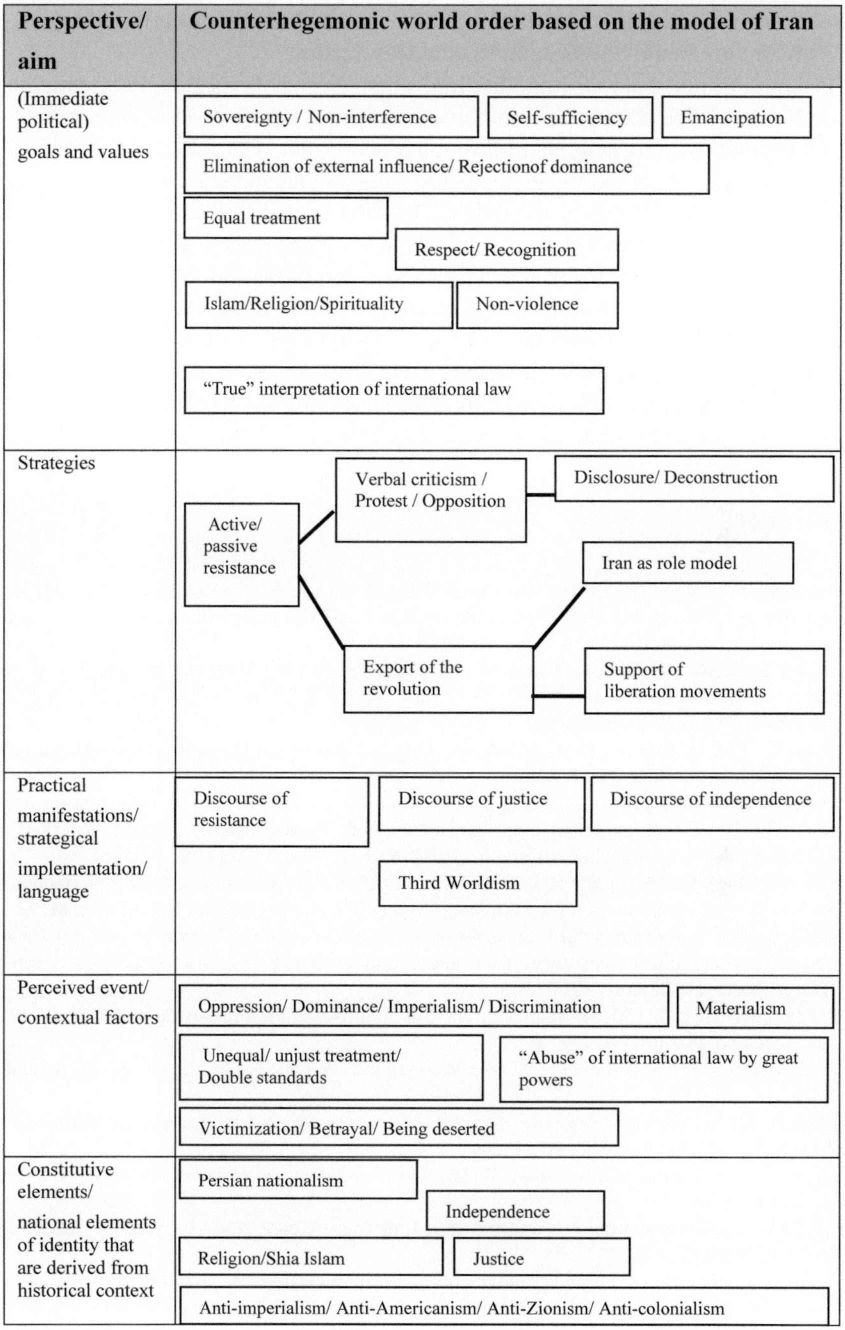

Fig. 6.4 Profile of Iran's normative world order vision and foreign policy identity

purely reactive measures that an actor, who sees his/her freedom of action endangered by international norms, uses to counteract them.

It should be noted at this point that Iran's behavior vis-à-vis global norms seem to be ambivalent: The country is torn between wishing to reform the given normative structures and overthrowing them through a revolution. The following chapter will shed more light on this ambivalent relationship in one specific subarea of international politics: Multilateral arms control. Does the country follow the argumentation suggested by AE2? Does it try to counter Western liberal norms, which are perceived as hegemonic interventions in the right of self-determination, by formulating subsidiary counter-norms? Does it act as a mere norm destroyer, as the "rogue" label and AE1 suggest? Or—as formulated in the thesis guiding this study—does Iran act as a norm entrepreneur who tries to constructively participate in the reform of current structures and to implement its visions of order within this framework?

References

Abdulrazaq, T. (2015). The axis of resistance. Time to put up, or shut up. *Middle East Monitor*. https://www.middleeastmonitor.com/articles/middle-east/16611-the-axis-of-resistance-time-to-put-up-or-shut-up. Accessed 28 April 2017.

Adabi-Moghaddam, A. (2012). Discourse and violence: The friend-enemy conjunction in contemporary Iranian-American relations. In A. Ehteshami (Ed.), *Iran and the international system* (pp. 150–167). London: Routledge.

Adebahr, C. (2014). *Tehran calling: Understanding a new Iranian leadership*. Brüssel: Carnegie Endowment for International Peace.

Ahmadinejad, M. (2007, September 25). Statement to the 62nd Session of the UNGA, New York.

Akbari, S. (2004). Iran zwischen amerikanischem und innenpolitischem Druck. Rückfall ins Mittelalter oder pragmatischer Aufbruch. *HSFK-Report*, 1/2004. Frankfurt a. M.

Akbari, S. (2006). Grenzen politischer Reform- und Handlungsspielräume in Iran. Die Bedeutung innenpolitischer Dynamiken für die Außenpolitik. *HSFK-Report* 9/2006. Frankfurt a. M.

Amirpur, K. (2010). Der iranische Schlüsselsatz. Süddeutsche Zeitung, 11 May 2010. https://www.sueddeutsche.de/kultur/umstrittenes-zitat-von-ahmadinedschad-der-iranische-schluesselsatz-1.287333. Accessed 28 April 2017.

Amnesty International. (2015). Jahresbericht 2015. https://www.amnesty.de/jahresbericht2015/iran. Accessed 28 April 2017.

Alborzi, M. R. (1998). Statement to the 3rd Session of the CWC CSP, The Hague, 16–20 November 1998.

Alfoneh, A. (2013). *Iran unveiled: How the revolutionary guards is turning theocracy into military dictatorship*. Washington, DC: AEI Press.

Algar, H. (1981). *Islam and revolution. Writings and declarations of Imam Khomeini*. Berkeley, CA: Mizan Press.

Ali, J. (2001). Chemical weapons and the Iran-Iraq war: A case study in noncompliance. *The Nonproliferation Review, 8*(1), 43–58.

Alikhani, A. (2012). Iran's religious fundaments and principles in interaction with the international system. In: A. Ehteshami & R. Molavi (Eds.) *Iran and the International System* (pp. 3–32). London: Routledge.

Ansari, A. (2006). *Confronting Iran: The failure of American foreign policy and the roots of mistrust*. London: C. Hurst & Co.

Ansari, A. (2007). *Iran under Ahmadinejad: The politics of confrontation*. Abingdon: Routledge.

Ardakani, A. S. (1980, October 10). Statement to the 35th Session of the UNGA, New York.
Axworthy, M. (2008). *A history of Iran: Empire of the mind*. New York, NY: Basic Books.
Begley. (2016). Read Donald Trump's Full Speech to AIPAC. Time. http://time.com/4267058/donald-trump-aipac-speech-transcript/. Accessed 26 October 2018.
Buchta, W. (2000). *Who rules Iran? The structure of power in the Islamic Republic*. Washington, DC: The Washington Institute for Near East Policy.
Byman, D. (2001). *Iran's security policy in the post-revolutionary era*. Santa Monica, CA: Rand.
Byman, D. (2008). Iran, terrorism, and weapons of mass destruction. *Studies in Conflict & Terrorism, 31*(3), 169–181.
Carter, J. (1977, December 31). Iran toasts of the president and the Shah at a state dinner, Tehran. http://www.presidency.ucsb.edu/ws/?pid=7080. 28 August 2015.
Chubin, S. (2002). *Whither Iran? Reform, domestic politics and national security*. London: IISS.
Claes, J. (2012). Protecting civilians from mass atrocities: Meeting the challenge of R2P rejectionism. *Global Responsibility to Protect, 4*(1), 67–97.
Cordesman, A., & Kleiber, M. (2007). *Iran's military Forces and warfighting capabilities: The threat in the Northern Gulf*. Washington, DC: Centre for Strategic and International Studies.
Cordesman, A., & Seitz, A. (2009). *Iranian weapons of mass destruction: Doctrine, policy and command* (Working Draft). Resource Document. http://csis.org/files/media/csis/pubs/090112_iran_wmd_policy.pdf. Accessed 28 April 2017.
Davenport, K. (2019, July). Timeline of Nuclear Diplomacy with Iran. Facht Sheets & Briefs. *Arms Control Association*. https://www.armscontrol.org/factsheet/Timeline-of-Nuclear-Diplomacy-With-Iran. Accessed August 30, 2019.
Ehteshami, A. (2009). *Machtstrukturen in Iran*. Bundeszentrale für politische Bildung. http://www.bpb.de/apuz/31564/machtstrukturen-in-iran?p=all. Accessed 28. April 2017.
Eisenstadt, M. (1998). *Chemical and biological weapons and deterrence. Case study 4 Iran*. Alexandria: Chemical and Biological Arms Control Institute.
Entezam, N. (1946, October 30). Statement to the 1st session of the UNGA, New York.
Fathi, N. (2006). Holocaust Deniers and Skeptics Gather in Iran. http://www.nytimes.com/2006/12/11/world/middleeast/11cnd-iran.html. Accessed April 28, 2017.
Firooz-Abadi, D. (2012). The Islamic Republic of Iran and the ideal international system. In A. Ehteshami & R. Molavi (Eds.), *Iran and the international system* (pp. 43–58). London: Routledge.
Frick, M. (2011). *Iran's Islamic revolutionary guards corps: An open source analysis*. National Defense University. http://www.dtic.mil/dtic/tr/fulltext/u2/a516529.pdf. Accessed 28 April 2017.
Fürtig, H. (2003). Globalization as a one-way-street? The case of the Islamic Republic of Iran. In H. Barrios, M. Beck, A. Boeckh, & K. Segbers (Eds.), *Resistance to globalization: Political struggle and cultural resilience in the Middle East, Russia, and Latin America* (pp. 34–51). Münster: LIT Verlag.
Geldenhuys, D. (2004). *Deviant conduct in world politics*. Houndmills: Palgrave Macmillan.
Gohari, N. (2012). Concluding thoughts. In A. Ehteshami (Ed.), *Iran and the international system* (pp. 207–211). London: Routledge.
Holliday, S. (2011). *Defining Iran: Politics of resistance*. Farnham: Ashgate Publishing.
International Affairs Department. (1995). An anthology of the speeches of Imam Khomeini (r) including an account of the events of the revolution. 1962–1978. Kawthar. Volume One. Tehran.
IRNA. (2008). President says Zionist regime of Israel faces dead end. Presidency of the Islamic Republic of Iran. Press Release. http://web.archive.org/web/20110716100837/http://www.president.ir/en/?ArtID=10114. Accessed 28 April 2017.
Juneau, T., & Razavi, S. (2013). Introduction: Alone in the world. In R. Juneau & S. Razavi (Eds.), *Iranian foreign policy since 2001: Alone in the world* (pp. 1–17). New York, NY: Routledge.
Katz, M. N. (2010). Iran and Russia. In R. Wright (Ed.), *The Iran Primer: Power, Politics and U.S. Policy*. Washington, DC: United States Institute of Peace.
Katzman, K. (1993). *The warriors of Islam: Iran's revolutionary guard*. Boulder, CO: Westview Press.
Khamenei, S. A. (1987a, September 22). Statement to the 42nd Session of the UNGA, New York.

Khamenei, S. A. (1990, March 30). *Supreme leader's address to government officials.*

Khamenei, S. A. (2000, October 25). *Supreme leader's speech in a meeting with officials and ambassadors of Islamic countries.*

Khamenei, S. A. (2005, August 20). *Supreme leader's speech to President and Cabinet members.*

Khamenei, S. A. (2006a, March 26). *Supreme leader's speech in meeting with students.*

Khamenei, S. A. (2006b, June 19). *Supreme leader's speech to government officials.*

Khamenei, S. A. (2006c, August 21). *Supreme Leader's speech to participants of 19th international conference on Islamic unit.*

Khamenei, S. A. (2007a, May 21). *Supreme leader's speech to Basiji members.*

Khamenei, S. A. (2007b, July 11). *Supreme leader's speech to members of Guardian Council.*

Khamenei, S. A. (2007c, September 14). *Supreme leader's friday prayer address.*

Khamenei, S. A. (2008a, May 3). *Supreme leader's speech to Basiji members.*

Khamenei, S. A. (2008b, May 22). *Supreme leader's speech to Armed Units in Shiraz.*

Khamenei, S. A. (2008c, September 19). *Supreme leader's friday prayer address.*

Khamenei, S. A. (2009a, February, 7). *Supreme leader's speech to airforce personnel.*

Khamenei, S. A. (2009b, September 11). *Supreme leader's friday prayer address Ramadhan 1388.*

Khamenei, S. A. (2009c, September 24). *Supreme leader's speech to members of the assembly of experts.*

Khamenei, S. A. (2010a, June 4). *Supreme leader's address to government officials and scientific and political figures.*

Khamenei, S. A. (2010b, September 7). *Supreme leader's speech meeting with entrepreneurs.*

Khamenei, S. A. (2010c, September 10). *Supreme leader's address to government officials and ambassadors of Islamic countries.*

Khamenei, S. A. (2010d, November 3). *Supreme leader's speech to students.*

Khamenei, S. A. (2014, July 23). *Supreme leader's speech in meeting with student.*

Kharrazi, K. (1999, September 24). Statement to the 54th Session of the UNGA, A/54/PV.12, New York.

Kharrazi, K. (2002, September 14). Statement to the 57th Session of the UNGA, New York.

Khatami, M. (2000, September 6). Statement to the 55th Session of the UNGA, A/55/PV.3, New York.

Khatami, M. (2001, September 10). Statement to the 56th Session of the UNGA, New York.

Khomeini, R. (1963, June 3). *The Afternoon of Ashur*a. In Algar 1981 (pp. 177–181).

Khomeini, R. (1964a, April 10). Speech Number Thirteen in International Affairs Department 1996, pp. 159–167.

Khomeini, R. (1964b, October 27*). The granting of capitulatory rights to the U.S.* In Algar 1981 (pp. 182–189).

Khomeini, R. (1967, April 16). *Open letter to Prime Minister Hoveyda.* In Algar 1981 (pp. 189–195).

Khomeini, R. (1971, October 31*). The incompatibility of monarchy with Islam.* In Algar 1981 (pp. 200–209).

Khomeini, R. (1972, July 10). *Message to the muslim students in North America.* In Algar 1981 (pp. 211–213).

Khomeini, R. (1978a, February 19). *In commemoration of the first Martyrs of the revolution.* In Algar *1981* (pp. 212–228).

Khomeini, R. (1978b, October 11). *In commemoration of the Martyrs of Tehran.* In Algar 1981 (pp. 239–242).

Khomeini, R. (1979, April 1). *The first day of God's government.* In Algar 1981 (pp. 267–269).

Khomeini, R. (1980a, January 2). *The religious scholars led the revolt. Interview with Khomeini.* In Algar 1981 (pp. 329–345).

Khomeini, R. (1980b, March 21). *New year's message.* In Algar 1981 (pp. 286–295).

Khomeini, R. (1981, March 21). *New year's message.* In Ramazani 2013 [1983].

Khomeini, R. (1983, February 15). *Imam Khomeini's last will and testament.* https://www.al-islam.org/imam-khomeini-s-last-will-and-testament/testament. Accessed 28 April 2017.

Lake, A. (1994). Confronting backlash states. *Foreign Affairs, 73*(2), 45–55.

Leverett, F., & Leverett, H. (2013). *Going to Tehran: Why the United States must come to terms with the Islamic Republic of Iran*. New York, NY: Metropolitan Books.

Litwak, R. (2007). *Regime change: U.S. strategy through the prism of 9/11*. Washington, DC: Woodrow Wilson Center Press with Johns Hopkins University Press.

Maloney, S. (2002). Identity and change in Iran's foreign policy. In S. Telhami & M. Barnett (Eds.), *Identity and foreign policy in the Middle East* (pp. 88116). Ithaca, NY: Cornell University Press.

Maloney, S. (2008). *Iran's long reach: Iran as a Pivotal State in the muslim world*. Washington, DC: United States Institute of Peace Press.

Mir-Khalili, M., (2008). Imam Khomeini's viewpoints on Iranian foreign policy. In *Iran review*, 26 May 2008. http://www.iranreview.org/content/Documents/Imam_Khomeini%E2%80%99s_Viewpoints_on_Iranian_Foreign_Policy.htm. Accessed April 28, 2017.

Monshipouri, M. (2013). Iran's foreign policy and Islamic ideology. In T. Juneau & S. Razavi (Eds.), *Iranian foreign policy since 2001: Alone in the world* (pp. 56–69). New York, NY: Routledge.

Moshirzadeh, H. (2007). Discursive foundations of Iran's nuclear policy. *Security Dialogue, 38*(4), 521–543.

Müller, H. (2015). Khameineis rote Linien. Eine Bewertung des Iran-Abkommens. HSFK-Report 2/2015. Frankfurt am Main.

Nincic, M. (2005). *Renegade regimes: Confronting deviant behavior in world politics*. New York, NY: Columbia University Press.

Pirseyedi, B. (2013). *Arms control and Iranian foreign policy: Diplomacy of discontent*. New York, NY: Routledge.

Polk, W. (2011). *Understanding Iran: Everything you need to know, from Persia to the Islamic republic, from Cyrus to Ahmadinejad*. New York, NY: Palgrave Macmillan.

Posch, W. (2008). *E pluribus unum: Decision-makers and decision-making in Iran*, EU Institute for Security Studies. ISS Policy Brief 02/2008. http://www.iss.europa.eu/uploads/media/PB_2-E_pluribus_unum.pdf. Accessed 28 April 2017.

Posch, W. (2010). Zwischen Ideologie und Pragmatismus. Grundlinien der iranischen Außenpolitik. ÖMZ 6/2010.

Posch, W. (2013). *The third world, global Islam and Pragmatism. The making of Iranian foreign policy*. SWP Research Paper 3/2013. Berlin.

Rajaee, F. (2013). Conclusion: Why "alone"? In T. Juneau & S. Razavi (Eds.), *Iranian foreign policy since 2001: Alone in the world* (pp. 208–222). New York, NY: Routledge.

Ramazani, S. (2013 [1983]). Khomeini's Islam in Iran's foreign policy. In A. Dawisha (Ed.), *Islam in foreign policy* (pp. 9–32). Cambridge: Cambridge University Press.

Ramazani, S. (2013 [1990]). Iran's export of the revolution. In J. Esposito (Ed.), *The Iranian revolution: Its global impact* (pp. 40–92). Miami: Florida International University Press.

Ramazani, S. (2013 [2001]). Reflection on Iran's foreign policy. In J. Esposito & R. K. Ramazani (Eds.), *Iran at the crossroads* (pp. 211–237). New York: Palgrave Macmillan.

Ramazani, R. K. (2005). Iran's hostage crisis: International legitimacy matters. *Comparative Studies of South Asia, Africa and the Middle East, 25*(2), 273–278.

Ramazani, R. K. (2013). *Independence without freedom: Iran's foreign policy*. Charlottesville: University of Virginia Press.

Rice, C. (2005). Opening Remarks by Secretary of State-Designate Dr. Condoleezza Rice, Senate Foreign Relations Committee, Washington, DC, 18 January 2005. http://2001-2009.state.gov/secretary/rm/2005/40991.htm. Accessed 28 August 2015.

Sachedina, A. (1981). *Islamic Messianism: The idea of Mahdīin Twelve Shī'ism*. Albany, NY: State University of New York Press.

Sadeghi, A. (2008). Genealogy of iranian foreign policy: Identity, culture and history. *The iranian journal of international affairs, 20*(4): 1–40.

Safiarian, S. (2011). *Pulverfass Iran: Wohin treibt der gottesstaat?* Freiburg: Herder.

Sands, A., & Johnson, P. (2001). CWC compliance issues. In J. B. Tucker (Ed.), *The chemical weapons convention: Implementation challenges and solutions* (pp. 17–22). Monterey: CNS.

Schweller, R. (1994). Bandwagoning for profit: Bringing the revisionist state back in. *International Security, 19*(1), 72–107.

Senn, M. (2008). *Rogue no more!? Die iranische Bedrohung in der Wahrnehmung der USA*. Resource document. IPG 3/2008. http://library.fes.de/pdf-files/ipg/ipg-2008-3/05_a_senn_d.pdf. Accessed 28 April 2017.

Senn, M. (2009). *Wolves in the woods: The rogue state concept from a constructivist perspective*. Baden-Baden: Nomos.

Singh, M. (2014). The case for zero enrichment in Iran. Arms Contrl Today, 4 March 2014. https://www.armscontrol.org/act/2014-03/case-zero-enrichment-iran. Accessed 28 April 2017.

Takeyh, R. (2007). Time for Détente with Iran. *Foreign Affairs, 86*(2), 17–32.

Takeyh, R. (2009). *Guardians of the revolution: Iran and the world in the age of the Ayatollahs*. New York, NY: Oxford University Press.

Thaler, D., Nader, A., Chubin, S., Green, J. D., Lynch, C., Wehrey, F., et al. (2010). *Mullahs, guards, and bonyads: An exploration of Iranian leadership dynamics*. Santa Monica, CA: Rand.

The Daily Beast. (2014). Iran and North Korea: The nuclear 'Axis of Resistance'. https://www.thedailybeast.com/iran-and-north-korea-the-nuclear-axis-of-resistance. Accessed 28 April 2017.

US Department of State. (1985). Patterns of Global Terrorism: 1984, November 1985. http://www.higginsctc.org/patternsofglobalterrorism/1984PoGt.pdf. Accessed 28 April 2017.

US Department of State Publication. (2016). Country Report on Terrorism 2015, June 2016, Washington, DC. https://www.state.gov/documents/organization/258249.pdf. Accessed 28 April 2017.

US Institute of Peace. (2014). *Khamenei at 25 years—Thoughts and edicts*. US Institute of Peace: The Iran Primer, 19.01.2014. https://iranprimer.usip.org/blog/2014/jun/03/khamenei-25-years-thoughts-and-edicts. Accessed 28 April 2017.

Velayati, A. A. (1983, September 30). Statement to the 38th Session of the UNGA, A/38/PV.13, New York.

Velayati, A. A. (1985, October 3). Statement to the 40th Session of the UNGA, A/40/PV.20, New York.

Velayati, A. A. (1989, October 5). Statement to the 44th Session of the UNGA, A/44/PV.13, New York.

Velayati, A. A. (1990, September 28). Statement to the 45th Session of the UNGA, A/45/PV.5, New York.

Velayati, A. A. (1991, September 23). Statement to the 46th Session of the UNGA, A/46/PV.5, New York.

Velayati, A. A. (1996, September 23). Statement to the 51st Session of the UNGA, A/51/PV.5, New York.

Ward, S. (2009). *Immortal. A military history of Iran and its armed forces*. Washington, DC: Georgetown University Press.

Wunderlich, C., Hellmann, A., Müller, D., Reuter, J., Schmidt, H.-J. (2013). Non-aligned reformers and revolutionaries. Egypt, South Africa, Iran, and North Korea. In H. Müller & C. Wunderlich (Ed.), *Norm dynamics in multilateral arms control, interests, conflicts, and justice* (pp. 246–295). Athens, GA: University of Georgia Press.

Yazdi (1979, October 4). Statement to the 34th session of the UNGA, A/34/PV.21, New York.

Chapter 7
Iran as a Norm Entrepreneur

While there are numerous accounts of the conflict surrounding Iran's nuclear program, scientific analyses of Iranian arms control policy are scarce and either tackle single weapon categories (e.g., Ali 1996) or remain superficial (e.g., Jones 1998, 2012). Bobi Pirseyedi was the first to provide a comprehensive account of Iran's arms control diplomacy, covering both conventional and weapons of mass destruction in the period from 1979 to 2003. The following sections as well as the analysis of instances of Iranian norm entrepreneurship build on and expand Pirseyedi's study through their own empirical data (partly published in Wunderlich et al. 2013; Wunderlich 2014, 2017). I share Pirseyedi's assessment that the lack of attention paid to Iranian arms control policy encourages factual misjudgments, simplifies Iran's policies, and therefore weakens the West's negotiation strategy in the long term. I also share his assumption that the main driver for Iranian policies is dissatisfaction with current structures. Yet, while Pirseyedi dismisses Iranian arms control policy first and foremost as political maneuvering and a propaganda instrument (Pirseyedi 2013: 1), I argue that it is also norm-driven and that an understanding of how Iran interprets key norms of multilateral arms control policy and how it seeks to propagate these norm interpretations is key to effective and fruitful diplomatic negotiations.

7.1 Basic Principles of Iranian Arms Control Policy

Before discussing three instances of Iranian norm entrepreneurship in the field of WMD arms control, I will briefly delineate the framework within which Iranian arms control policy unfolds.[1] Arms control policy is predominantly a matter of the political

[1] Information on decision-making and implementation procedures is scarce (Pirseyedi 2013: 4). The Iranian Foreign Ministry maintains a number of political research institutes which, inter alia, discuss arms control policy issues (Posch 2013: 9–11) and prepare information for an English-speaking audience. Yet, most arms control guidelines or position papers exist in Farsi only (but see Shababi 1994).

C. Wunderlich, *Rogue States as Norm Entrepreneurs*,
Norm Research in International Relations,
https://doi.org/10.1007/978-3-030-27990-5_7

elite (Pirseyedi 2013: 182, fn. 56). The decision-making authority rests with the Supreme Leader, while opinion-forming and deliberation processes are more inclusive. The Ministry of Foreign Affairs (particularly the Department for Disarmament and International Security), the Ministry of Defense, and affiliated institutions are responsible for diplomatic negotiations, technical issues, and the implementation of arms control policies. Moreover, various government agencies are responsible for implementation, such as the Atomic Energy Organization of Iran (AEOI), whose technical and scientific expertise finds its way into the Supreme National Security Council, the central body of political decision-making. These agencies are also involved in international negotiations, e.g., within the International Atomic Energy Agency (IAEA) (Pirseyedi 2013: 22). The Revolutionary Guards are responsible for the supervision and operational control of Iran's missile program, the nuclear program, and dual-use technologies (Cordesman and Seitz 2009: 18). Especially in connection with the controversial nuclear program, authors such as Ali Alfoneh have repeatedly pointed to the self-interest of the participating institutions, namely the AEOI and the Revolutionary Guards, describing the latter as "the engine of the Islamic Republic's nuclear program" (Alfoneh 2013: 248). Purportedly, many nuclear scientists have close relations to the Revolutionary Guards, which are even said to have their own laboratories and facilities (Tabatabai 2015)—a fact that has led some to question to whether the political leadership is informed about the exact dimensions of Iran's nuclear program at all (Chubin 2013: 24).

Arms control policy became a topic of public interest with the beginning of Khatami's term of office, when the political elite put particular emphasis in advocating the narrative of a right to peaceful use of nuclear energy (see Sect. 7.4). As a result, there is a regular public debate on matters of arms control. The use of chemical weapons against the Iranian population during the Iran–Iraq war has also triggered public interest in matters of WMD control; there is a vivid Iranian civil society actively working for the support of victims of chemical weapons attacks (see Sect. 7.2).

While the level of activism with regard to Iranian arms control depends on the political preferences of the respective president or foreign minister, the "red lines" of politics continue to be determined by a narrow circle surrounding the Supreme Leader—also with regard to how the nuclear program is depicted in the press (Thaler et al. 2010: 32; Nirumand 2015: 7). However, observers attest to a high level of continuity in Iranian arms control policy, independent of the respective political elite and even dating back to pre-revolutionary times. According to Pirseyedi, "the differences of view in the IRI about arms control policy have dealt more with the means of Iran's diplomatic operations than with their content or overall direction" (Pirseyedi 2013: 186, fn. 104).

Iran is part of all three regimes on the control of weapons of mass destruction: The Biological and Toxin Weapons Convention (BWC), the Chemical Weapons Convention (CWC), and the Nuclear Non-proliferation Treaty (NPT).

The Shah regime regarded the NPT as a promising instrument to limit the proliferation of nuclear weapons, to soften tensions between the major powers, and to initiate a global (nuclear) disarmament process (the following builds on Etemad

1987: 203). Back then, the political elite was not aware of the incisions on national sovereignty that the treaty would bring about; furthermore, the inequality enshrined into the treaty's structures, meaning that the nuclear weapon states (NWS) and non-nuclear weapon states (NNWS) had different rights and obligations, did not trigger meaningful domestic debates. Iran signed the NPT in July 1968 on the day of its submission. With the Parliament's ratification in February 1970, the country reaffirmed its categorical rejection of nuclear weapons or—broader: weapons of mass destruction in general—as un-Islamic and inhuman (e.g., Khalatbari 1978; Mousavi 1981: 551; Velayati 1994a; Kharrazi 1997: 25; Ahmadinejad 2005; Rouhani 2013a).[2] Iranian politicians often refer to an Islamic legal pronouncement—a fatwa—purportedly issued by Khamenei in October 2003, banning the production, storage, and use of WMD.[3]

In line with its categorical rejection of WMD as un-Islamic, Iran actively supported the efforts to outlaw biological and chemical weapons that had begun in the late 1960s (Pirseyedi 2013: 96). The BWC was signed in April 1972 and ratified by the Iranian Parliament in August 1973, long before the Convention officially entered into force (March 1975). After the removal of the Shah, the revolutionary regime maintained its positions: The use of WMD was considered "a great and unforgivable sin" (Khamenei, cited in European Dialogue 2012). The categorical rejection of WMD seemed as much a religious and humanitarian duty, as it was in the security interest of the country (Velayati 1983; Kazemi Kamyab 1984b).[4]

Even after the Islamic Revolution, Iran continued to advocate a chemical weapons ban within the Geneva Conference on Disarmament. After it had become victim of massive chemical weapons attacks by Iraq in the wake of the first Gulf War, this commitment intensified (e.g., Fartash 1979; Dabiri 1981; Sheikholeslam 1984; Nasseri 1990b). This experience, and the hesitant reaction of the international community, had a lasting impact on Iran's arms control policy, which lasts until today (see Sect. 7.1). Tehran signed the CWC shortly after the conclusion of negotiations and its adoption by the UN General Assembly in January 1993. However, it was not ratified until July

[2]As provided for in the NPT, Iran concluded a "Safeguards Agreement" with the IAEA in 1973 to ensure that the declared nuclear activities served peaceful purposes. There is a controversy as to whether the Shah, despite his willingness to cooperate, nevertheless wanted to keep the option of a military nuclear program open (see Patrikarakos 2012: 96–103).

[3]Then Supreme Leader Khomeini is said to have issued a fatwa outlawing the production and use of chemical weapons already during the war with Iraq. While the fatwa has been repeatedly referred to by religious and political leaders and even put into writing (Iran 2005e; Salehi 2012), skepticism remains regarding the prohibition's scope and legal status (Eisenstadt 2011; Tabatabai 2014).

[4]The data sample comprised a huge amount of statements uttered by revolutionary leaders and state representatives at various forums throughout the entire period of investigation. Reasons of space, however, allow for a selective reference to statements only.

1997 due to domestic political hurdles.[5] Since then, Iran has been an active member of the Organisation for the Prohibition of Chemical Weapons (OPCW).

While Iran stresses the equality of obligations emanating from the three WMD regimes, the country seems to put a stronger emphasis on measures aimed at eliminating WMD and fostering the peaceful use of technology in contrast to measures aimed at restricting the proliferation of such technologies, which are regarded rather as a means to the end of disarmament (e.g., Gharib Abadi 2011b: 3). Not unsurprisingly given the importance of justice in Iran's political culture and its historical experiences, Iran places particular emphasis on the "promotional dimension" (Iran 2009c) in all three WMD regimes and especially stresses the strengthening of what it perceives as "inalienable rights" to the peaceful use of dual-use technologies (e.g., for CW Iran 1997; for BW Soltanieh 2001; for NW see Sect. 7.4). Correspondingly, Iran holds that the treaty regimes oblige all State Parties to cooperate for these purposes, and complains about the inadequate implementation of this perceived stipulation accordingly (e.g., Nasseri 1994b; Mottaki 2006).

An analysis of Iran's policies in the respective treaty regimes as well as its position toward core regime norms reveals three thematic priorities of Iranian arms control policy with regard to which Iran showed extraordinary engagement across the individual regimes (for a more detailed description see Wunderlich et al. 2013: 263–272; Wunderlich 2014): (1) the goal of a world free of weapons of mass destruction, (2) equal access to dual-use goods/technology exchange for all contracting parties, and (3) security guarantees and protective measures in the event of a threat or attack with WMD.

Sections 7.2–7.4 will focus on these key points of Iranian engagement and assess whether the advocacy shown by Iran meets the criteria of norm entrepreneurship.

7.2 Iran's Support for Victims of Chemical Weapons

Iran was one of the first states to call for effective protection and assistance measures during the final negotiations of the CWC. Given that Tehran itself had repeatedly been victim of gas attacks by Iraq, this is not surprising. Indeed, Iran played a leading role in shaping the resulting Article X on measures to support and provide assistance in the event of a chemical weapons attack and has been working to strengthen it

[5] Representatives of the Iranian armed forces, the Revolutionary Guards, and conservative politicians feared that the CWC could restrict the country's military freedom of action. In view of neighboring countries striving for WMD, such as Israel, India, or Pakistan, and due to dissatisfaction with the design and implementation of the CWC, they demanded that Iran should maintain a chemical weapons option. In addition, Iran demanded that the USA and Russia ratified the treaty first (Pirseyedi 2013: 87–91). Ultimately, the Parliament reserved the right to withdraw from the CWC under certain circumstances, i.e., if contractual obligations were implemented incompletely or discriminatively or if peaceful uses of technology was disproportionately hindered. The declaration of reservation is available at http://www.geneva-academy.ch/RULAC/international_treaties.php?id_state=109. Accessed 28 August 2015.

ever since. Iran's commitment to the rights of victims of chemical weapons even exceeds the measures laid down in the treaty: On an Iranian initiative in 2006, the International Support Network for Victims of Chemical Weapons was established in 2011, underlining the humanitarian mission of the OPCW and drawing attention to the long-term (medical) needs of CW victims.

7.2.1 Background: Article X of the Chemical Weapons Convention

Even though the Geneva Protocol of 1925 had outlawed biological and chemical weapons as means of warfare, Iraq repeatedly used poison gas against Iranian military positions, but also against the Kurdish and Iranian civilian populations (Tucker 2007: 249–260; 279–286). Even though the international community reacted rather hesitantly at first, this incident was one of the triggers for negotiations on a comprehensive ban on chemical weapons in 1984, leading to the 1993 Chemical Weapons Convention, which entered into force in 1997 (see Robinson 1998 on the history of negotiations).

The CWC prohibits the development, production, storage, transfer, possession, and use of chemical weapons. It also requires member states to destroy existing stocks, regulates the peaceful trade in chemicals, and contains provisions for mutual assistance when a member is threatened or attacked with chemical weapons. The Organisation for the Prohibition of Chemical Weapons (OPCW), based in The Hague, has been entrusted with the verification of the treaty provisions and the coordination of cooperation and aid measures (Kenyon and Feakes 2007).

Like other provisions, Article X found its way into the treaty because the developing countries regarded it as a necessary concession and made their acceptance conditional upon its inclusion (Kenyon and Mashadi 2007: 240). But since Article X was introduced into the negotiations relatively late in the early 1990s—and because of the "politicization" (Kenyon and Mashadi 2007: 243) of the debate during the Iran–Iraq war, the provisions contained therein remain relatively vague, particularly with regard to the operationalization and implementation of assistance and protection measures (see Trapp 2014 for a legal interpretation).[6]

Article X of the CWC grants State Parties the right to receive assistance and protection in the event of an attack or threat with chemical weapons. It also commits them to exchange information on research for protection against chemical weapons. Each Party to the treaty is requested to provide the OPCW Technical Secretariat annually with information on national protection programs. Furthermore, in an emergency, members are requested to provide at short notice one or more protective measures (financial, technical, material, and personnel resources), which are registered by the OPCW. The Technical Secretariat is called upon to assist the states in developing

[6]http://www.opcw.org/protection/protection-against-chemical-weapons/. Accessed 28 August 2015.

national protection measures, inter alia through courses for medical experts or practical trainings. Each State Party is entitled to request assistance and protection from the OPCW should it have been threatened or attacked with chemical weapons. "Assistance" is defined as

> the coordination and delivery to States Parties of protection against chemical weapons, including, inter alia, the following: detection equipment and alarm systems; protective equipment; decontamination equipment and decontaminants; medical antidotes and treatments; and advice on any of these protective measures. (Article X.1)[7]

It is important to note that the measures provided for in Article X relate to future situations in the event of a chemical weapons attack and are primarily intended to provide short-term assistance in acute emergency situations. The provisions only came into force with the entry into force of the CWC 1997 and were therefore not applicable to victims of previous chemical weapons attacks.[8]

While State Parties agreed in principle on the need for such protective measures, the industrialized countries were careful not to enter into concrete legally binding measures, as they would have had to bear the main burden of the support to be made available. The final text of the treaty (Article X, paragraph 7a–c) therefore lists various options from which State Parties can choose (Kenyon 2000: 9): They can either pay into an assistance fund; conclude a bilateral agreement with the OPCW specifying possible assistance, or inform the OPCW of what measures they will make available unilaterally in the event of a request. Overall, implementation of these obligations was slow (Höhl and Kelle 2003: 18): At the time of writing, 47 out of 190 State Parties have made financial contributions; only 80 have so far implemented one of the three options (OPCW 2016: 18). Only Iran and Peru have concluded bilateral agreements with the OPCW.

7.2.2 *Raising Public Awareness Through Normative Framing and Practical Activities*

As already mentioned, Iran's engagement for the rights of chemical weapons victims is partly grounded in itself having experienced massive gas attacks without being equipped with adequate protection measures.[9] The Iraqi attacks on its own Kurdish population in Halabja in 1988 left a particularly deep imprint to the world. The global public has taken far less notice of the victims among the Iranian civilian population. According to Iranian sources, during the eight-year war, Iraq conducted a total of 600 poison gas attacks (30 of them on inhabited areas in Iran) using various chemical

[7]The text of the treaty is available at https://www.opcw.org/chemical-weapons-convention/download-convention. Accessed 28 August 2015.

[8]This was explained to me by former and current employees of the OPCW during the background conversations conducted in May and June 2015; see Interview Khateri 12 May 2015, The Hague; Mashhadi, 9 June 2015; Trapp 31 May 2015.

[9]Interview with Hassan Mashhadi, 9 June 2015.

warfare agents (sarin, tabun, VX, and mustard gas). Iran claimed over 100,000 dead and injured (including more than 7000 civilians; Mehmanparast 2012). According to the Iranian Veterans Foundation Janbazan, approximately 34,000 Iranians are still suffering from chronic health consequences (OPCW 2008).

While Iran already demanded a ban on chemical weapons during the rule of the Shah, the experiences during the war with Iraq fundamentally shaped Iran's policy priorities, in terms of both the vehemence with which the country has been committed to the complete destruction of chemical weapons ever since and the focus on effective assistance and protection mechanisms.

Accordingly, the advocacy for appropriate protection measures figured high for Iran during the CWC negotiations. Iranian delegates called for legally binding protection and assistance measures to be provided by the State Parties in case of an emergency (Kenyon 2000: 9). Tehran considered Article X to be one of the main pillars of the CWC (along with the disarmament norm, the verification norm, and the requirement for cooperation, e.g., Deghani 2009b), even though in its view, the provisions contained therein remained too vague and did not take sufficient account of the rights of the victims of chemical weapons (e.g., Iran 2003; Mottaki 2006; Gharib Abadi 2013). On closer examination, Iran's engagement in that regard covered two dimensions: Firstly, it was geared toward sensitizing the global public as to the extent of CW attacks, and to assert recognition of Iran's victimhood. Second, and relatedly, Iran sought to anchor victims' rights more firmly in the CWC or OPCW through an effective mechanism for providing assistance.

With regard to the creation of public awareness, Iranian delegates sought to put Iraq's norm violations on the agenda of the existing diplomatic forums by reporting on the extent of Iraqi attacks throughout the whole period as well as by calling for diplomatic condemnation of Iraq and firms that had supplied chemical precursors for Iraq's CW program. For these purposes, Iran launched a massive awareness campaign and also lobbied various international organizations involved in health issues, such as the World Health Organization, and organized bilateral meetings with like-minded countries.[10]

Iran first reported that Iraq had been carrying out CW attacks from the beginning of the war in June 1981 (Jalali 1981a: 31).[11] As the fighting intensified and the Iraqi CW program became more adept from 1984 onwards,[12] such references increased. Iranian delegates meticulously listed the number, date, and location of the attacks

[10]Telephone interview with Hassan Mashhadi, 9 June 2015.

[11]Tehran Radio reported the dropping of chemical bombs over the city of Susangerd already in November 1980 (Robinson and Goldblat 1984). According to official sources, Iraq began building a large-scale CW program in 1982 in order to counter Iran's conventional superiority (UN 2006). The first use of mustard gas is dated back to the summer of 1983. Beginning in 1984, Iraq carried out large-scale attacks with the nerve agent Tabun and mustard gas against Iranian positions (Karsh 1993: 37; Ali 2001: 47–48; Khateri 2010). While sources vary with regard to the exact dates, there is consensus that Saddam Hussein from 1984 to 1986 used unprecedented levels of toxic gas against both Iranian soldiers and civilians.

[12]By its own account, Iraq produced some 3850 tons of chemical warfare agents (mustard gas, tabun, sarin, and VX) between 1981 and 1991. Approximately, 3300 tons of agents were weaponized in

as well as the agents used. For example, in 1984 then Foreign Minister Velayati described the injuries resulting from 49 gas attacks in 40 Iranian border regions since the beginning of the war as follows:

> Among these victims, 26 were poisoned, 25 were suffocated, 69 suffered from nausea, 66 became dizzy, 11 had breathing problems, 362 suffered from vision problems with permanent or temporary blindness and 59 complained of skin ailments, while 100 others were severely injured in their testicles and legs. The pictures taken from those afflicted show vividly the traces of wounds, blisters, black and pink skin marks and physical malfunctions. (Velayati 1984: 10)

Delegates also vividly reported on the devastating humanitarian, moral, and ecological consequences on both the Iranian and Iraqi sides. Often, statements were accompanied by the distribution of photographs or first-hand reports of chemical weapons victims—forcefully underlining the need for action.[13] While in view of the extent of the attacks it is hardly possible to speak of a disproportionate "dramatization," Iran consciously sought to address the emotions of the audience as illustrated by the following speech on the occasion of the attack on the Iranian city of Sardasht on 28 June 1987—the world's first large-scale poison gas attack on inhabited territory in which hundreds of civilians, mainly women and children, died or were injured:[14]

> It is very essential that we should all for a moment imagine how a child would behave when he cries hard for survival, and with each cry, lumps of this lethal gas are pumped into his lungs. We should also imagine what the desperate mother could do – prevent the child from breathing, I mean suffocate him, or let her dear one die of mustard gas. (Larijani 1987: 11)

Despite Iran's massive efforts, the attack on Sardasht gained much less public attention than the one on the Kurdish city of Halabja on 16 March 1988.[15] Therefore, Iran has spent much energy in redirecting public perception, e.g., through commemoration ceremonies[16] and through linking the attack to historical precedents of "crimes against humanity" (Velayati 1988a) such as the nuclear bombings of Hiroshima and Nagasaki (Velayati 1987) or the holocaust (Mashhadi 1988; Velayati 1988a).

Iran also sought to influence global coverage of the events, e.g., through distributing information brochures of chemical weapons victims and inviting journalists to

---

different types of bombs, artillery munitions, and missile warheads. About 80 percent of these warfare agents were used from 1982 to 1990 (UN 2006).

[13] Interview with the former head of the Iranian disarmament delegation at the CD, 9 June 2015.

[14] Iraqi military dropped a total of seven mustard gas-filled bombs. According to official reports, more than half of the inhabitants of the village fell victim to the attacks; http://www.tehranpeacemuseum.org/files/pdf/Sardasht%20gas%20Attack-Foroutan.pdf. Accessed 28 April 2017.

[15] The attack is considered the worst toxic gas attack since the First World War—5000 people died, 7000 were injured, and 75 percent of them women and children.

[16] In 2011, Iran's efforts resulted in a decision of the OPCW's Executive Council to commemorate the annual attacks on Sardasht with an official ceremony. The importance attached to symbolic gestures is also illustrated by the Iranian proposal to name part of the OPCW site after the Iranian city of Sardasht in 2008. http://news/article/opcw-director-general-meets-deputy-foreign-minister-of-the-islamic-republic-of-iran. Accessed 28 April 2017.

Iranian cities affected by CW attacks (Ali 2001: 48).[17] Since the country itself did not have sufficient infrastructure to treat injured people, victims were flown to European countries (e.g., Sweden, Austria, Belgium, and Switzerland; CBW Events 2007: 5). Already during the war, Iran organized various international medical congresses dealing with the consequences of poisonous gas attacks and the treatment of victims. On these occasions, Iran shared footage and led victims report their experiences (Velayati 1984: 10). Confronting European countries with CW victims was considered an important aspect of moral awareness-raising and regarded as an instrument to enhance negotiations of a CW ban (Velayati 1987: 3). In almost every subsequent speech uttered in the context of the CWC, Iran refers to its victim status and in particular to the long-term consequences of the CW attacks in order to underline its own commitment to the CWC. In 2003, for example, a delegate at the 8th Conference of the Parties to the CWC declared:

> 13 years after cease-fire between the two countries, hardly a week still goes by without Iranian people losing one of their loved ones to chemical weapons after long years of agonizing pained suffering. Iran sustained 100,000 known victims to the use of different types of chemical agents (nerve agents, blistering agents and mixed agents), 35,000 of them are considered serious, due to suffering from long effects of chemical weapons deployed by Iraq (especially mustard gas). Ten percent of the victims whose cases are serious will have a definite, gradual and agonizing death awaiting them. [...] Our experience with chemical weapons has been and will continue to remain very costly to the Islamic republic of Iran in many respects. Therefore, the Islamic republic of Iran has good reasons beyond a mere legal ground to do its utmost in accomplishing the goals of the Convention and implementation activities of the OPCW. (Khoshroo 2003b)

Iran's efforts to raise awareness in diplomatic forums also served to persuade the international community to condemn Iraq's CW use as a breach of the Geneva Protocol and to hold Saddam Hussein accountable. From 1982 on Iran approached the UN for support and demanded investigations into the incidents.[18]

Between 1984 and 1988, several inspection missions were carried out which confirmed the use of mustard gas and nerve agents.[19] Despite Iran's massive publicity campaign, however, the reaction of the international community was rather cautious at first (Ali 2001: 50–51): The UN Security Council condemned the use of chemical weapons, calling on both parties to end the conflict and refrain from further gas attacks.[20] However, despite obvious evidence that Iraq had used chemical weapons

[17]Iran also invested in national education campaigns that were similar in both content and nature to international efforts. Yet, these measures were not included into the analysis because they are of no relevance for assessing global norm entrepreneurship.

[18]An overview of Iran's letters to the UN as well as the resolutions adopted and missions undertaken can be found at: http://www.un.org/en/sc/repertoire/studies/middle_east.shtml. Accessed 28 April 2017.

[19]Besides on-site inspections in Iran, medical experts also conducted clinical analyses of alleged victims brought to European hospitals for treatment purposes. A summary of the results of the UN investigations from 1984 to 1988 can be found in Findlay (1991: 139–143).

[20]Iran had already presented a draft resolution in September 1984 in which the Iraqi use of poisonous gas was condemned as a breach of the Geneva Protocol—but due to American opposition this initiative failed (Battle 2003). Security Council resolutions adopted before 1986 contained neither

against Iran and probably for political reasons,[21] the Security Council refrained from assigning clear responsibility to Iraq. Sanctions were not issued. Later, Iranian delegates argued that this cautious reaction—which constituted "an international conspiracy of silence" (Jalali 1981b) from Iran's perspective—had given Iraq "a carte blanche to continue and intensify its use of these weapons of mass destruction" (Velayati 1988a: 3). To Iran, the consequences of the international community's passivity stretched way beyond "innocent Iranians," but put "damage [...] to the common human conscience" (Kazemi Kamyab 1984a: 32). Condemning Iraq was framed as a moral duty for "all fair-minded people" (Velayati 1985: 9).

Iran also demanded accountability for those Western countries (in particular the UK, the USA, and the Soviet Union) and companies that had supplied Saddam Hussein with the chemicals and technologies needed to set up his chemical weapons program.[22] Both with the UN and the CWC, Iranian delegates used naming, blaming, and shaming strategies to condemn the accused countries and firms as "international merchants of death" (Velayati 1984, 1986). A rhetorical move which is often used by Iran consisted in highlighting their duplicity and double standards as illustrated in the following statement:

> It simply does not make sense that countries crying for humanity, peace and stability are generously arming, assisting and politically supporting such a criminal régime, regardless of its violation of international law and ignorance! Any assistance to the violator with the knowledge of its continuous violations is in itself a crime and constitutes participation in the crime. (Larijani 1987: 12)

Iranian delegates continued their demands for accountability and compensation after the war had ended (e.g., Mottaki 2006; Deghani 2009a). In fact, Iran is of the opinion that the CWC contains several regulatory gaps insofar as it neither defines the use of chemical weapons as a war crime (Sheikholeslam 1984) nor contains accountability provisions. Iran is of the opinion that such provisions address the humanitarian dimension and should thus become an integral part of the aid and protection measures available to member states. Furthermore, such provisions are perceived to be basic rights of victims of chemical weapons. Iran therefore repeatedly called on the CWC parties and the OPCW to address this gap, for example, by setting up a working group to investigate CW precursor supplies to Iraq. Tehran called on the Technical Secretariat to publish the names of the 15 countries that had supplied

---

references to the CW attacks nor named Iraq as the aggressor. Only in 1988, following the attacks on the Kurdish civilian population in Halabja, a UN Security Council resolution (A/RES/620) was passed that identified Iraq as aggressor.

[21] Fearing that the revolutionary Iranian regime would grow stronger, but also because of their trade relations with Iraq, many Western governments, particularly the USA, were reluctant to condemn Iraq or even impose sanctions. However, after public reporting had addressed the issue, some countries such as Australia, France, Japan, the UK, and later also the USA, restricted chemical trade with Iraq (Ali 2001: 49–50).

[22] Throughout the war, Iraq received political support and military assistance from the West. For the development of the chemical weapons program, Iraq needed foreign technologies, equipment, and raw materials, which were officially requested under the pretext of establishing a state pesticide production (UN 2006).

Iraq with raw materials for the manufacture of chemical weapons, "so that they will have guilty consciences in their lifetimes. They should also bear the burden of this tragic responsibility" (Gharib Abadi 2010: 2). While Iran's national interests are obvious, Iranian diplomats stress that that prosecution would also serve to prevent future crimes and that the victims of gas attacks are entitled to see the responsible actors be penalized (Najafi 2007: 13).

7.2.3 Strengthening Article X Through Institutionalization

Given its own experiences during the Iraq war, Iran's commitment to strong protective measures for CW victims already came to the fore in the CWC negotiations in Geneva (Kenyon 2000: 9). In the day-to-day business of other delegations, the issue played only a marginal role, if at all. Apart from Iran, only a few countries were committed to such provisions[23]—Iran's victim status placed the country in a unique position. The Iranian delegation made the scientific expertise that it had built in response to the national treatment of CW victims available during the negotiations by involving medical–technical experts in its national delegation. As Hassan Mashhadi, Head of negotiations and later Director of the OPCW's Assistance and Protection Branch, explained, Iran was

> the only country in the negotiations that knew what they were talking about, [the] only country having experienced quite vividly the effects of chemical weapons usage. [...] We wanted to make sure we could get some help in treating our CW victims, and that this does not happen again or if so, [that] countries are prepared.[24]

To Iran, countries that fall victim to the use of chemical weapons or threat thereof "should be assisted in every possible way to combat the effects of these horrible weapons by defensive and protective measures and [...] they should be equipped medically to provide care for the victims who have been so afflicted" (Kazemi Kamyab 1984b: 28). In particular, Iran demanded that the Executive Council should react immediately at the request of a State Party which claimed to have been the victim of a CW attack. Without prior political consultations, the Council should automatically send an inspection team and activate punitive mechanisms (Velayati 1990a). After an attack, the other State Parties should automatically be obliged to take predetermined assistance measures as is elaborated in the following remark by then Foreign Minister Velayati:

> With regard to article X, assistance in cases of use should be mandatory and comprehensive. The comprehensiveness and universality of the convention form the most important point. Upon the request of the Executive Council, following actual use of chemical weapons, when there is a need for urgent assistance, the assistance should be mandatory and automatic. In cases of the threat of use, assistance can be voluntary. (Velayati 1988a: 6)

---

[23]Pakistan also drafted several working papers on the issue matter (Kenyon and Mashhadi 2007).

[24]Hassan Mashhadi, telephone interview, 9 June 2015.

That assistance to CW victims should be automatic and mandatory is justified on humanitarian grounds, "because any delay in providing assistance such as antidotes, medical care and first aid would cost human lives" (Velayati 1989: 6). Accordingly, Iran regretted the weak contractual provisions relating to Article X in the CWC (Naimi-Arfa 1990; Najafi 2007). In particular, Iran did not consider the longer-term needs of victims of chemical weapons to be sufficiently taken into account in the CWC (Araghchi 2007; Deghani 2009b). Article X applies only to future CW attacks, and its provision does not foresee the treatment of CW victims that have been injured due to attacks prior to the entry into force of the Convention (1997).[25] Iran's efforts to provide information on the long-term consequences of poisonous gas attacks have to be seen against this background. Again and again delegates stressed the immense burden that Iran had to bear alone as a result of the poison gas attacks (Najafi 2007: 12).

As a consequence in 2006,[26] then Foreign Minister Manouchehr Mottaki proposed to establish an international support network for victims of chemical weapons under Article X (*Chemical Weapons Victim's International Funding & Assistance Network*). Some states (such as the USA, Meier 2008) warned against extending the mandate of the OPCW beyond disarmament assistance and argued that organizations such as the ICRC were responsible for covering the humanitarian aspects.[27] Iran, on the other hand, argued that the CWC also had a humanitarian task as was stressed in Mottaki's statement:

> We are not able to make up for those victims who have passed away, but could help alleviate the human suffering of the survivors of chemical weapons. To this end, I submit the establishment of a support network to mobilize international care, addressing their special needs. (Mottaki 2006)

The support network would not only strengthen the humanitarian mandate of the OPCW and the rights of victims of chemical weapons, but was also meant strengthen the implementation of the measures provided for in Article X (Ziaran 2008).

In 2010, Iran submitted a proposal to the Conference of State Parties (Iran 2010k) which specified the scope of the network's activities and called on the Executive Council to initiate its establishment. The Iranian proposal foresaw that the OPCW should set up a database, which should interrogate the medical needs of victims of chemical weapons, provide information on assistance offered by member states, and list relevant national, regional, and civil society organizations in the field of victim protection. Furthermore, the network should provide a platform for information and

---

[25] Interview Khateri, 12 May 2015, The Hague.

[26] By its own account, Iran had already called for establishing such a network in 2003 (Iran 2010h).

[27] The group of Western European and other states feared that the fund could be used politically to link the issue of the long-term consequences of chemical weapons use with possible questions about the responsibility of Western companies for chemical and technology supplies to Iraq. See Interview Mashhadi, 9 June 2015; interview with representatives of the Western group within the OPCW, May 2015. I could only find one speech in which during an Executive Council meeting South Africa on behalf of the African group expressed its support (South Africa 2011). Civil society and the OPCW welcomed the initiative and saw the establishment of the network as reasonable; see interviews with OPCW staff, arms control experts, and NGOs in The Hague in May 2015.

communication for victims of chemical weapons and help facilitate the practical coordination of assistance. Those affected should also be given the opportunity to participate in the network, e.g., by providing their experience reports and personal stories. The aid fund to be set up should not only fund information campaigns, but should also provide funds for research, for example, to organize seminars and workshops on treatment methods or for research grants for resource-poor developing countries. State Parties should agree to cooperate in the treatment of chemical weapons victims and facilitate the trade in protective equipment and technologies needed to treat chemical weapons victims. The proposal thus confirmed the support measures already provided for in Article X, paragraph 7. In order to substantiate the need for such a network, Iran referred to the common good:

> We are of the conviction that establishment of such a network is the least that the States Parties and the Organisation can do in order to display their sympathy for the victims of chemical weapons. This issue is not exclusively related to one country only and that at least several other countries have offered victims in this regard. (Gharib Abadi 2011b: 4)

In 2011, the State Parties finally decided to establish an international support network for victims of chemical weapons (OPCW 2011), which was largely in line with Iran's proposal. To implement the decision, the Parties were called upon to contribute financially to a voluntary assistance fund, to provide medical treatment for victims of chemical weapons in their countries, to organize national awareness-raising campaigns, to exchange information and experience on the treatment of victims of chemical weapons, and to facilitate the trade in materials and protective equipment (OPCW 2013).

In 2012, the Technical Secretariat established a voluntary trust fund to finance the network, to which Iran donated 15,000 euros (Gharib Abadi 2012).[28] Since 2013, a section on the OPCW web site is providing information on the activities of the network and the history of CW attacks. The web site also provides links to the web sites of (Iranian) NGOs.[29] In 2016, a medical manual was developed by experts involved in the network. The handbook covers both acute and long-term consequences of CW use, provides backgrounds, defines terminology, explains first-aid measures, and discusses treatment options.[30] While Iran welcomed the establishment of the support

---

[28] So far, the financial contribution of the signatory states has been modest: Iraq has failed to keep its promise of 5000 euros for the aid fund. See interview Khateri, 12 May 2015, The Hague. The OPCW donated a share of the Nobel Peace Prize money of 20,000 euros and Dr. Robert Matthews, winner of The Hague Award 2014 donated 45,000 euros for the network. http://www.gevans.org/speeches/speech562.html. Accessed 28 April 2017. Iran criticizes the reluctant financial participation and urges particularly those states to make a contribution that supplied Iraq with materials and technology (Gharib Abadi 2013).

[29] See https://www.opcw.org/special-sections/victims-of-chemical-weapons-network/. Accessed 28 April 2017.

[30] In addition to Iranian experts, scientists from Australia, Belgium, Germany, Japan, Spain, the UK, and the USA were involved in the preparation of the handbook; see https://www.opcw.org/fileadmin/OPCW/ICA/APB/Practical_Guide_for_Medical_Management_of_Chemical_Warfare_Casualties_-_web.pdf. Accessed 28 April 2017.

network, it called on the signatory states to take further practical steps and make further financial contributions to fully activate it (Iran 2013a; Jahangiri 2015).

Nevertheless, Iran's commitment has its limits: The country was relatively reluctant to engage with the Syrian ruler Assad in the summer of 2013 in the case of the confirmed use of chemical weapons (Sarin) against the Syrian civilian population. Iran regularly coordinates its positions in the Executive Council with the Syrian delegation and has tried to prevent condemnation of the allied Assad regime and a referral to the UN Security Council (Lynch 2015).[31] Sure, Iran maintains its position that the use of CW constitutes a crime against humanity and condemned the attacks (e.g., Jahangiri 2015). Also, Iranian delegates stress the need for assistance and support for the victims of the attack. For example, Iran demanded the right to use the fund set up for the support network to support civilian victims of "terrorist" chemical weapons attacks (Jahangiri 2015). However, Iran insists that Syrian rebels had used the poisonous gas (FARS News Agency 2013; Ministry of Foreign Affairs Iran 2013), even though investigations by the OPCW and intelligence reports suggested that the Assad regime was responsible for the operations.[32] In the Executive Council of the OPCW, Tehran repeatedly used disruptive action: In January 2015, it did not even shy away from diplomatic self-isolation in order to prevent a statement initiated by the USA and Russia, in which "serious concern" about the continued chlorine gas attacks was expressed and the Director-General of the OPCW was asked to refer the matter to the UN Security Council.[33] For the third time in the history of the OPCW, there was a vote, with only Tehran voting against the decision. Thus, Iran prevented the adoption of effective measures against the continued use of CW gas in Syria and thereby undermined its own commitment to the protection of CW victims. Iran also maintained this position in view of the more recent attacks in Syria in April 2017: While the West, in particular France, holds the Syrian regime responsible for the attack and the USA reacted with a missile attack on a Syrian air base, Iran stands firmly at President Assad's side together with Russia, who denies the use of chemical weapons and blames rebel groups for it.

7.2.4 *Practical Engagement*

The previous chapters have already touched upon some of the practical activities Iran has undertaken in the context of raising awareness for the extent of CW usage during the Iraq–Iran war as well as for the need for victim assistance. Throughout the whole investigation period, Iran participated regularly in the Conferences of the State

---

[31] Interviews with members of Western countries within the OPCW, 11 and 13 May 2015 in The Hague.

[32] See http://www.nti.org/learn/countries/syria/. Accessed 28 April 2017.

[33] A member of the Western group within the OPCW reported on the incident during my interview trip to The Hague.

Parties. Its level of engagement in the CWC negotiations and the regular meetings can be considered above-average.[34]

In order to commemorate the victims and to keep the urgency of banning chemical weapons in collective memory (Mehmanparast 2012), Iran puts emphasis on symbolic actions: On the anniversary of the attacks on Sardasht, which coincides with the entry into force of the CWC, several Iranian cities are hosting national commemorations accompanied by events (such as medical congresses, CWC seminars, press conferences, publication of victim statistics, anniversary publications, or international civil society meetings. In 2004, June 28 was declared "National Day for Campaign against Chemical and Biological Weapons" (Najafi 2012). Iran's donation of a monument to the victims of chemical weapons in the garden of the OPCW in 2012 also aimed to raise moral awareness (Gharib Abadi 2012). During the annual Conference of State Parties, Iran regularly organizes photograph exhibitions on the CW attacks in cooperation with Iranian NGOs and the OPCW. On the same occasions, a delegation of chemical weapons victims travels to The Hague to report on their experiences and long-term consequences.

Iran's active role in efforts to improve protection against chemical weapons is often dismissed by some political observers and Western diplomats as merely image-building, which serves only to satisfy its own interests (e.g., Thränert 2003: 25). However, Iran's commitment to providing assistance and protection measures in case of a CW attack or threat thereof, as listed in Article X, paragraph 7, is above average. On its web site, the OPCW praises Iran's practical activities and notes that "[t]he need to manage the treatment of [...] a large number of casualties has placed Iran's medical specialists in the forefront of the development of effective treatment regimes for chemical weapons victims, and particularly for those suffering from exposure to mustard gas."[35]

While the country does not participate in payments into the voluntary trust fund,[36] for a long time Iran was the only State Party to provide assistance available under Article X in a bilateral agreement with the OPCW—a fact that Iran does not get tired to emphasize and which it uses to call on other states to follow its example (e.g., Gharib Abadi 2010, 2011a). In the pledge, Iran undertakes at the request of a member state to accept up to 50 patients in its hospitals. In addition, two medical expert teams (consisting of five doctors) are to be sent to the attacked country in

[34]See background conversations with members of the OPCW in May 2015; telephone interview with Hassan Mashhadi, 9 June 2015 and email conversation with Dr. Ralf Trapp, 31 May 2015.

[35]"Genesis and Historical Development". http://www.opcw.org/chemical-weapons-convention/genesis-and-historical-development/. Accessed 28 August 2015.

[36]To date, only 45 countries have contributed to the aid fund, which has a budget of approximately EUR 1.5 million. This amount may be used by the OPCW in an emergency to assist a State Party. See Interview Khateri, OPCW employee, 12 May 2015 in The Hague.

such an emergency situation (OPCW 2000a).[37] Iran also commits itself to establish a regional training center in which medical courses for the treatment of victims of chemical weapons will be held.[38] From 1999 to 2008, Tehran organized a total of nine such courses in collaboration with the OPCW Technical Secretariat.[39] In a speech at the 2010 Executive Council meeting, an Iranian delegate explains that due to its own experience, Iran "insists on capacity building and [...] making available adequate resources in order to expeditiously meet the needs of the State Parties that have been exposed to chemical attacks." (Gharib Abadi 2010). Iranian experts and arms control officials also participated in two of the three practical exercises (ASSISTEX) organized by the Technical Secretariat, which served to improve the coordination of assistance and protection measures in chemical weapons attacks.[40] The willingness to pass on the expertise of Iranian medical personal on the treatment of CW victims via the OPCW to other countries is seen by employees of the OPCW as an important contribution to the capacity building of the treaty community.[41]

The scientific/medical expertise in the treatment of CW victims is also made available internationally. To this end, Iranian experts participate in training courses on Article X[42] organized by other member states, organize international medical congresses, or occasionally cooperate with international humanitarian organizations and civil society actors.[43] At the invitation of the Iranian Foreign Ministry, for example, a Swedish delegation of "Physicians for the Prevention of Nuclear War" spent

[37]The text "Memorandum of Understanding between the OPCW and the Government of the Islamic Republic of Iran regarding the Provision of Assistance" dated 02 July 1999 has been published in OPCW (2000).

[38]Interview with Shahriar Khateri, employee of the responsible OPCW department, 12 May 2015, The Hague.

[39]No further courses have been held since 2008. According to a member of the Assistance and Protection Branch, it is unclear why Iran suspended them. The OPCW had repeatedly expressed interest in resuming the courses, as Iranian expertise was irreplaceable. See interview Khateri, 12 May 2015, The Hague. Upon request, the head of Iran's national CWC Supervisory Authority cited as a reason the uncooperative behavior of the Director-General of the OPCW with regard to the allocation of offices within the Technical Secretariat. Apparently, there are no plans to resume the courses in the near future. To be fair, it should be noted that the OPCW has spent less money on capacity building in recent years than before, interview with a former OPCW employee, 09 June 2015.

[40]For ASSISTEX 1, which took place from 10 to 14 September 2002 in Zadar/Croatia, Iran provided a medical team of six and a field hospital; https://www.opcw.org/fileadmin/OPCW/ICA/APB/ASSISTEX_I_%20Croatia_2002/ASSISTEX1_CDQ_2003_No01.pdf. Accessed 28 April 2017. Iran also participated with a medical team in ASSISTEX 2, which took place from 10 to 14 September 2002 until 14 October 2005 in Lviv/Ukraine, interview Khateri, 12 May 2015. Iran did not participate in ASSISTEX 3 from 6 to 8 July 2010 in Tunisia.

[41]Interviews with Shahriar Khateri, 12 May 2015, The Hague; Ralf Trapp, 31 May 2015.

[42]The OPCW Technical Secretariat regularly conducts regional assistance and protection trainings in one of the countries of the region. Iran regularly participated in such courses and provided the expertise of Iranian doctors (Chemical Disarmament Quarterly 2008: 22).

[43]This is also done by the Baqiyatallah Hospital in Tehran granting scientists from all over the world access to chemical weapons victims and thus contributing to the scientific development of new treatment options (Vick 2012).

a four-day research stay in Tehran to investigate the long-term health consequences of Iranian soldiers and civilians exposed to poisonous gas attacks in the 1980s (NTI 2008).[44] According to a member of the assistance and protection branch of the OPCW, however, Iran's involvement has decreased since 2008.

Table 7.1 illustrates the range of Iranian activities in relation to assistance and protection measures:[45]

7.2.5 *Assessment*

According to the criteria set up for the purposes of this study (see Sect. 5.2.1) Iran's commitment to the protection of victims qualifies as norm entrepreneurship: Dissatisfied with the inadequate protection and assistance provided by the international community and in view of its hesitant reaction to Iraq's repeated poisonous gas attacks, Iran actively advocated the establishment of protection and support norm for those affected by chemical weapons. In addition, Iran considerably contributed to the shaping of Article X by providing its own experience and competences. Even after the CWC came into force, Iranian diplomats continued to support the institutional strengthening of victim protection.

Ultimately, Iran even succeeded in institutionally expanding the protection and support norm for chemical weapons victims: With the establishment of the assistance network, State Parties extended the scope of the OPCW's tasks to humanitarian concerns and recognized the need for regulation with regard to the long-term needs of victims of chemical weapons in principle.

Throughout the entire period under investigation, Iran played a prominent role—also in comparison with other countries—in establishing Article X and later in strengthening it. It is true that, in addition to Iran, other countries were also involved in the design of protection and support measures. On the basis of its own experiences, however, Iran acquired a unique position, which it was able to skillfully insert into the negotiations through active norm entrepreneurship. As shown above, the Iranian activities corresponded to the characteristics of typical norm entrepreneurship, both with regard to the strategies used for the normative framing and the practical measures. The extent of national resources (in particular medical expertise) used by the Iranian government to strengthen Article X is particularly striking.

---

[44] Iranian NGOs are involved in such measures. However, in a country like Iran governmental approval is necessary for international civil society exchanges. Therefore, such measures are seen as an indicator of government activities.

[45] Information on Iran's practical activities stems from secondary literature, primary sources, interviews, the annual reports of the OPCW as well as information from the CBW Bulletin (http://www.sussex.ac.uk/Units/spru/hsp/pdfbulletin.html. Accessed 28 April 2017) and the two journals Chemical Disarmament Quarterly and OPCW Today published by the OPCW.

Table 7.1 Practical activities to support chemical weapons victims

Type of activity	Date and title	Description
Actions within the CWC	1999	"Memorandum of Understanding between Iran and the OPCW on the provision of medical emergency assistance teams and treatment of chemical weapons casualties at Iranian hospitals according to Article X (7b)"
	2006	Proposal to establish a support network
National medical trainings in cooperation with the OPCW	1999/05/15–20, "First Course on Medical Defence against Chemical Weapons," 22 participants from 15 State Parties 2000/5 2000/10/23–26, 23 "Third Course on Medical Aspects of Defence against Chemical Weapons," participants from 19 State Parties 2002/10/14–17, 14 participants from 12 State Parties 2003/5/26–30 "Sixth annual course on the medical aspects of defense against chemical weapons," *International Medical Center for Training and Treatment against chemical Weapons* (IMCTTCW), 25 participants from eight State Parties 2004/4/17–21 2004/10/9–13 "Course on Aspects of Defence Against Chemical Weapons," Teheran 2006/11/4–8, "Eight Course on the medical aspects of defense against chemical weapons," 22 participants from 21 State Parties 2008/11/5–9, 22 participants from 21 State Parties	The courses are organized by the National CWC Supervisory Authority of Iran, the Ministry of Health and the Janbazan Veterans' Foundation in collaboration with the Technical Secretariat of the OPCW and are hosted at the International Medical Center for Training and Treatment against Chemical Weapons (IMCTTCW) in Tehran. They are intended to provide basic knowledge about chemical weapons and their effects as well as information about protective measures, including detection options for chemical attacks, comprehensive protection and treatment measures as well as necessary decontamination measures Description of the course in the invitation to member states by the OPCW: "The aim of the course is to provide an opportunity for participants to receive advice from Iranian doctors who have previously treated casualties of chemical weapons on the battlefield […] and who continue to provide medical care for them. This, it is intended, will enable participants to increase their understanding of the problems they may encounter during national or international responses to incidents involving chemical weapons. Participant also receive information on assistance and further training available through OPCW" (OPCW 2000b) During the courses, participants also meet victims of chemical weapons; participating medical personnel are given the opportunity to attend clinical training seminars in Iranian hospitals in which chemical weapons victims are examined with regard to long-term consequences. Participation in interactive, computer-based simulation courses is also planned

(continued)

Table 7.1 (continued)

Type of activity	Date and title	Description
Nationally held (international) conferences	1983 Medical Congress in Tehran 1984 Medical Congress 1986/03/17–18 "Seminar on chemical and biological warfare," Shiraz University 1995/03/15 "Seminar on the study of the effects of chemical weapons," *Kowsar Health Complex*, Teheran 1997/10/22 "Seminar on the adverse consequences of using chemical weapons against Iran" 2002/10/14 Seminar "Medical defences for chemical weapons," *Bagiatallah Medical Sciences University* 2004/06/30 Congress "Review of the Consequences of Application of Chemical Weapons" 2007 Two medical congresses in Mashhad and Isfahan 2007/10/22–23 International Seminar "The use of chemical weapons against the Islamic Republic of Iran, its impacts and consequences" 2008/10/22–23 Seminar "The Consequences of Chemical Weapons Attacks against Iran" 299/11/13 Workshop on prevention and medical operations during chemical, biological and nuclear attacks 2004/03/15 Seminar "Use of Chemical Weapons: Backgrounds and Outlooks"	Conferences dealing with the consequences of poison gas and the treatment of patients, during which participants also meet victims of chemical weapons attacks

(continued)

Table 7.1 (continued)

Type of activity	Date and title	Description
Scientific events	1999	Opening of the *International Centre for Training and Treatment of the Victims of Chemical Warfare* in Teheran
	2007/01/20 Teheran	Invitation of the Swedish section of the "International Physicians for the Prevention of Nuclear War" by the Foreign Ministry to spend four days conducting research on chemical weapons victims
Meetings with international civil society	Participation in various Pugwash meetings and invitation of international NGOs to national conferences Occasional involvement or participation in seminars with civil society within the framework of the OPCW Invitation and support for cooperation between Iranian and Japanese NGOs	
Symbolic actions	1999/03/16	Commemorative publication of the government-related magazine Kayhan International on the occasion of the commemoration of the poison gas attacks on the Kurdish city of Halabja
	2007/05/09 Seminar on "the Occasion of the 10th Anniversary of the EIF of the CWC" as well as various memorial ceremonies 2000/10/22 "Seminar on contents of CWC"	Issue of a special stamp and a special publication to mark the tenth anniversary of the CWC
	2007/06/30	Opening of the "Peace Park and Museum" in Tehran, which mainly exhibits works of art dealing with the Iraqi chemical weapons attacks
	2009 in the lobby of the *World Forum Conference Centre* in Den Haag	Photograph exhibition at the OPCW within the framework of Conferences of the State Parties

(continued)

Table 7.1 (continued)

Type of activity	Date and title	Description
	2012/11/26 during the 17th conference of the State Parties to the CWC	Foundation of a memorial to the victims of chemical weapons in the OPCW garden in The Hague
Commemoration ceremonies	Since 2004 every year on 28 June in various Iranian cities	Commemoration of the mustard gas attacks on the Iranian city of Sardasht
	2007/05/09 "Commemoration Ceremony with the attendance of Iranian officials and head of foreign missions and embassies in Tehran"	Commemoration of the 10th anniversary of the CWC and the 20th anniversary of the attacks on Sardasht

Table 7.2 summarizes Iran's norm entrepreneurship according to the established criteria.

7.3 Iran's Commitment to Nuclear Disarmament

As one of the three "pillars" of the NPT, nuclear disarmament can be considered as being a fairly entrenched norm. Yet while the overall validity of the norm of nuclear disarmament is hardly disputed, its concrete meaning and the behavioral consequences resulting from its normative provisions have been subject to contestation ever since the NPT was negotiated. Since its accession to the treaty, Iran has expressed its commitment to nuclear disarmament and sought to strengthen the norm (or more precisely, the meaning it attaches to it) through discursive and practical means.

7.3.1 *Background: The Norm of Nuclear Disarmament in the Context of the NPT*

The norm of nuclear disarmament enshrined in Article VI of the NPT requires each State Party

> to pursue negotiations in good faith on effective measures relating to cessation of the nuclear arms race at an early date and to nuclear disarmament, and on a treaty on general and complete disarmament under strict and effective international control.[46]

The wording remains rather vague, which opens the possibility for contestation regarding the exact requirements and the scope of the normative obligations (Burford 2015). Whether the normative commitment comprises concrete disarmament steps and how progress on this issue should be measured has been the subject of a dispute between NPT members for years (e.g., Joyner 2011; Kmentt 2013; Müller and Wunderlich 2018). Four times in the history of the NPT, discontent among non-nuclear weapon states with the implementation of the disarmament norm has also prevented the adoption of a consensual final document (1980, 1990, 2005, and 2015).

Basically, two interpretive positions can be discerned: With the exception of China, the nuclear weapon states and their allies hold the view that the NPT primarily serves to prevent the proliferation of nuclear weapons and that cooperation in the peaceful uses of nuclear energy and disarmament are of secondary relevance (hereinafter Müller 2012: 4–5). In contrast, the states of the Non-Aligned Movement (NAM) in particular argue that the NWS are not fulfilling their contractual obligation to disarm and plea for a treaty-bound path to nuclear disarmament. For the NAM, the elimination of nuclear weapons is a legal and moral obligation that must be implemented

[46]Treaty on the Non-Proliferation of Nuclear Weapons, Article VI, http://www.un.org/en/conf/npt/2005/npttreaty.html; 25 June 2018.

Table 7.2 Overview of the respective characteristics of norm entrepreneurship based on Sell and Prakash (2004: 153) in the case of "protection for victims of chemical weapons"

Norm entrepreneur case 1: Effective protection and assistance for victims of chemical weapons	
Period	1980–until today
Trigger (extrinsic/intrinsic)	– Own experiences during the Iran–Iraq war in the 1980s
Problem definition	– Existing protection and assistance measures for states attacked or threatened by chemical weapons are insufficient and ineffective – The long-term consequences of CW use are not sufficiently anchored in the (moral) consciousness of the international community
Preferred solution	– An effective mechanism to assist victims of chemical weapons in the framework of CWC
Normative framing	– Aid as a humanitarian measure – Moral responsibility of the international community, especially in the context of the involvement of Western companies in Iraq's chemical weapons program; ending double standards – Commitment to chemical weapons victims as a moral commitment – Mitigating the long-term consequences of the use of chemical weapons also serves the common good
National interests	– Assistance for own victims, especially with regard to the long-term consequences of the use of chemical weapons – Condemnation and sanctioning of Iraq; putting an end to CW attacks – Demonstrating responsibility of Western companies for chemicals and technology supplies to Iraq and thereby preventing future activities in this area – Strong Article X as a security guarantee for possible future CW attacks
Applied strategies	– Massive awareness campaign using naming, shaming, and blaming as well as emotionalization – Symbolic actions – Capacity building
Resources	– Technical and medical expertise – Practical support – Financial resources

(continued)

Table 7.2 (continued)

Norm entrepreneur case 1: Effective protection and assistance for victims of chemical weapons	
Allies	– NAM states – Various civil society actors – OPCW (personnel)
Normative transformation?	– Strengthening and specifying the norm of victim protection, in particular with regard to the long-term consequences – Contribution to moral awareness
Substantial change?	– Establishment of the support network by the OPCW 2011
Breaches or doubts about the credibility of the norm advocacy?	– Political support for the Syrian regime, even after alleged use of poisonous gas against the Syrian population

independently of the global security situation. This interpretation is also shared by Iran: Reaching general and complete disarmament is regarded as primary objective of the UN bodies dealing with disarmament and non-proliferation. Instead of advocating an international order based on the deterrent potential of nuclear weapons, Iran advocates a security order in which weapons of mass destruction play no role and military force should only be used for defensive purposes ("defensive security scheme"; Velayati 1992, 1994b; Nasseri 1993). In a speech in 1993, a delegate to the Geneva Conference on Disarmament argued that the aim should not be to reduce, but rather to eliminate nuclear arsenals. In analogy to the START treaties between the USA and Russia, which aimed to reduce strategic offensive arms, he instead called for a "STOP treaty, i.e., Strategic and nuclear arms Out of our Planet" (Nasseri 1993).

The NWS and many of their allies reject such a "big bang approach" (Müller 2012: 4) and advocate incremental disarmament steps instead . While the NAM argues that nuclear disarmament must be pursued independently of the political security situation, the nuclear weapon states argue that the current context is simply not ripe for "global zero" and demand that certain preconditions be in place before meaningful disarmament can occur.

Irrespective of this discursive rift, NPT member states have made quite significant efforts to work out a common language since 1995, resulting in the specification of Article VI (Müller et al. 2013: 55; Müller and Wunderlich 2018: 345–347). For example, the document on "Principles and objectives for nuclear non-proliferation and disarmament"[47] adopted at the 1995 Review and Extension Conference confirms that the NPT was designed to ensure the complete elimination of nuclear weapons and not merely negotiations "in good faith" (Tannenwald 2013: 302–303). It also interprets Article VI as prescribing the prompt conclusion of a Comprehensive

[47] Decision on Principles and objectives for nuclear non-proliferation and disarmament (NPT/CONF.1995/32/DEC.2); http://fas.org/nuke/control/npt/text/prin_obj.htm. Accessed 28 April 2017.

Nuclear-Test-Ban Treaty (CTBT), the start of negotiations on a treaty prohibiting the production of fissile material for weapon purposes (Fissile Material Cut-off Treaty, FMCT), and systematic measures to reduce nuclear arsenals on the part of the NWS (Dhanapala 2005).[48] During the 2000 RevCon, States Parties agreed on "13 practical steps for systematic and progressive efforts towards complete disarmament"[49] including the reduction of substrategic nuclear weapons, enhancing transparency, the irreversibility of disarmament measures, and an "unequivocal commitment of the NWS to abolish nuclear weapons (Simpson 2001). In 2009, on the initiative of the UK, the NWS began regular consultations in order to build the transparency and confidence regarded as being necessary conditions for nuclear disarmament.

In 2010, the measures adopted in 2000 were updated in an "action plan"[50] containing a total of 22 concrete disarmament steps, including restrictions on the development of new warheads, reducing the alert status of nuclear arsenals, progress with the ratification of the CTBT, and the revival of the UN disarmament machinery, in particular the Geneva Conference on Disarmament. Furthermore, the nuclear weapon states were "encouraged" to enter into negotiations on legally binding security guarantees and asked to report regularly and in a systematic manner on their arsenals and the disarmament steps they had actually undertaken (Johnson 2010).

Also outside the NPT, various proposals to strengthen the disarmament norm have been underway. Although the Conference on Disarmament remains blocked, the UN disarmament machinery has been reactivated when in 2010, on initiative of Austria, the UN General Assembly commissioned an open-ended working group to draw up proposals to advance multilateral disarmament negotiations (A/RES/67/56 of 2010). In 2013, the UN General Assembly held its first high-level meeting on nuclear disarmament (A/RES/67/39 of 2013). In parallel, a coalition of non-nuclear weapon states and civil society actors initiated the so-called "Humanitarian Initiative", which emphasized the devastating consequences of nuclear weapons use and invoked a new level of urgency for banning these weapons (Sauer 2015). With the support of more than two-thirds of the NPT membership, the initiative pushed the idea of a legal "ban" on nuclear weapons (Kmentt 2013) and ultimately led to the conclusion of the "Treaty on the Prohibition of Nuclear Weapons" in July 2017. Proponents of the ban see it as closing a legal gap by unequivocally confirming the illegality and illegitimacy of continued adherence to nuclear weapons by the NWS (among others Thakur 2017; Ritchie 2018). Certainly, the prohibition treaty has further specified the disarmament norm enshrined in Article VI of the NPT.

---

[48]This view was reinforced in 1996 when the International Court of Justice (ICJ) found that the threat and use of nuclear weapons was contrary to international law and confirmed the existence of a disarmament norm. Following that decision, some observers argued that Article VI acquired the status of customary international law (e.g., Joyner 2014).

[49]The "13 steps" are contained in the final document of the 2000 NPV Review Conference: NPT/CONF.2000/28 (part I), para. 15, 14–15.

[50]Available at http://www.reachingcriticalwill.org/images/documents/Disarmament-fora/npt/revcon2010/FinalDocument.pdf. Accessed 28 April 2017.

7.3.2 Iran's Normative Framing: Nuclear Disarmament as Humanitarian Mission

Iran's demand for universal and comprehensive nuclear disarmament has become a foreign policy mantra which is reflected in the rhetoric of the foreign policy elite and that of the Supreme Leader himself. A qualitative analysis of the content of Iranian speeches and working papers during the NPT Review Conferences and within the UN bodies concerned with disarmament (First Committee, Conference on Disarmament, UN Special Sessions on Disarmament 1978, 1982, 1988) shows that Iran has consistently advocated the implementation and strengthening of the disarmament norm. The constant rhetorical activation or confirmation of the disarmament norm serves to emphasize the importance attached to it. At the same time, Iran tries to anchor its particular interpretation of Article VI and the obligations resulting from it into the final documents of NPT Review Conferences.

Iran perceives the mere existence of nuclear weapons as constituting a threat to world peace. Thus, in its view, only the complete abolition of these "anti-human weapons" (Mousavi 1981: 551) would guarantee safety for humankind. Even though Iran's arms control policy is also guided by security and status considerations (Pirseyedi 2013: 126), the religious and moral rejection of weapons of mass destruction represents a continuous element of Iranian rhetoric that goes back to pre-revolutionary times (e.g., Fartash 1975; Khalatbari 1978). Until today, "Iran considers the acquiring, development and use of nuclear weapons inhuman, immoral, illegal and against its very basic principle" (Iran 2005a).

If security concerns are raised, they are usually embedded in humanitarian reasoning. At the height of the Cold War, the Shah regime called for an end to the arms race and repeatedly warned of a "nuclear holocaust" (e.g., Ghods Nakhai 1961: 84), a recurrent phrase that was used until the late 1990s (e.g., Velayati 1996: 27; Khamenei 2010). Consequently, Iran welcomed the fact that in 1996, the International Court of Justice classified the threat of nuclear weapons or their use as being contrary to international law, and has ever since referred to the advisory opinion on a regular basis (e.g., Zarif et al. 1996; Kharrazi 2000; Iran 2005a).

Notwithstanding the fact that Iranian delegates officially emphasize the equivalence of the NPT's three pillars and resulting obligations, Article VI is repeatedly described as the most important contractual obligation, with nuclear disarmament being the treaty's overarching goal (e.g., Nasseri 1990a: 19; Iran 2005d, 2010a). In order to document this to the outside world, in 2010, Ahmadinejad even proposed renaming the NPT as "Nuclear Disarmament and Non-Proliferation Treaty (D.N.P.T.)" (Ahmadinejad 2010b). Iran considers the disarmament obligation of the nuclear weapon states to be a quid pro quo—and thus a matter of justice—for the non-nuclear weapon states to renounce a nuclear option, and argues that nuclear abolition must take place independently of the goal of general and complete disarmament (e.g., Aram 1962; Fartash 1975: 47; Dabiri 1980b: 119; Iran 1990).

7.3.3 *Iranian Support for Measures Aimed at Facilitating Nuclear Disarmament*

Iran primarily advocated a strengthening of the disarmament norm through rhetorical affirmation or activation of Article VI and the obligations that in Iran's view result from it. In addition, together with other non-nuclear weapon states, Iran supports various measures which are seen as being necessary steps on the way to a nuclear weapon-free world—most of which have been agreed upon by the treaty community as a whole or have been initiated by other countries.

Iran is particularly strongly committed to promoting the entry into force of a comprehensive test ban treaty. In fact, the country played an active role in establishing the anti-test norm. The Shah regime had already spoken out in favor of banning all nuclear weapons tests in the 1960s, a measure that was regarded a necessary condition for ending the nuclear arms race (e.g., Ghods Nakhai 1961; Aram 1962). In 1963, a limited test ban treaty was passed, which banned nuclear explosions in the atmosphere, under water and in space, but allowed underground nuclear tests to continue. Iran regarded this as being inadequate and advocated a comprehensive and non-discriminatory ban on explosive and non-explosive tests under international control (e.g., Fartash 1979; Dabiri 1980a; Mashhadi 1988; Zarif 1991; Nasseri 1994a). Iran was actively involved in the CTBT negotiations that began in 1994 (by presenting various draft treaties) and was particularly active in developing verification procedures and establishing a worldwide seismological monitoring network ((International Monitoring System, IMS; see also Johnson 2009: 103–104; Pirseyedi 2013: 131–136) in the framework of the so-called Group of Governmental Experts (GSE). In this context, Iran offered to set up various (seismological) monitoring stations in the country (e.g., Nasseri 1994a; Velayati 1996).[51] Nuclear testing was framed not only as a security threat, but also as a threat to the environment and health. According to Tehran, existing test sites were to be closed and the associated infrastructure to be irreversibly destroyed (e.g., Mashhadi 1987).

In the final round of negotiations in February 1996, Iran presented its own draft treaty (Iran 1996a) which contained a comprehensive ban on all nuclear explosions but allowed "peaceful nuclear explosions" under certain conditions. The preamble to the Iranian draft text even included a commitment to nuclear disarmament within a certain timeframe. With the draft, Tehran wanted to explore possible compromises (Velayati 1996). And indeed, Rebecca Johnson (2009: 103) concludes the Iranian draft helped the Disarmament Conference to reach agreement on a treaty text.

Yet Iran was of the opinion that the final treaty text did not reflect the negotiations correctly. Together with India, it unsuccessfully tried to prevent the final report from being forwarded to the UN General Assembly (Johnson 2009: 138; Pirseyedi 2013: 136). Notwithstanding these shortcomings (in particular with regard to the provisions on entry into force and the disarmament commitment), Iran signed the CTBT in

[51] At present (November 2018), Iran operates a seismic monitoring station in Tehran and two further aid stations in Kerman and Shushtar. A radionuclide station and an infrasonic station are planned. See http://www.ctbto.org/verification-regime/station profiles/. Accessed 28 November 2018.

September 1996 when the treaty was opened for signature. While Iranian delegates have ever since continuously advocated for its swift entry into force, Iran itself has not yet ratified the treaty—and says it will do so only when the USA has ratified the CTBT.

Iran also took part in several other measures aimed at strengthening nuclear disarmament and contributed its own proposals to the debate. During the 2010 NPT Review Conference, President Ahmadinejad proposed that an independent body be entrusted with the preparation of guidelines to operationalize the obligations resulting from Article VI and that a temporary disarmament plan should be submitted (Ahmadinejad 2010b). The demands went well beyond the measures provided for in Article VI: Ahmadinejad called for the suspension of any research, development, or modernization of nuclear weapons. To underline the urgency of his demands, he also proposed renaming the NPT the "Nuclear Disarmament and Non-Proliferation Treaty (D.N.P.T.)" (Ahmadinejad 2010b: 6) and placing disarmament obligations at the center of the non-proliferation regime. However, the proposal has not been taken up again, either by other member states or by Iran itself.

In line with the position of the non-aligned countries, Iran also advocated the idea of a time-bound framework for disarmament as early as the 1970s and 1980s (Fartash 1975: 48; Dabiri 1980b; Zarif 1999; Iran 2010a, among others). In this context, Iranian delegates reaffirmed Iran's positive attitude toward a future Nuclear Weapons Convention.[52] Iranian diplomats have repeatedly pleaded for an ad hoc committee on nuclear disarmament to be set up and given a negotiating mandate within the Conference on Disarmament (Velayati 1995; Ahmadinejad 2010b, among others). Beginning in 2005, Iran submitted a draft resolution to the CD, which reaffirmed these demands and resulted in corresponding UN resolutions.[53] In 2011 and 2013, Iran co-sponsored draft resolutions (A/C.1/66/L.42 and A/C.1/68/L.36) calling on UN member states to negotiate a nuclear weapons convention. Iran also actively participated in the UN General Assembly's Open-Ended Working Group on Nuclear Disarmament (Daryaei 2013; Iran 2013c) which was established in 2012, while in September 2013, it attended the first High-Level Meeting of the UNGA on Nuclear Disarmament, which was initiated by non-aligned countries (under Iranian chairmanship). President Rouhani presented a three-point plan, which was finally adopted by the UN General Assembly (A/RES/68/32 of 2013 and follow-up resolution A/RES/69/58 of 2014). Therein, Rouhani proposed declaring 26 September the "International Day for the Complete Abolition of Nuclear Weapons". The intention was that the international community should use this day to reaffirm its commitment to the vision of a world free of nuclear weapons (Rouhani 2013b). He also reiterated his call for negotiations on a nuclear weapons convention to begin swiftly within the-Conference on Disarmament. Consequently, Iran participated in the negotiations of the Treaty on the Prohibition of Nuclear Weapons that commenced in March 2017, and voted in favor of its adoption on 7 July 2017.

[52]For example by supporting the relevant action plan that the non-aligned countries submitted during the 2010 NPT Review Conference (NAM 2010).

[53]See A/Res/60/70 of 2005; A/Res/62/24 of 2007; A/Res/64/31 of 2009 and A/Res/66/28 of 2011.

7.3.4 Naming, Blaming, and Shaming of the Nuclear Weapon States

Iran advocated a strengthening of the disarmament norm not only through rhetorical affirmation of Article VI and supporting measures to foster nuclear disarmament. It also used a strategy that norm researchers subsume with the label "naming, blaming, and shaming," i.e., fierce criticism directed toward the nuclear weapon states, and above all the USA, for not living up to their disarmament obligations as stipulated in Article VI.

Iranian politicians perceive the adherence to nuclear weapons as a continuation of imperialism and thus as a morally reprehensible attempt by the NWS to attain hegemony. Iran therefore frames its commitment to a world free from nuclear weapons in the tradition of anticolonialism (e.g., Dabiri 1980b; Mahallati 1983; Mashhadi 1986). During the 1980s in particular, Iranian speeches were charged with calls for non-aligned countries not to run counter the doctrine of nuclear deterrence by developing their own nuclear weapon capabilities. Instead, Iran called into question the symbolic value of nuclear weapons as status objects and advocated a commitment to multilateral disarmament. The fact that Iran linked its willingness to accept further non-proliferation measures to the proper implementation of Article VI (e.g., Dabiri 1980b; Zarif 1995; Iran 2010a) should be seen in this context. A central element of Iran's advocacy for strengthening the disarmament norm is therefore the persistent naming, shaming, and blaming of the nuclear weapon states' combined misconduct.

Criticism regarding inadequate treaty provisions and the lack of implementation of the nuclear disarmament norm on the side of NWS have been a central element of Iranian speeches since the first NPT Review Conference in 1975.[54] Two thematic clusters can be discerned.

First, Iran complained that in practice, the nuclear weapon states have hardly taken any disarmament steps (e.g., Dabiri 1980b; Kharrazi 2000, 2005b; Ahmadinejad 2010b). These accusations were already voiced in the UN disarmament bodies before the NPT came into force and were linked to the demand for general and complete disarmament (e.g., Pahlavi 1970; Fartash 1975; Mahallati 1983; Mashhadi 1987). Besides inadequate implementation of the obligations resulting from Article VI, Iran also missed progress with regard to efforts that had been agreed upon in final documents as follow-on or additional measures to foster nuclear disarmament (i.e., negotiations of a CTBT, politically binding negative security assurances, a NWFZ in the Middle East; Dabiri 1980b; Velayati 1990b: 49–50, 1995).

Second, Iranian delegates criticized the nuclear weapon states for upgrading and modernizing their arsenals both quantitatively and qualitatively (e.g., Dabiri 1980b; Shahabi Sirjani 1985b; Nasseri 1990a; Moradi 1995; Kharrazi 2005a).

[54]Earlier, the Shah regime had criticized the superpowers' continuing arms race and their unwillingness to enter into serious disarmament negotiations (e.g., Hoveyda 1972: 3). Although moderate in tone and careful not to blame the superpowers all too clearly, Iran called on them to live up to their responsibility.

In Iran's reading, the lack of implementation of the disarmament norm not only constituted a violation of the Treaty; it also hindered the universality of the NPT (Fartash 1975; Dabiri 1980b: 120; Mahallati 1988). Over and over again, Iran criticized the mismatch between words and deeds of the "Nuclear Greats" and objected that "the participating governments are really hypocritical [...] no one is interested in reducing the burden of the arms race, but rather that each state or group of states is seeking only to disarm the others, while ensuring the maintenance of its own weapons mix" (Fartash 1977: 59, 58). In 1985, an Iranian delegate lamented the fact that

> the gap between perception and expectation which had existed during the first five years of the Treaty had widened considerably. [...] Through the continuing nuclear arms race and the lack of any serious negotiations to halt and reverse it, the nuclear-weapon States had continued to undermine the expectations and good faith upon which the non-nuclear-weapon States had relied when they had acceded to the Treaty. The non-nuclear-weapon States had been humiliated by the abuse of their trust and confidence. (Shababi Sirjani 1985a: 181)

Consequently, in Iran's view, it would only be a matter of time before the non-aligned countries no longer felt bound by their treaty obligations. In fact, it claimed that the irresponsible attitude of the NWS called into question the continued existence of the treaty regime (e.g., Fartash 1975: 48; Iran 1990; Nasseri 1990a; Kharrazi 2005a).

While Iran welcomed the bilateral disarmament negotiations between the USA and the USSR (SALT I and SALT II) that took place in the 1970s and late 1980s (Mashhadi 1986; Velayati 1988b), the country regarded several practices as violating the provisions laid down in Articles I and II of the NPT: The adherence to the doctrine of nuclear deterrence, particularly the stationing of nuclear weapons on allies' territory and the concept of nuclear sharing (Dabiri 1981; Velayati 1988b). The stalled negotiations over the conclusion of a comprehensive test ban treaty and the refusal of the NWS to accept legally binding negative security assurances were also repeated causes for Iranian criticism. However, it is above all "the lack of a clear commitment to a zero option by all nuclear-weapon states" (Zarif 1995: 5) that Iran complains about time and again.

Iran shifted its strategy from criticism to blackmail when it announced that its approval of the indefinite extension of the 1995 treaty would depend, among other things, on progress on the disarmament issue. The nuclear weapons tests carried out by China and France in 1996 had been interpreted as an indication of the lacking will to disarm of the nuclear weapon states and as a warning signal that the NNWS would lose any means of exerting pressure by agreeing to the indefinite extension of the NPT (e.g., Nasseri 1995). Ultimately, Iran did not suit the action to the word. After all, the "Principles and Objectives" adopted at the 1995 Extension and Review Conference as well as the resolution calling to establish a NWFZ in the Middle East were regarded as appropriate means to strengthen nuclear disarmament. In addition, the "package proposal" consisting of the indefinite extension, the resolution on the Middle East, and the "principles and objectives" put the responsibility of the NWS on record (Nasseri 1995).

At the 2000 RevCon, then Foreign Minister Kharrazi noted "a mix of satisfaction and frustration" (Kharrazi 2000) with regard to the implementation of these decisions.

In particular, he deplored the nuclear tests by India and Pakistan, the rejection of the CTBT by the US Senate (even though following diplomatic practice, he refrained from naming these countries), and he warned against a new nuclear arms race:

> Despite the ever-growing call for nuclear disarmament, the nuclear weapon states have shown no sign of relenting. They still believe that holding on to extremely risky nuclear arsenals would secure them a prominent international status forever. It should be noted that the NPT has never meant to perpetuate a permanent classification of some states as nuclear-weapon states. (Kharrazi 2000)

In his speech, he blamed the South Asian nuclear tests on frustration with the lack of progress in disarmament. This would have become clear from intensive discussions with both countries, which Tehran had undertaken with the purpose to persuade them to stop their activities (Kharrazi 1998: 3).

Iran welcomed the "13 steps" set out in the final document of the 2000 Review Conference which included a "clear commitment" by the nuclear weapon states to disarm their nuclear arsenals. Iran once again reiterated the view that "nuclear-weapon states have an international obligation to cease the manufacture of nuclear weapons, liquidate all their existing stockpiles and eliminate nuclear weapons and their means of delivery from their national arsenals" (Kharrazi 2000: 3). In the following years, criticism of the non-implementation of these measures was thus fierce. It became much sharper for various reasons: Due to the escalating nuclear crisis and in order to reverse the accusations put forward against Tehran, but also in response to the increasingly hostile US position on nuclear disarmament since George W. Bush had taken office in 2001. During the NPT preparatory conference in April 2003, the USA accused Iran of secretly working on an own nuclear weapons capability. Iran's Deputy Secretary of State Ali Khoshroo responded with a series of sharp rhetorical counter-questions which are a prime example of Iranian naming, blaming, and shaming:

> How many nuclear weapon states other than the United States have prescribed the use of nuclear weapons in conventional conflicts and developed new types of nuclear weapons compatible with its combat scenarios? None. Which other nuclear weapon states have named non-nuclear weapon states parties to the NPT as the targets of their nuclear weapons? None. Which other nuclear weapon states have sought to utilize outer space for nuclear purposes more than the United States? None. How many NPT nuclear weapon states other than the United States have legally rejected the CTBT and practically doomed its future? Why did the United States through its unilateral withdrawal from the ABM and its abrogation of step 7 of the 13 steps threaten the strategic stability of the world? Which NPT party other than the United States has left such a record of undermining so many international instruments, on disarmament and other issues alike? None. (Khoshroo 2003a: 12)

While in the past, Tehran had adhered to the diplomatic practice of not citing individual states by name,[55] a tendency to officially name the USA is observable

[55] An exception is the reference to Israel's suspected nuclear weapon status and the related demand that Israel should abandon its nuclear weapons program and join the NPT as NNWS. During the Iran–Iraq war, there are also repeated passages calling explicitly for Iraq to be condemned. Usually, more general terms such as "the nuclear weapon states" or "a certain nuclear weapon state" are used.

concurrent with the escalating nuclear crisis between Iran and Western states. For example, during the 2005 NPT RevCon, then Foreign Minister Kamal Kharrazi not only complained about the lack of progress in implementing the "13 steps" adopted in 2000, but also officially criticized "that the legacy of Mr. Bolton remains to be pursued and pronounced in this Conference by stressing that the USA does not have particular obligations under Article VI of the treaty" (Iran 2005d: 5). He also accused the nuclear weapon states of having violated the spirit and letter of the NPT: First, by upgrading the role of nuclear weapons in their national security doctrines; second, by reversing the principle of the destruction of nuclear weapons toward their decommissioning; third, by terminating the Anti-Ballistic Missile Treaty; and fourth, by adhering to concepts of nuclear sharing. Kharrazi also mentioned the stationing of nuclear weapons on the territory of third countries, the continued nuclear cooperation with Israel, the rejection of the CTBT, and the blockade of the negotiations on an FMCT. He saw additional indications in the development of new types of nuclear weapons and in the lacking willingeness to negotiate security assurances for non-nuclear weapon states (Kharrazi 2005a). Iran's closing statement, in which then UN ambassador of Iran, Javad Zarif, demanded "[a]ny increase in nuclear capability should equal a reduction in political credibility," made that point even clearer. He obviously blamed the USA for having caused the failure of negotiations through its "obstructionist moves" (Zarif 2005). It is striking that no equivalent mention is made of the modernization programs of the non-Western nuclear weapon states. This could simply be interpreted as an indication of Iran's traditional anti-Americanism. Yet it also shows that Iran's criticism (and particularly its fierceness) is related to the nuclear crisis. In fact, there are indications that Iran's references to double standards and the NWS's hypocrisy, in particular that of the USA, are increasing to the extent that Iran has been accused of violating treaty obligations.

In this vein, an Iranian delegate lamented in 2008:

> Those who hypocritically preach that others should comply are themselves guilty of serious non-compliance in the context of article I, II, IV and VI of the NPT and the agreements reached at the 2000 NPT Review Conference. That has given rise to the pervasive concern that some nuclear-weapon States have no genuine will to accomplish the disarmament part of the NPT bargain. (Al Habib 2008)

In 2010, on the occasion of the "Tehran International Conference on Disarmament and Non-Proliferation," revolutionary leader Khamenei even accused the USA of having committed unforgivable war crimes through the atomic bombing of Hiroshima and Nagasaki ("a major nuclear crime," "the ultimate nuclear offence," Khamenei 2010). At the same conference, Ahmadinejad called for the expulsion of the USA and other nuclear weapon states from the IAEA and the establishment of an international body to implement and monitor the nuclear disarmament process (Al Arabyia 2010; Rajiv 2010). However, this proposal also did not lead to a more far-reaching initiative.

During the 2010 NPT RevCon, Iran put the blame for the failed 2005 RevCon on the disarmament hostility of "certain Nuclear Weapon States" (Iran 2010e), i.e., the USA and France. In a working paper, Iran once again accused the NWS of failing to comply with their treaty obligations,[56] and their adherence to the doctrine of deterrence is described as a threat to humanity:

> The continued existence of thousands of such bombs in the stockpiles of the United States and other nuclear powers has kept the fate of civilization and of humanity itself under horror and panic. By insisting on keeping nuclear bombs or merely decommissioning part of them, nuclear-weapon States themselves are the source of proliferation. As long as one nuclear-weapon State or nuclear power outside of the Treaty insists on maintaining the nuclear option, the other nuclear-weapon States will do the same, and this vicious circle will never end. Thus the non-nuclear-weapon States that have already forgone the nuclear option are rightly asking why these terrible weapons exist. Under what circumstances and for what purpose would the use or threat of use of the world's most destructive mass-terror weapons be justified. (Iran 2010g)

Tehran's vehement criticism continued throughout the conference, clearly surpassing that of the always critical non-aligned states (Johnson 2010). Teheran's fierceness almost led to the failure of the conference, when it rejected the wording of the final declaration because it would paint too "rosy" a picture of disarmament progress (Iran 2010e). Iran was not willing to see President Obama's efforts on "Global Zero" as a positive step toward nuclear disarmament. On the contrary, it felt that since he had entered into office, the US efforts to disarm had continued to diminish.

7.3.5 Practical Activities in Support of Nuclear Disarmament

As already mentioned, Iran is actively engaged in the multilateral disarmament discourse. This is demonstrated by the numerous speeches in the relevant UN bodies: Nuclear disarmament is addressed in almost every statement. Tehran's participation in the 1978, 1982, and 1988 UN special sessions on disarmament and the initiation of the first high-level meeting of the UN General Assembly on disarmament issues in 2013 also demonstrates the importance Iran attaches to the issue. An evaluation of Iran's voting behavior in the First Committee and the UN General Assembly shows that the country continuously supported resolutions dealing with nuclear disarmament. Iran has also occasionally sponsored draft resolutions.

During the NPT preparatory and review conferences, Iranian delegates also called for nuclear disarmament with above-average vigor. Independent observers attest that Iran has a comparatively high degree of activity with regard to nuclear disarmament: For the period from 2007 to 2015, Iran clearly leads the list of speeches on the subject of nuclear disarmament drawn up by the NGO Reaching Critical Will with 38 statements.[57] Since 2002, Iran has also been complying with the transparency measure set

---

[56]The USA, France, and Great Britain are explicitly mentioned, whereas China and Russia are not referred to.

[57]For comparison, here are the quotas of some particularly disarmament friendly countries: Austria 15, Brazil 22, Egypt 20, Germany 10, Ireland 3, Mexico 23, Sweden 8, South Africa 21, New Zealand 24. http://www.reachingcriticalwill.org/resources/profiles, 28 November 2018. For the analysis, I

out in the final document of the 2000 NPT Review Conference, which calls on states to report annually on their implementation of Article VI.[58] The Japanese Center for the Promotion of Disarmament and Non-Proliferation (CPDNP), which has been evaluating state commitment to nuclear disarmament, non-proliferation, and nuclear safety since 2012, places Iran in the lower midfield of all countries analyzed.[59]

In addition to rhetorically reaffirming the nuclear disarmament norm in multilateral forums, Iran undertook some unilateral activities aimed at promoting nuclear disarmament. Not surprisingly, Iran also criticizes the inadequate disarmament practices of the nuclear weapon states on a national level, e.g., in the context of Friday prayers, in speeches by the Supreme Leader or in the form of research work and publications by think tanks close to the government.[60] Rather than providing scientific expertise, these measures are intended to influence international opinion. Two international disarmament and non-proliferation conferences held in 2010 and 2011, for example, stated that they were pursuing the goal "[to] examine the current challenges towards the implementation of nuclear disarmament commitments and finding mechanisms to realize the lofty goal of a nuclear-weapon-free world" (Iran 2010f). In the context of these conferences, Iran presented itself as "a forerunner in the global campaign against nuclear armaments" (Ministry of Foreign Affairs Iran 2010) and continued its criticism of the lack of disarmament practice in the nuclear weapon states. For example, President Ahmadinejad called for future disarmament negotiations to be convened by non-nuclear weapon states such as Iran (Ahmadinejad 2010a). The conference ended with a 12-point communiqué reaffirming several measures geared toward fostering disarmament, i.e., the entry into force of the CTBT and the adoption of a comprehensive, legally binding nuclear weapons convention.[61] A follow-up conference held in June 2011 reflected the setting and central contents

---

have refrained from quantifying the proportion of text passages relating to the issue of nuclear disarmament in comparison with the total amount of text itself. Firstly, the completeness of the data basis could not be guaranteed, as not all documents were accessible (in particular for the early review conferences). Secondly, the analysis showed that Iran referred to this aspect in almost every speech or working paper, thus also placing other issues in the broader context of nuclear disarmament.

[58] See the annual reports on the implementation of Articles VI: Iran (2004, 2005a, 2007b, 2008a, 2009b, 2010f, 2012, 2015a, b, c).

[59] The (rhetorical) commitment to nuclear disarmament is evaluated in the categories "Commitment to achieving a world without nuclear weapons"; "Role and significance of nuclear weapons in the national security strategies and policies"; "CTBT"; "FMCT"; "engagement in research and development for verification of measures of nuclear weapons reductions"; "irreversibility"; "disarmament and non-proliferation education and cooperation with civil society" (Hiroshima Report 2012, 2014). A problem is that in some cases participation in initiatives whose membership is circumscribed to an inclusive circle is also evaluated—which negatively affects the level of Iranian engagement (as well as that of other countries who are excluded from such arrangements).

[60] Examples for publications by governmental think tanks are Shahabi (1994); Zarif et al. (1996) or the overviews on the homepages of the Center for Strategic Research and the Institute for Political and International Studies: http://www.csr.ir/center.aspx?lng=en and http://www.ipis.ir/index.aspx?siteid=9. Accessed 28 November 2018.

[61] See http://cms.mfa.gov.ir/cms/cms/Tehranicd/en/ConclusionofDiscussion. Accessed 2 November 2014.

of the previous year.[62] Both conferences took place in the presence of (selected) civil society (i.e., international disarmament experts and NGOs concerned with the issue), which Iran had invited in advance. Throughout the entire period under investigation, it is striking that Iran—at least rhetorically—seems to be clearly committed toward working together with civil society actors (e.g., Zarif 2005). The country also made repeated attempts to approach international disarmament initiatives and in these contexts to promote its own activities or collaborative proposals which it supported.[63]

7.3.6 Assessment

In conclusion, the rhetorical commitment and practical activities which Iran deployed to foster nuclear disarmament correspond to the indicators for norm entrepreneurship set out in Sect. 5.2.1: Throughout the entire period of analysis, Iran has been committed to strengthening the disarmament norm. Together with like-minded actors, Tehran promoted the implementation of the proposed measures within various institutional forums and at various levels (national, regional, international). Iran expressed its dissatisfaction with the implementation of the disarmament norm by the nuclear weapon states through repeated verbal criticism. Iranian delegates also took every opportunity to denounce the misconduct of the nuclear weapon states, which Tehran considered to be a violation of treaty obligations.

Yet the analysis shows no indication that Iran aimed to undermine current regime structures as suggested by alternative explanation 1. While it made repeated use of naming, shaming, and blaming, these were primarily directed against the lack of disarmament efforts by nuclear weapon states. The country used destructive strategies to underline its demands (e.g., initiation of counter-events, deconstruction of opposing frameworks, verbal provocation, and stigmatization). By that, it wanted to hold the nuclear weapon states accountable and demanded that they act in compliance with the norms—its activities were thus aimed at strengthening the disarmament norm.

This also disproves the validity of alternative explanation 2: Iran's engagement was not merely a reaction to an international norm, which was perceived as a threat to its own autonomy and countered with the formulation of subsidiary norms. It is true that the lack of implementation of Article VI was criticized as hegemonic behavior and power politics of the nuclear weapon states. But rather than being based on alternative normative meanings, Iran's efforts to strengthen the disarmament norm were closely linked to the meaning enshrined in the NPT.

While the case at hand seems to qualify as Iranian norm advocacy, it has to be noted that the norm entrepreneurship was comparatively weak. Iran made use of the typical framing strategies and, in addition, resorted to various practical activities

[62] Key topics were the establishment of a NWFZ in the Middle East and the conference in Helsinki scheduled for 2012. According to participants, the first priority for Iranian government members was to demand Israel's unconditional accession to the NPT; confidential participation report of a Western NGO representative.

[63] Email conversation with a participating scientist 20 July 2011; see also Press TV (2010).

that meet the criteria of norm entrepreneurship. However, in several respects, Iran fulfilled these requirements only weakly during the period of investigation: For example, it participated only selectively in some of the measures aimed at strengthening nuclear disarmament. Iran is one of the most ardent supporters of disarmament within the Non-Aligned Movement and has shown above-average commitment. However, Iran's activities do not stand out from the mass of non-aligned countries and are surpassed, for example, by the proactivism of Egypt, Brazil, Indonesia, Mexico, and South Africa (e.g., Hanson 2012: 57; Wunderlich et al. 2013). This is particularly evident from the fact that the latter are trying to adopt bridge-building positions and are participating in heterogeneous initiatives that specifically seek to overcome the North–South divide by working out consensual solutions. Iran's cooperation with civil society has also been extremely selective—which also has to be alluded to the NGOs themselves, who—for several reasons—often shy away from cooperating with Iran (Westberg 2010). Apparently, some regard it as too risky to endanger their own objectives by cooperating with an alleged norm breaker. That Iran's norm entrepreneurship in this case is rather weak is further underlined by the fact that some proposals put forward by Iran seemed to be mere symbolic politics—they caused a furor in the disarmament debates but were not taken up again. An example is Ahmadinejad's suggestion in 2010 to establish guidelines for the implementation of Article VI.

Does this mean that Iranian norm entrepreneurship is less relevant or even to be disqualified due to competing (and more active) norm entrepreneurs? Or is it irrelevant to the quality of norm entrepreneurship that there are other "competing" actors who are committed to strengthening a norm? These questions will be taken up again in the concluding chapter.

Table 7.3 summarizes Iran's norm entrepreneurship with regard to nuclear disarmament according to the criteria for norm entrepreneurship discussed in Sect. 5.2.1.

7.4 Iran's Advocacy for a Right to Uranium Enrichment

Iran holds the view that the NPT guarantees non-nuclear weapon states a right to the peaceful uses of nuclear energy, including uranium enrichment. While Tehran's advocacy for such a right can be traced back to the Shah era, the formal recognition of this right is a central element of the nuclear negotiations between Iran and the West that started in 2003. Over the years, Iranian diplomats have carefully crafted a "narrative avowing Iran's right to nuclear energy" (Farhi 2009: 3), which is used as justification for the mastery of the full nuclear fuel cycle. At the same time, this right is framed as a central norm of the nuclear non-proliferation regime and as serving the common good of all treaty members. Iran's engagement is not aimed at building a new norm. Rather, Tehran seeks to implement and codify its own interpretation of the norm of technological cooperation (which it claims to be the originally intended meaning of the norm) into the discourse. Eventually, Iran intends to specify the meaning of the norm.

Table 7.3 Overview of the respective characteristics of norm entrepreneurship based on Sell and Prakash (2004: 153) for the case of "nuclear disarmament"

Norm entrepreneur case 2: Iran's commitment to strengthening the norm of nuclear disarmament	
Period	– Demand existed already prior to the establishment of the NPT – Within the NPT: 1979 until today
Trigger (extrinsic/intrinsic)	– No concrete reason; general religious/moral/security concerns against WMD and increasing frustration at the lack of progress in nuclear disarmament by the NWS
Problem definition	– According to Iran the nuclear weapon states are not fulfilling their obligation of Article VI to disarm their arsenals completely and irreversibly under international control – Interim measures until general and complete disarmament has been achieved are not implemented or blocked by NWS
Preferred solution	– Implementation of Article VI by complete abolition of NWS' nuclear arsenals; ideally by adopting a nuclear weapons convention with a certain timeframe – Strengthening Article VI through interim measures, e.g., CTBT, FMCT, transparency measures
Normative framing	– Holding on to the possession of nuclear weapons is immoral, un-Islamic, inhuman, and illegal – The best protection against the use of nuclear weapons is disarmament – Moral responsibility of the international community, in particular the nuclear weapon states which have a special role due to grand bargain enshrined in the NPT; ending double standards
National interests	– National interests in the Middle East (Israel's nuclear status, regional hegemony) – Disarmament as a cover for secret nuclear weapons capabilities? – Political interests: criticism of the USA as the "arch-enemy"
Applied strategies	– Fierce naming, blaming, and shaming as well as emotionalizing language – Rhetorical demands – Public relations – Cooperation with like-minded states and civil society

(continued)

Table 7.3 (continued)

Norm entrepreneur case 2: Iran's commitment to strengthening the norm of nuclear disarmament	
Resources	– Diplomacy – Scientific expertise
Allies	– NAM states – Civil society actors
Normative change?	– Specification of the obligations resulting from Article VI, but not as a credit for Iran's commitment. However, Iran had its share in further inciting displeasure among the non-aligned regarding the NWS' unwillingness to disarm
Substantial change?	– With regard to the specific norms supported by Iran (CTBT and the Nuclear Weapons Convention), no progress can be attributed to Iran's activities
Breaches or doubts about the credibility of the norm entrepreneurship?	– Accusations regarding the establishment of a secret nuclear program associated with violations of safeguards obligations – Inconsistencies regarding perceived or discontinued policy initiatives – Exemplary proposals were not followed by follow-up actions/initiatives

7.4.1 *Background: The Controversy Over the "Inalienable Right to the Peaceful Use of Nuclear Energy"*

In order to make sense of Iran's advocacy, it is necessary to understand the norm dynamics within the nuclear non-proliferation regime, particularly with regard to the controversy surrounding the relative hierarchy and meaning of the NPT's core norms which impose different rights and obligations on the member states:

(1) Articles I and II form the core of the non-proliferation norm: Nuclear weapon states pledge neither to transfer nuclear materials and technologies to non-nuclear weapon states nor to assist them in developing nuclear weapons. NNWS undertake to refrain from acquiring, developing, and possessing nuclear weapons. In order to verify compliance with this obligation, they agree to subject all fissile materials in their possession to IAEA verification measures (safeguards) (Article III, 1).

(2) Article IV acknowledges the "inalienable right" of State Parties to research, develop, and use nuclear energy for peaceful purposes. It also calls for the "fullest possible exchange" of nuclear-related information and technology between NWS and NNWS (norm of technological cooperation). Article III, 2 states that civilian nuclear technology and fissile materials may only be exported to countries which are subject to IAEA safeguards.

(3) Finally, in Article VI, State Parties commit themselves to pursuing nuclear disarmament.

Originally, treaty negotiations focused on curbing the spread of nuclear weapons. Nuclear disarmament and technological cooperation in the civilian uses of nuclear technology were not mentioned in the early drafts between the Soviet Union and the USA (on the history of negotiations, see Shaker 1980: vol. 1–3). However, the NNWS demanded concessions for the renunciation of a nuclear option and for voluntary submission to the IAEA inspection regime. In return, NWS were required to commit themselves to disarming their arsenals and facilitating exchange and cooperation in the realm of civilian uses of nuclear energy. This was meant to prevent the NPT enshrining a policy of "nuclear apartheid" (Singh 1998). Consequently, Article IV codifies the "inalienable right of all the Parties to the treaty to develop research, production and use of nuclear energy for peaceful purposes without discrimination and in conformity with Articles I and II". State Parties agree to "facilitate, and have the right to participate in, the fullest possible exchange of equipment, materials and scientific and technological information for the peaceful uses of nuclear energy". Furthermore, member states are requested to cooperate with the aim of further developing the use of nuclear energy for peaceful purposes. Particular reference is made to the "needs of the developing regions of the world".[64]

There is disagreement, especially with regard to the meaning and scope of the provisions formulated in Article IV (Franceschini 2012), particularly as to whether "research, production and use of nuclear energy" includes a legal right to access enrichment and reprocessing (ENR) technology. Attempts by non-nuclear weapon states to explicitly include language on such provisions in the treaty text were not successful (Shaker 1980: 293–299). Against this background, it has been argued that there is no right to uranium enrichment (and reprocessing) simply because the treaty does not explicitly refer to it (e.g., Ford 2009; Makovsky and Misztal 2012; Sherman 2013). Others counter that what is not explicitly prohibited is allowed (e.g., Joyner 2013: 289; Beeman 2013).[65]

The controversy also affects the implementation of the norm of technological cooperation. Questions arise as to what extent technologically advanced states are obliged to make sensitive technologies available and under which conditions nuclear exports are to take place. Supporters of a rather restrictive interpretation of Article IV call into question the existence of an unconditional legal right to enrichment and reprocessing technologies. Basically, three "camps" can be distinguished:

---

[64] Apart from the discriminatory division into nuclear haves and have-nots, a second asymmetry of the NPT is that about three dozen states possess sophisticated nuclear capabilities, while those of the majority of treaty members are limited (Franceschini 2012: 3). This is why it is particularly important for the latter to implement the arrangements set out in Article IV, i.e., to enable cooperation. Controversies reign especially with regard to the scope of trade in civilian nuclear energy.

[65] Confusion results from the fact that the "inalienable right" formulated in Article IV is conditional upon the State Party behaving in conformity with the obligations set out in Articles I and II: These prohibit the parties from any activities aimed at the acquisition or production of nuclear weapons. In particular, it is contested which measures already violate the requirement laid down in Article II not to "manufacture or acquire nuclear weapons or other nuclear explosive devices".

(1) The majority of states hold the view that compliant NPT member states may develop full fuel cycle capabilities for peaceful purposes. In the 1970s, this position was particularly advocated by Western nuclear energy countries, including Germany (Fey et al. 2014). Indeed, Article IV, paragraph 2 links the "inalienable right" to the peaceful uses of nuclear energy to behavior in "accordance with Articles I and II," which prohibit State Parties to produce, acquire, and proliferate nuclear weapons. Conversely, deviant NPT members forfeit these rights. Yet, it is unclear who decides about compliance or/non-compliance: Some NPT members, particularly those belonging to the Non-Aligned Movement (Potter and Mukhatzhanova 2012: 104), argue that a state's legal right of access to sensitive technologies depends solely on the IAEA's judgment, i.e., if it could be proven beyond any doubt that a country had violated its safeguards agreement with the IAEA or its NPT commitments. A precedent for proponents of this position occurred in November 2006, when the IAEA rejected a request for technical assistance from Iran and suspended a great deal of its cooperation program with the country with reference to doubts about Iran's compliance with its NPT obligations and violations of UN resolutions (Boureston and Lacey 2007). Other states, e.g., those belonging to the Nuclear Suppliers Group (NSG), hold that the decision to grant access to sensitive technologies ought to be the matter of the respective exporting country. Since 1977, members of the NSG are obliged to exercise restraint when trading in ENR technologies (Strulak 1993: 3).

(2) The US government favors a particularly strict model of "technology governance" (Franceschini 2012: 6). According to this view, Article IV contains some legal loopholes that non-nuclear weapon states could exploit to develop military capabilities under the guise of civilian use of nuclear energy. They therefore demand strict trade restrictions for proliferation-related technologies and materials (e.g., Ford 2009: 24). In 1978, the USA supported by several Western countries decided that nuclear trade would only be conducted with countries whose activities would be subject to full-scope safeguards of the IAEA. Several other measures were introduced that aimed at restricting trade in sensitive technologies (Müller et al. 2013: 56). Today, the USA still follows a restrictive approach in the form of bilateral trade agreements and measures for the export of ENR technologies within the NSG (e.g., Müller et al. 2014: 27). In light of these policies, "the Bush administration distorted the nature of the peaceful uses pillar to make it appear as a gift rather than an obligation" (Graham 2012: 138). In 2004, George W. Bush even proposed that NSG members should "limit access to and control of sensitive technologies to an exclusive group of established technology owners" (Bush 2004). Ultimately, this attempt to reinterpret Article IV (Lantis 2015; Tannenwald 2013) failed—Bush abandoned his position during his second term of office. The proposal had created too much resistance, especially among non-aligned NSG members such as Argentina, Brazil, and South Africa.

(3) A third "camp" argues that a country's right to enrichment depends on its needs. Accordingly, only non-nuclear-weapon states with large nuclear energy pro-

grams would have a right to access ENR technologies. All other cases, i.e., enrichment or reprocessing without requirements, are seen by proponents of this position as an indication of military intentions (e.g., Singh 2014).

The view that access to ENR technologies should be subject to certain conditions is particularly contested by the non-aligned NNWS, who refer to national sovereignty rights and the right to development. In their view, enrichment and reprocessing should be regarded as unconditional, i.e., truly "inalienable" rights of all NPT member states and therefore non-negotiable. They interpret Article IV as entailing an obligation to cooperate, which legally obliges nuclear advanced states to facilitate trade in dual-use goods. What is today a position of the developing countries has historically been of concern to Western holders of nuclear technology. The attempt by the USA to strictly limit access to and trade in sensitive nuclear goods and technologies was regarded as illegal and discriminatory by countries such as Germany and Belgium (Shaker 1980: 293–299; Müller et al. 2013: 55–56; Fey et al. 2014). Today, it is primarily non-aligned countries that reject restrictive export control regimes, proposals to limit access to ENR technologies, and considerations on the multilateralization of the fuel cycle (Joyner 2011: 59). While only few of them support Iran's position that export controls in and of itself are to be rejected as discriminatory means, most NAM states accept measures such as making export conditional upon the acceptance of full-scope safeguards. Yet their argumentation rests on their belief that Article IV entails an inherent right to the full fuel cycle and that the development of ENR technologies is a matter of national sovereignty. Accordingly, it must not be made dependent on the credibility of their respective nuclear energy policies or withdrawn on the pretext of non-compliance (Franceschini 2012: 6–7; Tannenwald 2013: 306–308).

Despite the political and scientific controversy that has been simmering for years, the international community has so far failed to reach consensus on "Nuclear Technology Rights and Wrongs" (Ford 2009). In this context, Iran's persistent commitment to a right to uranium enrichment can be seen as an attempt to contribute to the specification of Article IV.

7.4.2 Iran's Narrative of "Nuclear Rights" in the Context of Its Nuclear Program

Iran's advocacy for the right to the full use of peaceful nuclear energy, including sensitive technologies, can be traced back to pre-revolutionary times and is closely linked to the development of indigenous nuclear capabilities.[66] Shah Reza Pahlavi aspired to transform his country into a model of modernity (Pahlavi 1968: 132–133).

[66] Iran is not the only country that interprets Article IV of the NPT as entailing an inherent right to enrichment and reprocessing. Today, Brazil, Mexico, and Romania in particular share this concern. During the treaty negotiations, Western countries such as Belgium, Germany, Italy, and Switzerland had spoken out in favor of more explicit language (Shaker 1980: 293–299). Back then, Iran was not yet a member of the negotiation forum and thus did not participate.

At a time when nuclear energy was considered synonymous with scientific progress and an expression of "Western" lifestyle (which the Shah desperately tried to imitate; Patrikarakos 2012: 43), Iran initiated a comprehensive nuclear energy program in 1957. The West, especially the USA, played a major role in the development of Iran's nuclear infrastructure. After Iran had promised to use the supplied materials and technologies exclusively for peaceful purposes, comprehensive civilian nuclear cooperation began in 1974 covering technical assistance as well as the supply of enriched uranium. With the support of various foreign suppliers, Iran slowly developed its own capacities and nuclear expertise and soon began exploration of national uranium reserves (Etemad 1987: 205)—the first stage of the fuel cycle. The Shah (and the revolutionary regime that succeeded him) justified the nuclear program with reference to economic reasons, energy diversification, the necessity to keep up with technological progress, and an expression of national sovereignty (Pahlavi 1968: 307–308; Etemad 1987: 209–210; Ministry of Foreign Affairs of Iran 1994: 242).

According to Akbar Etemad, the first president of the AEOI and "father of Iran's nuclear program" (Nufer 2012), the Shah had been interested in building his own fuel cycle, which he saw as a sovereign right, from the start (Etemad 1987: 222). The foundations of Iran's narrative of nuclear rights can already be found in early speeches by Iranian delegates during NPT and IAEA conferences. Statements contain repeated references to the importance of Article IV, the inclusion of which in the treaty document constituted the necessary condition for developing countries to accede to the treaty (Ameri 1975: 269; Fartash 1975). Iran placed particular hope in the IAEA, the primary task of which was perceived to be to support the member states in their use of civil nuclear energy. Importantly, the Shah regime advanced the view that trade in civilian nuclear materials and technologies should only be made with countries that accepted IAEA safeguards (Pirseyedi 2013: 119).

The language used by the Shah regime can be described as moderate when compared with that of the Islamic regime that was to follow. Back then, systematic and repeated references to the "inalienable right to the peaceful uses of nuclear energy" were almost completely lacking. This is surprising given the fact that the cooperation granted to the Shah by the West was not unlimited. Concerned about a risk of proliferation, the USA was skeptical about Iran acquiring domestic ENR capacities right from the start. It therefore insisted that additional bilateral controls be carried out in addition to IAEA safeguards (Milani 2010). Indeed, the AEOI not only began to explore uranium mining and research on laser enrichment in 1976; the Shah had also expressed interest in plutonium reprocessing. Eventually, however, he gave in to Western pressure and refrained from establishing a national ENR program, even though rhetorically, he adhered to the idea of an inherent right (Milani 2010).

With the 1979 Islamic Revolution, nuclear cooperation with the West came to an abrupt end (Etemad 1987: 208), although nuclear research, particularly with regard to the exploration of uranium deposits as well as mining and conversion continued (partly without informing the IAEA). The USA stopped supplying highly enriched uranium and in subsequent years thwarted various cooperation projects between Iran and non-Western supplier countries (e.g., Argentina or China).

Due to the increased demand for energy and the efforts to further expand national technical and scientific expertise on nuclear issues, the nuclear program was officially relaunched in 1982. The Iranian regime, which due to its radical stance faced international isolation, tried in vain to win cooperation partners for the completion of its nuclear infrastructure. The start of a national enrichment program in 1985 has been justified by Iran as a reaction to the systematic denial of access to nuclear technology by the West.[67]

From that time on, the nuclear program became an integral part of the self-definition of the Islamic Republic (Patrikarakos 2012: 169). For the revolutionary regime, it was a symbol of resistance against Western hegemony. 1985 was the first time that Iran in a speech at the IAEA General Conference referred to its "inalienable" right to a civil nuclear energy program explaining

> [...] that *all countries had the right to plan, implement and develop peaceful nuclear programmes*, having regard to their own resources, needs and priorities, and that they had likewise *an absolute and unlimited right of access to supplies, services and know-how in the domain of nuclear science and technology.* [...] All States should respect the rights and decisions of others relating to fuel cycle programs as well as the policies adopted by others for the peaceful use of nuclear energy; the conditions for the transfer of technology for the peaceful use of nuclear energy should not be incompatible with the independence and sovereignty of countries wishing to benefit from that technology. (Amrollahi 1984; my emphasis)

Due to international trade restrictions, Iran turned to the network of Pakistani nuclear scientist Abdul Qadeer Khan from which it purchased blueprints and components for gas centrifuge enrichment plants. From 1987 to 1993, Tehran secretly conducted intensive research and development in the field of centrifuge technology.[68] Since official Western procurement channels were denied, the regime sought nuclear technology cooperation with China and—after Beijing had succumbed to American pressure—with Russia until it was stopped in 1995 (Patrikarakos 2012: 196–204).

In 2002, an Iranian opposition group, the *People's Mujahedin*, revealed that the regime had already begun construction of a heavy-water reactor in Arak and an enrichment plant in Natanz during the 1990s.[69] In subsequent years, it became apparent that Iran had over a longer period of time and repeatedly violated its Safeguards Agreement with the IAEA (for an overview El Baradei 2011: Chaps. 5, 9, 11, 12).[70] Although the country continued to adhere to the rhetoric of peaceful uses of nuclear

[67] See http://nuclearenergy.ir/history/. Accessed 2 November 2014. Unfortunately, the web site has now been put offline, but it can be reconstructed via Internet archives such as the Wayback Machine (https://web.archive.org/).

[68] Iran justified its behavior by saying that the centrifuges had been used to produce fuel for the operation of the Bushehr reactor, which at that time had been destroyed by Iraqi attacks. See nuclearenergy.ir/history. Accessed 2 November 2014 or Amrollahi (1986) and Soltanieh (2008).

[69] This is not illegal in itself, but falls within Article IV, which allows research, production, and use of nuclear energy for peaceful purposes. However, under the IAEA Safeguards Agreement, Iran would have been obliged to inform the organization of the facility, at least 90 days before it was to be equipped with nuclear materials. After the revelation, Tehran argued that there was no such reporting obligation and that it had intended to inform the IAEA later that year (IAEA 2003).

[70] For an overview of IAEA reports on Iran's nuclear program see http://www.iaea.org/newscenter/focus/iran/iaea-and-iran-iaea-reports. Accessed 28 April 2017.

energy, doubts arose due the lacking economic rationale for the nuclear program, a deteriorating regional security context, and increased arms expenditures and political threats by Iran. There was also growing concern about Tehran's intentions because efforts to clarify the situation were blocked by Iran with political maneuvering and deception (El Baradei 2011: Chap. 5).[71]

Ultimately, the USA and Europe sought to persuade Iran to abandon its enrichment program.[72] Beginning in 2003, the IAEA Board of Governors had adopted several resolutions calling on Iran to suspend all enrichment and reprocessing activities until outstanding questions on the military dimension of its program had been resolved. In 2006, the Security Council also imposed a comprehensive sanctions regime, including travel restrictions, trade embargoes, and financial measures. It also contained references to Chapter VII of the UN Charter, should Iran fail to comply with the required enrichment stop (Davenport 2012). In February 2008, the IAEA announced that there was no evidence that Iran was still working on a military dimension (IAEA 2008). Similarly, a report by the US National Intelligence Council in December 2007 concluded that it was "highly likely" that Iran had maintained a nuclear weapons program until the fall of 2003 but "almost certainly" had not re-started it (New York Times 2007).

The revelation of undeclared nuclear activities not only provoked the ongoing crisis between Iran and the West. It also prompted Iran to demand and promote the right to uranium enrichment even more intensively than before. Faced with accusations that its nuclear program violated international law, President Khatami launched a massive campaign, which linked elements of Iran's argumentation into a systematic narrative of nuclear rights. Iran's quest to control the complete fuel cycle was basically framed as a legitimate and unconditional right of a member state of the NPT. In Iran's view, the nuclear activities undertaken were within the civilian uses of nuclear energy permitted by the NPT. Enrichment and reprocessing were not explicitly prohibited in the NPT and were therefore allowed. In 2004, Khatami demanded "that our right to enrichment be recognized by the international community because it is our legal right and in accordance with the Nuclear Nonproliferation Treaty" (quoted after Fathi 2004). IAEA and UN Security Council resolutions calling on Iran to suspend its enrichment activities were regarded as violating Article IV and as a means to deny Iran "a natural right to possess the fuel cycle" (Rouhani 2005).

The issue of enrichment soon became the crux of the multilateral nuclear negotiations that lasted for more than ten years. The tension between the West's desire to put

[71] It took almost six months for the IAEA to gain access to the facilities in Arak and Natanz. In the years that followed, Iran withheld information and used tactical maneuvering. In the course of the attempts to clarify the situation, even more dubious activities came to light, e.g., the supply of construction plans for P-2 centrifuges by the Khan network (IAEA 2004a) or experiments with polonium-210, which can trigger a chain reaction necessary for a nuclear explosion (Patrikarakos 2012: 280–281.

[72] How to achieve that aim was contested. While Europe pleaded for diplomacy, Washington favored strong condemnation and a referral of the case to the UN Security Council. In the eyes of some Europeans, by resuming enrichment activities, Iran had not violated its NPT commitments but the safeguards agreement with the IAEA (El Baradei 2011: Chap. 9; Patrikarakos 2012: 255–263).

a halt to Iran's enrichment program and Iran's insistence on the formal recognition of a right to uranium enrichment was already evident in the first phase of negotiations between Iran and the EU3 (France, Germany, and the UK). The "Tehran Declaration" of October 2003, in which Iran agreed to temporarily suspend all enrichment and reprocessing activities and to sign and voluntarily implement the IAEA Additional Protocol (BBC 2003), put on the record a vague right of Iran to develop civilian nuclear energy within the framework of the NPT. However, the text remained as vague as the NPT on the question of what exactly this right entailed. In the "Paris Agreement" of November 2004, the three European states reaffirmed their readiness "[to] recognize Iran's right under the NPT exercised in conformity with its obligations under the treaty, without discrimination" (IAEA 2004b). In return, Iran agreed to suspend all enrichment and reprocessing activities from mid-2004 to July 2005 and reaffirmed its willingness to cooperate and allow inspections by the IAEA.[73] Yet the West, especially the USA, continued to demand "zero enrichment" and in August 2005 called on Tehran "not to pursue fuel cycle activities other than the construction and operation of light water power and research reactors" (Governments of France, Germany and United Kingdom 2005). All attempts to resolve the dispute over Iran's nuclear program by diplomatic means eventually failed because the positions regarding the right to uranium enrichment seemed irreconcilable: Tehran insisted on the formal recognition of its narrowly defined nuclear rights and refused to give up uranium enrichment altogether. The West was not willing to let this happen (Mousavian 2013).[74]

During the presidency of Ahmadinejad, Iran's position became even more rigid. In light of the lack of progress in the negotiations, the political leadership criticized the concessions to the West, suspended the IAEA Additional Protocol until Iran's right to the peaceful uses of nuclear energy was recognized (Patrikarakos 2012: 309), and resumed uranium enrichment in 2006 (the decision had already been made during Khatami's term of office). At that time, all Security Council members plus Germany ("EU3+3") were involved in the negotiations to resolve the nuclear crisis with Iran.

In Iran, the nuclear program had long since acquired symbolic status. Notwithstanding disagreement as to the concrete negotiation strategies, there was broad political consensus regarding the claim to a legal right to the full fuel cycle (Farhi 2009: 4). In April 2006, Tehran finally achieved a breakthrough in uranium enrichment up to 3.5%. President Ahmadinejad proudly announced "Iran has joined the

---

[73]In the meantime, Iran's nuclear program continued to make progress. In 2005, Rouhani, the chief negotiator at the time, admitted that Iran had entered into concessions only in areas in which there were no more technical problems. The main aim had been to gain time in order to make progress in mastering the full fuel cycle and to prevent a referral to the UN Security Council (Rouhani 2005).

[74]A nuclear proposals timeline published on the government-related Web site http://nuclearnenergy.ir shows that "Recognition of Right to Enrichment" was a recurring element of Iran's negotiating position; http://nuclearenergy.ir/wp-content/uploads/2013/11/negotiationsfinal.jpg. Accessed 2 November 2014. Apart from agreements in October 2003, February and November 2004, however, offers from the West did not include the required recognition so that Tehran refused the proposals. In addition, the USA has long called for a ban on enrichment as a precondition for negotiations. Iran, on the other hand, was at best willing to accept a (temporary) suspension as a result of negotiations.

club of nuclear countries" (quoted in CNN 2006) and declared that the country would continue to expand its enrichment activities. The government declared the day as "National Day of Nuclear Technology" and placed it in the context of the fight against discrimination. In the words of then president Ahmadinejad: "[Western nations] have tried their utmost to prevent Iran from going nuclear, but Iran has gone nuclear. [....] Nobody will be able to stop it" (Ahmadinejad quoted according to Deutsche Welle 2013). The slogan "Nuclear energy is our inalienable right" became the mantra of the entire Iranian population (Vick 2012). The right to uranium enrichment had become a question of national identity.

In a gesture of goodwill, Iran informed the IAEA of the existence of a hitherto unknown underground uranium enrichment plant in Fordo in 2009. Yet when the request to the IAEA for the supply of 20% enriched uranium for medical purposes and a suggestion to exchange reactor fuel with Russia failed, Iran announced in February 2010 that it planned to enrich uranium to 20% (Patrikarakos 2012: 353). During the 8th NPT Review Conference in May 2010, Tehran unexpectedly agreed to a fuel swap deal arranged by Turkey and Brazil. In a joint declaration, Iran agreed to hand over 1200 kg of low enriched uranium to Turkey and to receive 120 kg of 20% enriched uranium in exchange from the USA, Russia, France, and the IAEA (Iran et al. 2010). The statement even referred to "the right of all State Parties, including the Islamic Republic of Iran, to develop research, production, and use of nuclear energy (as well as nuclear fuel cycle including enrichment activities) for peaceful purposes without discrimination" (Iran et al. 2010).

However, as the West continued to insist on zero enrichment, this agreement also failed. As a result, neither UN resolutions nor a tightened sanctions regime or acts of sabotage (such as the Stuxnet cyberattack) prevented Iran from steadily expanding its enrichment program from 2009 to 2012. In 2010 and 2011, negotiations between Iran and the EU3+3 again failed because Tehran made unlimited access to the full fuel cycle and the right to uranium enrichment a precondition for any negotiated solution.

In 2012, for the first time, the West offered Iran the prospect of "allowing" enrichment at a low level (Richter 2012). With the inauguration of President Hassan Rouhani (who had been chief negotiator in the nuclear dispute from 2003 to 2005), new hopes were awakened for a solution to the nuclear crisis. In 2013, after decades of hostility, direct bilateral talks between Iran and the USA took place for the first time. In November 2013, the negotiating parties reached a milestone on the way to a solution to the nuclear conflict: Iran and the EU3+3 agreed on the so-called "Geneva Action Plan" (EEAS 2013). As a result, in April 2015, Iran agreed to substantially reduce its nuclear program and to implement far-reaching transparency measures (e.g., limiting the extent and degree of enrichment and verification). In return, the EU and the USA wanted to gradually relax sanctions. There were, however, differences of opinion as to how the text of the agreement relates to Iran's right to uranium enrichment. The wording does not explicitly recognize a legal claim. It simply states: "a comprehensive solution [...] would involve a mutually defined enrichment program with mutually agreed parameters" (EEAS 2010: 4). Nevertheless, Iranian government representatives celebrated the agreement as a milestone. In a television address, President Rouhani declared: "Iran's right to uranium enrichment on its soil was accepted in this nuclear deal by world powers. Let anyone make his own reading, but this right is clearly stated in the text of the agreement that Iran can continue its enrichment" (Rouhani, quoted in USIP 2013b). President Obama, on the other hand, reaffirmed: "In terms of the end state, we do not recognize a right for Iran to enrich uranium" (quoted in USIP 2013a). And Secretary of State John Kerry confirmed this position: "There is no right to enrich. We do not recognize a right to enrich. It is clear, in the […] NPT […] it's very, very [clear] that there is no right to enrich" (quoted in Blake 2013).

At the end of July 2015, the negotiating parties finally succeeded in reaching a "Joint Comprehensive Plan of Action" (JCPOA). The comprehensive action plan not only marked the breakthrough in the crisis surrounding Iran's nuclear program. It can also be interpreted as an at least implicit success of Tehran's efforts to gain a recognition of its right to uranium enrichment. In fact, the agreement represents a win–win situation for both sides: For the first time, Iran agreed to massive concessions which severely limit its nuclear energy programs and practically rule out the path to a nuclear bomb (e.g., Kerry 2017).[75] In return, the agreement holds that the "successful implementation of this JCPOA will enable Iran to fully enjoy its right to nuclear energy for peaceful purposes […], and the Iranian nuclear programme will be treated in the same manner as that of any other non-nuclear weapon state party to the NPT" (JCPOA 2015: 3). With that formulation, the West "accepted Iran's right to a peaceful use of nuclear energy and thus also the right to enrich uranium and agreed to the suspension of sanctions" (Nirumand 2015). Iranian politicians also interpret the agreement in this sense. The government stated: "After 22 months, the government consolidated Iran's right to enrichment" (The Guardian 2015). The subsequent UN Resolution 2231 of 20 July 2015 formally codified Iran's right to uranium enrichment and was interpreted as another means of recognition (Zarif 2015). While the JCPOA was specifically tailored to solve the Iranian nuclear crisis, it is safe to assume that it has broader implications (see already Meier 2014).

7.4.3 Normative Framing at the International Level

While Iran's advocacy for nuclear rights has to be seen in the context of its own nuclear program, Iran's engagement goes beyond the domestic context and is explicitly embedded in a common-good-oriented normative framework.

[75] Iran agreed to reduce the number of centrifuges from 190,000 to 6000 for a period of six years; to keep only 300 kg of the 12,000 kg enriched uranium in the country over a period of 15 years; to modify the heavy-water reactor Arak, so that it becomes unusable for weapons purposes; to suspend enrichment in the Fordo underground research facility for a period of 15 years and use centrifuges only for research purposes. It is allowed to retain Natanz as the only enrichment facility and to enrich uranium to only 3.67% over a period of 15 years. The agreement also provides for comprehensive IAEA verification measures. In addition, Iran agrees to allow inspections of military installations, subject to certain conditions. In the preamble, Tehran also renounces forever the development or acquisition of nuclear weapons. This obligation is unprecedented and goes beyond the provisions of the NPT, which in Article X contains a withdrawal clause (Müller 2015).

At the international level, especially within the IAEA and the NPT, Iran demands unhindered access to peaceful nuclear technology, including uranium enrichment: Whereas Article IV of the NPT is seen as providing the legal framework, the IAEA is considered responsible for facilitating the widest possible exchange and cooperation in this field. Consequently, from 1975 onwards, Iran regularly refers to the relevance of Article IV and the importance of the IAEA's technical assistance program in both forums (e.g., Fartash 1975; Amrollahi 1983; Nasseri 1990b; Amrollahi 1994; Kharrazi 2000; Iran 2010g). As indicated in the previous section, Iran assumes that as a member of the NPT, it has a legitimate right to master the full fuel cycle, including enrichment and reprocessing. Iranian delegates also claim that the NPT in Article IV, paragraph 2 obliges nuclear developed countries to cooperate with the respective materials and technologies and they frame this provision as a matter of equitable justice and a moral requirement (Fartash 1975; Amrollahi 1985; Nasseri 1990a; Ayatollahi 1995a; Kharrazi 2000; Iran 2010d). The "inalienable right" is interpreted as an inherent right that is unconditional and non-negotiable, and of which a state cannot be deprived. That speeches uttered during the reign of the Shah lack systematic references to a legal right to the peaceful uses of nuclear energy can probably be explained by the fact that at that time, nuclear cooperation with the West was relatively unhindered.

Iran opposes trade restrictions imposed by strict export control measures based on a restrictive interpretation of Article IV, which it regards as a politically and economically motivated violation of the "spirit and letter of the NPT" (Aghazadeh 2004). Non-proliferation measures designed to limit the risk of proliferation of sensitive technologies are regarded as a reinterpretation of treaty norms and an attack on inherent rights. For example, a working paper presented by Iran to the NPT Review Conference in 2005 states: "The interpreting of Article IV in a way that limits the rights derived from this Article to mere 'benefits of nuclear energy' is clearly in contravention of the very wording of the treaty and is totally unacceptable" (Iran 2005c: 3). Besides being illegal, the denial of "nuclear rights" is also regarded as discriminatory. In 2010, President Ahmadinejad complained that

> none of the non-nuclear weapon States has ever been able to exercise their inalienable and legal rights for peaceful uses of nuclear energy without facing pressures and threats. [...] One of the gravest injustices committed by the nuclear weapon States is equating nuclear arms with nuclear energy. As a matter of fact, they want to monopolize both the nuclear weapons and the peaceful nuclear energy, and by doing so to impose their will on the international community. The aforementioned issues are all against the spirit of the NPT and in flagrant violation of its provisions. (Ahmadinejad 2010b)

Consequently, from Tehran's point of view, all NPT treaty members should benefit equally from the exchange and cooperation in the peaceful use of nuclear energy. In fact, as an Iranian delegate put it during the IAEA General Conference on 1991 "[t]he so-called 'new world order' could only be meaningful if mankind were able to benefit from the progress of technology without prejudice. All men should have an equal share in the benefits of modern technologies and [...] in their potential risks" (Amrollahi 1991: 31). Against this background, Iran stylizes itself as fighting for collective concerns and embeds its argumentation in a collective action frame that is particularly shared by non-aligned countries. Indeed, Tehran sees itself as "a model depicting the capability of a nation to resist pressure, to preserve independence, and to break the scientific monopoly of some arrogant powers," as the Vice President and Chairman of the Iranian nuclear energy organization, Dr. Fereydoun Abbasi, declared to the IAEA in 2012 (Abbasi 2012). In order to make up for their delayed development, developing countries are regarded as particularly dependent on cooperation in the civilian uses of nuclear technology. Contrary to its own rhetoric of fair treatment, Iran therefore calls for preferential access rights to be granted to these countries (e.g., Amrollahi 1985, Soltanieh 1990a; Iran 2000a, 2005c). Iran has also repeatedly demanded that special assistance funds be set up by the IAEA and urges the Director-General of the organization to report on the implementation of technology transfers—the denial of which Iran considers to be a violation of Article IV.[76]

In its argumentation, Iran repeatedly refers to metanorms, such as the right to development and national sovereignty. Time and again, Iranian delegates demanded that the international community "[respect] the national choices, decisions and policies of all States Parties to work in all safeguarded nuclear activities, including fuel cycle without discrimination" (Iran 2010d: 4). The same formulation can be found in joint declarations of the NAM, in their respective national statements, but also in final documents of past NPT Review Conferences. References to the right to economic and technological development are even more frequent. For example, in 2005 Kharrazi declared that "[t]he inalienable right of the States to develop nuclear technology for peaceful purposes emanates from the universally accepted proposition that scientific and technological achievements are the common heritage of mankind" (Kharrazi 2005b: 4). In a speech to the UN General Assembly, President Ahmadinejad even linked scientific and technological development with human rights:

> How can one talk about human rights and at the same time blatantly deny many the inalienable right to have access to science and technology with applications in medicine, industry and energy and through force and intimidation hinder their progress and development? Can nations be deprived of scientific and technological progress through the threat of use of force and based on mere allegations of possibility of military diversion? We believe that all countries and nations are entitled to technological and scientific advancement in all fields, particularly the peaceful technology to produce nuclear fuel. Such access cannot be restricted to a few, depriving most nations and by establishing economic monopolies, use them as an instrument to expand their domination. (Ahmadinejad 2005)

What appears to be a rhetoric of self-assertion on the domestic level can be perceived of as an element in the discursive counter-hegemonic struggle against imperialism. Restrictive non-proliferation measures are interpreted by Iran as attempts by industrialized countries to create a monopoly on the production of nuclear fuel—a strategic and critical commodity (Aghazadeh 2006). In a speech to the IAEA, Head

[76]While Iran was initially open to the possibility of multilateral fuel arrangements (e.g., Amrollahi 1986), it became increasingly skeptical about such considerations. Even against the background of its own experience, Tehran argues that one cannot rely on international promises. In 2010, then Iranian IAEA ambassador Soltanieh described plans to establish fuel banks as "nuclear apartheid" (quoted in CNN 2010) which would further exacerbate already existing discrimination.

of the Iranian nuclear energy organization Abbasi describes Iran's uranium enrichment capabilities as "an intellectual gift to all humanitarian nations in the world and a beginning to peaceful cooperation aimed at human beings' welfare and health" (Abbasi 2012).

Figure 7.1 shows how often Iranian delegates linked the "inherent right to the peaceful uses of nuclear energy" to specific framings such as "injustice/discrimination," "technological/scientific development," "national sovereignty," "counter-hegemonic resistance," "security," and "national interests" in NPT and IAEA speeches in the period under investigation (total number: 163).[77]

The demand for access to Iran's full fuel cycle was most frequently framed as an inherent right to be granted unconditionally (122 mentions).[78] The legal claim is often linked to justice-based arguments and to the norm of technological cooperation, which (in Tehran's view) stems from Article IV of the NPT (injustice/discrimination 59, technological/economic development 46 mentions).

The claim to a legal right was least often backed with security-related or interest-based arguments (2 and 1 mention, respectively). Ultimately, it is always in the national interest to demand the right to civilian use of nuclear energy. However, the analysis shows that this motive is firmly embedded in normative reasoning aimed to foster the common good. It is striking that Iran's advocacy for a right to uranium enrichment within the IAEA and NPT intensified in parallel to the escalating nuclear crisis. Some experts see this connection as an indication that Iran's commitment

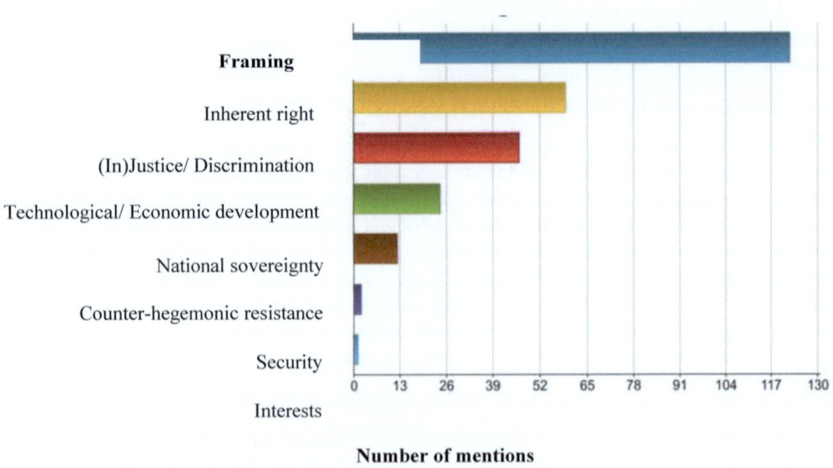

Fig. 7.1 Frequency of thematic links between the legal claim to peaceful uses of nuclear energy in the analyzed NPT and IAEA documents

[77]This figure does not claim to be complete, as I did not have access to all statements/documents issued by Iran. For the analysis, I drew on verbatim records provided by Iran where possible. In some cases, especially for the early NPT documents, only summary records were available.

[78]The coding scheme is available upon request.

is mainly motivated by interests (e.g., Farhi 2009; Tabatabai 2012, 2014). However, Iran has advocated this right since the Shah's time and justified its advocacy above all with common-good- and justice-related arguments. The frequency with which Iran sought to strengthen the "inalienable right of all State Parties to nuclear technology for peaceful purposes without discrimination" (Iran 2010d) through activation in speeches and working papers rose sharply over the period of investigation parallel to the beginning of the nuclear crisis (2003), as Fig. 7.2 illustrates.[79]

As the nuclear crisis intensified, the passages justifying the Iranian enrichment program as an exercise of "sacred rights" grew longer, increasingly specifying the scope of Article IV from Tehran's point of view. For example, a working paper presented at the 2005 NPT Review Conference states:

> 'Peaceful purposes' is the only limit the Treaty lays on the exercise of the inalienable right of States parties to nuclear energy. Neither the NPT negotiations nor the text of the Treaty even slightly imply any limit on any specific field of nuclear technology, including the enrichment and fuel cycle fields. The practice of the States parties is also a confirmation of this understanding of the Treaty. (Iran 2005c)

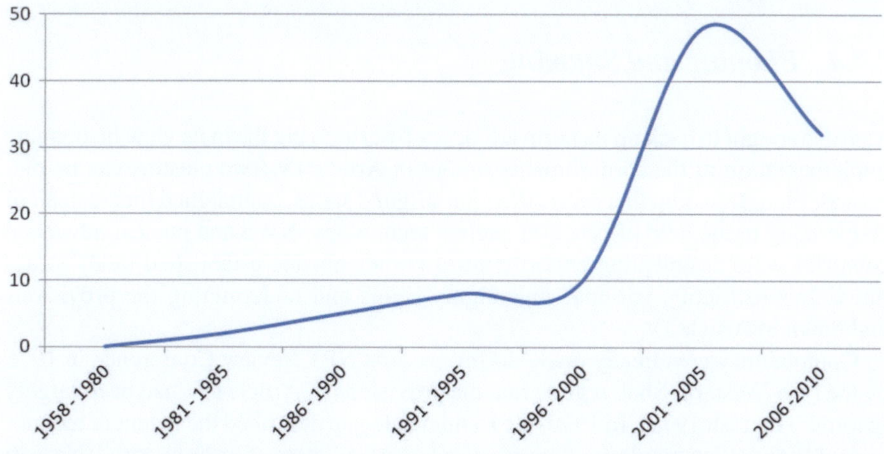

Fig. 7.2 Verbal references to the "inalienable right" to the peaceful uses of nuclear energy (number of mentions from 1958 to 2010)

[79]The figure shows this trend over time. The comparability of the primary data is only limited: During the NPT Review Conferences, which are held periodically every five years, a large number of speeches and working papers are presented, resulting in an accumulation of nominations in 1995, 2000, 2005, and 2010 (no references could be found in 1975, 1980, and 1990). In contrast, IAEA General Assemblies are held annually and only last a few days. Here, it was only in 1985 that Iran first referred to its "inalienable right". At the time of the evaluation, no statements were available for the most recent NPT Review Conference 2015. Politicians involved in the negotiations explained the decline in the framing of "inalienable rights" from 2005 to 2010 with the fact that Iran has put all available diplomatic resources into resolving the nuclear conflict and has thus made fewer statements in both forums in purely quantitative terms during this period. See interviews with Soltanieh, 25 April 2012, Vienna; Mousavian, 3 May 2012, Vienna.

Iran also sought to strengthen its cause by referring to the wording of the consensually adopted final documents of earlier review conferences, which confirmed the "inalienable right of all the State Parties to the treaty to develop research, production and use of nuclear energy for peaceful purposes without discrimination". That this should take place "in conformity with Articles I, II and III of the treaty" was, however, not mentioned (e.g., Iran 2005c, 2010b, 2015d; Salehi 2013). Iran's effort to further consolidate its narrative of nuclear rights is also reflected in the language of working papers that Iran periodically submitted to the main committee III of the NPT which deals with peaceful uses of nuclear energy. The genealogy of the formulation of the title of these papers signals that Tehran tried to specify and anchor the scope of Article IV in the contractual language of the review conferences: Until 2008, the papers traded under the name "Peaceful Uses of Nuclear Energy". In 2009 and 2010, the title was "Peaceful research, production and use of nuclear energy"; since 2012, the working paper has been entitled "The inalienable right to develop research, production and uses of nuclear energy for peaceful purposes" (Iran 1998, 2000a, 2005c, 2007a, 2008b, 2009a, 2010d, 2012, 2013b, 2015d).

7.4.4 Blaming and Shaming

Iran also sought to back up its norm advocacy by criticizing the in its view inadequate implementation of the commitments set out in Article IV. Two clusters can be discerned: First, Iran, together with other non-aligned states, complained that instead of cooperating in the field of peaceful nuclear technology, NWS and nuclear advanced countries were establishing export control bodies outside established treaty structures, thus restricting national sovereignty rights and undermining the provisions laid down in Article IV.

Complaints were already made during the first NPT Review Conference in 1975 by the (pro-Western) Shah regime that the provisions of Article IV "had been largely ignored" (Fartash 1975). In 1990, the Iranian delegate described the extent of technological cooperation granted as "minimal and, in many cases, discriminatory" (Nasseri 1990a). Iranian delegates within the IAEA were concerned about a shift in "balance between its promotional and verification activities" (Ayatollahi 1995a; Iran 2005b). In order to ensure "that the technological cooperation program remains firm, sustainable and predictable" (Iran 2005b), Iran called on the international community to provide the Technical Cooperation Fund with the necessary financial and human resources (Iran 2000a). Developing countries so far had not benefited from the granted benefits of civilian nuclear energy. They were also confronted with "growing and often insurmountable constraints […] imposed by the industrialized countries" (Nasseri 1990a)—a criticism that dates back to the time of the Shah as well (Hoveyda 1977: 13).

Instead of complying with their treaty obligations on technological cooperation in the peaceful uses of nuclear technology, nuclear weapon states would try to reinterpret Article IV:

> In past few years [sic!], some efforts have been made to undermine the main principles of the NPT in order to change it to a single-goal treaty. In this context, unfortunately the nuclear disarmament obligations have been totally overlooked and access to peaceful nuclear materials and technologies has been denied. At the same time, obligations of the NNWSs [sic!] on non-proliferation have been overemphasized as if the NPT has no other provision. With such an approach, certain countries have tried to impose more extreme and deeper restrictions on access to peaceful nuclear technology and sought to monopolize such technology only to NWSs [sic!] and a few staunch allies even in some cases if they are non-parties to the NPT. (Iran 2010c)

Iran was particularly critical of Bush's (2004) proposal "to limit the access to peaceful nuclear technology to an exclusive club of technologically advanced states under the pretext of non-proliferation" (Kharrazi 2005a). Trade restrictions justified as non-proliferation instruments would ultimately limit the legitimate and inalienable right (Velayati 1995) to nuclear energy for peaceful purposes.

The in Iran's view exclusive and arbitrary composition of most export control bodies complicated matters further (Kharazzi 2000). Iran therefore called for the abolition of closed door clubs that would operate "on an informal and secretive basis" (Baeidinejad 1995: 24) outside formal treaty structures. Instead, the existing export control bodies should be replaced by "transparent international mechanisms with the participation of all States parties to the Treaty" (Ayattollahi 1995b: 10–11). Iran also called for the establishment of international procedural mechanisms that would sanction infringements resulting from the lack of implementation of Article IV and regulate how technology transfer denials should be compensated (e.g., Nasseri 1990a; Iran 2008c, 2010b).

This leads to the second cluster of criticism identified in the analysis: Tehran accuses the Western supplier states, especially the USA, of applying double standards and interpreting the central norms of the NPT according to their own preferences: It claims that while countries such as Iran are excluded from trade in civil nuclear technology on the basis of false accusations, Western states engage in trade with non-NPT members, thus undermining the credibility of the treaty regime and violating the non-proliferation norm enshrined in Articles I and III of the NPT (e.g., Fartash 1975; Dabiri 1980b; Amrollahi 1985).[80] In this context, Iran also regularly complains about the tacit acceptance of Israel's nuclear weapons capability and subsequent trade agreements (e.g., Aghazadeh 2004: 5). Iranian delegates also vehemently criticized the US "nuclear deal" with India in 2008. By lifting the supply embargo against India imposed in 1998, the NSG was giving the country access to legal trade in civilian nuclear technology. This "infamous decision" (Iran 2010b) was regarded as a violation of core NPT norms (especially Article III, paragraph 2), but above all a de facto recognition of India as a nuclear power (Iran 2009a, 2012, 2015d).

---

[80] See also interviews with Soltanieh, 25 April 2012, Vienna; Mousavian, 3 May 2012, Vienna.

7.4.5 Practical Activities

The importance that Iran attaches to advocating the right to the peaceful uses of nuclear energy is aptly illustrated by the amount of speeches devoted to the subject as well as in the working papers on the subject, which are regularly presented to main committee III at NPT RevCons. In addition, Iran supported all relevant draft resolutions on this subject presented to the UN General Assembly.[81]

Iran's practical engagement also comes to the fore with regard to pledges to implement existing programs for technological cooperation more adequately. Already during the Shah's time, Iranian delegates called on IAEA member states to allocate resources to the Technical Cooperation Fund and they regularly emphasized Iran's voluntary contributions in that regard (e.g., Etemad 1974: 2; Ameri 1975). Later, criticism regarding IAEA structures prevailed: Iran demanded that the departments entrusted with verification tasks, i.e., the safeguards department, should be financed from the regular budget and not via extra-budgetary contributions in order to prevent politically motivated withholding of payments (e.g., Soltanieh 1984; Ayatollahi 1995a; Iran 2000a, 2010d). In the same vein, Iran supported the establishment of a special aid fund for developing countries (Ayatollahi 1995b). However, it did not partake in other initiatives, such as the International Project on Innovative Nuclear Reactors and Fuel Cycles (INPRO) set up in 2000 or the Peaceful Uses Initiative (PUI) founded in 2010, which aimed to provide extra-budgetary contributions to support the IAEA's work on the peaceful use of nuclear energy.

In addition to providing financial resources, Iran promoted its interpretation of nuclear rights through public outreach and cooperation with like-minded states. Back in the 1960s and 1970s, this included industrialized NNWS who were also concerned that restrictive non-proliferation measures could hinder their economic and technological development and strengthen the nuclear weapon states' monopoly on the civilian use of nuclear energy. In April 1977, Iran hosted the Iran Conference on the Transfer of Nuclear Technology with the aim of bringing together supplier and recipient countries. The objective was to provide joint advice on how to deal with the increasingly restrictive non-proliferation policy, in particular the recently founded NSG. The event was organized jointly with the American Nuclear Society, the European Nuclear Society, and the Nuclear Society of Japan, and it was the first conference worldwide to deal with the topic of nuclear technology transfer from an economic, technical, and political perspective. Iran played an active role, drawing particular attention to developing countries' "legitimate needs for technology transfer" (Etemad 1977: 17). Export control measures were not criticized per se; in order to secure supply, Iran even considered them to be useful. However, as the head of

[81] From 1977 to 1980, a UN resolution on "Peaceful use of nuclear energy for economic and social development" was put to the vote (A/RES/32/50 of 1977; A/RES/33/4 of 1978; A/RES/34/63 of 1979; A/RES/35/112 of 1980). From 1981 to 1997 there was a resolution on "United Nations Conference for the Promotion of International Co-operation in the Peaceful Uses of Nuclear Energy" (A/RES/36/78 of 1981; A/RES/37/167 of 1982; A/RES/38/60 of 1983; A/RES/39/74 of 1984; A/RES/40/95 of 1985; A/RES/41/21/212B of 1986; A/RES/42/24 of 1987).

the AEOI made clear, they should be developed collectively and be "consistent with the ideals of the NPT and the Statute of the International Atomic Energy Agency" (Etemad 1977: 17). The Iranian speakers (in particular the head of the AEOI) harshly criticized the "club diplomacy" (Etemad 1977: 18) and the discriminatory approach of the supplier countries, which they considered to be aiming at consolidating their monopoly position (Etemad 1977: 17, 18; Hoveyda 1977: 13–4). The approximately 500 participants from 41 countries, including government officials, scientists, industry representatives, and IAEA staff, were unable to agree on a final declaration. Nevertheless, the nuclear "emerging countries" present were able to clarify their position vis-à-vis the USA and formed a strategic alliance.[82]

Iran also actively participated in the International Fuel Cycle Evaluation process initiated by the US government, which took place from 1977 to 1980 (Barnaby 1980; Skjöldebrand 1980). Together with Germany and France, Iran chaired Working Group 2 on enrichment availability (Commission of the European Communities 1980). Iran had also placed its hopes in the United Nations Conference for the Promotion of International Co-operation in the Peaceful Uses of Nuclear Energy (UNCPICPUNE), which was convened in 1980 by a resolution of the UN General Assembly (UN A/RES/32/50 of 1977). Already during the meetings of the Preparatory Committee, however, Iran expressed criticism of the lack of willingness of the nuclear weapons states to cooperate (Amrollahi 1983: 18–19) and felt disappointed when the participants failed to agree on principles of international cooperation (Soltanieh 1990a, b: 306).

Iran also used national platforms to promote its right to uranium enrichment, e.g., in Friday prayers or speeches by the revolutionary leader.[83] Under Rouhani's presidency, Iran launched a massive (digital) publicity campaign in this context. In November 2013, a web site was launched dedicated to the topic of the peaceful uses of nuclear energy—in Iran, but also in general.[84] Even though the Iranian government never officially admitted to operate the web site, observers saw it as a part of the massive public diplomacy campaign. The web site, the design and language of which is aimed at a Western audience, does not only provide a detailed account of the development of the Iranian nuclear program ("the nuclear saga").[85] It also addresses controversial and legal issues as well as historical facts and figures which are accompanied by extensive visual material and ideological content, for example, a commemorative section for the murdered nuclear scientists. At the same time, Iran launched a Twitter and Facebook campaign in which high-ranking politicians campaigned for Iran's "nuclear rights". For example, through his official Twitter account, Rouhani stated that the government does not intend to "retreat one iota

[82]In May 1977, a follow-up event entitled "Nuclear Power and its Fuel Cycle" took place in Salzburg. Another follow-up conference that Iran had agreed to host in 1981 fell victim to the Islamic Revolution and was instead held in Geneva without Iranian participation.

[83]See a compilation "The Supreme Leader's view on nuclear energy", available at http://farsi.khamenei.ir/speech-content?id=101,442. Accessed 28 April 2017.

[84]See http://nuclearenergy.ir. Accessed 2 November 2014.

[85]This is the title of the opening banner on the web site http://nuclearenergy.ir. Accessed 2 November 2014.

from protecting rights of Iranian nation incl. right to peaceful nuclear technology".[86] The campaign also served to demonstrate Tehran's determination to the West and domestic political critics. A video message from Foreign Minister Javad Zarif, in which he justified Iran's right to uranium enrichment, can also be seen in this light.[87]

National activities were also directed at Iran's allies and the world public. In April 2010, Iran hosted the Tehran International Conference on Disarmament and Non-Proliferation. Under the motto "Nuclear Energy for Every-One, Nuclear Weapons for No-One"[88] Iran advocated the two NPT norms that the country regards as central: nuclear disarmament and the peaceful uses of nuclear energy. However, the conference was also interpreted as an attempt by Tehran to restore its own credibility (before international and national audiences alike) and to prevent further sanctions (Rajiv 2010). Observers have argued that Iran had intended the conference to counter the USA-initiated "Nuclear Security Summit," which had taken place only a few days earlier in Washington and for which Iran had been denied participation (Butters 2010; Posch 2013). For its own summit, Iran had invited around 60 states, in particular those from the Non-Aligned Movement and representatives of international and regional organizations as well as NGOs.[89] In addition to nuclear disarmament, which has been dealt with in Sect. 7.3, questions of nuclear cooperation were of particular importance. In his opening speech, Ayatollah Khamenei addressed the developing countries in the region directly and described them as "thirsting for peace, security and progress" and as "hav[ing] the right to ensure the economic position and prosperity of the future generations" (Khamenei 2010). Iran once again stylized itself as a frontrunner of the developing countries: Doubts about the peaceful intentions of Iran's nuclear program and about countermeasures such as sanctions were presented as a means "to hold back the nations of the region from paying serious attention to this natural and important right of theirs" (Khamenei 2010). In contrast, the Iranian president reaffirmed "the inalienable rights of nations under article IV of NPT in having the nuclear fuel cycle" (Ahmadinejad 2010a). In the final declaration which was registered as an official document at the IAEA (2010), the conference president reaffirmed the legal right of access to the full fuel cycle (Mottaki 2010). Other (non-

---

[86]Hassan Rouhani, 25.2.2014 (11:34 a.m.) tweet: "To dear ppl of #Hormozgan: Gov will not retreat one iota from protecting rights of Iranian nation incl. right to peaceful nuclear technology". Similarly Rouhani, Hassan (Hassan Rouhani). "As NPT signatory, what we pursue in the final#nuclear agreement is for #Iranian nation to exercise all its rights under international law.", February 23, 2014, 9:15 a.m. Tweet.

[87]http://www.youtube.com/watcz?v=Ao2WH6GDWz4. Accessed 28 August 2015.

[88]The conference program, a list of participants, and individual speeches can be found on the homepage of the Iranian Ministry of Foreign Affairs, available at http://cms.mfa.gov.ir/cms/cms/Tehranicd/en. Accessed 28 August 2015.

[89]The list of participants circulating on the homepage of the Ministry of Foreign Affairs does not correspond to the actual composition. While Tehran had not even invited the USA because of the lack of diplomatic relations, the EU refused to participate, as Iran apparently wanted to deny it an active role that went beyond being present at the opening ceremony (Westberg 2010). According to participating NGO members, Western countries would have participated in the 2011 follow-up conference, but only "incognito," email conversation with a participating scientist 20 July 2011.

aligned) states and the spokesman of the Organization of Islamic Cooperation also supported this view (Ihsanoglu 2010; Natalegawa 2010).

In June 2011, Iran held a follow-up conference, which also linked the demand for universal nuclear disarmament with a right to the peaceful uses of nuclear energy. This topic became particularly controversial in view of the accident at the Japanese nuclear power plant Fukushima in March 2011. Despite the obvious dangers of nuclear energy, Iran continued to advocate an unrestricted right of full access to the fuel cycle.[90]

Table 7.4 illustrates the range of activities that Iran conducted in order to enforce the perceived right to the full fuel cycle:[91]

7.4.6 Assessment

In summary, Iran's strong commitment to the right to the peaceful uses of nuclear energy, including the right to uranium enrichment, can be qualified as norm entrepreneurship according to the indicators set out in Sect. 5.2.1.

Even though Tehran was not directly involved in the negotiations on the design of Article IV in the Eighteen Nation Committee on Disarmament, it actively promoted the recognition of nuclear rights to which it sees itself (and the entire treaty community) entitled. Throughout the entire period under investigation, Iranian delegates actively promoted their interpretation of the NPT, according to which the NPT contains an inherent right to the peaceful uses of nuclear energy, including sensitive technologies, and a requirement for cooperation on the side of technology holders. Iranian delegates tried to discursively anchor this interpretation in the various arms control forums. They also tried to put their favored wording to the record in the politically binding final documents and other official statements.

[90]Unfortunately, I could not find speeches or press releases for the follow-up conference. The information cited here is based on background discussions with participating civil society representatives, e.g., email conversation with a participating scientist on 20 July 2011 and conversations during the preparatory commission for the 2015 NPT Review Conference in Vienna from 30 April to 11 May 2012.

[91]Due to the scope of the topic, it was not possible to search all potential sources for indications of Iranian activities regarding the peaceful uses of nuclear energy. The information listed here is based on interviews, evaluated primary sources within the IAEA and the NPT Review Conferences, IAEA annual reports, and a literature analysis. Iran also contributed to the Technical Cooperation Fund through voluntary financial contributions (Ameri 1975; Etemad 1974). In cooperation with the IAEA, the country also organized a series of technical workshops and training courses, in particular on medical nuclear research. In addition, Iranian delegates reaffirmed their willingness to make their nuclear expertise available to other states (Salehi 2009, 2010). The annual reports give an overview of each country's activities within the IAEA in the area of technical cooperation. See https://www.iaea.org/technicalcooperation/Pub/Ann-Reports/index.html. Accessed 28 April 2017. Since these activities did not serve directly to advocate the right to the peaceful uses of nuclear energy, they are not listed in Table 7.4.

Table 7.4 Practical activities of Iran with regard to the right to uranium enrichment

Title/type of conference	Date and location	Description
National conferences		
International seminar on civil nuclear programs financed by AEOI	29 October 1986 in Ramsar at the Caspian Sea	
Nationally hosted international conferences		
International Conference on the Transfer of Nuclear Technology	10–14 April 1977 in Shiraz and Persepolis	Conference in response to the establishment of the NSG; participants expressed their opposition to further restrictions on the transfer of nuclear technology In addition to the NAM, also Western, nuclear energy holders participated Organized by: Atomic Energy Organization of Iran together with the Japanese Atomic Energy Society, American Nuclear Society and the European Nuclear Society
First Tehran International Conference on Disarmament and Non-Proliferation	2010	
Second Tehran International Conference on Disarmament and Non-Proliferation	2011	
International conferences attended by Iran		
International Fuel Cycle Evaluation	1977–1980	
United Nations Conference for the Promotion of International Cooperation in the Peaceful Uses of Nuclear Energy	23 March–10 April 1987	

In doing so, Iran relied on all of the typical strategies of norm entrepreneurship specified in Sect. 5.2.1. It is particularly striking that the Iranian government not only rhetorically promoted its interpretation of the norm, but also invested massive national resources in order to implement its nuclear rights narrative in practice. Even though Iran is not the only country that has advocated a right of access to the full fuel cycle and that sees a requirement for cooperation stemming from Article IV, Iran's commitment can be described as outstanding. Iran's activities also meet the criteria for proactivism—a central element of norm entrepreneurship—set out by Becker et al. (2008: 820): Tehran did advocate the propagated norm (interpretation) in various forums and across various audiences. Its commitment continued throughout the entire period under investigation and even dates back to the time of the Shah regime. It has to be admitted, though, that the international conferences on the subject organized by Iran are less impressive, with a 33-year break between 1977 and 2010. However, this can at least partly be explained by the deterioration in international relations as a result of the Islamic revolution and the nuclear crisis. Overall, the degree of activity rose in parallel with the nuclear crisis in the 2000s, and from the mid-1990s on, the Iranian government began to systematically develop its nuclear rights narrative in an effort to change the meaning of the current norm. However, the country has by no means been interested in destroying the norm. The use of naming, shaming, and blaming and destructive tactics do not contradict this. While the secret development of an own enrichment program and proven violations of Iran's safeguards agreement cast some doubts on Iran's credibility as a norm entrepreneur, this behavior can also be interpreted as being part of its advocacy. Iran's willingness to fully investigate past breaches of norms in the course of the nuclear agreement negotiated in July 2015 also does not indicate that the country seeks to overthrow existing structures. Consequently, part of Iran's behavior regarding the propagation of the nuclear rights narrative can be interpreted in light of the second alternative explanation: Tehran interprets the interpretation of norms by NWS and the Western supplier countries as unjustified interference with national sovereignty rights. Iran tries to counter the denial of the right to uranium enrichment and the denial of access to corresponding technologies with an alternative norm interpretation. The normative framing of the nuclear rights narrative also contains elements that refer to norm subsidiarity (national sovereignty; counter-hegemonic resistance; injustice; discrimination). Nevertheless, Tehran's commitment goes beyond purely reactive behavior. This is demonstrated by the resources deployed by Iran—in particular its attempts to convince norm supporters—and on the other hand by the continuity of engagement over time (as well as regime type) and arms control forums. Table 7.5 summarizes Iran's advocacy for a right to uranium enrichment along the criteria for norm entrepreneurship:

7.5 Strategies and Resources of Iranian Norm Entrepreneurship

In the previous sections, I discussed three empirical cases in which Iran has made disproportional efforts to establish or strengthen global norms. All of these cases—albeit to various extents—meet the criteria of typical norm entrepreneurship as set out in Sect. 5.2.1. What then are the peculiarities of Iranian norm advocacy with regard to the strategies and resources used to foster its normative aims?

First, and maybe most importantly, Iran's activism rests on an exceptionally high level of scientific and technical expertise which has provided the country with considerable influence. For one, Iranian delegates have used their knowledge as a resource in negotiations both in the process of agenda setting as well as with regard to putting

Table 7.5 Overview of the relevant characteristics of norm entrepreneurship based on Sell and Prakash (2004: 153) in the case of "right to uranium enrichment"

Norm entrepreneur case 3: Iran's advocacy for a right to uranium enrichment	
Period	– Already during the reign of the Shah; within the NPT: 1970 until today
Trigger (extrinsic/intrinsic)	– Development of an indigenous nuclear energy program
Problem definition	– According to Iran, Article IV of the NPT contains an inherent right to the full fuel cycle, including enrichment and reprocessing capabilities – Non-proliferation measures aimed at restricting sensitive technologies constitute discriminatory measures in Iran's view and violate the requirement for cooperation laid down in Article IV
Preferred solution	– Full implementation of Article IV and official recognition of the right of each contracting state to full access to sensitive technologies – The abolition of discriminatory export control bodies and all trade barriers through discursive and political integration and norm linkage
Normative framing	– Access to nuclear technology as part of a right to development, particularly for disadvantaged developing countries – Access to nuclear technology as an act of equitable justice for the abandonment of a nuclear weapons option upon accession to the NPT – The maintenance of an indigenous nuclear energy program is a question of national sovereignty; restrictive non-proliferation measures are rejected as interference with national sovereignty – The application of double standards in trade with non-NPT members is unfair
National interests	– Mastery of sensitive technologies possibly with the aim of building a nuclear weapons capability, both status and security interests – National self-sufficiency and avoidance of external dependencies with regard to own energy supply – Political interests: Criticism of the USA as "arch-enemy" also serves to strengthen its own identity and role, securing power; counter-reaction to accusations that Iran is secretly striving for an atomic bomb

(continued)

Table 7.5 (continued)

Norm entrepreneur case 3: Iran's advocacy for a right to uranium enrichment	
Applied strategies	– Rhetorical demands and affirmation of Iran's interpretation of Article IV – Public relations and digital campaigns – Critique through naming, shaming and blaming – Thematic link (nuclear disarmament, criticism of Israel) to established (meta)norms (right to development, national sovereignty, justice) – Cooperation with like-minded countries
Resources	– Diplomacy – Scientific expertise – Capacity building
Allies	– In the 1960s and 1970s emerging Western nuclear energy holders; thereafter primarily NAM states
Normative transformation?	– Reaffirmation of the right to uranium enrichment as part of Article IV in final documents of the Group of Non-Aligned States and in various agreements between the West and Iran (although very vague in wording)
Substantial change?	– In the negotiations with Iran, the West has now deviated from the position of zero enrichment and has recognized Iran's right to uranium enrichment. Nevertheless, the West is trying to avoid a precedent and extending Article IV in the context of the NPT to include a right of access to sensitive technologies – Still no obligation to cooperate
Breaches or doubts about the credibility of norm entrepreneurship?	– Accusations that Iran has built up a secret nuclear weapon program associated with violations of safeguards obligations – Close entanglement of the nuclear rights narrative with national interests and intensification of the demands parallel to the nuclear crisis suggest purely strategically motivated action

emphasis on issues which Iran felt should gain priority. This became particularly apparent during the final round of negotiations of the CWC[92]: In contrast to all other State Parties and as a corollary of the Iraqi gas attacks, Iran had built considerable medical–technical expertise in the treatment of chemical weapons victims and with regard to protective measures. This led to Iran playing a decisive role in the formulation of Article X of the CWC.

But Iran not only surpassed its non-aligned fellow states with its high degree of technical and political competence. The Iranian delegation was also one of the largest among non-aligned states, if not the largest at certain times (and with technical expertise that was otherwise only available to some of the Western European countries).[93] These resources enabled Iran to actively participate in numerous expert groups on all aspects of the CWC. Iran's influence is also evident in the fact that Hassan Mashhadi, who had led the Iranian delegation during the CWC negotiations, was released for work within the Preparatory Commission of the OPCW. He became Head of the Department for Government Relations and Political Affairs from 1993 until 1997. Later, he built up the Assistance and Protection Branch of the OPCW, which he headed until 2006.

Iran's expertise also stretched to the UN bodies dealing with nuclear disarmament as well as to the NPT. During NPT Review Conferences, for example, the country was generally one of the most active and strongest delegations in terms of numbers and was represented by high-ranking government representatives—mostly at presidential level, at least at foreign minister level.[94] In addition, Iran's above-average scientific and technical expertise allowed the country to assume influential offices such as the chairing of working groups or negotiations.[95]

Observers also attest great negotiating skills to Iran. In interviews, several individuals who were involved in multilateral arms control negotiations highlighted that Iranian delegates were usually exceptionally well prepared, equipped with extensive technical and scientific knowledge and often one step ahead of other negotiating parties.[96] Iran's geostrategic position as well as the expertise which it was willing to share also gave the country an influential position within the Non-Aligned Movement (Ogilvie-White 2012: 261; Potter and Mukhatzhanova 2012: 31).[97]

In relation to the cognitive resources and personnel which lay the groundwork for Iran's norm entrepreneurship, the country invested in the practical support of

[92]The following information is based on conversations with Ralf Trapp, 31 May 2015, and Hassan Mashhadi, 9 June 2015.

[93]See interview Trapp, 31 May 2015.

[94]See http://www.reachingcriticalwill.org/resources/profiles. Accessed 28 April 2017 and talks with observers of the negotiations during field research at the OPCW in The Hague in May 2015.

[95]For example, Iran assumed the role of "friends of the chair/president" during the 1978 special session on disarmament or in the NPT negotiations in 1995 or 2010, interviews with Soltanieh on 25 April 2012; Kmentt 24 April 2012; Mousavian 18 March 2015.

[96]Interviews with various IAEA staff members who had been involved in the negotiations with Iran (14 March 2012, 16 and 17 April 2012, Vienna) and various arms control officials who participated in CWC and NPT negotiations.

[97]Interview Trapp, 31 May 2015.

favored norms: An unparalleled example of this is the capacity building in the context of the treatment of possible chemical weapons victims. In addition, the Iranian government also supported scientific analysis regarding the treatment of chemical weapons victims, studies on nuclear disarmament, and the peaceful uses of nuclear energy, which the country also made available internationally. By contrast, the financial support that Iran provided to the organizations in charge of implementing the relevant treaty norms was rather modest. With regard to both IAEA and OPCW, Iran's financial contributions are only average. Yet in the IAEA, Iran belongs to the group of countries which constantly call for increases in the organization's budget for technological cooperation.

Bridge-building activities, which are identified in the literature as typical for norm entrepreneurs, do not belong to the standard repertoire of Iranian diplomats. An exception are efforts to mediate between India and Pakistan after both states had conducted nuclear weapon tests in 1998 (Kharrazi 1998; Ziaran 1998). As will be discussed in more detail below, by contrast Iran often assumes a spoiler role and tends to follow its normative mission rather uncompromisingly.

In order to convince potential addressees of the actual validity and normative and practical necessity of Iran's favored norm (or interpretation thereof) and to anchor and institutionalize these into the discourse, in all three cases Iran made ample use of prototypical norm entrepreneurial strategies: In order to convince followers, Iranian diplomats pursued active lobbying and formed strategic alliances with like-minded states and occasionally with civil society actors. Moreover, Iran resorted to framing strategies to highlight the urgency of its concern and to put pressure on actors that held other opinions. Some components of the framing used by Iranian delegates (diagnostic, prognostic, motivational framing; emotionalization/dramatization; normative fit; reference to metanorms; naming, blaming, and shaming; rhetorical activation) have already been discussed in the previous sections. Therefore, the following paragraph focuses on the common features of the collective action frames used by Iran.

In all three cases of Iranian norm entrepreneurship, Iran's normative framing can be described as collective action frame, which consists of three components: firstly, the description of the current normative structure as an untenable because unjust state of affairs; secondly, the formulation of an active component to overcome it; and thirdly, the construction of dichotomous identities (Gamson 1992; Klandermans 1997). Iran's argumentation was particularly linked to framings which were shared by the non-aligned countries.

In all three cases, Iran related the need and urgency to change the respective normative structure to perceptions of injustice. As shown in Sect. 6.3, the pursuit of global justice is deeply rooted in Iran's political identity. Iran's self-stylization as a "standard bearer of a just government" (Sadjadpour 2009: 10) was also conceivable in its norm advocacy: Particularly in the context of the NPT, Iran's norm entrepreneurship was directed at leveling formal and informal privileges of the nuclear weapon states and their allies, above all the USA and Israel. Tehran criticized in particular the discriminatory, unbalanced structure of the NPT, and the lack of implementation of contractual obligations (nuclear disarmament and access to the full fuel cycle). Iranian diplomats also criticized the application of double standards regarding cooperation with non-NPT-members and the interpretation of core norms of the NPT. In the case of the protection of chemical weapons victims, Iran also deplored the application of double standards: For example, the fact that Western companies had supplied Iraq with chemical precursors and materials, but were not held accountable, or that Saddam Hussein escaped sanctions, even though Iraq had (repeatedly) violated the Geneva Protocol.

The Iranian government used justice-based arguments not only to justify the development of its indigenous nuclear fuel cycle capabilities. It also considered the full implementation of the norm of technological cooperation, including the right to sensitive technologies, and the strengthening of the disarmament norm as a central element of the bargain underlying the NPT. The lack of implementation of both norms is considered to be unjust and a violation of the treaty. Tehran blamed the nuclear weapon states and developed nuclear energy holders which in its view had a special moral responsibility toward the treaty community as a whole, and the disadvantaged countries in the global South in particular.

In all three cases, Iranian delegates used belligerent rhetoric to highlight the magnitude of grievances. They actively named, blamed, and shamed the nuclear weapons states, in particular the USA for the failure to implement their disarmament obligations (NPT and CWC) and—in Iran's view—for misinterpreting core norms (i.e., nuclear disarmament and the norm of technological cooperation). Israel has also repeatedly been the focus of fierce criticism.

But Iran not only demanded justice and equal treatment for itself. The country also sees itself as an advocate of developing countries in the fight against discrimination and Western dominance (Wunderlich et al. 2013: 263–272). Iranian argumentation is embedded in and can thus be connected to traditional principles of non-aligned states such as independence, national sovereignty, non-interference in internal affairs, anti-imperialism, and compensatory justice. This is particularly evident in the fight for what Iran perceives to be its "nuclear rights," i.e., access to sensitive technologies.

Even though the non-aligned are probably the most important reference group of Iran, even with regard to its norm advocacy, Iran's position within the non-aligned countries is not uncontroversial. Some NAM members have been quite skeptical about a possible military dimension of the Iranian nuclear program. Nevertheless, Ogilvie-White (2010) rightly observes that the non-aligned were relatively united in their criticism of how the West has approached Iran in the long-standing nuclear conflict. From the perspective of the NAM, it has to be seen as yet another unlawful encroachment on national sovereignty if the nuclear weapon states deprive them of basic nuclear rights—especially if these rights are granted to other members and non-parties to the NPT whose nuclear programs are not even under IAEA safeguards.

So while the justice motive constitutes the most important frame referred to by Iran, Iran's normative framing also relates to other metanorms, i.e., national sovereignty and—in the case of the peaceful uses of nuclear technology—the right to development. What is also striking, though not surprising given the interrelated nature of the phenomena at hand, is that Iran actively creates linkages between the propagated norms: For example, statements aimed at strengthening the disarmament norm generally include references to the inalienable right to cooperate in the peaceful uses of nuclear energy. The following statement aptly demonstrates such linkage strategies:

> The world is currently witnessing discrimination. On one hand, using nuclear energy for peaceful purposes is limited while at the same time, countries which possess nuclear weapons do not allow nations to access nuclear energy. These countries allow themselves to use nuclear weapons and announce that they will not hesitate to use these arms against other nations. This can lead to a collective effort. The international community would like to set in motion a real move to enjoy nuclear technology for peaceful purposes and for national development. We are witnessing big threats by possessors of nuclear weapons. They are boldly threatening to use nukes. Any use of nuclear weapons to harm humanity is condemned.[98]

It is striking that Iran tried to demonstrate its competence and credibility as committed actor and norm entrepreneur across all arms control fields by invoking its own status as a victim of chemical weapons. Corresponding references can be found not only in speeches within the CWC, but also in those aimed at strengthening the norm of technological cooperation in the peaceful uses of nuclear energy and the disarmament norms within the BWC and NPT as well as in the various UN forums.

In addition to these prototypical strategies described in the literature on norms entrepreneurship, however, Iran also relied on a number of other more confrontational strategies and tactics that resemble the "negative" or destructive strategies identified by Bob (2012: 34): blockade and dragging techniques, repeated disruptive maneuvers and interventions, procedural filibuster, rhetorical derailments, and diplomatic blackmail strategies. They seem to be primarily aimed at discrediting opposing positions which are perceived as unfair, sabotaging negotiations, and successfully asserting one's own position. In line with these more confrontationist strategies, in all analyzed cases, in the propagation of favored norms, Iran showed little willingness to deviate from its principles. It repeatedly risked the failure of negotiations and thus isolated itself rather than deviating from its positions. For example, in 1995 Iran made its approval of the unlimited extension of the NPT conditional on the nuclear weapon states' willingness to give greater prominence to the disarmament norm and the norm of technological cooperation (even though Iran did not follow these announcements when the conditions were not fulfilled). Also, several NPT Review Conferences almost failed to adopt a consensual final document because of Iranian opposition. In 1985, for example, Iran threatened to block consensus if no mention of the Iraqi attack on the Iranian nuclear facility Bushehr was included in the final document (Iran 1985; Shababi 1985b). In 1995, Iran's displeasure led to an almost two-hour delay in negotiations in the face of a reaffirmation of the Israeli—Palestinian peace process contained in the resolution on the Middle East (Rauf and Johnson 1995: 30). In 2010, too, the adoption of a consensual final document almost failed due to Iran's refusal to accept what was regarded as weak language in the field

[98] Statement of then spokesperson of the Foreign Ministry, Ramin Mehmanparast, during an interview with the Iranian state television station PressTV on the sidelines of the "Tehran International Conference on Disarmament and Non-Proliferation 2010" on April 28, 2010 (quoted from Press TV 2010).

of disarmament (Johnson 2010: 4; Müller 2010: 8).[99] Some Iranian politicians, e.g., the chairman of the parliamentary committee responsible for national security and foreign policy, Alaeddin Boroujerdi, even launched the withdrawal from the NPT as a means of exerting pressure on the nuclear negotiations with the West (Mousavian 2012: 74–75).[100] Although Tehran's strategies in dealing with the nuclear crisis must be separated from arms control diplomacy,[101] the issue is closely linked to Iran's advocacy of a right to uranium enrichment. Former chief nuclear negotiator Rouhani warned in a speech to the United Nations in May 2005 that:

> termination of fuel cycle activities as demanded of Iran means you have killed the NPT. If you take out Article IV, all developing countries will step out of the treaty. […] Termination is war between the North and the South. The Americans say forget about Article IV, forget about the disarmament promised in Article VI […]. The U.S. today is trying to create a second discrimination, one between those that have peaceful nuclear technology and those not allowed to have peaceful nuclear technology. (Rouhani 2005, cited after Perkovich 2005)

Although less pronounced, Iran also resorted to destructive strategies in the context of the CWC, insisted on voting procedures, even if it became apparent that Iran would cast the only negative vote, or tenaciously blocking consensus decisions (although this did not directly concern the propagation of the protection norm for chemical weapons victims).

Some observers have described Iran's recourse to confrontational or destructive strategies as "uncompromising radicalism" (Müller 2011: 225) or "diplomatic obstructionism" (Pirseyedi 2013: 136). Such behavior is also regarded as characteristic of Iran's insidiousness, "reducing Iran's arms control diplomacy to political maneuvering" (Pirseyedi 2013: 1). With respect to the cases under investigation here—and leaving out the nuclear crisis—it must however be acknowledged that cooperative and confrontational strategies seem to balance each other out. While

---

[99]This was also confirmed by former Iranian IAEA Ambassador, Ali Asghar Soltanieh, in an interview with the author on 25 April 2012 in Vienna. In both cases, a compromise solution was found at the last minute: In 1985, the Australian delegation persuaded Iran to add the reference to an appendix to the final document; in 2010, the non-aligned under the leadership of Egypt succeeded in persuading Iran to compromise. In 2010, Iran was also concerned with preventing condemnation or criticism of its nuclear programme (Müller 2010: 8). Rebecca Johnson therefore ascribes to Tehran a strategy of "block[ing] without being blamed" (Johnson 2010: 4).

[100]So far, however, no such statements have been made in government circles. On the contrary, Tehran was keen to reject concerns and underline its commitment to the NPT (Shirazi 2013).

[101]In interviews when I asked about Iran's "destructive strategies," I was repeatedly reminded by arms control experts and IAEA representatives that a distinction must be made between Tehran's behavior in the nuclear negotiations and its arms control diplomacy. What Tanya Ogilvie-White calls "belligerent approach to nuclear diplomacy" (Ogilvie-White 2012: 149), i.e., "making and breaking commitments, playing cat and mouse with the IAEA and international negotiators, periodically appearing to climb down, and all the while pursuing an independent nuclear deterrent" (Ogilvie-White 2010: 120), applies exclusively to the former. An IAEA staff member who was involved in the Iran negotiations said: "Iran is only obstructionist, where the military dimension of its program is concerned, and by the way, which party would not?" On the multilateral level, by contrast, Iran has presented itself as a skilled and sometimes difficult negotiating partner, but by no means exclusively acts as a troublemaker. Background talks with IAEA staff and representatives of various groups of States, 14 and 16 March 2012, 16 and 17 April 2012 in Vienna.

Iran's confrontational stance increased under President Ahmadinejad, both his predecessor Khatami and his successor Rouhani adopted a much more moderate tone and conciliatory political style.

It thus seems more apt to interpret Iran's recourse to strategic disruptive maneuvers as an expression of "shrewd diplomatic and procedural maneuvering" (Rauf and Johnson 1995: 32) and thus negotiation skills. At the end of the day, Iran mostly bowed to compromise solutions, sometimes winning concessions, thereby preventing the failure of negotiations. As one interview partner put it: "They are tough negotiators, super prepared but not obstructionist [and] not the ones who prevent consensus at the end of the day."[102] This is also backed by observations of several participants of CWC conferences who reported that Iran had played a key role in negotiating compromise solutions during the three review conferences.[103]

As far as the selection of organizational platforms is concerned, Iran has located its norm entrepreneurship most of all within the UN arms control architecture. Above all, the Geneva-based Conference on Disarmament provided a platform to point out the lack of implementation of individual treaty norms. Iran also actively participated in the establishment of the CWC and the OPCW. Since the respective treaty regimes came into force, these have been the main forums for Iran's commitment.

Outside the treaty regimes, Iran also acted as a norm advocate through various practical activities. For example, Iranian delegates engaged in what has been described in the literature as rhetorical "activation" (Rublee 2008), both at the national and regional levels. Iran used the regular summits of the Non-Aligned Movement—the country's main reference group—to promote the propagated norms and their interpretation. In all three cases under investigation, the analysis revealed speech patterns in which Iran emphasized or reaffirmed its close ties to the non-aligned countries. Iran worked closely with NAM partners in all arms control forums. Within the movement, Iran belongs to the hardliners and therefore stands out from the majority of the non-aligned because of its much more aggressive rhetoric (Ogilvie-White 2010, Potter and Mukhatzhanova 2012: 15, 34; Wunderlich et al. 2013: 2). This notwithstanding, strategic alliance with non-aligned states rests on adherence to principles such as national sovereignty, independence from external interference, anti-imperialism, and aversion to discriminatory regime structures. Also with regard to substance, most non-aligned states take positions similar to those advocated for by Iran, i.e., the demand for time-bound nuclear disarmament or for the broadest possible technological cooperation in the peaceful uses of dual-use technologies. This is particularly true for Iran's commitment to the right to uranium enrichment which gained broad NAM support.[104] In addition to Iran, other developing countries

[102] Background conversation with a member of the EU3 negotiating team.

[103] The compromise of the first review conference was negotiated by the USA, the UK, Iran, and India. The agreements reached at the second conference were agreed by a group of 23 states in which Iran and India played key roles. See interview Soltanieh 25 April 2012; Trapp 31 May 2015.

[104] Indeed, Iran's nuclear rights narrative is not novel: India took this position during the treaty negotiations. New Delhi finally refrained from membership of the NPT because it feared that the treaty could establish a kind of new "nuclear apartheid regime". Other non-aligned states were also actively involved in the wording of Article IV during the treaty negotiations, such as Romania.

also have an interest in access to the fuel cycle (e.g., South Africa), or they already have such technologies (such as Argentina and Brazil). It is therefore that Iran was able to repeatedly present itself as an advocate of the non-aligned (Wunderlich et al. 2013: 266; Wunderlich 2014).

All cases under investigation here show that Iranian diplomats sought support for their positions primarily through informal multi- and bilateral meetings at various diplomatic levels. Iran has repeatedly used NAM meetings to put favored issues on the organization's agenda or to gain support for its proposals. For example, the final communiqué adopted at the 16th Non-Aligned Summit in Tehran confirmed Iran's interpretation of Article IV of the NPT as "including the inalienable right of each State Party, if it so decides, to develop, for peaceful purposes, a full national nuclear fuel cycle in accordance with its rights and obligations under the treaty on the Non-Proliferation of Nuclear Weapons" (NAM 2012: 64). Even Egypt, a traditional rival of Iran for leadership within the non-aligned and for supremacy in the region, repeatedly defended Iran's claim to the establishment of the complete fuel cycle (Arms Control Association 2008). In the CWC, too, Iran primarily sought the support of the non-aligned countries, but seemed also prepared to enter into temporary tactical coalitions with like-minded states if this seemed expedient.[105]

As far as cooperation with civil society is concerned, the conclusion is more ambivalent: Although Iran rhetorically reaffirmed its efforts to cooperate with civil society actors on several occasions, foreign NGOs and experts were invited to national conferences in all three cases and organized NGO briefings during the review conferences. However, some observers believe that this is mainly lip service, as cooperation is predominantly superficial in nature.[106]

References

Abbasi, F. (2012, September 17). Statement to the 56th Session of the IAEA General Conference, GC/56/OR.1, Vienna.

AEOI (1977). *Iran Conference on the Transfer of Nuclear Technology, Persepolis/Shiraz*, Iran, April 10–14, Volume I. http://lib.aeoi.org.ir/Content/downloads/EBooks_Files/shiraz_confrences/20757-transfer%20of%20nuclear%20technology%20v.1%20.pdf. Accessed April 28, 2017.

Aghazadeh, R. (2004. September 20). Statement to the 48th Session of the IAEA General Conference, GC/48/OR.1, Vienna.

Aghazadeh, R. (2006, September 18). Statement to the 50th Session of the IAEA General Conference, GC/50/OR.1, Vienna.

[105]Interview Mashhadi 9 June 2015; also background conversation with a member of Western Group to OPCW, 11 May 2015 and Trapp 31 May 2015. During the CWC treaty negotiations, Iran cooperated mainly with Argentina, Brazil, China, India, Indonesia, Cuba, Malaysia, Mexico, Nigeria, and Pakistan, in recent years particularly closely with Syria and—with the exception of India—with the BRICS states (Brazil, Russia, India, China, and South Africa).

[106]For example, interviews with members of Western delegations to the OPCW conducted in May 2015.

Ahmadinejad, M. (2005, September 17). Statement to the 60th Session of the UNGA, A/60/PV.10, New York.

Ahmadinejad, M. (2010a, April 17). *Text of President's Speech at the 1st International Conference on Disarmament and Non-Proliferation*. http://www.president.ir/en/pring.php?ArtID=21266. Accessed October 1, 2010.

Ahmadinejad, M. (2010b, May 3). Statement to the 2010 NPT RevCon, New York.

Al Arabyia. (2010, April 17). *Suspend 'Atomic Criminal' US from IAEA Iran*. http://www.alarabiya.net/articles/2010/04/17/106085.html. 28 April 2017.

Alfoneh, A. (2013). *Iran unveiled: How the revoluationary guards i turning theocracy into military dictatorship*. Washington, DC: AEI Press.

Al Habib, E. (2008, October 9). Statement to the 63rd Session of the UNGA 1st Committee. A/C.1/63/PV.7, New York.

Ali, J. (1996). *Iran, a case study: Chemical and Biological Arms Control Institute*. Alexandria, VA: Chemical and Biological Arms Control Institute.

Ameri, H. (1975, May). Statement to the 1st NPT RevCon, NPT/CONF/C.II/SR.5, Geneva.

Amrollahi, R. (1983, October 13). Statement to the 26th Session of the IAEA General Conference, GC/XXVII/OR.253, Vienna.

Amrollahi, R. (1984, September 26). Statement to the 28th Session of the IAEA General Conference, GC(XXVIII)/OR.260, Vienna.

Amrollahi, R. (1985, September 24). Statement to the 29th Session of the IAEA General Conference, GC/XXIX/OR.271,Vienna.

Amrollahi, R. (1986, September 30). Statement to the 30th Session of the IAEA General Conference, GC/XXX/OR.284, Vienna.

Amrollahi, R. (1991, September 16). Statement to the 35th Session of the IAEA General Conference, 1GC/XXXV/OR.334, Vienna.

Amrollahi, R. (1994, September 20). Statement to the 38th Session of the IAEA General Conference, GC/XXXVIII/OR.3, Vienna.

Araghchi, R. (2007, November 5). Statement Before the 12th Session of the CWC CSP, The Hague.

Aram, A. (1962, September 24). Statement to the 17th Session of the UNGA. New York.

Arms Control Association. (2008). The Middle East and nonproliferation: An interview with Nabil Fahmy, Egypt's Ambassador to the United States, 01.09.2008. *Arms Control Today*. http://www.armscontrol.org/act/2008_09/Fahmy. Accessed April 28, 2017.

Ayatollahi, M. S. (1995a, April 24). Statement to the 1995 NPT RevCon, NPT/CONF.1995/MC.III/SR.2, New York.

Ayatollahi, M. S. (1995b, May 2). Statement to the 1995 NPT RevCon, NPT/CONF.1995/MC.II/SR.3, New York.

Barnaby, F. (1980). Nuclear needs and risks of misuse: The final INFCE report. *Ambio, 9*(2), 101–102.

Battle, J. (2003). Shaking hands with Saddam Hussein: The U. S. tilts toward Iraq, 1980–1984. *The National Security Archive*. http://nsarchive.gwu.edu/NSAEBB/NSAEBB82/index2.htm. Accessed April 28, 2017.

Becker, U., Müller, H., & Wisotzki, S. (2008). Democracy and nuclear arms control—Destiny or ambiguity? *Security Studies, 17*(4), 810–854.

Beeman, W. (2013). Does Iran have the right to enrichment? The answer is yes. Resource document. *The World Post*, 31.10.2013. http://www.huffingtonpost.com/william-o-beeman/does-iran-have-the-right-_b_4181347.html. Accessed April 28, 2017.

Blake, A. (2013). Kerry on Iran: We do not recognize a right to enrich. *Washington Post*, 24.11.2013. http://www.washingtonpost.com/news/post-politics/wp/2013/11/24/kerry-on-iran-we-do-not-recognize-a-right-to-enrich/. Accessed April 28, 2017.

Bob, C. (2012). *The global right wing and the clash of world politics*. New York: Cambridge University Press.

Boureston, J., & Lacey, J. (2007). Nuclear technical cooperation: A right or a privilege? Resource document. *Arms Control Today*, 01.09.2007. https://www.armscontrol.org/act/2007_09/NuclearCoopFeature. Accessed April 28, 2017.

Burford, L. (2015). Defining the Nuclear Disarmament Norm. Paper presented to the conference "*Reassessing the Global Nuclear Order*", hosted by MIT (Cambridge, MA) and RMIT (Melbourne). Accessed January 9, 2015.

Bush, G. W. (2004, February 11). *President announces new measures to counter the threat of WMD*. Remarks by the President George W. Bush on Weapons of Mass Destruction Proliferation, National Defense University, Fort Lesley J. MC Nair, Washington, DC. http://2001-2009.state.gov/t/isn/rls/rm/29290.htm. Accessed April 28, 2017.

Butters, A. (2010). Ahmadinejad's answer to Obama's nuclear summit. *Time*, 19.04.2010. http://content.time.com/time/printout/0,8816,1982962,00.html. Accessed April 28, 2017.

CBW Events. (2007). A chronology of events relating to Iraq and chemical & biological warfare, 1984, First Quarter, Sample File. www.cbw-events.org.uk/EXIQ84Q1.PDF. Accessed April 28, 2017.

Chubin, S. (2013). Command and control in a nuclear-armed Iran. In collaboration with the Atomic Energy Commission CEA, Proliferation Papers 45, ifri Security Studies Center). http://www.ifri.org/sites/default/files/atoms/files/pp45chubin.pdf. Accessed April 28, 2017.

CNN. (2006, April 12). *Iran says it joins "Countries with Nuclear Technology"*. http://edition.cnn.com/2006/WORLD/meast/04/11/iran.nuclear/. Accessed April 28, 2017.

CNN. (2010, December 5). *Iran calls fuel bank "nuclear apartheid"*. http://edition.cnn.com/2010/WORLD/meast/12/04/iran.nuclear. Accessed April 28, 2017.

Commission of the European Communities. (1980). Final report, INFCE COM (80) 316, June 1980.

Cordesman, A., & Seitz, A. (2009). Iranian weapons of mass destruction: Doctrine, policy and command (working draft). Resource Document. http://csis.org/files/media/csis/pubs/090112_iran_wmd_policy.pdf. Accessed April 28, 2017.

Dabiri. (1980a, April 29). Statement to the CD, CD/PV.61, Geneva.

Dabiri. (1980b, August 19). Statement to the 1980 NPT RevCon, NPT/CONF.II/SR.12, Geneva.

Dabiri. (1981, February 19). Statement to the CD, CD/PV.108, Geneva.

Daryaei, M. H. (2013, May 15). Statement to the UNGA Open-ended Working Group on "Taking forward Multilateral Nuclear Disarmament Negotiations", Geneva.

Davenport, K. (2012). *Fact sheet: Security Council resolutions on Iran*. https://www.armscontrol.org/factsheets/Security-Council-Resolutions-on-Iran. Accessed April 28, 2017.

Deghani, G. (2009a, November 30). Statement at the 13th Session of the CWC CSP, The Hague.

Deghani, G. (2009b, December 1). Statement at the 14th Session of the CWC CSP, C-14/NAT.19, The Hague.

Deutsche Welle. (2013, April 9). *Iran celebrates national nuclear day with two new projects*. http://www.dw.com/en/iran-celebrates-national-nuclear-day-with-two-new-projects/a-16730190. Accessed April 28, 2017.

Dhanapala, J. (2005). *Multilateral diplomacy and the NPT: An insider's account, with Randy Rydell*. Geneva: UNIDIR.

EEAS. (2013, November 24). *Joint plan of action der EU3+3, Geneva*. http://eeas.europa.eu/statements/docs/2013/131124_03_en.pdf. Accessed April 28, 2017.

El Baradei, M. (2011). *The age of deception: Nuclear diplomacy in treacherous times*. New York: Metropolitan Books/Henry Holt and Co.

Eisenstadt, M. (2011). Religious ideologies, political doctrine, and nuclear decisionmaking. In M. Eisenstadt & M. Khalaji (Eds.), Nuclear fatwa: Religion and politics in Iran's proliferation strategy (1–12). The Washington Institute. https://www.washingtoninstitute.org/uploads/Documents/pubs/PolicyFocus115.pdf. Accessed April 28, 2017.

Etemad, A. (1974, September 17). Statement to the 18th Session of the IAEA General Conference GC/XVIII/OR.170, Vienna.

Etemad, A. (1977). *Speech to the Iran Conference on the Transfer of Nuclear Technology*. In: AEOI 1977, 15–19.

Etemad, A. (1987). Iran. In H. Müller (Ed.), *A European non-proliferation policy: Prospects and problems* (pp. 203–227). Oxford: Clarendon Press.

Farhi, F. (2009). Ahmadinejad's nuclear folly. *Middle East Report*, 252. Resource Document. http://www.merip.org/mer/mer252/ahmadinejads-nuclear-folly. Accessed April 28, 2017.

FARS News Agency. (2013, April 29). *Iranian Deputy FM. US seeking to impose no fly zone, 29.04.2013*. http://www.highbeam.com/doc/1G1-327930076.html. Accessed April 28, 2017.

Fartash, M. (1975, May 7). Statement to the 1975 RevCon, NPT/CONF/SR.4, Geneva.

Fartash, M. (1977). The disarmament "Club" at work. *Bulletin of the Atomic Scientist, 1,* 55–62.

Fartash, M. (1979, January 26). Statement to the CD, CD/PV.6, Geneva.

Fathi, N. (2004). Iran reasserts its right to enrich uranium as standoff persists. Resource document. *New York Times*, 27.11.2004. http://www.nytimes.com/2004/11/28/world/middleeast/iran-reasserts-its-right-to-enrich-uranium-as-standoff.html. Accessed April 28, 2017.

Fey, M., Melamud, A., & Müller, H. (2014). The role of justice in compliance behavior: Germany's early membership in the nuclear non-proliferation regime. *International Negotiation, 19*(3), 459–486.

Findlay, T. (1991). *Chemical weapons and missile proliferation: With implications for the Asia/Pacific Region*. Boulder, CO: Rienner.

Ford, C.A. (2009). *Nuclear technology rights and wrongs: The NPT, Article IV, and non-proliferation*. Hudson Institute, Washington, DC. https://www.hudson.org/…/20090601-ford-nuclearrightsandwrongs.pdf. Accessed April 28, 2017.

Franceschini, G. (2012). *The NPT review process and strengthening the treaty: Peaceful uses (Non-proliferation Policy Papers 11, EU Non-proliferation Consortium)*. Resource Document. SIPRI. https://www.sipri.org/sites/default/files/0000116074-EUNPC_no-11.pdf. Accessed April 28, 2017.

Gamson, W. (1992). The social psychology of collective action. In Morris, A., & Mc Clurg Mueller, C. (Eds.), *Frontiers in social movement theory* (pp. 3–76). New Haven, CT: Yale University Press.

Gharib Abadi, K. (2010, June 29). Statement to the OPCW at the 61st Session of the EC, EC-61/NAT.15, The Hague.

Gharib Abadi, K. (2011a, February 15). Statement to the OPCW at the 63rd Session of the EC, EC-63/NAT.12, The Hague.

Gharib Abadi, K. (2011b, May 3). Statement to the OPCW at the 64th Session of the EC, EC-64/NAT.10, The Hague.

Gharib Abadi, K. (2012, November 26). Statement to the 17th Session of the CWC CSP, C-17/NAT.24, The Hague.

Gharib Abadi, K. (2013, December 2). Statement to the OPCW at the 18th Session of the CWC CSP, C-18/NAT.15, The Hague.

Ghods Nakhai, H. (1961, September 22). Statement to the 16th Session of the UNGA, New York.

Governments of France, Germany and the United Kingdom. (2005, August 5). Full text of the E3 (France, Germany, and United Kingdom) proposal for a Framework for a long-term agreement between the E3 and Iran. http://www.acronym.org.uk/docs/0508/EU050808.pdf. Accessed April 28, 2017.

Graham, T., Jr. (2012). Interpreting the nuclear non-proliferation treaty. *The Nonproliferation Review, 19*(1), 137–141.

Hanson, M. (2012). Advocating the elimination of nuclear weapons: The role of key individual and coalition states. In T. Ogilvie-White & D. Santoro (Eds.), *Slaying the nuclear dragon. Disarmament dynamics in the twenty-first century* (pp. 56–84). Athens, GA: University of Georgia Press.

Höhl, K., & Kelle, A. (2003). *Die multilaterale Rüstungskontrolle von chemischen Waffen am Scheideweg. Das Chemiewaffen-Übereinkommen und seine erste Überprüfungskonferenz*. HSFK-Report 15/2003. Frankfurt a. M.

Hoveyda, F. (1972, November 1). Statement to the UNGA 1st Committee, A/C.1/PV.1881.

Hoveyda, A. A. (1977). Address by Amir Abbas Hoveyda. In: *Prime Minister of Iran, to the Iran Conference on the Transfer of Nuclear Technology, AEOI (1977)* (pp. 11–14).

IAEA. (2003, June 6). *Implementation of the NPT safeguards agreement in the Islamic Republic of Iran, GOV/2003/40, Vienna*. https://www.iaea.org/sites/default/files/gov2003-40.pdf. Accessed April 28, 2017.

IAEA. (2004a, February 24). *Implementation of the NPT safeguards agreement in the Islamic Republic of Iran, GOV/2004/11, Vienna*. https://www.iaea.org/sites/default/files/gov2004-11.pdf. Accessed April 28, 2 017.

IAEA. (2004b, November 26). *Communication dated 26 November 204 received from the permanent representatives of France, Germany, the Islamic Republic of Iran and the United Kingdom concerning the agreement signed in Paris on 15 November 2004, INFCIRC/637, Vienna*. https://www.iaea.org/sites/default/files/publications/documents/infcircs/2004/infcirc637_fr.pdf. Accessed April 28, 2017.

IAEA. (2008, February 22). *Implementation of the NPT safeguards agreement and relevant provisions of security council resolutions 1737 (2006) and 1747 (207) in the Islamic Republic of Iran, GOV/2008/4, Vienna.*

IAEA. (2010, May 7). *Communication dated 28 April 2010 received from the permanent mission of the Islamic Republic of Iran to the Agency regarding the Tehran Conference on Disarmament and Non-Proliferation, Vienna, INFCIRC/794*. https://www.iaea.org/sites/default/files/publications/documents/infcircs/2010/infcirc794.pdf. Accessed April 28, 2017.

Ihsanoglu, E. (2010, April 17). *Statement of the Secretary General of the OIC at the International Conference on Disarmament and Non-Proliferation: World Security without Weapons of Mass Destruction, Tehran*. http://www.oic-oci.org/topic_print.asp?t_id=3643. Accessed October 1, 2010.

Iran. (1985, September 19). Amendment by the Islamic Republic of Iran to the Draft Resolution NPT/CONF.III/L.4. Tabled by Iraq, NPT/CONF.III/L.5, Geneva.

Iran. (1990, August 31). *Suggested Elements for Final Document Language on Article III of the NPT*. Working Paper, NPT/CONF.IV/MC.II/WP.11, Geneva.

Iran. (1997, December 3). Declaration of the Islamic Republic of Iran upon ratification of the convention on the prohibition of the development, stockpiling and use of chemical weapons and on their destruction, C-II/NAT.2, The Hague.

Iran. (1998, May 5). *Cluster three: Peaceful uses of nuclear energy*. Working Paper, NPT/CONF.2000/PC.II/20, New York.

Iran. (2000a, May 4). *Peaceful uses of nuclear energy*. Working Paper, NPT/CONF.2000/MC.III/WP.10, New York.

Iran. (2004, May 4). *Implementation of Article VI*, Report, NPT/CONF.2005/PC.III/33, New York.

Iran. (2005a, April 18). *Implementation of Article VI*, Report, NPT/CONF.2005/4, New York.

Iran. (2005b, May 19). Working paper submitted by Iran for Main Committee II, NPT/CONF.2005/WP.48, New York.

Iran. (2005c, May 19). *Peaceful use of nuclear energy.* Working Paper, NPT/CONF.2005/WP.50, New York.

Iran. (2005d, May 20). Statement to the 2005 NPT RevCon, Main Committee I, On Compliance with Article I and VI, New York.

Iran. (2005e, September 15). Communication dated 12 September 2005 from the PERMANENT MISSION OF THE Islamic Republic of Iran to the IAEA, INFCIRC 657, Vienna.

Iran. (2007a, May 9). *Implementation of Article VI*, Report, NPT/CONF.2010/PC.I/13, New York.

Iran. (2007b, May 11). Peaceful Uses of Nuclear Energy, Working Paper, NPT/CONF.2010/PC.I/WP.75, New York.

Iran. (2008a, April 24). *Implementation of Article VI*, Report, NPT/CONF.2010/PC.II/7.

Iran. (2008b, April 25). *Peaceful uses of nuclear energy.* Working Paper, NPT/CONF.2010/PC.II/WP.6, Geneva.

Iran. (2008c, May 5). *Non-proliferation*. Working Paper, NPT/CONF.2010/PC.II/WP.28, Geneva.

Iran. (2009a, April 23). *Peaceful research, production and use of nuclear energy.* Working Paper, NPT/CONF.2010/PC.III/WP.7, New York.

Iran. (2009b, April 21). *Implementation of Article VI*, Report, NPT/CONF.2010/PC.III/6, New York.

Iran. (2009c, August 21). Working Paper on International Cooperation & National Measures I, BWC/MSP/2009/MX/WP.21, Geneva.

Iran. (2010a, May 3). *Nuclear disarmament.* Working Paper, NPT/CONF.2010/WP.49, New York.

Iran. (2010b, May 3). *Peaceful research, production and use of nuclear energy.* Working Paper, NPT/CONF.2010/WP.53, New York.

Iran. (2010c, May 10). Statement to the 2010 NPT RevCon, Main Committee II, New York.

Iran. (2010d, May 11). Statement to the 2010 NPT RevCon, Main Committee III, New York.

Iran. (2010e, May 28). *Statement at Final Session of the 2010 NPT RevCon*, New York.

Iran. (2010f, June 5). *Implementation of Article VI*, Report, NPT/CONF.2010/34, New York.

Iran. (2010g, June 5). Working Paper on the Issue of Non-Compliance with Articles I, III, IV and VI of the Treaty, NPT/CONF.2010/WP.62.

Iran. (2010h, November 29). Proposal by Iran on the establishment of "International Support Network for the Victims of Chemical Weapons", C-15/NAT.2, The Hague.

Iran. (2012, April 26). The inalienable right to develop research, production and uses of nuclear energy for peaceful purposes, NPT/CONF.2015/PC.I/WP.31, Vienna.

Iran. (2013a, April 8). Protection and assistance (Article X), RC-3/NAT.11, The Hague.

Iran. (2013b, April 19). The inalienable right to develop research, production and uses of nuclear energy for peaceful purposes. Working Paper, NPT/CONF.2015/PC.II/WP.39, Geneva.

Iran. (2013c, July 15). Taking forward multilateral nuclear disarmament negotiations. Working Paper submitted to the OEWG to develop proposals to take forward multilateral nuclear disarmament negotiations for the achievement and maintenance of a world without nuclear weapons, A/AC.297/WP.6, Geneva.

Iran. (2015a, March 31). *Implementation of Article VI*, Report, NPT/CONF.2015/20, New York.

Iran. (2015b, April 19). *Implementation of Article VI*, Report, NPT/CONF.2015/PC.II/6, Geneva.

Iran. (2015c), April 28). Implementation of Article VI, NPT/CONF.2015/PC.III/11, New York.

Iran. (2015d, April 29). *The inalienable right to develop research, production and uses of nuclear energy for peaceful purposes* [Working Paper]. NPT/CONF.2015/WP.43, New York.

Iran, et al. (2010, May 17). *Joint declaration by Iran, Turkey and Brazil.* https://fas.org/nuke/guide/iran/joint-decl.pdf. Accessed April 28, 2017.

Jahangiri, A. (2015, March 17). Statement to the OPCW on Behalf of the NAM and China to the EC, The Hague.

Jalali. (1981a, June 18).Statement to the CD, CD/PV.130, Geneva.

Jalali. (1981b, November 3). Statement to the 36th Session of the UNGA 1st Committee, A/C.1/36/PV.24, New York.

Johnson, R. (2009). *Unfinished business: The negotiation of the CTBT and the end of nuclear testing*. Geneva: UNIDIR.

Johnson, R. (2010). Assessing the 2010 NPT review conference. *Bulletin of the Atomic Scientists, 66*(4), 1–10.

JCPOA. (2015). *Joint comprehensive plan of action, Vienna 14 July 2015*. http://www.eeas.europa.eu/statements-eeas/docs/iran_agreement/iran_joint-comprehensive-plan-of-action_en.pdf. Accessed April 28, 2017.

Jones, P. (1998). Iran's threat perceptions and arms control policies. *The Nonproliferation Review, 6*(1), 40–55.

Jones, P. (2012). Learning to live with a nuclear Iran. *The Nonproliferation Review, 19*(2), 197–217.

Joyner, D. (2011). *Interpreting the nuclear non-proliferation treaty*. Oxford: Oxford University Press.

Joyner, D. (2013). Iran's nuclear program and international law. *Penn State Journal of Law & International Affairs, 2*(2), 282–292.

Joyner, D. H. (2014). The legal meaning and implications of Article VI of the Non-Proliferation Treaty. In G. Nystuen, S. Casey-Maslen, & A. Golden Bersage (Eds.), *Nuclear weapons under international law* (pp. 397–417). Cambridge: Cambridge University Press.

Karsh, E. (1993). Rational ruthlessness: Non-conventional and missile warfare in the Iran-Iraq war. In E. Karsh, M. S. Navias, & P. A. Sabin (Eds.), *Non-conventional weapons proliferation in the Middle East* (pp. 30–47). Oxford: Clarendon Press.

Kazemi Kamyab, N. (1984a, March 29). Statement to the CD, CD/PV.254, Geneva.

Kazemi Kamyab, N. (1984b, August 30). Statement to the CD, CD/PV.286, Geneva.

Kenyon, I. (2000). Chemical weapons in the twentieth century: Their use and their control. *The CBW Conventions Bulletin, 48*, 1–15. Resource Document. http://www.fas.harvard.edu/~hsp/bulletin/cbwcb48.pdf. Accessed April 28, 2017.

Kenyon, I., & Feakes, D. (2007). *The creation of the organization for the prohibition of chemical weapons: A case study in the birth of an intergovernmental organization*. The Hague: T.M.C. Asser Press.

Kenyon, I. & Mashhadi, H. (2007). Helping those threatened or attacked: Article X. In I. Kenyon & D. Feakes (Eds.), *The creation of the organisation for the prohibition of chemical weapons: A case study in the birth of an Intergovernmental Organisation.*

Kerry, J.F. (2017, September 29). The Iran deal is working: Here's how we know. *The Washington Post*. https://www.washingtonpost.com/opinions/the-iran-deal-is-working-heres-how-we-know/2017/09/29/d138b070-a44c-11e7-b14f-f41773cd5a14_story.html?utm_term=.ed5164333f66. Accessed November 8, 2017.

Khalatbari, A. A. (1978, June 6). Statement to the 10th Special Session of the UNGA, A/S-10/PV.18, New York.

Khamenei, S. A. (2010, April 17). *Speech at the Tehran Conference on Nuclear Disarmament and Non-Proliferation, Tehran*. http://cms.mfa.gov.ir/cms/cms/Tehranicd/en/Files/PresidentSpeech. Accessed August 28, 2015.

Kharrazi, K. (1997, September 22). Statement to the 52nd Session of the UNGA, A/52/PV.6, New York.

Kharrazi, K. (1998, June 4). Statement to the CD, CD/PV.796, Geneva.

Kharrazi, K. (2000, April 25). Statement to the 2000 NPT RevCon, NPT/CONF.2000/SR.4, New York.

Kharrazi, K. (2005a, May 3). Statement to the 2005 NPT RevCon, NPT/CONF.2005/SR.3, New York.

Kharrazi, K. (2005b, May 3). Statement to the 2005 RevCon (Verbatim), New York.

Khoshroo, G. (2003a, April 29). Statement to the 2nd PrepCom for the 2005 NPT RevCon, NPT/CONF.2005/PC.II/SR.4, Geneva.

Khoshroo, G. (2003b, April 30). Statement to the 1st RevCon of the States Parties to the CWC, The Hague.

Klandermans, B. (1997). *The social psychology of protest*. Oxford: Blackwell.

Kmentt, A. (2013). How divergent views on nuclear disarmament threaten the NPT. *Arms Control Today*. Resource Document. http://www.armscontrol.org/act/2013_12/How-Divergent-Views-on-Nuclear-Disarmament-Threaten-the-NPT. Accessed April 28, 2017.

Lantis, J. (2015). Nuclear technology and norm stewardship: US nonproliferation policies revisited. *International Studies Perspectives, 16*(4), 423–445.

Larijani, A. (1987, June 30). Statement to the CD, CD/PV.417, Geneva.

Mahallati. (1983, March 15). Statement to the CD, CD/PV.203, Geneva.

Mahallati. (1988, October 26). Statement to the 43rd Session of the UNGA 1st Committe, A/C.1/43/PV.15, New York.

Makovsky, M., & Misztal, B. (2012). Iran has no "right" to enrich uranium. Resource document. *The Wall Street Journal*, 08.07.2012; https://www.wsj.com/articles/SB10001424052702304141204577508442031058860. Accessed April 28, 2017.

Mashhadi, H. (1986, October 29). Statement to the 41st Session of the UNGA 1st Committee, A/C.1/41/PV.24, New York.

Mashhadi, H. (1987, October 22). Statement to the 42nd Session of the UNGA 1st Committee, A/C.1/42/PV.17, New York.

Mashhadi, H. (1988, April 26). Statement to the CD, CD/PV.460, Geneva.

Mehmanparast R. (2012, October 1). Statement at the OPCW high-level meeting on "fifteen years of the Chemical Weapons Convention: Celebrating success, committing to the future", New York.

Meier, O. (2008). News analysis: Chemical weapons parlay's outcome uncertain. *Arms Control Today*, 03/2008. https://www.armscontrol.org/print/2774. Accessed April 28, 2017.

Meier, O. (2014). Crisis as opportunity: Implications of the Nuclear conflict with Iran for the Nuclear Non-Proliferation Regime. *SWP Research Paper.* November 2014, Berlin.

Milani, A. (2010). The Shah's atomic dreams. *Foreign Policy*. http://foreignpolicy.com/2010/12/29/the-shahs-atomic-dreams/. Accessed April 28, 2017.

Ministry of Foreign Affairs of Iran. (1994). Positions. *The Iranian Journal of International Affairs, 6*(1), 241–272.

Ministry of Foreign Affairs of Iran. (2010, October 4). Spokesman Terms Iran "Forerunner of Campaign against N. Armaments" [Press Release]. http://zan1400.blogfa.com/post-166.aspx. Accessed April 28, 2017.

Ministry of Foreign Affairs Iran. (2013, August 25). *Intl community should react to use of chemical weapons [Press Release]*. http://www.mfa.gov.ir/?siteid=3&siteid=3&pageid=1997&newsview=7574. Accessed April 28, 2017.

Moradi, B. (1995, April 20). Statement to the 1995 NPT RevCon, Main Committee I, NPT/CONF.1995/MC.I/SR.2, New York.

Mottaki, M. (2006, December 6). Statement to the 11th Session of the CWC CSP, The Hague.

Mottaki, M. (2010, April 17). *Statement at the Tehran International Disarmament Conference*. http://www.president.ir/en/print.php?ArtID=21266. Accessed August 28, 2015.

Mousavi, M. H. (1981, October 5). Statement to the 36th Session of the UNGA, A/36/PV.26, New York.

Mousavian, S. (2012). *The Iranian nuclear crisis: A memoir*. Washington, DC: Carnegie Endowment.

Mousavian, S. (2013). Globalising Iran's fatwa against nuclear weapons. *Survival: Global Politics and Strategy, 55*(2), 147–162.

Müller, H. (2010). *Der nukleare Nichtverbreitungsvertrag nach der Überprüfung*. HSFK-Report 3/2010: Frankfurt a. M.

Müller, H. (2011). A nuclear nonproliferation test: Obama's nuclear policy and the 2010 NPT review conference. *The Nonproliferation Review, 18*(1), 219–236.

Müller, H. (2012). *The NPT review process and strengthening the treaty: Disarmament, EU non-proliferation consortium (Non-Proliferation Papers No. 10)*. Resource Document. https://www.sipri.org/publications/2012/eu-non-proliferation-papers/npt-review-process-and-strengthening-treaty-disarmament. Accessed April 28, 2017.

Müller, H. (2015). *Khameneis Rote Linien: Eine Bewertung des "Iran-Abkommens"*. HSFK-Report 2/2015: Frankfurt a. M.

Müller, H., Becker-Jakob, U., & Seidler-Diekmann, T. (2013). Regime conflicts and norm dynamics: Nuclear, biological, and chemical weapons. In H. Müller & C. Wunderlich (Eds.), *Norm dynamics in multilateral arms control: Interests, conflicts, and justice* (pp. 51–81). Athens, GA: University of Georgia Press.

Müller, H., & Wunderlich, C. (2018). Not lost in contestation: How norm entrepreneurs frame norm development in the nuclear nonproliferation regime. *Contemporary Security Policy, 1*(29), 341–366.

Müller, H., Wunderlich, C., Fey, M., Ricke, K., & Schaper, A. (2014). *Global Non-proliferation "clubs" vs. the NPT* (Resource document. Report 2014(04) Swedish Radiation Safety Authority Stockholm: 02/2014). http://www.stralsakerhetsmyndigheten.se/Publikationer/Rapport/Icke-spridning/2014/201404/. Accessed April 28, 2017.

Naimi-Arfa, B. (1990, October 17). Statement to the 45th Session of the UNGA 1st Committee, A/C.1/45/PV.6, New York.

Najafi, R. (2007, October 23). Statement to the 62nd Session of the UNGA 1st Committee, A/C.1/62/PV.14, New York.

Najafi, R. (2012, October 22). Statement at the 67th Session of the UNGA 1st Committee, New York.

NAM. (2010, April 28). *Elements for a Plan of Action for the Elimination of Nuclear Weapons*. Working Paper, NPT7CONF.2010/WP.47, New York.

NAM. (2012, August 31). Final Document adopted at the 16th Summit of Heads of State or Government of the Non-Aligned Movement, NAM 2012/Doc.1/Rev.2, Tehran. http://www.iranwatch.org/sites/default/files/nam-tehrandeclaration-083012.pdf. Accessed August 28, 2015.

Nasseri, S. (1990a, August 24). Statement to the 1990 NPT RevCon, NPT/CONF.IV/SR.8, New York.

Nasseri, S. (1990b, August 30). Statement to the CD, CD/1039, Geneva.

Nasseri, S. (1993, August 10). Statement to the CD, CD/PV.659, Geneva.

Nasseri, S. (1994a, June 23). Statement to the CD, CD/PV.683, Geneva.

Nasseri, S. (1994b, September 26). Statement to the Special Conference of the BWC, BWC/SPCONF/SR.3, Geneva.

Nasseri, S. (1995, May 11). Statement to the 1995 RevCon, NPT/CONF.1995/PV.17, New York.

Natalegawa, M. M. (2010, April 17). *Statement by the Minister for Foreign Affairs of Indonesia at the International Conference on Disarmament and Non Proliferation, Tehran*. http://kemlu.go.id/Pages/SpeechTranscriptionDisplay.aspx?IDP=498&l=en. Accessed October 1, 2010.

New York Times. (2007, December 4). Iran's President Clarifies Stand on Holocaust. It's a European Myth. https://www.nytimes.com/2005/12/15/world/middleeast/irans-president-clarifies-stand-on-holocaust-its-a.html. Accessed April 28, 2017.

Nirumand, B. (2015). *Kein Zurück mehr für Iran*. Resource document. Heinrich-Böll-Stiftung, 15.07.2015. https://www.boell.de/de/2015/07/15/kein-zurueck-mehr-fuer-iran. Accessed April 28, 2017.

NTI. (2008). *Iran chemical chronology*, last update 10/2008. https://www.nti.org/media/pdfs/iran_chemical.pdf?_=1316555748. Accessed April 28, 2017.

Nufer, C. (2012). Der Vater des iranischen Atomprogramms mit Schweizer Vergangenheit. *Tagesanzeiger*, 22.08.2012. http://www.tagesanzeiger.ch/ausland/naher-osten-und-afrika/Der-Vater-des-iranischen-Atomprogramms-mit-Schweizer-Vergangenheit/story/25588153. Accessed April 28, 2017.

Ogilvie-White, T. (2010). The defiant states: The nuclear diplomacy of North Korea and Iran. *The Nonproliferation Review, 17*(1), 117–138.

Ogilvie-White, T. (2012). The defiant states. North Korea and Iran. In T. Ogilvie-White & D. Santoro (Eds.), *Slaying the nuclear dragon: Disarmament dynamics in the twenty-first century* (pp. 249–278). Athens, GA: University of Georgia Press.

OPCW. (2000a, May 17). *Report of the organisation on the implementation of the convention*, The Hague.

OPCW. (2000b, July November). An invitation to propose candidates for a course on medical aspects of defence against chemical weapons, Tehran, Islamic Republic of Iran, 23–26 October 2000, S/199/2000, The Hague.

OPCW. (2008, November 9). Ninth international course on medical defense against chemical weapons, The Hague. https://www.opcw.org/news/article/ninth-international-course-on-medical-defence-against-chemical-weapons/. Accessed February 14, 2015.

OPCW. (2011, December 2). Decision: The establishment of the international support network for victims of chemical weapons and the establishment of a voluntary trust fund for this purpose, C 16/DEC.13, The Hague.

OPCW. (2013, September 9). *Report by the Director-General: Status of Implementation of the International Support Network for Victims of Chemical Weapons*, EC-74/DG.12, C-18/DG.13, The Hague.

OPCW. (2016, November 30). *Report of the OPCW on the Implementation of the CWC in 2015*, C-24/4, The Hague.

Pahlavi, A. (1970, November 11). Statement to the UNGA 1st Committee, A/C.1/PV.1756, New York.

Pahlavi, M. R. (1968). *Mission for my country*. London: Hutchinsons & Co.

Patrikarakos, D. (2012). *Nuclear Iran: The birth of an atomic state*. London: I.B. Tauris.

Perkovich, G. (2005). For Tehran, nuclear program is a matter of national pride. *Yale Global*, 23.05.2005. http://carnegieendowment.org/2005/03/23/for-tehran-nuclear-program-is-matter-of-national-pride. Accessed April 28, 2017.

Pirseyedi, B. (2013). Third world, global islam and pragmatism. In *Arms control and Iranian Foreign Policy: Diplomacy of discontent*. New York, NY: Routledge.

Posch, W. (2013). The third world, global islam and pragmatism. The making of Iranian Foreign Policy. SWP Research Paper 3/2013. Berlin.

Potter, W., & Mukhatzhanova, G. (2012). *Nuclear politics and the non-aligned movement. principles vs. pragmatism*. Abingdon: Routledge.

Press TV. (2010). *Salehi during 2nd Conference on Disarmament and Non-Proliferation. US, "Israel" Violating NPT*. http://edition.presstv.ir/detail.fa/184296.html. Accessed April 28, 2017.

Rajiv, S. C. (2010). *Iran and the NPT RevCon 2010 (IDSA Comment)*. http://www.idsa.in/idsacomments/IranandtheNPTRevCon2010_sscrajiv_040510. Accessed April 28, 2017.

Rauf, T., & Johnson, R. (1995). After the NPT's indefinite extension: The future of the global nonproliferation regime. *The Nonproliferation Review, 3*(1), 28–42.

Richter, P. (2012). U.S. signals major shift on Iran nuclear program. *Los Angeles Times*, 27.04.2012. http://articles.latimes.com/2012/apr/27/world/la-fg-iran-nuclear-20120428. Accessed April 28, 2017.

Ritchie, N. (2018). The diplomacy of resistance: Power, hegemony and nuclear disarmament. *Global Change Peace & Security, 2*(30), 121–141.

Robinson, J. P. (1998). The negotiations on the Chemical Weapons Convention: A historical overview. In M. Bothe, N. Ronzitti, & A. Rosas (Eds.), *The negotiations on the Chemical Weapons Convention: Implementation and prospects* (pp. 17–36). The Hague: Kluwer Law International.

Robinson, J. P., & Goldblat, J. (1984). Chemical warfare in the Iran-Iraq-war 1980–1988. *SIPRI Fact Sheet*. http://www.iranchamber.com/history/articles/chemical_warfare_iran_iraq_war.php. Accessed April 28, 2017.

Rouhani, H. (2005, September 30). Text of speech by Supreme National Security Council Secretary Hassan Rohani to the Supreme Cultural Revolution Council. Beyond the challenges facing Iran and the IAEA concerning the nuclear dossier, Rhabord (in Persian), 7–38 (FBIS-IAP20060113336001), translated in 2006 by the Foreign Broadcast Information Service.

Rouhani, H. (2013a, September 24). Statement to the 68th Session of the UNGA, New York.

Rouhani, H. (2013b, September 26). Statement on behalf of NAM at the high-level meeting of the UNGA on Nuclear disarmament, New York.

Rublee, M. (2008). Taking stock of the nuclear nonproliferation regime: Using social psychology to understand regime effectiveness. *International Studies Review, 10*(3), 420–450.

Sadjadpour, K. (2009). *Reading Khamenei: The world view of Iran's most powerful leader*. Washington: Carnegie Endowment for International Peace.

Salehi, A. A. (2009, September 14). Statement to the 53rd Session of the IAEA General Conference, GC/53/OR.1, Vienna.

Salehi, A. A. (2010, September 20). Statement to the 54th Session of the IAEA General Conference, GC/54/OR.1, Vienna.

Salehi, A. A. (2012, April 12). Iran. We do not want nuclear weapons. *Washington Post*. https://www.washingtonpost.com/opinions/iran-we-do-not-want-nuclear-weapons/2012/04/12/gIQAjMNnDT_story.html?utm_term=.5f0c16cc6510. Accessed April 28, 2017.

Salehi, A. A. (2013, September 16). Statement to the 57th Session of the IAEA General Conference, GC/57/OR.1, Vienna.

Sauer, T. (2015). *The NPT and the humanitarian initiative: Towards and beyond the 2015 NPT review conference (Deep Cuts Working Paper No. 5)*. Resource Document. http://deepcuts.org/images/PDF/DeepCuts_WP5_Sauer_UK.pdf. Accessed April 28, 2017.

Sell, S. K., & Prakash, A. (2004). Using ideas strategically: The contest between business and NGO networks in intellectual property rights. *International Studies Quarterly, 48*(1), 143–175.

Shababi S. (1985a, September 4). Statement to the 1985 NPT RevCon, NPT/CONF.III/SR.13/Add.1, Geneva.

Shababi S. (1985b, September 21). Statement to the 1985 NPT RevCon, NPT/CONF.III/SR.16, Geneva.

Shababi, S. (1994). Arms control and non-proliferation policies of Iran. *The Iranian Journal of International Affairs, 6*(1–2), 278–281.

Shaker, M. (1980). *The nuclear non-proliferation treaty: Origin and implementation 1959–1979*. London.

Sheikholeslam. (1984, April 26). Statement to the CD, CD/PV.262, Geneva.

Sherman, W. R. (2013, October 3). Senate hearing 113–152. Reversing Iran's nuclear program, hearing of State Secretary Wendy R. Sherman before the Committee on Foreign Relations, United States Senate. 113th Session, Washington. http://www.gpo.gov/fdsys/pkg/CHRG-113shrg86351/html/CHRG-113shrg86351.htm. Accessed August 28, 2015.

Shirazi, N. (2013). Relax, Iran isn't going to withdraw from the NPT. Resource Document. Wide Asleep in America. http://www.wideasleepinamerica.com/2013/07/iran-withdraw-npt-mousavian.html. Accessed April 28, 2017.

Simpson, J. (2001). The 2000 NPT review conference. In Disarmament Armaments & International Security (Eds.), *SIPRI yearbook* (pp. 487–502). Oxford: Oxford University Press.

Singh, J. (1998). Against nuclear apartheid. *Foreign Affairs, 77*(5), 41–52.

Singh, M. (2014). The case for zero enrichment: Iran arms control today. Resource Document. *Arms Control*, 04.03.2014. https://www.armscontrol.org/act/2013_03/The-Case-for-Zero-Enrichment-in-Iran. Accessed April 28, 2017.

Skjöldebrand, R. (1980). The international nuclear fuel cycle evaluation—INFCE. *IAEA Bulletin, 22*(2), 30–33.

Soltanieh, A. A. (1984, September 25). Statement to the 28th Session of the IAEA General Conference, GC/XXVIII/COM.5/OR.35, Vienna.

Soltanieh, A. A. (1990a, August 28). Statement to the 1990 NPT RevCon, Main Committee III, NPT/CONF.IV/MC.III/SR.2, Geneva.

Soltanieh, A. A. (1990b, August 29). Statement to the 1990 NPT RevCon, Main Committee II, NPT/CONF.IV/MC.II/SR.3, Geneva.

Soltanieh, A. A. (2001, November 19). Statement to the 5th BWC RevCon, Geneva.

Soltanieh, A. A. (2008, September 29). Statement to the 52nd Session of the IAEA General Conference, GC/52/OR.2, Vienna.

South Africa. (2011, February 16). Statement on Behalf of the African Group of States Parties at the 63rd Session of the EC, EC/63/NAT.10, The Hague.

Strulak, T. (1993). The nuclear suppliers group. *The Nonproliferation Review*, 2–10.

Tabatabai, A. (2012). The audience war: The challenges of Iran's nuclear rhetoric. *RUSI Analysis, 29*(3), 2012.

Tabatabai, A. (2014). Iran's evolving narrative. Resource Document. http://www.belfercenter.org/publication/irans-evolving-nuclear-narrative. Accessed August 28, 2015.

Tabatabai, A. (2015, February 13). Where does the Islamic revolutionary guard corps stand on nuclear negotiations? *Bulletin of the Atomic Scientists*. http://thebulletin.org/where does iran%E2%80%99s supreme leader really stand nuclear negotiations7987. Accessed April 28, 2017.

Tannenwald, N. (2013). Justice and fairness in the nuclear nonproliferation regime. *Ethics & International Affairs, 27*(3), 299–317.

Thakur, R. (2017, November 20). *Nuclear norms and the UN Ban Treaty (Australian Strategic Policy Institute)*. https://www.aspistrategist.org.au/nuclear-norms-and-the-un-ban-treaty/. Accessed November 28, 2018.

Thaler, D., Nader, A., Chubin, S., Green, J. D., Lynch, C., Wehrey, F., et al. (2010). *Mullahs, guards, and bonyads: An exploration of Iranian leadership dynamics*. Santa Monica, CA: Rand.

The Guardian. (2015, July 14). Vienna nuclear deal. A new opportunity both for Iran and the world. http://www.theguardian.com/world/2015/jul/14/iran-nuclear-deal-political-figures-react-landmark-agreement. Accessed April 28, 2017.

Thränert, O. (2003). *Der Iran und die Verbreitung von ABC-Waffen*. Berlin: SWP-Studie.

Trapp, R. (2014). Article X: Assistance and protection against chemical weapons. In W. Krutzsch, E. Myjer, & R. Trapp (Eds.), *The Chemical Weapons Convention: A commentary* (pp. 333–350). Oxford: Oxford University Press.

Tucker, J. (2007). *War of nerves: Chemical warfare from World War I to Al-Qaeda*. New York, NY: Anchor Books.

UN. (2006, May 30). United Nations Monitoring, Verification and Inspection Commission, S/2006/342, New York.

USIP. (2013a, November 24). *Geneva Deal II. President Obama on Merits of Talks*. http://iranprimer.usip.org/blog/2013/nov/24/geneva-deal-ii-president-obama-merits-talks. Accessed April 28, 2017.

USIP. (2013b, November 24). *Geneva Deal III: Iranian Reaction*. http://iranprimer.usip.org/blog/2013/nov/24/geneva-deal-iii-iranian-reaction. Accessed April 28, 2017.

Velayati, A. A. (1983, September 30). Statement to the 38th Session of the UNGA, A/38/PV.13, New York.

Velayati, A. A. (1984, February 16). Statement to the CD, CD/PV.242, Geneva.

Velayati, A. A. (1985, May 16). Statement to the CD, CD/PV.308, Geneva.

Velayati, A. A. (1986, February 27). Statement to the CD, CD/PV.343, Geneva.

Velayati, A. A. (1987, July 28). Statement to the CD, CD/PV.425, Geneva.

Velayati, A. A. (1988a, March 31). Statement to the CD, CD/PV.453, Geneva.

Velayati, A. A. (1988b, June 1). Statement to the 15th eisenSpecial Session on Disarmament of the UNGA, A/S-15/PV.3, Geneva.

Velayati, A. A. (1989, July 4). Statement to the CD, CD/PV.514, Geneva.

Velayati, A. A. (1990a, March 15). Statement to the CD, CD/PV.543, Geneva.

Velayati, A. A. (1990b, September 28). Statement to the 45th Session of the UNGA, A/45/PV.5, New York.

Velayati, A. A. (1992, September 25). Statement to the 47th Session of the UNGA. A/47/PV.6, New York.

Velayati, A. A. (1994a, January 9). Statement to the CD, CD/PV.690, Geneva.

Velayati, A. A. (1994b, January 9). Statement to the CD, CD/PV.690, Geneva.

Velayati, A. A. (1995, April 21). Statement to the 1995 NPT RevCon, NPT/CONF.1995/SR.8, New York.

Velayati, A. A. (1996, February 22). Statement to the CD, CD/PV.726, Geneva.

Vick, K. (2012, January 16). In their own words. For Iranian, negotiations = stalling time. *Time*. http://world.time.com/2012/01/16/in-their-own-words-for-iranians-negotiations-stalling. Accessed April 28, 2017.

Westberg, G. (2010). *Report on the Tehran Conference on Nuclear Weapons, April 10*. Resource Document, 05.05.2010. http://www.oldsite.transnational.org/Area_MiddleEast/2010/Westberg_TehranConf.html. Accessed April 28, 2017.

Wunderlich, C. (2014). A "rogue" gone norm entrepreneurial? Iran within the nuclear nonproliferation regime. In W. Wagner, W. Werner, & M. Onderco (Eds.), *Deviance in international relations: "Rogue states" and international security* (pp. 83–104). Basingstoke: Palgrave Macmillan.

Wunderlich, C. (2017). Delegitimisation à la Carte: The "Rogue State" label as a means of stabilising order in the nuclear non-proliferation regime. In S. Gertheiss, S. Herr, K. Wolf, & C. Wunderlich (Eds.), *Resistance and change in world politics: International dissidence* (pp. 143–189). Cham: Palgrave Macmillan.

Wunderlich, C., Hellman, A., Müller, D., Reuter, J., & Schmidt, H. J. (2013). Non-aligned reformers and revolutionaries: Egypt, South Africa, Iran, and North Korea. In H. Müller & C. Wunderlich. 246–295.

Zarif, J. (1991, October 16). Statement to the 45th Session of the UNGA 1st Committee, A/C.1/45/PV.5, New York

Zarif, J. (1995, January 24). Statement at the 4th Session of the PrepCom for the 1995 RevCon, NPT/CONF.1995/PC.IV/SR.3, New York.

Zarif, J. (1999, February 2). Statement to the CD. CD/PV.812, Geneva.

Zarif, J. (2005, May 27). Statement at the 2005 NPT RevCon, Concluding Statement, New York.

Zarif, J. (2015, July 15). UNSC to recognize Iran's right for enrichment activities. en.mfa.ir/index.aspx?siteid=3&fkeyid=&siteid=3&fkeyid=&siteid=3&pageid=1997&newsview=349184. Accessed April 28, 2017.

Zarif, J., Mqmtaz, J., & Mirzaee, S. (1996). Impermissibility of the use or threat of use of nuclear weapons: A case for an advisory opinion from the International Court of Justice. *Iranian Journal of International Affairs, 8*(1), 1–33.

Ziaran, B. (1998, June 2). Statement to the CD, CD/PV.795, Geneva.

Ziaran, B. (2008, April 7). Statement to the 2nd Special Session of the CSP to Review the Operation of the CWC, The Hague.

Chapter 8
Comparing Prototypical and Unorthodox Norm Advocacy

8.1 Recap: Applying the Norm Entrepreneurial Label to Iran

The previous chapters demonstrated that parts of Iranian activities in the realm of multilateral arms control can be qualified as norm entrepreneurship. According to the criteria set out in Sect. 5.2.1, norm entrepreneurs should be perceived as actors who—dissatisfied with the prevailing normative order—actively seek to put into practice certain ideas or normative meanings which they deem particularly important or more appropriate than existing ones. Their ultimate objective is by means of rhetorical and practical lobbying to anchor their particular norm interpretation as a new standard of appropriateness.

In the analyzed cases, Iran acted as a norm entrepreneur particularly with regard to consolidating already established norms: With regard to the norm of nuclear disarmament, Iran called for the appropriate implementation of Article VI or for measures to strengthen it. Yet Iran was not directly involved in the establishment of new normative regulations. While it supported the idea of a nuclear weapons convention within the group of non-aligned states, it did not start independent initiative to support it (see Sect. 7.3). Pertaining to the peaceful use of nuclear energy, Iran's activities were also aimed at strengthening or specifying an already established norm: Here, Tehran took the view that Article IV was incorrectly interpreted and implemented and tried to anchor its own interpretation (a right to uranium enrichment) through persistent discursive interventions. In both cases, however, Iran was not directly involved in establishing new norms.

Also, in both cases, Iran did not act in isolation: With regard to the norm of nuclear disarmament, its concern was shared by a heterogeneous group of disarmament-friendly states to which Iran referred in its argumentation. It also has to be noted that some non-aligned countries, Iran's most important reference group, also made a more consistent and organized commitment to nuclear disarmament (e.g., Brazil, South

C. Wunderlich, *Rogue States as Norm Entrepreneurs*,
Norm Research in International Relations,
https://doi.org/10.1007/978-3-030-27990-5_8

Africa, and Mexico). The advocacy for a right to the peaceful uses of nuclear energy is also not new, but was already put forward in the 1960s and 1970s by Western industrialized countries and by the non-aligned, in particular non-NPT member, India.

It was only with regard to the commitment for the protection and assistance of victims of chemical weapons that Iran's norm entrepreneurship already started in the early phase of norm construction.[1] In fact, Article X of the CWC was largely designed through Iranian suggestions, even though Iran was not the only driving force. In addition, Iran was able to put the Iraqi chemical weapons attacks and the devastating consequences for the CW victims onto the international agenda and mobilized international support. Since from Iran's point of view, protection and assistance measures provided by Article X were not sufficient, the country continued to advocate the strengthening of these provisions even after the CWC had entered into force. The attempt to institutionalize the norm finally led to the establishment of a network of supporters for victims of chemical weapons.

In its norm-promoting activities, Iran made use of classical norm entrepreneurial strategies, as discussed in the previous chapter. Iran's repertoire of actions is characterized by a mixture of rhetorical and practical activities. Persuasion strategies were mainly based on (emotionalizing) framing, verbal criticism, and massive resort to naming, shaming, and blaming. But it also turned to unconventional, destructive tactics and blocking strategies to enforce its positions. For example, some of the strategies used to strengthen the disarmament norm or the right to uranium enrichment particularly aimed to counteract the activities of other actors. A case in point is the Tehran International Conference on Disarmament and Non-Proliferation in April 2010, which was conceived of as a counter-initiative to President Obama's Nuclear Security Summit and his commitment to a world without nuclear weapons. This conference and the following one in 2011 not only served Iran as a platform for its norm entrepreneurship and an opportunity to present itself as "forerunner in the global campaign against nuclear armaments" (Ministry of Foreign Affairs Iran 2010). They also provided an arena for diplomatic counter-attacks regarding the accusation that Tehran was working on a military nuclear program (Butters 2010; Rajiv 2010).

It is striking that Iran's activities with regard to the CWC differ from the engagement shown in the realm of the NPT. Although in order to advocate more effective protection measures for victims of chemical weapons, Iran also relied on intensive naming, shaming, and blaming, it did so with less vigor. Perhaps this more moderate stance can be explained with reference to the discriminatory structure of the NPT: Like many other non-aligned NNWS, Iran feels it has been treated unfairly, which in turn is manifest in a confrontational tone and leads to a "diplomacy of discontent" (Pirseyedi 2013: 164).

[1]This does not mean, though, that Iran is not a "genuine" norm entrepreneur seeking to construct new norms. Such norm entrepreneurship can be seen in other policy areas, for example President Khatami's initiative for a "dialogue among civilizations" in 2000 (Bettiza and Dionigi 2014). With his efforts for a "World against Violence and Violent Extremism" (WAVE) in 2013, President Rouhani tried to tie in with Khatami's norm entrepreneurship.

What is the résumé regarding the element of proactivism typical for norm entrepreneurship? As has been set out in Sect. 5.2.1, the actions of norm entrepreneurs are typically characterized by a high degree of consistency in word and deed and are purposeful, intentional, and change-oriented while displaying a consistently high level of activity. The strategies used are rather anticipatory and more active than reactive.

In all three cases, Iranian engagement showed a high level of continuity over time and regime type (pre-revolutionary as well as after the revolution) as well as across various forums (national, regional, international). All in all, Iran's proactivism with regard to the CWC exceeded the one displayed in the non-proliferation regime. This fact is probably connected with the West's doubts about Iran's own nuclear program, which limited Iran's possibilities.

Iranian activities were also intentional and change-oriented, albeit with varying degrees of success. The only criterion which is hard to prove is that of innovation: While Iran was one of the first states to stand up for the protection of victims of chemical weapons, the argumentation put forward was not new. Neither was it in the case of nuclear disarmament and the fight for a right to uranium enrichment. In both cases, Iran drew heavily on already established patterns of norm advocacy.

Norm entrepreneurship is also characterized by a high degree of consistency in rhetoric and action. Observers of Iranian arms control policy, however, have repeatedly argued that Iran's proactive rhetorical commitment to strengthening regime norms does not always match its actions (e.g., Thränert 2003: 26–27; Pirseyedi 2013: 167). These contradictions raise doubts about the credibility of Iranian norm entrepreneurship and suggest that it serves the purpose of prestige advertising rather than symbolizing genuine commitment.

Such inconsistencies also came to the fore in the cases under investigation. On the one hand, the fact that Iran had secretly worked on a military nuclear program until 2003 stands in striking contrast to Iranian statements that weapons of mass destruction are un-Islamic and immoral. Its possible nuclear weapons intentions not only overshadow its commitment to nuclear disarmament. They also suggest that the demand for a right to uranium enrichment might only be strategically motivated to promote national interests. This is further supported by the fact that Iran has systematically expanded its nuclear rights narrative parallel to the nuclear conflict with the West. Instead of setting a good example, Tehran did not follow its own rhetorical demands, a behavior that was justified with reference to the perceived systematic injustices inherent to the NPT. An example of such "scapegoating tactics" (Pirseyedi 2013: 167) is that although Iran repeatedly calls on the nuclear weapons states to join the CTBT, it makes its own ratification dependent on that of the USA. Perceptions of injustice are also reflected in the criticism directed toward the USA and Israel, which Iranian diplomats expressed in all speeches and which led Iran to block negotiations on several occasions. Even Iran's commitment to the protection of chemical weapons victims was not free of interest-based ambivalences—in particular, with regard to the unbroken loyalty to the Syrian ruler Assad, who has reportedly used chemical weapons against his own population.

It can therefore not be dismissed that Iran might have advocated norms for purely strategic reasons. But does self-interest in establishing and promoting a norm per se exclude a humanitarian or normative motivation? While advocating for norms on the protection of chemical weapons victims and the right to uranium enrichment undoubtedly served the national interests of Iran, the country backed and justified its normative engagement by referring to the idea that it also served the common good. The analysis revealed that Iran refers to justice-based and welfare-oriented arguments quite consistently (Wunderlich 2014: 92), which seems to indicate that Iranian norm entrepreneurship is in fact also based on "ideational commitment" (Finnemore and Sikkink 1998: 898). Another indicator in favor of genuine, norm-driven commitment is that Iran has continuously advocated the propagated norms in various forums over a long period back to the Shah's times.

To sum up, Iran's activities in the analyzed cases match the criteria for norm entrepreneurship. How then can Iran's actions be evaluated with regard to the alternative explanations set out in Sect. 5.2.2?

Obviously, the alternative explanation that "rogue states" are to be understood primarily as norm breakers whose words and actions are aimed at undermining and destroying the prevailing normative order (AE1) cannot be upheld. It may be true that Iran demonstrated its opposition to the (US-shaped) normative order in words and deeds. To this end, Iranian delegates occasionally resorted to destructive practices that were intended to undermine existing norms and/or negotiation processes. Nevertheless, Iran did not merely act as a norm breaker.

In some cases, Iran acted as a classic norm entrepreneur. With regard to the protection of victims of chemical weapons, Iran's activities covered a broad spectrum of norm entrepreneurial activities including norm construction, promotion, and institutionalization. Iran's commitment to nuclear disarmament can be located at later stages of the norm life cycle, i.e., constantly reaffirming and monitoring the proper implementation of an already established norm as well as supporting additional measures to further strengthen nuclear disarmament.

In the case of the right to uranium enrichment, Iran advocated the establishment of subsidiary normative meanings. The norm advocacy here can in part be interpreted as an attempt to counter a Western liberal hegemonic interpretation. Yet since Tehran's activities go beyond pure reaction, they do not confirm alternative explanation 2 and instead qualify as classic norm entrepreneurship according to the criteria set out in Sect. 5.2.1.

In conclusion, the findings illustrate that the norm entrepreneurial concept can be applied to the supposed "rogue state" Iran. However, there are inconsistencies that cast doubt on Iran's normative credibility. In order to gain further insights into the peculiarities of Iranian norm entrepreneurship, in the following sections, I will compare the findings with two contrasting cases.

Section 8.2 will take a closer look at the prototypical norm entrepreneur, Sweden. A comparison will bring to the fore differences to Iranian norm advocacy, and it will reveal insights regarding the question of how credibility relates to norm entrepreneurship, to be discussed in the concluding chapter.

In order to avoid the impression that norm entrepreneurship is arbitrary and can be attributed to every state, Iranian arms control diplomacy will be compared to North Korea, another alleged "rogue state." Doing so also makes it possible to address alternative explanation 2.

8.2 "Good Cop, Bad Cop": Comparing Sweden and Iran

This section provides a (cursory) overview of how Sweden—which has been designated a norm entrepreneur many times—tries to promote norms pertaining to the control of nuclear weapons. To this end, I will not trace individual instances of norm entrepreneurship. My goal is rather to illustrate the full range of Swedish norm entrepreneurship in this policy field and to shed light on the strategies and resources used for this purpose. Within the nuclear non-proliferation regime, Iran and Sweden focus on similar normative priorities. However, the two countries differ in terms of their strategies.

Sweden is generally considered a prototypical norm entrepreneur. In policy fields as diverse as human rights (Ingebritsen 2002; Brysk 2009), environmental protection (Ingebritsen 2002), development cooperation (Ingebritsen 2002), or international security (Björkdahl 2002, 2008, 2013; Rublee 2009; Youde and Slagter 2013; Wunderlich 2013), various authors have traced Swedish norm-setting and norm-promoting activities. Sweden's reputation as a good international citizen with a general welfare orientation also transcends to the field of multilateral arms control (Becker-Jakob et al. 2013: 224–231).

Sweden was considered a "force for good in the world" (Dahl 2002: 140) long before Olof Palme coined the term "active internationalism" in the 1970s. For many years, the Nordic country has pursued a norm-based foreign policy characterized by a preference for multilateralism, cooperation, international solidarity, and justice, as well as the protection and promotion of international law. Sweden's political identity is based on social democratic and Protestant values, which also led the country to advocate social justice and solidarity with less privileged countries on a multilateral level (Bergman 2007: 84). A central component of this active foreign policy was the policy of neutrality pursued for many years, which enabled Sweden to play a mediating role between the superpowers and lay the ground for its global reputation and credibility (Agius 2006: Chap. 4; Bjereld et al. 2008: Chap. 1). But neutrality and active internationalism also served to promote national interests, as Sweden was able to gain international influence and participate in the development of a cooperative security architecture (Agius 2006: 61).

Sweden's (self-imposed) role as a "moral superpower" (Nilsson 1991; transl. CW) or "global conscience" (Bjereld et al. 2008: 21) is reflected in its multilateral arms control policy. While leaving open an own nuclear option from the mid-1950s to the 1970s, Sweden began to become actively involved in international disarmament negotiations and was able to use its technical nuclear expertise to strengthen its negotiating position (Prawitz 1995: 12). Ultimately, the government decided that the best protection against a nuclear attack was global disarmament (Wallin 1991: 37). Active commitment to nuclear disarmament and non-proliferation of WMD was therefore not only a moral requisite, but it was also in the immediate national interest of the country.

Swedish diplomats were soon among the driving forces behind various disarmament initiatives in international forums, gaining respect and authority that transcended the small country's material resources. Ever since, Sweden has actively been involved in constructing and strengthening the NPT (Prawitz 1995: 27) and has become "a non-proliferation and disarmament powerhouse" (Bergenäs 2010). Indeed, Sweden's commitment to nuclear disarmament and non-proliferation is impressive, as the following overview shows.

8.2.1 Sweden's Commitment to Nuclear Disarmament and Effective Verification: Normative Demands and Practical Activities

Sweden's disarmament activism flourished between 1962 and 1994, when a well-equipped disarmament delegation led the negotiations and advised the government on relevant issues. The importance attached to disarmament is also reflected at the institutional level: Until the 1990s, Sweden had a disarmament minister.[2] Alva Myrdal, who held the post from 1967 to 1973 and who later won the Nobel Peace Prize for her work for disarmament, contributed significantly to Sweden's increasing influence over international disarmament and non-proliferation efforts. Within the UN disarmament machinery, Sweden took on the role of spokesperson of the non-aligned states,[3] acted as a persistent critic of the superpowers, and kept on urging them to comply with their disarmament obligation stemming from Article VI of the NPT.

Sweden's efforts to achieve a world free from nuclear weapons date back to the 1960s, when in 1961 then Foreign Minister Östen Undén proposed to establish a nuclear weapon-free club. Its members were to commit themselves neither to acquire nuclear weapons nor to have them stationed on their territory (Brodin 2016). In 1965, Sweden submitted a package proposal to the Conference on Disarmament

[2]In 1974, Inga Thorsson was appointed undersecretary of state for disarmament. A few years later in 1982, Maj Britt Theorin was granted the status of disarmament ambassador. In 1991, the post was finally abolished by the Bildt government and transferred to the responsibility of the Foreign Ministry. The liquidation of the post in the 1990s was accompanied by a gradual devaluation of the importance attached to nuclear disarmament. While Sweden continued its commitment to multilateral arms control, the level of activities decreased during the 1990s and shifted toward non-proliferation.

[3]During the Cold War, the members of the Conference on Disarmament formed three groups: the Western Group, the Eastern Group, and the Group of 21 non-aligned states (G21). Until 1995, Sweden—like Iran—was officially a member of the G21. With its accession to the EU, this was no longer possible. Since then, Sweden has been outside any group formation while maintaining close ties to the Western Group and the G21.

containing various measures aimed at preventing the spread of nuclear weapons as well as providing for quantitative and qualitative restrictions on existing nuclear arsenals (Birnbaum 1965: 308). After the proposal was rejected by the NWS, the country worked with the non-aligned states on a draft treaty based on the Irish resolution of 1961, which formed the basis for the later NPT. It contained demands that were to become basic tenets of Swedish nuclear diplomacy: The commitment to achieve a Comprehensive Nuclear Test-Ban Treaty, combined with a ban on the production of fissile material for weapons purposes, negative security assurances, effective verification measures based on comprehensive IAEA safeguards and a time-bound plan for complete disarmament (Gierow 1990: 10; Alani 1995: 10; Prawitz 2003: 62).[4]

Swedish advocacy was also instrumental with regard to integrating an obligation to nuclear disarmament (Article VI) equivalent to the commitment to the non-proliferation norm into the draft treaty text of the NPT—even if the results were much weaker than Sweden had hoped for (Lomas 1991: 194; Thunborg 2005: 32). Referring to the role Sweden played during the negotiation of the NPT, Lars van Dassen asserts that "when it is sometimes stated that the NPT is an 'Irish baby' it also has to be said that Sweden is one of the treaty's uncles or aunts" (van Dassen 1998: 21). By ratifying the NPT in January 1970, Sweden confirmed its final renunciation of nuclear weapons (Jonter 2001; Rublee 2009: 169–184). Sweden's conscious decision against the nuclear option helped to consolidate the role attributed to the country from outside. From then on, the NPT was regarded as the cornerstone of Swedish disarmament policy, which is reflected, among other things, in the determined efforts to universalize and strengthen the treaty institutionally and in the persistent criticism of the nuclear weapons states' unwillingness to disarm (Wunderlich 2008).

In the 1970s and 1980s in particular, Sweden worked closely with non-aligned countries (Garris 1973: 201). In fact, it shared many positions with the developing countries, such as calling on the superpowers to put an end to the nuclear arms race and instead giving priority to general and complete disarmament. Sweden also shared the demand for time-bound disarmament. In practice, however, the country has always been committed to a balanced weighting of the three pillars of the NPT: disarmament, non-proliferation, and the peaceful uses of nuclear energy. Foreign Minister Anna Lindh summarized this position in 2000:

> the NPT is based on balanced commitments. The majority of states have agreed to forego the nuclear option in return for negotiations in good faith, chiefly among the five nuclear weapon states, towards nuclear disarmament. Our common goal is a nuclear weapon-free world. This is the foundation of the global non-proliferation regime. The absence of negotiations on disarmament would risk eroding the NPT regime. (Lindh 2000)

The commitment to non-proliferation, particularly in the form of effective verification, was regarded as an integral part of this policy (e.g., Sweden et al. 1985). This led the Swedish government to propose or support various initiatives in the field of

[4]The data sample comprised a huge amount of statements uttered by revolutionary leaders and state representatives at various forums throughout the entire period of investigation. Reasons of space, however, allow for a selective reference to statements only.

export controls: Since 1971, Sweden has coordinated its export policies within the Zangger Committee and has been a member of the Nuclear Suppliers Group since 1977. Within the latter, it was one of the first states to demand full-scope safeguards as a condition for nuclear supply (Alani 1995: 16; van Dassen 1995, 1996: 269–270).[5] From the outset, Stockholm was committed to strengthening the safeguards and, like Iran, called for them to be extended to cover the civilian nuclear industries of NWS as well, thereby "placing the nuclear industries of the nuclear weapon and non-nuclear weapon States on an equal footing" (Bodström 1985: 30).

Since 1980, Sweden has been a member of the Vienna Group of Ten (G11 since 1991),[6] which has advocated the strengthening of non-proliferation measures, more effective safeguards, and strong export control guidelines as well as multilateral fuel cycle arrangements (e.g., Sweden et al. 1995; 2000; Sweden 2010). A number of improvements in the area of verification and export controls are based on G11 proposals, including the introduction of comprehensive safeguards by the IAEA as a precondition for nuclear exports or the requirement to recognize the Additional Protocol as a verification standard (Müller et al. 1994: 57). Sweden also played a leading role in the negotiations on the IAEA Additional Protocol (Rublee 2008: 183, footnote 149; Jonter 2003: 18).

Outside the NPT, Sweden was also actively involved in nuclear disarmament: In the early 1970s, then Minister of Disarmament Myrdal opposed the conventionalization of "mini-nukes" (nuclear weapons with a blast of less than five kilotons) (Myrdal 1977: 45–48). In the 1980s, Prime Minister Olof Palme called for a ban on the use of nuclear weapons in the UN General Assembly and co-founded the Six Nations Initiative (also known as Five Continent Initiative) in 1984.[7] The initiative was mainly concerned with promoting nuclear disarmament and demanded above all that a nuclear freeze and negotiations on a comprehensive test ban should be introduced. It also advocated banning the arms race in outer space and called on the nuclear weapon states to enter into a meaningful dialogue (Lomas 1991: 195; Prawitz 1995: 32). Palme also headed the "Independent Commission on Disarmament and Common Security Issues," whose final report (UN 1983) was discussed during the second UN Special Session on Disarmament in 1982. Among other things, it proposed the establishment of a nuclear weapon-free corridor which was met with great public response in Central Europe, but, as expected, was rejected by NATO states (Müller et al. 2015: 19–20).

---

[5]Sweden's national export control legislation even goes beyond the NSG guidelines and European legislation (van Dassen 1995: 190). Sweden is one of the few European countries to carry out end-use controls on its nuclear exports. The re-export of exported materials also requires prior government approval, including within the EU (Berkol and Moreau 2009: 15, 20).

[6]In 1991, Hungary joined the group, also known as White Angels. Its members meet informally in the run-up to NPT Review Conferences to coordinate their positions and prepare joint working papers on verification, export control, and the peaceful uses of nuclear energy.

[7]Apart from Sweden, members were Argentina, Greece, India, Mexico, and Tanzania. Palme led the group until his assassination in 1986.

Sweden's long-standing commitment to a Comprehensive Test-Ban Treaty is also impressive. Despite Myrdal's intensive efforts to safe a compromise negotiations (Theorin 2003: 48) on a test ban failed in the 1960s due to different views on verification. All the USA and the Soviet Union could agree on was a limited test ban (Partial Test-Ban Treaty, PTBT). In order to make the PTBT as strong as possible, Sweden contributed valuable technical nuclear expertise for the development of strong verification measures (for a detailed description, see Mallin 1994; Wunderlich 2008). In 1965, Myrdal proposed to establish an international cooperation program for seismic verification, the so-called "seismic detection club" (Sweden 1965). In 1976, an Ad Hoc Group of Scientific Experts to Consider International Co-operative Measures to Detect and Identify Seismic Events (GSE) was founded on the initiative of Sweden, whose work served as a basis for establishing a worldwide seismic monitoring system (International Monitoring System, IMS; Schmalberger 1991: 61).[8] After setting up a seismic station at Hagfors in 1968), Sweden agreed to provide one of four International Data Centers to collect and analyze raw data in advance and then distribute the results to the States Parties. From 1983 onward, Sweden also presented various draft texts for a CTBT at the Conference on Disarmament (others followed in 1991 and 1993; Sweden 1983, 1991, 1993). When the nuclear weapon states except China announced test moratoria in the summer of 1993, Sweden took advantage of the emerging window of opportunity and presented a new draft text to the Conference on Disarmament. Treaty negotiations were opened just a few months later (Mallin 1994).

Sweden's strong commitment to nuclear disarmament did not decrease with its accession to the EU on 1 January 1995. On the contrary, as van Dassen states, Article VI showed "how it was hard to align a Swedish tradition or enthusiasm and activity with the common non-proliferation objectives that the EU seeks to implement" (van Dassen 1998: 22, footnote 62). This became particularly clear during the 1995 NPT extension conference when Sweden, together with Austria and Ireland, abandoned the joint EU position which declared the arms race to be over and purported that the nuclear weapon states, in particular France and Great Britain, had made significant progress in disarmament (Johnson 1995). The Swedish delegates not only insisted on their interpretation of the disarmament norm, according to which "the non-proliferation treaty contained the first and, so far, the only *contractual commitments* by the nuclear weapon States to negotiate in good faith on nuclear disarmament" (Ekwall 1995b: 2; emph. CW). In view of the hesitant disarmament practices of the nuclear weapon states and with reference to recommendations of the Commission on Global Governance[9] chaired by Swedish Prime Minister Carlsson, they also called

[8]From 1976 to 1996, Swedes chaired the group (1976–1982 Dr. Ulf Ericsson; 1981–1996 Dr. Ola Dahlman). The GSE was dissolved in 1996 but continued its activities in Working Group B of the Test Ban Committee of the Disarmament Conference, which Dahlman chaired until 2006. See https://www.ctbto.org/verification-regime/background/interview-ola-dahlmanchairman-ctbto-working-groupon-verification-wgb-1996-2006/dahlman-1/. Accessed 28 August 2015.

[9]In its report "Our Global Neighborhood," the Commission called on the international community to initiate a program to eliminate all nuclear weapons within ten to fifteen years (Alani 1995: 17). The report is available at http://www.centerforunreform.org/?q=node/243. Accessed 28 April 2017.

for a disarmament timetable (Eliasson 1995). This was a demand otherwise reserved for the more radical non-aligned states and difficult to reconcile with the positions of the European nuclear weapons states and their allies. Sweden insisted on its vision of a world free of nuclear weapons and also set itself apart from its EU partners in its own working paper (Sweden 1995).

This stance was maintained in the years to follow. Sweden reserved the right to present initiatives and statements in national capacity that went beyond the common EU positions. Even more so, Sweden sought to establish its political priorities within the EU: To this day, the country is one of the few to support the withdrawal of tactical nuclear weapons from Europe (Lindh 2000; Finland and Sweden 2002; Freivalds 2005; Bildt 2010; Bildt and Sikorski 2010). Swedish politicians have also been instrumental in raising the EU's arms control profile. In 2003, Foreign Minister Anna Lindh initiated the "EU Strategy against the Proliferation of Weapons of Mass Destruction" (EU Council 2003) and advocated for the Union to take on a proactive role in the field of nuclear disarmament.

In 1998, Sweden, together with six other disarmament-friendly states, founded the New Agenda Coalition (NAC).[10] The group's main concern was to bring about steps toward a world free of nuclear weapons and to mediate between the opposed camps in the NPT (NWS vs. NAM). The NAC's agenda included "an unequivocal undertaking by the nuclear weapon states to accomplish the total elimination of their nuclear arsenals"; the reduction of tactical nuclear weapons; legally binding negative security guarantees; the universalization of the NPT, the early entry into force of the CTBT; and the continuation of bilateral disarmament negotiations, among other things (NAC 1998). Membership of the NAC gave Sweden's disarmament activism a further boost until the mid-2000s.

The country also worked to strengthen the disarmament norm at the national level. In 2003, the Swedish government established the Weapons of Mass Destruction Commission chaired by Hans Blix, former IAEA Director-General (1981–1997) and Head of the UN Disarmament Commission for Iraq (UNMOVIC, 2000–2003). The Commission was to give new impetus to international disarmament and non-proliferation efforts by drawing up viable proposals to completely eliminate the threat posed by nuclear weapons.[11]

However, Sweden's impressive disarmament activism also shows that state norm entrepreneurship is not based on political tradition only, but is also dependent on the respective domestic political constellation: With the assumption of office by the coalition government in 2006, Sweden's disarmament activism declined significantly in comparison with its policy of non-proliferation. During Fredrik Reinfeldt's term of office, Sweden focused most of its efforts on preventing the proliferation of weapons of mass destruction within the framework of the EU.[12]

[10]Other founding members were Egypt, Brazil, Ireland, Mexico, New Zealand, and South Africa. Slovenia left the NAC due to American pressure and its accession to NATO.

[11]See the final report "Weapons of Terror - Freeing the World of Nuclear, Biological and Chemical Arms" published in June 2006; https://fas.org/irp/offdocs/wmdcomm.html. Accessed 28 April 2017.

[12]EU membership did change the framework for action, with the result that Sweden had to coordinate its arms control policy with European partners. However, this did not lead to a limited radius

Instead of being a "disarmament beacon," Sweden was perceived internationally only as one voice among many, as a passive voice in the EU choir (Tolf 2013: 2). Disarmament idealism and the willingness to act as uncomfortable critic had apparently given way to political pragmatism and the need to foster European integration and security cooperation with NATO. At the NPT Review Conferences, the country appeared only as a shadow of itself and largely refrained from national positions that went beyond those of the EU.

Sweden was quickly replaced in its role as a mediator between opposing camps. Countries such as Norway or Austria had adopted Sweden's position as a disarmament diplomat par excellence. Sweden even left the NAC in 2013 (Svensson 2013). Another indicator for Sweden's declined engagement can be seen in the fact that it did not use the opportunity to put nuclear disarmament on the agenda when it held the EU Council Presidency in 2009. Back in 2001, Stockholm had used its presidency to introduce an action plan against weapons of mass destruction. On the national level, a lack of disarmament activism translated into budgetary cuts within the disarmament department as well as the funding for the Stockholm International Peace Research Institute (SIPRI) and in the winding-up of the Blix Commission in 2009. To be fair, Sweden followed traditions by co-sponsoring an initiative for the rapid entry into force of the CTBT[13] and a Polish-Swedish initiative for the withdrawal of tactical nuclear weapons from Europe (Bildt and Sikorski 2010).

Sweden's declining disarmament activism was met with considerable criticism from local civil society, as disarmament engagement is deeply rooted in the country's political identity. Consequently, this was one of the issues that helped the Social Democrats win the elections in 2014. The announcement that Sweden would "return to a leading position in disarmament issues" (Ahlin 2010)[14] was immediately followed by action by the minority government of the Greens and Social Democrats: Sweden joined the so-called Humanitarian Initiative only two weeks after taking office. Former Foreign Minister Carl Bildt had dismissed this as a "dead track" and a "symbolic policy" in which "actually no serious states" participate (e.g., Söderlund 2013).

---

of action. On the contrary, membership of the Union has even increased Sweden's influence in promoting the non-proliferation norm, as with the strategy against the proliferation of weapons of mass destruction the EU has adopted a common policy in 2003. The situation is, however, different in the realm of disarmament, where the tripartite division of EU members into NWS, alliance-free non-nuclear weapon states and NATO non-nuclear weapon states has so far prevented an agreement on far-reaching disarmament steps (Müller et al. 2013: 325).

[13] See the press release on the web site of the Swedish Embassy in Vienna: http://www.swedenabroad.com/en-GB/Embassies/Vienna/Current-affairs/News/Sweden-promotes-the-entry-into-force-of-the-CTBT/. Accessed 28 April 2017.

[14] In their "12-point programme for disarmament" (Socialdemokraterna 2010) adopted in 2010, the Social Democrats announce, among other things, their commitment to further reducing nuclear arsenals, reducing the role of nuclear weapons in military doctrines, and initiating consultations with like-minded states within the UN in order to discuss the conditions for a nuclear weapons convention.

Similarly, Swedish delegates to the 2015 NPT Review Conference tied in both qualitatively and quantitatively with the former activity profile and, among other things, launched an initiative to strengthen nuclear disarmament together with neighboring Nordic countries.[15]

8.2.2 *Strategies, Resources, and Practical Activities of Swedish Norm Entrepreneurship*

As this overview has shown, Swedish norm entrepreneurship has made a significant contribution to the development of the non-proliferation regime. Motivated by "ideational commitment" (Finnemore and Sikkink 1998: 898) and out of concern for maintaining regime effectiveness, Sweden continuously campaigned for the strengthening of the NPT—in particular the disarmament norm—and together with like-minded countries advocated the implementation of the proposed measures within various institutional forums and at various levels (national, regional, international). While its practical commitment decreased for a short period between 2006 and 2014, when the new government came to office old positions were taken up again. This attitude stems from a "missionary instinct"[16] together with sensitivity for injustice and the political culture of the country, which is characterized by active internationalism and neutrality. As a result, the country has been actively engaged in the destruction of weapons of mass destruction, which it considers to be an immoral threat to the common good.

The resources and strategies used by Sweden correspond to those of classic norm entrepreneurship: Through active lobbying and the formation of strategic alliances with like-minded partners, Swedish diplomats have worked for the strengthening and implementation of the disarmament norm. Rhetorically, they used various framing strategies for this purpose, appealing in particular to the moral responsibility of the international community in general and that of the nuclear weapon states in particular. Sweden also used its technical and scientific expertise in many ways to strengthen the regimes, for example, through capacity building, financial and personnel contributions, mediation services, setting an example, and implementing treaty provisions.

Within the UN bodies dealing with disarmament issues and in the NPT Review Conferences, Sweden showed a high level of activism, both in terms of rhetorical and practical activities. The years 2006–2014 under Reinfeldt, however, form an exception to that. The importance that the country attaches to disarmament and non-proliferation diplomacy can also be illustrated by the fact that Sweden has a well-staffed disarmament department and was (and is) usually represented at review conferences by high-ranking government representatives (ministers of state or foreign minister level).[17]

---

[15]The newly elected government immediately reversed some arms control decisions of its predecessors: For example, Sweden declared its re-entry into the so-called de-alerting group, which advocates putting nuclear weapons off high alert (Regeringskansliet 2015).

[16]Email conversation with Alyson Bailes, 2 October 2007.

[17]See also the activity profile prepared by Reaching Critical Will; http://www.reachingcriticalwill.org/resources/profiles. Accessed 28 April 2017.

Sweden’s extensive commitment is based not only on its identity but also on the national technical and scientific expertise and research infrastructure that the country had built up in the 1950s and 1960s. This expertise helped Sweden build “soft power” that exceeded the material capabilities of the small country and provided it with extraordinary opportunities, e.g., to influence agenda setting processes within the various disarmament bodies. This is particularly demonstrated by Sweden’s involvement in setting up the verification system for a Comprehensive Test-Ban Treaty. Experts from the Ministry of Defense’s research institute (Totalförsvarets Forskningsanstalt, FOI) have always been an integral part of Swedish disarmament delegations and have thus contributed to the strength and persuasiveness of Swedish proposals. Examples include the detailed draft treaties for a test-ban treaty which Sweden submitted to the Conference on Disarmament in 1983, 1991, and 1994 and which significantly influenced the negotiations (Mallin 1994; Johnson 2009: 303, Footnote 17). FOI experts have repeatedly been called into international expert groups, for example, as part of the preparation of UN studies. Sweden fed background technical reports, in particular on verification issues, into the treaty regimes and also supported the various treaty organizations through capacity building in the form of extra-budgetary financial, human and technical contributions such as the organization of training sessions or workshops.[18]

Sweden’s role within the G-10/11 at NPT Review Conferences was also largely based on the country’s technical expertise. The fruitful cooperation with non-aligned countries during the Cold War also benefited from Swedish knowledge and Stockholm’s willingness to make this know-how available to countries with weak resources (Sundelius 2001: 251–252). Overall, Sweden’s expertise increased its diplomatic weight and therefore the credibility and authority attributed to it. Very often Swedish delegates held senior posts at NPT Review Conferences,[19] UN disarmament bodies[20] or other international organizations relevant to multilateral arms control.[21]

The Swedish government has also tried to insert its expertise into international opinion-forming through various initiatives, such as the initiation of various commissions, disarmament education measures and research, e.g., studies on the risks

[18] Sweden organized various seminars in 2001 to demonstrate the reliability of the CTBT verification system (Lindh 2001). It is also active in nuclear safety measures and supports the successor states of the Soviet Union in particular through practical measures within the IAEA, the G8 Global Partnership Against the Spread of Weapons of Mass Destruction or through disarmament assistance for chemical and nuclear weapons stocks (Blom 2001; van Dassen and Wetter 2006: 256–57).

[19] Inga Thorsson chaired the NPT RevCon in 1975, in 1985 (Rolf Ekéus), and in 1990 (Carl-Magnus Hyltenius) Swedes chaired the Drafting Committee. In 2002, Henrik Salander chaired the first meeting of the Preparatory Committee for the 2005 Review Conference, at which Elisabeth Borsiin-Bonnier took over the chairmanship of Main Committee III.

[20] Swedish delegates were often involved as friends of the chair during the CTBT negotiations (1994 Bertil Roth, 1995 and 1996 Richard Ekwall) or, based on their national expertise, headed the CTBTO GSE or Working Group B dealing with questions of verification.

[21] So far, two Swedes have held the post of IAEA Director-General: Sigvard Eklund from 1961 to 1981 and Hans Blix from 1981 to 1997. The latter also headed the United Nations Monitoring, Verification and Inspection Commission (UNMOVIC), which was responsible for monitoring Iraq’s weapons of mass destruction program.

and dangers associated with nuclear weapons (Andrén 1996: 221). These studies were not only meant to provide information to the international community,[22] but also served to influence public opinion.

Sweden tried to strengthen the treaty regimes, in particular the norm of nuclear disarmament, by making concrete proposals and by rhetorically reaffirming Article VI, but also by naming, blaming, and shaming. In both national capacity and as part of the NAC, Sweden has repeatedly voiced strong criticism of the NWS's lacking commitment to nuclear disarmament and of developments that threatened the stability of the non-proliferation regime, e.g., nuclear tests by France, China, India, and Pakistan, the NWS's refusal to ratify the CTBT, or North Korea's withdrawal from the NPT.[23] Overall, however, criticism remains moderate. Harsh blaming is rather rare. Swedish delegates repeatedly praised positive progress in disarmament (e.g., bilateral disarmament negotiations between the USA and the USSR in the 1970s or Obama's initiative on Global Zero; e.g., Bodström 1985; Ekwall 1995a; Freivalds 2004; Bildt 2010).

The collective action frames underlying Swedish argumentation closely resemble the positions advocated for by the non-aligned countries: Nuclear armament is regarded as a "dangerous and shortsighted attitude" (Theorin 1985), a violation of basic treaty obligations, which risks undermining the credibility of the NPT. While overall Sweden's tone remains comparatively moderate, the country seeks to underline its displeasure by using dramatizing and emotionalizing rhetoric: For example, Swedish delegates described nuclear weapons as "weapons of Armageddon" (Theorin 1991) or appealed urgently to the moral responsibility of nuclear weapon states. As early as 1977, Myrdal described the NPT as a highly discriminatory agreement (Myrdal 1977: 215). In this context, Swedish delegates often criticize the injustice of inadequate nuclear disarmament and the double standards applied by nuclear weapon states in the field of technological cooperation (Bodström 1985). In Sweden's understanding, the NNWS had a significant role to play in taking the NWS on their promise (Myrdal 1977).

Even if Sweden (like Iran) does not shy away from self-isolation,[24] the criticism expressed is mostly constructive. Stockholm refrains from using confrontational strategies and tactics. While it has repeatedly presented the preservation of a nuclear option until the 1950s as a negotiation strategy in order to wrest further concessions

---

[22]The establishment of SIPRI in 1966 served similar aims: As a non-governmental institution, SIPRI makes a major contribution to the international disarmament debate through its comprehensive research program and the publication of numerous publications (e.g., the SIPRI Yearbook, which provides an overview of the state of international disarmament).

[23]At the beginning of the 1990s, the number of critical comments decreased for a short time, but increased again over the years. The brief decline can be explained by the fact that Sweden did not want to nip progress in the heyday of arms control after the end of the Cold War with ongoing criticism. See interviews with Jan Prawitz, 24 October 2007; Maj Britt Theorin, 25 November 2007; Hans Blix, 11 September 2010, and Rolf Ekéus 13 September 2010.

[24]Sweden's accession to the EU did not, for example, prevent Prime Minister Carlsson from strongly condemning the French nuclear tests (van Dassen and Wetter 2006: 259).

from the nuclear weapon states (Garris 1973: 201; Agrell 1984: 170), this is the only instance which comes close to "diplomatic blackmail."

Despite vehement criticism, Sweden most often seemed willing to abandon principles rather than risk the failure of negotiations.[25] Instead of confrontational strategies or diplomatic pressure, Swedish politicians resort to dialogue and mediation, a fact that is demonstrated by its bridge-building activities between the superpowers and between these and non-aligned states in the 1970s. After the end of the Cold War, the country continued this role in various constellations: Within the framework of the NAC to mediate between nuclear weapon states and non-nuclear weapon states, or between the non-aligned and the industrialized non-nuclear weapon states. Sweden also acted as a mediator within the Western camp: For example, during the negotiations to strengthen IAEA safeguards, when it convinced skeptical Western nuclear suppliers of the benefits of these measures (van Dassen 1998: 23), or within the EU between the disarmament-friendly states and the European nuclear weapon states.

The fact that Sweden prefers to act in coalition with like-minded states was already demonstrated during the 1980s when it co-founded the Six Nations Initiative, but also by its traditional cooperation with the non-aligned countries or its Nordic neighbors. The cooperation within the G-10/11 and the establishment of the NAC in 1998 also indicate that the country considers joining forces with other like-minded states as an opportunity to pool resources. Cooperation with civil society actors and NGOs is also a well-established element of Swedish activism. And with regard to that Sweden has been advocating the norm to opening up to civil society actors even within the EU.

8.2.3 Comparing Iranian and Swedish Norm Entrepreneurship

In line with its identity as a good international citizen, Sweden acted as a norm entrepreneur in several aspects: It was involved in both the construction of norms and their further strengthening. Even though Sweden's proactivism experienced a brief period of stagnation during the term of the coalition government, Stockholm's overall activity profile is impressive and can, as expected, be regarded as a blueprint for prototypical norm entrepreneurship.

In terms of content, Swedish norm entrepreneurship and Iranian norm entrepreneurship show some interesting similarities, for example, with regard to the emphasis on the norm of nuclear disarmament or with regard to the sensitivity to unjust regime structures. In the NPT in particular, both states promoted similar

[25] For example during the CTBT negotiations, Swedish disarmament ambassador Theorin called on the other parties to show flexibility and to deviate from maximum demands: "Sweden has a clear position on what should ideally be the content of a mandate of an ad hoc committee. Nevertheless, in order to allow for the urgently needed multilateral consideration to start, my delegation is ready to go along with any mandate that is acceptable to other delegations" (Theorin 1988).

measures: for example, the reduction of the role of nuclear weapons; negative security assurances; a Comprehensive Test-Ban Treaty; a ban on the production of fissile materials for weapons purposes; the call on the nuclear weapon states to comply with their disarmament obligations; and an aversion to unfair regime structures. Substantial differences can be seen in the weighting of the treaty pillars: While Sweden advocated a balanced interpretation of treaty obligations and also advocated non-proliferation measures, Iran subordinated them to the norms of nuclear disarmament and technological cooperation.

The commitment of both countries is guided by both interests and norms. However, in the literature on Sweden, there is a tendency to explain Swedish policies primarily with reference to normative convictions. Accordingly, most observers focus on the country's reputation as a good international citizen and "force for good in the world" (Dahl 2002: 140): Sweden's credibility and moral authority as a norm entrepreneur appear to be beyond doubt.

By contrast, political observers question Iran's authenticity due to its dubious nuclear program and its reputation as a "rogue state" and dismiss its activities to promote norms as purely interest-led image cultivation. In contrast, the "dark sides" of Swedish norm entrepreneurship usually remain unconsidered. On the one hand, it is often neglected that in the 1960s and 1970s Sweden was regarded as a "problem country" by the US government due to its presumed nuclear ambitions (Bunn 1992: 68). Secondly, the country's record in humanitarian arms control is more ambivalent than its exceptional commitment to the elimination and non-proliferation of weapons of mass destruction. This imbalance reveals that even in the Swedish case national interests may at times override moral motives (Becker-Jakob et al. 2013: 229–230). For example, at a time when Sweden was pursuing an active policy of neutrality, it was also investing in the development of a strong arms industry that was heavily dependent on exports.[26] According to SIPRI, in the period from 1950 to 2016, Sweden ranks in 13th place among the world's leading arms exporting countries. Once oriented toward defensive purposes and the preservation of national sovereignty (but also prestige and competitiveness), Swedish arms export policy today aims to secure "participation of Sweden in strategically important cooperations" (Manga 2010: 3) and to maintain its interoperability with NATO partners (Swedish Ministry for Foreign Affairs 2014: 10). The country has one of the most restrictive national trade laws and can boast a particularly transparent export policy (Garcia 2006: 153). Nevertheless, repeatedly reports of the Swedish government's secret arms deals overshadow the success story of Swedish norm entrepreneurship. One example is the 1986 bribery affair between India and the Swedish company Bofors AB, which was accused to supply Swedish weapons to regimes accused of human rights violations (e.g., B. Bahrain, Pakistan). Another example is the participation of the Swedish Ministry of Defense in the construction of an arms factory in Saudi Arabia in 2012 (Holmström 2006; Svenska Freds 2012; Olsson and Åkerman 2012; Goldmann 2015).

Both Iran and Sweden used similar norm entrepreneurial framing strategies, in particular by referring to the common good and collective action frames linked to

[26]See http://armstrade.sipri.org/armstrade/html/export_toplist.php. Accessed 28 April 2017.

injustice and full with verbal criticism. Both countries worked closely with like-minded states (although Sweden was much more diverse and broadly based here, i.e., collaborating with heterogeneous actors and the quantity of its studies and initiatives clearly exceeded that of Iran) and sought contact with civil society actors. On the other hand, in the literature, Iran is often accused of paying lip service to its cooperation with civil society and the international scientific community rather than pursuing this as a genuine strategy. Similarly, while Iranian interview partners were extremely helpful, open and willing to share information, access to relevant interviewees proved comparatively difficult, required repeated efforts in some cases and even failed in others. With regard to resources, the commitment of both countries was based on a high level of technical and scientific expertise and well-equipped disarmament delegations.

Iran and Sweden differ most strikingly in the strategies used: Sweden's commitment was primarily aimed at strengthening regime stability and effectiveness. To this end, Stockholm relied on compromise-oriented strategies and attempts at persuasion based on the better argument. More than once, Swedish diplomats acted as mediators between opposing positions and offered their own resources to support weaker parties. In doing so, the country profited significantly from its reputation as moral authority (Prawitz 2003: 58). It appeared as a persistent critic and often used naming, blaming, and shaming strategies. Compared to Iran, however, Sweden's criticism remained moderate. Sweden's blaming statements were less sharp than Iran's, which sometimes contained aggressive undertones. There seemed to be too much concern that blaming could undermine the stability of the non-proliferation regime (and Sweden's reputation).[27] Overall, Sweden sees itself primarily as a norm reformer seeking to improve the current normative order within existing structures.

Iran, on the other hand, used confrontational tactics in addition to the classic norm entrepreneurial strategies and was often unwilling to deviate from its positions. Iranian diplomats often risked the failure of negotiations by employing blocking or delaying tactics, even if they often bowed to last-minute pressure from like-minded states. All in all, Tehran's norm entrepreneurship seems to aim at a more or less radical change of the existing normative structure. Feeling deceived and unfairly treated by the nuclear weapon states and rejecting any Western hegemony, Iran's norm entrepreneurship sometimes went beyond a reformist attitude. As a result, Tehran's strategies were often less active than reactive in undermining opposing positions.

To conclude, Sweden assumes a role as a proactive reformer of norms, primarily aimed at consensus-based solutions to regime conflicts. It wants to reinforce the effectiveness of the non-proliferation regime. On the other hand, dissatisfaction with the current normative structure prompts Iran to show a mixture of reform-oriented and revolutionary norm entrepreneurship. In the concluding chapter, I will further elaborate on this distinction.

---

[27]So the former Head of the Department for Disarmament and Non-Proliferation, Dr. Christer Ahlström, in a background conversation, 7 September 2010, Stockholm.

8.3 "Rogue'n Roll": Comparing North Korea and Iran

This study is guided by the question whether "rogue states" can act as norm entrepreneurs. As the previous chapters have demonstrated, under closer scrutiny Iranian arms control diplomacy does indeed reveal some instances of norm entrepreneurship. Does this mean that the concept can be applied to all ("rogue") states? In order to shed light on this question, in this section will apply the concept to another prototypical "rogue state"—the Democratic People's Republic of Korea (DPRK)—and analyze its attitude toward norms on the control of weapons of mass destruction. Since North Korea is also known for rejecting Western liberal ideas of world order, this contrasting case study also serves to assess the explanatory power of alternative explanation 2 (see Sect. 5.2.2). Similar to the previous section on Sweden, here too the objective is not to present a detailed process tracing of possible instances of North Korean norm advocacy in the realm of multilateral arms control. Rather, the analysis is meant to determine whether the country generally operates as a norm entrepreneur.

8.3.1 North Korea as Outcast of the International Community

North Korea is considered a prototype in the literature as well—in contrast to Sweden's good international citizenship, the DPRK is considered "a charter member of the countries that the USA has designated as rogue states" (Litwak 2012: 138; similar Sigal 1998: 11; Geldenhuys 2004: 174; Schmittchen 2006: 15). Like Iran, the North Korean regime led by the Kim dynasty is labeled an outsider to the international community of states, particularly by the USA. Often, the attribute "villain" alone is not considered sufficient to capture the presumed deviancy of the country. Instead, the authors use qualifications such as "blackmailing rogue" (Henriksen 2012: 103), "incalculable (rogue) actor" (Senn 2009: 65), "rogue outlaw" (Bleiker 2003: 720), "red rogue" (Bechtol 2007) or emphasize the irrationality, which the West ascribes to the regime and which lies at the heart of the threat perception, e.g., "paranoid peninsula" (French 2005: 1).

As early as 1985, then US President Reagan identified North Korea together with Iran and several other states to form a "confederation of terrorist states" (quoted after Klare 1995: 26). From the perspective of the USA, North Korea's revisionist foreign policy, including the pursuit of weapons of mass destruction, its aggressive external behavior, including terrorist actions, especially toward its neighbor South Korea, and the authoritarian rule of the Kim dynasty, make it a "rogue state" (e.g., Bechtol 2009; Senn 2009: 58–69; Henriksen 2012: Chap. 4).

North Korea is not only regarded as a paradigmatic "rogue," but also as the world's most isolated regime, which established its reputation as hermit kingdom long before the division of Korea. While North Korea's "retreat from international politics" (French 2005: 2) has to be seen in the light of its experiences of foreign rule and colonization, self-isolation and the quest for independence are today regarded as instruments to preserve the system (e.g., Waldenström 2005: 9). Roland Bleiker characterizes North Korea as "[t]otalitarian and reclusive, ideologically isolated and economically ruined" characteristics that make it "the inherent 'other' in a globalized and neoliberal world order" (Bleiker 2003: 719). Senn (2009: 58–59) traces North Korea's antagonistic attitude and revisionist foreign back to (mutual) threat perceptions: Since the Korean War, the country has been confronted with a (conventional and nuclear) military superiority of US military troops stationed in South Korea.

North Korea's opposition to the current normative order is at least partly grounded in the Juche ideology proclaimed by "great leader" Kim Il-Sung in the 1950s. Incorporated into the country's constitution in the 1970s, this ideology mixes Marxist–Leninist teachings and nationalist elements and strives for ideological, economic, political, and military self-sufficiency (French 2005: 30–47; Waldenström 2005). Although North Korea tried to propagate Juche in Asia, Africa, and Latin America, especially in the 1960s and 1970s, the ideology is more inward than universalist and aims above all at consolidating or maintaining the system (Waldenström 2005: 12). After Kim Il-Sung's son Kim Jong-Il took the lead in 1994, the principle of military independence gained increasing priority: In 2009, Juche was supplemented by the principle of "military first" (Songun) and a massive arms buildup was initiated both with regard to conventional as well as nuclear capabilities.

By the late 1990s, North Korea's economic situation had declined considerably, so that it eventually decided to seek to "normalize" relations with the West. In return for economic cooperation and recognition by the USA, North Korea was willing to enter into negotiations on its nuclear program (Geldenhuys 2004: 174). This rapprochement did not change anything regarding the ideologies of Juche and Songun, which continued to form the basis of North Korean identity. As a consequence, Juche ideology is also reflected in the following foreign policy priorities: First, sovereignty, second, the right to self-determination, third, the rejection of political influence and domination, and, fourth, the demand for equal recognition and respect (Waldenström 2005: 14). North Korea's rejection of any imperialism is of course particularly directed toward the presence of the USA in South Korea and manifests itself in an anti-American attitude (Senn 2009: 60) that resembles that of Iran.

Another similarity to the case of Iran is that research on North Korea focuses primarily on its "persistent rule-breaking behavior" (Geldenhuys 2004: 168). Studies most often refer to North Korea's nuclear deviance and the initially secret, meanwhile open buildup of a nuclear weapons program as well as to the anti-imperialist attitude and self-isolation of the country. Analyses of North Korea's arms control diplomacy that go beyond this are rather scarce. An exception is a study on the arms control policies of various states belonging to the non-aligned movement, conducted at the Peace Research Institute Frankfurt (PRIF) in which I was significantly involved (Wunderlich et al. 2013).[28] The following section is therefore based on the findings of this study.

[28]The chapter also covered the arms control policies of Egypt, Iran, and South Africa. The section on the DPRK was written by Hans-Joachim Schmidt in collaboration with Andrea Hellmann. Yet, they arrive at a different assessment of the DPRK's status as a norm entrepreneur.

8.3.2 *Background: The Conflict Surrounding North Korea's Nuclear Program*

North Korea's attitude to multilateral arms control must be seen in the context of the Juche ideology and the mutual threat perception with the USA, which has shaped the relationship since the Korean War (Wunderlich et al. 2013: 273). Analyzing North Korean positions toward norms on the control of weapons of mass destruction is difficult due to political decision-making structures that are difficult to grasp for outsiders,[29] but also due to an aura of secrecy buildup by the North Korean leadership. The lack of information leaves other states in the dark when it comes to foreign and security policy objectives and is geared toward increasing the DPRK's deterrent potential (Senn 2009: 65; Wunderlich et al. 2013: 273).

North Korea's arms control diplomacy takes place within the UN bodies dealing with disarmament and—until the country's withdrawal in 2003—the NPT. The CWC was never even signed by North Korea. Although it joined the BTWC and the Geneva Protocol in 1987 and 1989, it has not taken up a visible role in negotiations in either regime. It hardly participates in the review conferences, it boycotts the confidence-building measures provided for in the BTWC and for several years has entirely refrained from participating in the Conferences of States Parties. Official denials notwithstanding, it is considered proven that North Korea possesses considerable stocks of chemical weapons (Crisis Group 2009). Political observers also suspect the country of maintaining a clandestine biological weapons program and of possessing weapon-grade biological agents. Based on the scarcity of data for the other regimes, the following analysis of North Korea's arms control diplomacy focuses on its nuclear arms control policy.

Like Iran, North Korea is widely regarded as seeking to undermine the nuclear non-proliferation regime (Hilpert and Meier 2013: 4). This is mainly due to the nuclear weapons program pursued since the 1980s, the beginnings of which date back to the 1960s (Park 2006: 38; Suk 2011: 278).[30] Pressured by the Soviet Union, the DPRK joined the NPT together with South Korea in 1985. In 1992, following the withdrawal of US tactical nuclear weapons from South Korea, North Korea signed a safeguards agreement with the IAEA and, together with South Korea, a joint declaration on the denuclearization of the Korean peninsula.[31] After initial inspections revealed evidence of a secret plutonium program (Hecker 2010: 45–46; El Baradei 2011: Chap. 2), the DPRK refused IAEA inspectors access to the reactor in Yongbyon.

---

[29]The decision-making process is in the hands of a small circle of party officials, the army, and central intelligence officials. The "Supreme Leader" is considered to be the highest authority. Especially since the transfer of power to Kim Jong-Un, it is assumed that high-ranking military and family members are significantly involved in important decisions (Niksch 2007). See Park (2010); Gause (2013) on the political decision-making process, particularly with regard to arms control.

[30]On the history of the North Korean nuclear program, see among many Mansourov (1995); Habib (2011); Suk (2011).

[31]Joint Declaration on the Denuclearization of the Korean Peninsula, 1992; http://www.nti.org/media/pdfs/aptkoreanuc.pdf. Accessed 28 April 2017.

In 1993, North Korea threatened to withdraw from the NPT. Only the promise of negotiations with the USA eventually dissuaded the country at the last minute.[32] In return for the prospect of an easing of relations and economic incentives, Pyongyang undertook to gradually reduce its enrichment program.

In fact, North Korea's nuclear ambitions primarily seem to be motivated by security interests. In speeches, delegates regularly refer to the military presence of American forces on the Korean peninsula, as well as to the tense relationship with South Korea. Both leave the country with no choice but to seek nuclear weapons as a deterrent. Official North Korean rhetoric adheres to the idea of denuclearization and points to several measures which it pretends figure high on the DPRK's political agenda, such as the establishment of a nuclear weapon-free zone in the region and the overriding goal of nuclear disarmament (Han 1994; Kim 1995; Ri 1995). At the same time, however, North Korea uses the nuclear program as a tactical lever for obtaining economic advantages and international aid (Schmidt 2012: 17). Time and again, external observers have argued the primary addressee of North Korean arms control diplomacy to be not the international community, but the USA. In their view, recognition and status satisfaction are the DPRK's utmost policy objectives (Waldenström 2005: 9; Schmidt 2012: 18; Müller 2013: 359; Wunderlich et al. 2013: 277–278).

In the mid-1990s, North Korea pursued a "dual strategy of confrontation and cooperation" (Schmidt 2012: 1): After the Clinton government had promised security guarantees, nuclear cooperation, the supply of oil and the normalization of relations, North Korea committed itself to the Geneva Framework Agreement in 1994 in which it pledged to discontinue its plutonium program in the long term and to cooperate in clarifying the uncertainties in its material balances (Schmidt 2012: 11). At the same time, however, Pyongyang continued to expand its nuclear infrastructure: After revelations in 2002, North Korea confirmed that with the help of the Khan network it began work on a uranium enrichment program at the end of the 1990s (Harrison 2005: 99–110; El Baradei 2011: 102).

With the entering into office of George W. Bush, the situation was further exacerbated. Favoring a confrontational approach, the USA stopped cooperation with regard to nuclear technology and oil supplies. In return, North Korea expelled all IAEA inspectors from the country, put the plutonium plant back into operation, and declared its withdrawal from the NPT in 2003 (Schmittchen 2006: 15; Schmidt 2012: 12).[33] Pyongyang justified its decision with the confrontational attitude of the USA, which is perceived as endangering its national sovereignty. That the USA had labeled North Korea a member of the "axis of evil" increased threat perceptions. According

[32]Article X of the NPT states that each state party has the right to withdraw from the treaty if "extraordinary circumstances" make it impossible for it to remain in the treaty regime. In such a case, however, the respective member states are obliged to announce its intention to resign three months in advance. North Korea "suspended" the withdrawal decision one day before the deadline.

[33]Whether the withdrawal is legally binding is subject to controversy. North Korea referred to the suspended declaration of withdrawal of 1993, justifying its action within the necessary three-month period. In addition, North Korea had informed the UN Secretary-General but not the treaty community of its intention to withdraw. Some states therefore do not recognize the withdrawal (Bunn and Timerbaev 2005; Hilpert and Meier 2013: 5).

to the state news agency KCNA, Bush's speech to the nation in which the reference had been made was regarded as "little short of a declaration of war" (BBC 2002). In fact, "[b]randing North Korea as a 'rogue' meant 'denial of recognition' of the North Korean regime as a negotiating partner" (Kim 2014: 130) and further sparked the DPRK's nuclear ambitions. As a delegate of the DPRK to the UNGA First Committee declared in 2004:

> If the United States had not listed the Democratic People's Republic of Korea in the 'axis of evil', and named it as a target for nuclear preemptive strikes, thus aggravating the situation, the question of our nuclear deterrence would not have arisen. (Pak 2004: 12).

In 2003, the so-called "Six-party Talks" between North Korea, South Korea, Japan, China, Russia, and the USA were initiated, aiming toward reaching a negotiated solution to the denuclearization of the Korean peninsula (Buszynski 2013: 33).[34] After all, North Korea had succeeded in being accepted as a legitimate interlocutor, even if it would have preferred bilateral talks with the USA (Schmidt 2012: 13). Subsequently, there were several rounds of talks, which, however, remained largely fruitless due to divergent positions with the exception of joint declarations of intent.

In 2005, North Korea publicly declared itself a nuclear power (Huntley 2006: 724) and underlined its determination through a missile test in June 2006 and a test—if only moderately successful—of a nuclear explosive device in October 2006 (Schmidt 2012: 1). When faced with strong international sanctions, Pyongyang indicated willingness to come back to the negotiating table: In exchange for food and oil supplies, it even suspended its plutonium program. In April 2009, however, North Korea canceled the six-party talks again, tested the second nuclear explosive device in May the same year, and instead of cooperation, increasingly opted for isolation. One of the reasons given by political observers is that the regime was internally occupied with the succession of the "beloved leader" Kim Jong-Il by his son Kim Jong-Un (Schmidt 2012: 14).

In 2012, the DPRK offered to stop all missile and nuclear tests as well as the uranium enrichment program. However, this offer was soon withdrawn, enrichment and reprocessing plants were put back into operation and a further, largely successful nuclear test was announced in February 2013 (Davenport 2013). In the years that followed, the situation escalated further: Not only did Pyongyang carry out two more nuclear tests in 2016, in July 2017 it successfully tested its first intercontinental ballistic missile and in September it claimed to having tested a thermonuclear weapon.

Quite surprisingly, after years of heightened tensions, at the time of writing (as of December 2018), the crisis surrounding the North Korean nuclear program seems to be over: In March 2018, Kim Jong-Un announced the regime's willingness to enter negotiations on a denuclearization, to refrain from further nuclear and missile tests and asked for a bilateral meeting with US President Donald Trump. For the first time ever, in June leaders of both countries met at a summit in Singapore in

[34]From the outset, US treatment of North Korea differed from the predominantly confrontational punitive measures alleged "rogue states" were subjected to. Instead of isolation and containment, a strategy of "limited engagement by necessity" was used (Litwak 2000: 198).

the context of which the DPRK reaffirmed its commitment to work for the complete denuclearization of the Korean peninsula. It remains to be seen where the dialogue will lead to—so far, North Korea has taken few concrete steps to abandon its nuclear program.

The brief overview of the development of North Korea's nuclear program already reveals motives underlying the country's position within the nuclear non-proliferation regime: striving for security and threat perceptions, insisting on mutual commitments, the desire for recognition as an equal negotiating partner, and—seemingly paradoxically—the overriding objective of nuclear disarmament (Wunderlich et al. 2013: 275–277).

8.3.3 North Korea's Arms Control Diplomacy: Lip Service and Self-centeredness

North Korea's main hope from joining the NPT was that the country's security situation would improve. Thus, during the 1990 Review Conference, the North Korean delegate justified this decision by saying that the danger of nuclear war was to be prevented and nuclear disarmament to be promoted (DPRK 1990a). North Korea considers the disarmament obligation laid down in Article VI to be the overriding norm of the treaty, superior to the other two pillars.[35] In its view, complete disarmament of nuclear weapons is a joint responsibility of the treaty community:

> The international community must never allow a single super-Power the privilege which will allow it to produce, upgrade, sell or deploy on foreign soil weapons of mass destruction, particularly nuclear weapons, chemical weapons and inter-continental ballistic missiles. All this constitutes the source of all the evil in our world. (Ri 1993: 9)

In 1999 North Korea even stated its view that nuclear disarmament constituted a right to be granted to the NNWS (Ri 1999). In their statements, North Korean delegates repeatedly call on the nuclear weapon states to comply with their disarmament obligation and to abandon their policy of nuclear deterrence. Yet, the naming, blaming, and shaming used by North Korea is mainly directed against the USA which is accused of using unequal standards. In 2004 a North Korean delegate declared:

> In essence the nuclear super-Power has abused the NPT in order to achieve its absolute security by threatening and blackmailing non-nuclear weapons, States [sic!] with nuclear weapons at the cost of their security. It cannot be acceptable to anyone that a country advocates nuclear non-proliferation while it accumulates nuclear weapons in one corner of the globe and seeks their qualitative improvement. (Pak 2004: 11)

---

[35]Surprisingly, there are few references to Article IV in North Korean statements, although the country has a civilian nuclear program and has complained the lack of cooperation. To be sure, there are references to the need for technological support and to the view that the requirement for cooperation constitutes a sovereign right of non-nuclear weapon states which must not be restricted by unfounded and "fabricated" accusations (e.g., Choe 2009). Yet North Korea's argumentation does not go beyond references to its own nuclear program, a missionary instinct is completely missing.

However, North Korea's argumentation is not based on references to the common good, but rather is self-referential: Although the statements contain repeated accusations, proposals for overcoming these grievances that go beyond the rhetorical support of disarmament measures are missing. North Korea shares the position of non-aligned states and demands the entry into force of a CTBT, legally binding negative security assurances and time-bound nuclear disarmament (e.g., DPRK 1990b; DPRK et al. 1995). The demand for the establishment of a nuclear weapon-free zone on the Korean peninsula was primarily motivated by the objective to get rid of US nuclear weapons (DPRK 1986,1987, 1989). For similar reasons, North Korea also supported the demand by non-aligned countries to ban the stationing of nuclear weapons on foreign territory and to include nuclear weapons in the UN register of conventional weapons (Kim 1990; Ri 1990).

Usually, the criticism of the lack of implementation of the treaty provisions or the discriminatory nature of the NPT leads to references to the unfair treatment of North Korea (Kim 1995; Choe 2009). Deviant behavior by the nuclear weapons states also gives the North Korean regime the opportunity to justify its own treaty violations. Norm-breaking in the view of North Korea is a matter of reciprocity (Wunderlich et al. 2013: 277).

Building up indigenous nuclear capacities not only contradicts the North Korean argumentation that nuclear disarmament is an absolute priority. It further undermines the criticism that they maintain their policy of nuclear deterrence (e.g., Han 1996; Li 1998). Rhetorically, however, North Korea remained committed to nuclear disarmament even after it had withdrawn from the NPT (KCNA 2006; DPRK 2007, 2010). At the same time, North Korean delegates use the international disarmament forums to justify the development of the nuclear program, such as the test in 2006, as necessary self-defense measures against the growing American threat (Choe 2007; Hong 2007). The USA is being made the scapegoat:

> [T]he main cause of the destruction of international peace and security that also has a serious impact on the disarmament process is none other than the nuclear super-Power's policy of nuclear threats, based on highhandedness and unilateralism. Countries are designated as comprising an 'axis of evil' and are thus targets for preemptive nuclear strikes, while unilateral military attacks against foreign States are perpetrated under the pretext of suspicion over the possession of weapons of mass destruction. (Pak 2004: 12)[36]

North Korean delegates use a significant part of their speeches to respond to statements and proposals from other states by means of the "right to reply." They use almost every statement to draw attention to their own perceived threat situation and the unjustified policy toward their own country. Their criticism of the discriminatory, unjust character of the NPT, "that has accepted the legitimate right to the possession and use of nuclear weapons by nuclear weapon states but imposed unreasonable non-proliferation obligations on the non-nuclear weapon states" (Pak 1994), is also embedded in this narrative.

---

[36]North Korea goes even further in its argumentation by framing the development of its own nuclear capabilities as a common good: "[O]ur deterrent is no danger anyway, but rather contributes to maintaining peace and security on the Korean peninsula and in its surroundings" (Hong 2007).

Delegates repeatedly demand "to discuss sincerely and frankly the issues of peace and security and justice and impunity" (Jon 2003; Ri 2007). North Korea feels unfairly treated and inadequately perceived as a threat.

The possibility of returning to the NPT—in fact, norm compliance—is made subject to the condition that the USA abandon the nuclear umbrella for South Korea (e.g., Choe 2007; Kang 2008). The regime also keeps on calling for negative security guarantees (e.g., Kim 1998; So 2011), which it itself is not prepared to give until the USA makes a first move.[37]

This attitude is symptomatic of North Korea's arms control diplomacy: It is not the international community, but rather the USA, that seems to be the primary target for North Korean rhetoric and for the proposed measures. Pyongyang links the willingness to engage in verification measures to compensatory measures (Wunderlich et al. 2013: 279). As a consequence, it supports the demand for non-proliferation of nuclear weapons rhetorically, but does not act accordingly.[38] For North Korea, the demand is primarily based on the premise that the NWS—in particular the USA—no longer station nuclear weapons on foreign territories, abandon their doctrine of deterrence, accept negative security assurances, and meet their disarmament obligations (e.g., Pak 2004: 12).

8.3.4 North Korea's Attitude to International Norms: Between Rejection, Non-compliance, and Non-conformity

The overview of North Korea's attitude to the norms of the nuclear non-proliferation regime shows an ambivalent picture: On the one hand, North Korea criticizes the asymmetric and discriminatory character of the NPT and rhetorically advocates the strengthening of the norm of nuclear disarmament and supporting measures in this regard. On the other hand, the country rarely turns its words into practical activities in the form of initiatives to reform the treaty regime. The proposals formulated in the past to establish new norms (a nuclear weapon-free zone on the Korean peninsula, the ban on the stationing of nuclear weapons on foreign territory) are primarily aimed

[37]Instead, North Korean delegates claim that the nuclear weapons program does not serve as a threat, but "only" as a deterrent and to refrain from the first use of nuclear weapons (e.g., DPRK 2007).

[38]North Korea is suspected of having repeatedly violated Article III(2) of the NPT, which prohibits the transfer of nuclear materials to countries that have not concluded safeguards agreements with the IAEA. These include the export of nuclear know-how and related materials to countries such as Iran and Syria (Albright 2013; or https://www.armscontrol.org/factsheets/northkoreaprofile. Accessed 28 April 2017). At the same time, North Korea claims to comply with the treaty. Pollack quotes a statement by the North Korean Foreign Ministry in October 2009, shortly after the second nuclear test: "We will always sincerely implement our international commitment in the field of nuclear non-proliferation as a responsible nuclear[weapons] state"; quoted after Pollack (2009: 269).

at satisfying national interests and are not driven by a common-good orientation—an important criterion for norm entrepreneurship.

All in all, North Korea's attitude to regime norms appears to be predominantly self-referential in nature and less geared to reforming regime structures than to promoting national security and interests (recognition by the USA). According to the indicators set out in Sect. 5.2.1, North Korea's behavior cannot be described as norm entrepreneurship:

Although Pyongyang is dissatisfied with the discriminatory nature of the nuclear non-proliferation regime and criticizes the fact that, from a North Korean perspective, its basic norms are not being implemented, it is not trying to change the perceived grievances within the given structures or to strengthen the inadequately implemented norms through practical activities.

The North Korean government is not actively seeking allies, nor is it trying to further the debate with own proposals[39] or to get involved through practical measures, such as the provision of expertise or the assumption of offices. Nor does North Korea seek contact with civil society, which is a quite vivid participant at NPT Review Conferences. The non-aligned movement can be seen as North Korea's normative reference group, with which the country also shares central positions with regard to the NPT norms. In fact, North Korea also supports attempts by the non-aligned to establish new norms, such as the demand for a nuclear weapons convention. Within the movement, however, the country does not hold a particularly active position.[40] Moreover, North Korea shows a consistently low level of activity in the UN bodies dealing with disarmament and the NPT Review Conferences.[41] Since its withdrawal from the NPT, North Korean diplomats have hardly taken part in any review conferences or preparatory commissions. In line with that, I was not able to meet North Koreans for background conversations. This might again be an illustration of the intentional lack of transparency about North Korea's nuclear expertise which prevents it from actively contributing existing knowledge to arms control forums. The analysis suggests that North Korea has little interest in this either.

Overall, the impression prevails that North Korean arms control diplomacy is less focused on the further development of existing regime structures. Rather, its purpose is to create channels of communication with the USA and to influence its own position in the conflict on the Korean peninsula. North Korea's actions in the NPT are designed solely to provide the international community with information on national threat perception and are therefore used exclusively for its own purposes.

Also, other prototypical strategies and resources of norm entrepreneurs cannot be identified for North Korea: The normative frameworks used are predominantly self-referential: Although an appeal to the moral conscience of the international

[39] In the early years of its NAM membership (admission in 1975), North Korea tried to play an active role. Shim concludes "that it had the capacity to play an active and effective role in international diplomacy" (Shim 2014: 4). Nevertheless, already back then it was suspected to use the NAM context merely as platform rather than a forum of like-minded states (Krishnan 1981).

[40] This was confirmed to me by various IAEA staff and arms control officials from various states during my interviews in Vienna in spring 2012.

[41] See http://www.reachingcriticalwill.org/resources/profiles#. Accessed 28 April 2017.

community or the NWS can be found now and then, generally common-good-oriented arguments are rare. Some elements of the collective action frames shared by non-aligned countries could be identified, particularly with regard to perceived injustices. However, an action component that goes beyond mere accusations is completely missing in North Korean framings. Naming, shaming, and blaming do exist, but are neither presented consistently nor supplemented by constructive proposals for solutions or subsidiary norms. North Korean rhetoric is dominated by mere accusations against the USA and verbal (defensive) reactions to Washington criticizing North Korea or disseminating statements that it did not believe were true. The rationale underlying such statements is to justify North Korean policies. Pyongyang not only accuses the USA of inadequately fulfilling its disarmament obligation. Much more vehement is it criticism that this hinders the Korean peace process.

When it comes to strategies, North Korea relies mainly on confrontational tactics aimed at promoting national interests rather than disseminating or strengthening international norms. First and foremost, the government is striving to negotiate concessions in the talks over the North Korean nuclear program by resorting to diplomatic blackmail strategies. In addition to "saber-rattling threats" (Henriksen 2012: 103), North Korea uses "brinkmanship-cum-blackmail" in particular (Geldenhuys 2004: 196; also French 2005: Chap. 9; Senn 2009: 67–68) to extort the international community, above all the USA. Examples include the threat of withdrawal from the NPT in 1993, which was only "suspended" one day before the deadline expired; repeated threats that attempts by the West to "unlawfully" limit the North Korean nuclear program would have devastating consequences for world peace and international security (e.g., DPRK 2007); the various missile and nuclear tests or the conscious cultivation of the "rogue" image and the repeated demonstration of nuclear capabilities to demonstrate the country's deterrent potential. By resorting to "deft diplomacy, if not blackmail, Pyongyang has managed to persuade major international actors to rely more on co-operative than coercive responses to the worst instances of its rule-breaking behavior" (Geldenhuys 2004: 168). Apparently, North Korean diplomats use deviating behavior as negotiation tactics (Wunderlich et al. 2013: 277) and act as skillful strategists: Henriksen calls the regime a "consummate poker player" (Henriksen 2012: 104). Pyongyang sometimes deliberately transgresses the rules of the current structures, for example, by withdrawing support for previously supported resolutions or refusing to participate in decision-making processes because, in their view, the situation on the ground was presented inappropriately (e.g., DPRK 1995; Jon 2003).

North Korean proactivism in the nuclear non-proliferation regime is therefore out of the question. Although North Korea acts purposefully and intentionally, it is less innovative and rather reactive than active. Furthermore, the rhetorical affirmation of the norm of nuclear disarmament and the demand for corresponding measures (e.g., the conclusion of a CTBT) are in stark contrast to the development of own military nuclear capacities and the associated policies. North Korea's own non-compliance with the NPT norms reflects its rejection of the current regime norms: Article III, paragraph 2 of the NPT obliges the contracting states not to engage in nuclear trade with such states that have not submitted to IAEA safeguards. North Korea has repeatedly stated that it will only comply with these conditions if the nuclear weapon states comply with their disarmament obligations and also accept legally binding negative security assurances. Wunderlich et al. (2013: 279) describe this attitude as weak norm entrepreneurship. However, North Korea's behavior does not meet the criteria of norm entrepreneurship formulated in this study. North Korea seems to regard violating contractual norms as a legitimate means to express its dissatisfaction with the current treaty structures. In North Korean reading, the lack of implementation of the disarmament norm overrides the validity of the non-proliferation norm and is used as justification for the establishment of a nuclear weapons program and withdrawal from the NPT in violation of the treaty.

Although North Korea (now) openly admits to develop a nuclear weapons capability, it blames the USA for this (e.g., Han 1994; So 2003; Pak 2004). The fact that the country itself has so far neither given any negative security assurances nor signed the CTBT stands in stark contrast to the rhetorical demand to strengthen the disarmament norm as well as to build up its own weapons capabilities. This behavior shows that North Korea's attitude to the NPT norms is characterized by incoherence and implausibility. In criminal sociology, behavior that deviates from the norm, which is ultimately intended to bring about a change in the transgressed norm, is called nonconformist behavior (Lamnek 2001: 300): North Korea, however, is less concerned with reforming the nuclear non-proliferation regime than with concessions by the USA (negative security guarantees, nuclear disarmament on the Korean peninsula) and the recognition of North Korea as a partner on an equal footing.

The fact that the superordinate addressee of North Korean action does not appear to be the international community, but the USA, is a further proof against North Korea's classification as a norm entrepreneur (Wunderlich et al. 2013: 277). Some authors assume that North Korea uses norm-based arguments only to obtain recognition by the USA. Following this position, it might be likely that North Korea would drop the favored norms in return for political concessions (Park 2006: 42; Buszynski 2013: 176; Wunderlich et al. 2013: 280). While such assumptions are mere speculations (Geldenhuys 2004:194; Senn 2009: 6), it has to be emphasized that norm entrepreneurship presupposes long-term visions. In this respect, North Korea's lack of interest in the debate on Article IV, for example, indicates that the country is not particularly motivated to strengthen even those norms that serve its own interests (Wunderlich et al. 2013: 281). For these reasons, North Korea's behavior can also not be described as an attempt to formulate subsidiary norms.[42]

---

[42]The establishment of a nuclear weapons capacity could be interpreted as a reaction to unjustified intervention in national sovereignty and would thus come close to the concept of norm subsidiarity. However, no such argumentation could be found in the analyzed North Korean speeches.

8.3.5 Contrasting North Korea and Iran

Instead of acting as a norm entrepreneur, North Korea indeed appears primarily as a norm antipreneur who rejects the current (nuclear) order (see alternative explanation AE1). Instead of reforming unjust structures, the country seems to be primarily interested in undermining them. Thus, it seems to correspond to the image of the norm-breaking "rogue state" as maintained in the literature. Unlike Iran, North Korea is not actively involved in the promotion of norms—even if this would be in the interest of the country (e.g., with regard to Article IV of the NPT). Although both countries are united in their quest for recognition, North Korea—unlike Iran—does not shy away from isolation and self-isolation.

However, North Korea and Iran share similar positions with regard to the content of the favored norms: Both states share the view that nuclear disarmament is an overriding objective of the NPT. They therefore strongly criticize the lack of implementation of Article VI by nuclear weapon states. The discriminatory structure of the NPT and the perceived unequal treatment and application of double standards are also a thorn in their side.

The demand for equal treatment, respect for national sovereignty and justice play an important role in the rhetoric of both countries. Their membership in the movement of non-aligned states manifests itself in the rejection of dominance and injustice, but also in a pronounced imperialism/anti-Americanism and in the reaffirmation of measures aimed at nuclear disarmament, for example the conclusion of a CTBT or a time-bound disarmament plan and a nuclear weapons convention. Both North Korea and Iran share the impression of not being treated as equal negotiation partners, especially by the USA, and reject attempts to limit their nuclear programs as unjustified interferences in national sovereignty and as a new form of imperialism. Both countries' arms control diplomacy attaches great importance to being accepted as a formally equal and respectable negotiating partner by the USA.

With regard to the strategies used, both states are similar in their use of rather confrontational, sometimes destructive practices and diplomatic blackmail. The widespread opinion that "rogue states" should be regarded as irrational actors contradicts the observation that both Iran and North Korea are regarded as clever strategists and skillful negotiating partners. The description of the "diplomacy of discontent" (Pirseyedi 2013: 164) given by Pirseyedi for Iran also applies to North Korea's arms control policy. It is true that North Korea acts and argues in a much more self-referential manner here and, unlike Iran, shows no common-good-oriented attempts of norm entrepreneurship.

However, both countries also use multilateral arms control forums to defend themselves against allegedly unjustified accusations. Furthermore, both show a sometimes considerable discrepancy between proactive declaratory commitment and their own activities. While this calls Iran's proactive commitment into question and at least raises doubts about Iran's credibility as a norm maker, North Korea completely disqualifies itself as a credible norm-promoting actor: not only through its lack of practical commitment, but also through open nuclear tests and the proclamation as a nuclear power (Wunderlich et al. 2013: 279).

While Iran acts as a norm entrepreneur in some areas, with the aim of reforming current regime norms that the country perceives as unjust or inadequate, North Korea predominantly argues and acts on its own initiative. Regardless of all similarities in terms of confrontational strategies, Iran does not seem willing to place itself outside the regime structures. Despite its aggressive rhetoric, Iran is in most cases ready to join in consensus decisions, albeit at the last minute. Its desire to be recognized as a "normal" member of the international community and not "singularized" seems to be too important.

Moreover, Iran not only works closely with like-minded states and seeks cooperation with civil society; Tehran also sees itself as an advocate of the non-aligned movement and uses this association to promote preferred norms. North Korea, on the other hand, has chosen the path of isolation: The withdrawal from the NPT and the open demonstration of its nuclear weapons status demonstrate this willingness clearly. North Korea refuses to play by the rules of the system, and at the same time, its behavior is predominantly reactive. While Iran is thwarted between the reform of the current order perceived as unjust and its overthrow, North Korea does not seem to seek to change this order within the given parameters. Instead, it looks as if Pyongyang expects the current order to bow to the facts it has created and accept the country's status as a "responsible" nuclear power (Choe 2009).

It is possible that these differences, as well as the different findings regarding norm entrepreneurship, are due to the different ideologies or political identities of the countries: Thus, Islamic Khomeinism contains a clearly outward-looking, universalistic element in the form of the dictum of the export of the revolution, which is explicitly anchored in the constitution. In contrast, the North Korean Juche ideology is much more inward-looking. Even though North Korea, like Iran, claims a "self-image of exceptionality" (Wunderlich et al. 2013: 273) and saw itself—especially in the 1960s and 1970s—as "savior of the non-American world and collapsing multipolar international system" (Mansourov 2003: 90), this self-perception manifests itself less in the form of active norm entrepreneurship. While the export of the Juche ideology is also laid down in the North Korean constitution, already at its peak in the 1960s and 1970s it was mainly concentrated on the Korean peninsula (Geldenhuys 2004: 185). For example, the regime supported liberation movements with far less verve (and success) than Iran. As Kim (2014: 15) notes, North Korea seeks to maintain national sovereignty through non-interference and isolation rather than belonging to the international community. It is therefore primarily concerned with defending itself against unlawful interference in perceived sovereignty rights, instead of reforming the current order in line with own normative convictions. The following chapter discusses the theoretical and conceptual conclusions from the finding that Iran is a norm entrepreneur, while this does not apply to North Korea.

References

Agius, C. (2006). *The social construction of Swedish neutrality: Challenges to Swedish identity and sovereignty*. Manchester: Manchester University Press.

Agrell, W. (1984). The bomb that never was: The rise and fall of the Swedish nuclear weapons programme. In N. Gleditsch & O. Njølstad (Eds.), *Arms races. Technological and political dynamics*, (pp. 154–174). London: Sage Publications.

Ahlin, U. (2010). Interpellationsdebat: Sveriges agerande i frågan om nedrustning och icke-spridning, interpellation 2009/10:465 av Urban Ahlin (S). http://www.riksdagen.se/sv/Debatter–beslut/Interpellationsdebatter1/Debatt/?did=GX10465&doctype=ip. Accessed 28 August 2015.

Alani, B. (1995). Sverige och de globala kärnvapenfrågorna. NPT-konferensen: resultat och konsekvenser (UD informerar 1995:2). Stockholm: Utrikesdepartementet.

Albright, D. (2013). *A dangerous nexus: Preventing Iran-Syria-North Korea Nuclear and Missile Proliferation*. Prepared testimony of David Albright, President, Institute for Science and International Security (ISIS) before the House Foreign Affairs Committee, Subcommittee on the Middle East and North Africa and Subcommittee on Asia and the Pacific, April 11. http://isis-online.org/uploads/conferences/documents/Testimony_House_Subcommittees_11April2013_final.pdf. Accessed April 28, 2017.

Andrén, N. (1996). *Maktbalans och alliansfrihet. Svensk utrikespolitik under 1900-tale*. Stockholm: Norstedts Juridik.

BBC. (2002, February 2). *Bush's "evil acis" comment stirs critics*. http://news.bbc.co.uk/2/hi/americas/1796034.stm. Accessed April 28, 2017.

Bechtol, B. (2007). *Red Rogue: The Persistent challenge of North Korea*. Washington, DC: Potomac Books.

Bechtol, B. (2009). Creating instability in dangerous global regions: North Korean proliferation and support to terrorism in the Middle East and South Asia. *Comparative Strategy, 28*(2), 99–115.

Becker-Jakob, U., Hofmann, G., Müller, H., & Wunderlich, C. (2013). Good international citizens: Canada, Germany and Sweden. In H. Müller & C. Wunderlich (Eds.), *Norm dynamics in multilateral arms control, interests, conflicts, and justice* (pp. 207–245). Athens, GA: University of Georgia Press.

Bergenäs, J. (2010). *The rise of a White Knight State: Sweden's nonproliferation and disarmament history*. Resource Document. NTI Articles, 10.02.2010. http://www.nti.org/analysis/articles/swedens-nonproliferation-history/. Accessed 28 April 217.

Bergman, A. (2007). Co-constitution of domestic and international welfare obligations: The case of Sweden's Social Democratically inspired internationalism. *Cooperation and Conflict, 41*(1), 73–99.

Berkol, I., & Moreau, V. (2009). *Post-export controls on arms transfers: Delivery verification and end-use monitoring*. Resource Document. GRIP, 2009/4. http://archive.grip.org/en/siteweb/dev_e17906a2.asp.html. Accessed 28 April 2017.

Bettiza, G., & Dionigi, F. (2014). *Beyond constructivism's liberal bias: Islamic norm entrepreneurs in a post-secular world society*. EUI Working Paper MWP 2014/10. http://cadmus.eui.eu/bitstream/handle/1814/31692/MWP_WP_Bettiza_Dionigi_2014_10.pdf?sequence=1. Accessed 28 April 2017.

Bildt, C. (2010, May 3). Statement to the 2010 NPT RevCon, New York.

Bildt, C., & Sikorski R. (2010, February 1). Next, the Tactical Nukes. *New York Times*. http://www.nytimes.com/2010/02/02/opinion/02iht-edbildt.html?_r=0. Accessed 28 August 2015.

Birnbaum, K. (1965). Sweden's nuclear policy. *International Journal, 20*(3), 297–311.

Bjereld, U., Johansson, A., & Molin, K. (2008). *Sveriges säkerhet och världens fred. Svensk utrikespolitik under kalla kriget*. Stockholm: Santérus Förlag.

Björkdahl, A. (2002). *From idea to norm: Promoting conflict prevention*. Lund: Lund University.

Björkdahl, A. (2008). Norm advocacy: A small state strategy to influence the EU. *Journal of European Public Policy, 15*(1), 135–154.

Björkdahl, A. (2013). Ideas and norms in Swedish peace policy. *Swiss Political Science Review, 19*(3), 322–337.
Bleiker, R. (2003). A Rogue is a Rogue is a Rogue: US foreign policy and the Korean nuclear crisis. *International Affairs, 79*(4), 719–737.
Blom, F. (2001). *Non-proliferation and disarmament assistance to Russia, Swedish peace and arbitration society*. Stockholm.
Bodström, L. (1985, August 28). Statement to the 1985 NPT RevCon, NPT/CONF.III/SR.2, Geneva.
Brodin, K. (2016). The Undén Proposal. *Cooperation and Conflict, 1*(4), 18–29.
Brysk, A. (2009). *Global good Samaritans: Human Rights as foreign policy*. Oxford, NY: Oxford University Press.
Bunn, G. (1992). *Arms control by committee: Managing negotiations with the Russians*. Stanford, CA: Stanford University Press.
Bunn, G., & Timerbaev, R. (2005). The right to withdraw from the nuclear non-proliferation treaty (NPT): The views of two NPT negotiators. *Yaderny Kontrol, 10*(1–2), 20–29.
Buszynski, L. (2013). *Negotiating with North Korea. The six party talks and the nuclear issue*. New York, NY: Routledge.
Butters, A. (2010). *Ahmadinejad's answer to Obama's nuclear summit*. Resource Document. Time, 19 April 2010. http://content.time.com/time/printout/0,8816,1982962,00.html. Accessed 28 April 2017.
Choe, I. Y. (2007, October 31). Statement to the 62nd Session of the UNGA First Committee, A/C.1/62/PV.23, New York.
Choe, I. Y. (2009, October 27). Statement to the 64th Session of the UNGA First Committee, A/C.1/64/PV.19, New York.
Crisis Group. (2009). *North Korea's Chemical and Biological Weapons Programs*. International Crisis Group ICG, Asia Report 167, 26, Brüssels.
Dahl, A. (2002). Activist Sweden: The last defender of non-alignment. In A. Dahl & N. Hillmer (Eds.), *Activism and (Non)alignment. The relationship between foreign policy and security doctrine* (pp. 139–150). Stockholm: Utrikespolitiska institutet.
Davenport, K. (2013, February 28). *North Korea conducts nuclear test*. https://wwwarmscontrol.org/act/2013_03/North-Conducts-Nuclear-Test. Accessed 28 August 2015.
DPRK. (1986, June 30). Statement of the Government of the Democratic People's Republic of Korea, S/18191, New York.
DPRK. (1987, July 15). Statement by the Ministry of Foreign Affairs of the DPRK, S/18981, New York.
DPRK. (1989, September 13). Statement by the Ministry of Foreign Affairs of the DPRK, S/20964, New York.
DPRK. (1990a, August 31). Proposal by the DPRK Concerning the Safeguards Agreement and an Agreement to Assure the DPRK against the Use of the Threat of Use of Nuclear Weapon, NPT/CONF.IV/33, New York.
DPRK. (1990b, August 30). Suggested Elements to be Included in the Final Declaration, NPT/CONF.4/MC.I/WP.3, Geneva.
DPRK. (1995, May 9). Letter Addressed to the President of the 1995 RevCon, NPT/CONF.1995/30, New York.
DPRK. (2007, January 24). Right of reply by the Democratic people's Republic of Korea at the CD, Geneva. http://www.reachingcriticalwill.org/images/documents/Disarmament-fora/cd/2007/statements/1session/Jan24_DPRK.pdf. Accessed 28 August 2015.
DPRK. (2010, March 2). Statement to the CD, Geneva, Unofficial Transcript. http://www.reachingcriticalwill.org/images/documents/Disarmament-fora/cd/2010/statements/part1/2Mar_ROK.pdf. Accessed 28 August 2015.
DPRK., et al. (1995, May 5). *Extension of the treaty on the non-proliferation of nuclear weapons*. Submitted together with Indonesia, Iran, Jordan Malaysia, Mali, Myanmar, Nigeria, Papua New Guinea, Thailand and Zimbabwe: Draft Decision, NPT/CONF.1995/L.3, New York.

Ekwall, R. (1995a, April 25). Statement to the 1995 NPT RevoCon, Main Committee I, NPT/CONF.1995/MC.1/SR.2, New York.

Ekwall, R. (1995b, May 1). Statement to the 1995 NPT RevCon, Main Committee I, NPT/CONF.1995/MC.1/SR.6, New York.

El Baradei, M. (2011). *The age of deception: Nuclear diplomacy in treacherous times*. New York: Metropolitan Books/Henry Holt and Co.

Eliasson, J. (1995, April 20). Statement to the 1995 RevCon, NPT/CONF.1995/SR.7, New York.

EU Council. (2003, December 12). *Strategy against the proliferation of weapons of mass destruction*. Adopted by the European Council, Brüssel. http://eur-lex.europa.eu/legal-content/EN/TXT/?uri=URISERV:l33234. Accessed 28 August 2015.

Finland, & Sweden. (2002, April 11). Statement by H.E. Mr. Markku Reimaa on behalf of Finland and Sweden on non-strategic nuclear weapons at the Preparatory Committee for the 2005 NPT RevCon, New York.

Finnemore, M., & Sikkink, K. (1998). International norm dynamics and political change. *International Organization, 52*(4), 887–917.

Freivalds, L. (2004, March 16). Statement to the CD, CD/PV.951, Geneva.

Freivalds, L. (2005, May 3). Statement to the 7th NPT RevCon, New York.

French, P. (2005). *North Korea: The paranoid Peninsula. A modern history*. London: Zed Books.

Garcia, D. (2006). *Small arms and security: New emerging international norms*. London/New York.

Garris, J. (1973). Sweden's debate on the proliferation of nuclear weapons. *Cooperation and Conflict, 8*(4), 189–208.

Gause, K. (2013). *North Korean leadership dynamics and decision-making under Kim Jong-Un: A first year assessment*. CNA Analysis & Solutions.

Geldenhuys, D. (2004). *Deviant conduct in world politics*. Houndmills: Palgrave Macmillan.

Gierow, K. (1990). Sverige och icke-spridningen av kärnvapen. UD informerar 1990:2. Stockholm: Utrikesdepartementet.

Goldmann, K. (2015). Samsyn och kompromissvilja nickel till framgång i Tunisien. Resource Document. UI-bloggen, Utrikespolitiska Institutet. http://www.ui.se/blog/uibloggen/2015/9/15/samsyn-och-kompromissvilja-nyckel-till-framgang-i-tunisien.aspx. Accessed 28 August 2015.

Habib, B. (2011). North Korea's nuclear weapons program and the maintenance of the Songun system. *The Pacific Review, 24*(1), 43–64.

Han, C. O. (1994, June 30). Statement to the CD, CD/PV/684, Geneva.

Han, C. O. (1996, March 21). Statement to the CD, CD/PV.731, Geneva.

Harrison, S. (2005). Did North Korea cheat. *Foreign Affairs, 84*(1), 99–110.

Hecker, S. (2010) *A return trip to North Korea's Yongbyon nuclear complex*. Reource Document. CISAC Report, 20 November 2010. http://people.duke.edu/~myhan/kaf1007.pdf. Accessed 28 April 2017.

Henriksen, T. (2012). *America and the Rogue states*. St. New York, NY: Martin's Press.

Hilpert, H., & Meier, O. (2013). *Charting a new course on North Korea's nuclear programme?* The options and the non-proliferation treaty. SWP Comments 19, June 2013. https://www.swp-berlin.org/fileadmin/contents/products/comments/2013C19_hlp_mro.pdf. Accessed 28 April 2017.

Holmström, M. (2006). *Palme försökte aktiv säljas Boforskanoner*. Resource Document. Svenska Dagbladet, 23.4.2006. http://www.svd.se/palme-forsokte-aktivt-salja-boforskanoner. Accessed 28 April 2017.

Hong, J. R. (2007, October 9). Statement to the 62nd Session of the UNGA First Committee, A/C.1/62/PV.3, New York.

Huntley, W. (2006). Rebels without a cause. North Korea, Iran and the NPT. *International Affairs, 82*(4), 723–742.

Ingebritsen, C. (2002). Norm entrepreneurs: Scandinavia's role in world politics. *Cooperation and Conflict, 37*(1), 11–23.

Johnson, R. (1995). Indefinite extension of the non-proliferation treaty: Risks and reckonings. Acronym Report No. 7. http://www.acronym.org.uk/old/archive/acrorep/acro7.htm. Accessed 28.

Johnson, R. (2009). *Unfinished business. The negotiation of the CTBT and the end of nuclear testing*. UNIDIR, Geneva.
Jon, Y.-R. (2003, November 6). Statement to the 46th Session of the UNGA First Committee, A/C.1/58/PV.23, New York.
Jonter, T. (2001). *Sweden and the bomb: The Swedish plans to acquire nuclear weapons, 1945–1972*. SKI Report, 01(33), Stockholm.
Jonter, T. (2003). *Making a historical survey of a State's nuclear ambitions IAEA task ID: SWE C 01333, Impact of historical development of a state's national nuclear non-proliferation policy on additional protocol*. SKI Report 2003. Stockholm.
Kang, M. C. (2008, October 31). Statement to the 63rd Session of the UNGA First Committee, A/C.1/63/PV.22, New York.
KCNA. (2006, October 3). North Korean Foreign Ministry clarifies stand on new measure to bolster war deterrent. *Korean News KCNA*. http://www.kcna.co.jp/item/2006/200610/news10/04.htm#1. Accessed 28 August 2015.
Kim, C. G. (1990, October 20). Statement to the 46th Session of the UNGA First Committee, A/C.1/46/PV.20, New York.
Kim, C. G. (1995, January 27). Statement to the Preparatory Committee of the 1995 NPT RevCon, NPT/CONF.1995/PC.IV/SR.8, Geneva.
Kim, S. Y. (1998, October 15). Statement to the 53rd Session of the UNGA First Committee, A/C.1/53/ PV.7, New York.
Kim, J. (2014). *The North Korean nuclear weapons crisis. The nuclear taboo revisited?*. London/ New York: Palgrave Macmillan.
Klare, M. (1995). *Rogue states and nuclear outlaws: America's search for a new foreign policy*. New York, NY: Hill and Wang.
Krishnan, R. R. (1981). North Korea and the Non-Aligned Movement. *International Studies, 20*(1–2), 299–313.
Lamnek, S. (2001 [1979]). *Theorien abweichenden Verhaltens*, 7. Aufl., München: Wilhelm Fink Verlg.
Li, H. C. (1998, October 16). Statement to the 53rd Session of the UNGA First Committee, A/C.1/53/PV.7, New York.
Lindh, A. (2000, April 25). Statement to the 6th NPT RevCon, New York.
Lindh, A. (2001, November 11). Statement at the Conference on Facilitating the Entry into Force of the CTBT, New York.
Litwak, R. (2000). *Rogue states and U.S. foreign policy: Containment after the Cold War*. Washington, DC: Woodrow Wilson Center Press with Johns Hopkins University Press.
Litwak, R. (2012). *Outlier states: American strategies to change, contain, or engage regimes*. Washington, DC: Woodrow Wilson Center Press with Johns Hopkins University Press.
Lomas, P. (1991). Sweden. In H. Müller (Ed.), *How Western European nuclear policy is made: Deciding the atom* (pp. 190–208). Houndmills: MacMillan.
Mallin, M. (1994). *The June, 1993 Swedish draft comprehensive nuclear test-ban treaty: Implications and issues for negotiations*. McLean/ VA: Science Applications International.
Manga, E. (2010). Swedish arms export. From National interest to global Utopia. *New Routes, 15*(3), 3–6.
Mansourov, A. (1995). The origins, evolution, and current politics of the North Korean nuclear program. *The Nonproliferation Review, 2*(3), 25–38.
Mansourov, A. (2003). *The Hermit Mouse Roars: North Korea's Response to U.S. Security Policies*, Asia-Pacific Center for Security Studies, March 2003.
Ministry of Foreign Affairs Iran. (2010, October 4). Spokesman Terms Iran "Forerunner of Campaign against N. Armaments". Press statement. http://zan1400.blogfa.com/post-166.aspx. Accessed April 28, 2017.
Müller (2013). Conclusion: Agency is central. In H. Müller, & C. Wunderlich (Eds.), *Norm dynamics in multilateral arms control, interests, conflicts, and justice* (pp. 337–366). Athens, GA: University of Georgia Press.

Müller, H., Below, A., & Wisotzki, S. (2013). Beyond the state: Nongovernmental organizations, the European Union, and the United Nations. In H. Müller & C. Wunderlich (Eds.), *Norm dynamics in multilateral arms control, interests, conflicts, and justice* (pp. 296–336). Athens, GA: University of Georgia Press.

Müller, H., Fischer, D., & Kötter, W. (1994). *Nuclear non-proliferation and global order*. New York, NY: Oxford University Press.

Müller, H., Franceschini, G., Melamud, A., Müller, D., Péczeli, & Schaper, A. (2015). *A nuclear weapon-free zone in Europe: Concept–Problems–Chances*. PRIF Resource Document. http://www.bmeia.gv.at/fileadmin/user_upload/Zentrale/Aussenpolitik/Abruestung/NWFZE_Finalversion.pdf. Accessed 28 April 2017.

Myrdal, A. (1977). *The game of disarmament: How the United States and Russia run the arms race*. Manchester: Manchester University Press.

NAC. (1998, June 9). Towards a nuclear-weapon-free world: The need for a new agenda. Joint Declaration by the Ministers for Foreign Affairs of Brazil, Egypt, Ireland, Mexico, New Zealand, Slovenia, South Africa and Sweden, A/53/138.

Niksch, L. (2007, January 3). North Korea's nuclear weapons development and diplomacy (CRS Report for Congress) Washington, DC.

Nilsson, A.-S. (1991). *Den moraliska stormakten: En studie av socialdemokratins internationella activism*. Stockholm: Timbro.

Olsson, T., & Åkerman, M. (2012). *FOI stod bakom bulvanen*. Resource Document. SvD Näringsliv, 7.3.2012. http://www.svd.se/foi-stod-bakom-bulvanen_6908035; 28 April 2017.

Pak, G. Y. (1994, October 21). Statement to the 49th Session of the UNGA First Committee, A/C.1/49/PV.8, New York.

Pak, G. Y. (2004, October 12). Statement to the 59th Session of the UNGA First Committee, A/C.1/59/PV.7, New York.

Park, H. (2006). The rationales behind North Korean foreign policy. In L. Hagström & M. Söderberg (Eds.), *North Korea policy: Japan and the great powers* (pp. 38–52). London: Routledge.

Park, P. (2010). The future of the Democratic People's Republic of Korea. *Journal of Contemporary Asia, 31*(1), 104–120.

Pirseyedi, B. (2013). *Arms control and Iranian foreign policy: Diplomacy of discontent*. New York, NY: Routledge.

Pollack, J. (2009). North Korea's nuclear weapons program to 2015. In N. Busch & D. Joyner (Eds.), *Combating weapons of mass destruction: The future of international nonproliferation policy* (pp. 263–280). Athens, GA: University of Georgia Press.

Prawitz, J. (1995). *From nuclear-option to non-nuclear promotion: The Sweden case*. Research Report no 20. Stockholm: Swedish Institute of International Affairs.

Prawitz, J. (2003). Arms controller Alva Myrdal: Word power for world politics. In P. Wallensteen (Ed.), *Alva Myrdal in international affairs* (pp. 55–68). Uppsala: Uppsala Publishing House.

Rajiv, S. (2010). *Iran and the NPT RevCon 2010*. Resource Document. IDSA Comment. http://www.idsa.in/idsacomments/IranandtheNPTRevCon2010_sscrajiv_040510. Accessed 28 April 2017.

Regeringskansliet (2015, April 27). Från svensk sida är vi måna um att kunna bidra konkret, här och nu. *Sydsvenskan*.http://www.regeringen.se/debattartiklar/2015/04/fran-svensk-sida-ar-vi-mana-om-att-kunna-bidra-konkret-har-och-nu/. Accessed 28 August 2015.

Ri, T. (1990, November 30). Statement to the 1990 NPT RevCon, NPT/CONF.IV/SR.6, Geneva.

Ri, T. (1993, March 23). Statement to the CD, CD/PV.647, Geneva.

Ri, T. (1995, June 29). Statement to the CD, CD/PV.710, Geneva.

Ri, T. (1999, June 24). Statement to the CD, CD/PV.829, Geneva.

Ri, J. G.(2007, October 31). Statement to the 62nd Session of the UNGA First Committee, A/C.1/62/PV.23, New York.

Rublee, M. (2008). Taking Stock of the nuclear nonproliferation regime: Using social psychology to understand regime effectiveness. *International Studies Review, 10*(3), 420–450.

Rublee, M. (2009). *Nonproliferation norms: Why states choose nuclear restraint*. Athens, GA: University of Georgia Press.

Schmalberger, T. (1991). *In pursuit of a nuclear test Ban treaty: A guide to the debate in the conference on disarmament*. New York, NY: UNIDIR.

Schmidt, H.-J. (2012). Nordkorea als Nuklearmacht—Chancen der Kontrolle. HSFK Report 1/2012. Frankfurt a. M.

Schmittchen, D. (2006). "Rogue States"—"Schurkenstaaten". Ein stringentes US-Konzept im Kampf gegen Terrorismus und Proliferation von ABC-Waffen? Resource document. Forschungsgruppe Sicherheitspolitik. Berlin.

Senn, M. (2009). *Wolves in the woods: The Rogue state concept from a constructivist perspective*. Baden-Baden: Nomos.

Shim, D. (2014). *Visual politics and North Korea: Seeing is believing*. New York, NY: Routledge.

Sigal, L. (1998). *Disarming strangers: Nuclear diplomacy with North Korea*. Princeton/NY: Princeton University Press.

So, S. P. (2003). *February 13). Statement to the CD*. CD/PV.919, Geneva:

So, S. P. (2011, March 10). *Statement to the UN and Other International Organizations at the Conference on Disarmament*, Geneva.

Socialdemokraterna. (2010). Socialdemokraternas tolvpuntksprogram för nedrustning. En svensk offensiv mot massförstörelsevapen och för nedrustning, Stockholm. http://www.socialdemokraterna.se/upload/Internationellt/Dokument/nedrustningsprogram.pdf. Accessed 28 August 2015.

Söderlund, A. (2013, June 26). Carl Bildt överraskade—ringde "Ring P1". Aftonbladet. http://aftonbladet.se/nyheter/article16728776.ab?service=print. Accessed April 28, 2017.

Suk, A. (2011). What is the root cause of the North Korean nuclear program? *Asian Affairs. An American Review, 38*(4), 175–187.

Sundelius, B. (2001). The makers of Swedish security policy. In B. Huldt, T. Tiilikainen, T. Vaahtoranta, & A. Rågård-Helkama (Eds.), *Finnish and Swedish security: Comparing national policies* (pp. 232–258). Helsinki/Stockholm: Swedish National Defence College and the Programme on the Northern Dimension of the CFSP.

Svenska Freds. (2012). *Sweden is planning to help Saudi Arabia build an arms factors*. Resource Document. http://www.svenskafreds.se/sweden-is-planning-to-help-saudi-arabia-build-an-arms-factory. Accessed 28 April 2017.

Svensson, F. (2013). *Sverige lämnar nedrustningssamarbete*. Resource Document. OmVärlden, 24.4.2013. http://www.omvarlden.se/varlden/Briefing/Sverige-lamnar-nedrustningssamarbete/. Accessed 28 April 2017.

Sweden. (1965, September 2). Memorandum on International Cooperation for the Detection of Underground Nuclear Explosions, ENDC/154, Geneva.

Sweden. (1983, June 14). Draft Treaty Banning any Nuclear Weapon Test Explosion in Any Environment, Submitted to the CD, CD/381, Geneva.

Sweden. (1991, July 31). Text of a Draft Comprehensive Test-Ban Treaty and its annexed Protocols, Submitted to the CD, CD/1089, Geneva.

Sweden. (1993, December 6). Text of a Draft Comprehensive Nuclear Test Ban Treaty and its Annexed Draft Protocol, Submitted to the CD, CD/1232, Geneva.

Sweden. (1995, n. d.). Proposed language on the Review of Article VI and the Eighth to Twelfth Preambular Paragraphs, NPT/CONF.1995/MC.I/CRP.14, New York.

Sweden. (2010, March 19). *Multilateral approaches to the nuclear fuel cycle*. Working paper, NPT/CONF.2010/WP.7, New York.

Sweden et al. (1985, July 15). Letter dated 15 July 1985 addressed to the provisional secretary-general of the Third NPT RevCon. Together with Denmark, Finland, Island and Norway, NPT/CONF.III/16, New York.

Sweden et al. (1995, April 21). *Article III—Safeguards*. Working Paper. Together with Australia, Austria, Canada, Denmark, Finland, Hungary, Ireland, the Netherlands, New Zealand, and Norway. NPT/CONF.1995/MC.II/WP.2, New York.

Sweden et al. (2000, April 27). *Export controls*. Working paper. Together with Australia, Austria, Canada, Denmark, Finland, Hungary, Ireland, the Netherlands, New Zealand, and Norway, NPT/CONF.2000/MC.II/WP.4, New York.

Swedish Ministry of Foreign Affairs. (2014, March 13). Strategic Export Control in 2013—Military Equipment and Dual-Use Items, Government Communication 2013/14:114. Stockholm. http://www.government.se/legal-documents/2014/01/comm.-201314114/. Accessed April 28, 2017.

Theorin, M. B. (1985, February 5). Statement to the CD, Geneva.

Theorin, M. B. (1988, February 2). Statement to the CD, Geneva.

Theorin, M. B. (1991, July 25). Statement to the CD, Geneva.

Theorin, M. (2003). Alva Myrdal and the Peace Movement. In P. Wallensteen (Ed.), *Alva Myrdal in international affairs* (pp. 43–54). Uppsala: Uppsala Publishing House.

Thränert, O. (2003). *Der Iran und die Verbreitung von ABC-Waffen*. Berlin: SWP-Studie.

Thunborg, A. (2005). Swedish nuclear non-proliferation and disarmament policy and the European Union. *Foreign Policy in Dialogue, 17*, 31–35.

Tolf, A. (2013). Sverige och arbetet för kärnvapennedrustning—självständig aktör eller passiv medsångare i EU: skör? Stockholm: Svenska läkare mot kärnvapen, No. 123, March–April 2013.

UN. (1983, April 8). Report of the Independent Commission on Disarmament, A/CN.10/38, New York.

van Dassen, L. (1995). Sweden. In H. Müller (Ed.), *Nuclear export controls in Europe* (pp. 181–206). Brüssel: European Interuniversity Press.

van Dassen, L. (1996). Sweden. In H. Müller (Ed.), *European non-proliferation policy 1993–1995* (pp. 265–279). Brüssel: European Interuniversity Press.

van Dassen, L. (1998). *Sweden and the making of nuclear non-proliferation: From indecision to assertiveness*. SKI Report 98(16). Stockholm: Norstedts Tryckeri AB.

van Dassen, L., & Wetter, A. (2006). Nordic nuclear non-proliferation policies: Different traditions and common objectives. In A. J. K. Bailes, G. Herolf. & B. Sundelius (Eds.), *The Nordic countries and the European security and defence policy* (pp. 252–266), Oxford: Oxford University Press.

Waldenström, L. (2005). *North Korea's juche ideology and its implications on Pyongyang's relations with Washington 1994–2004. A North Korean perspective*. Umea: Swedish Defense Research Agency.

Wallin, L. (1991). Sweden. In R. Cowen Karp (Ed.), *Security with nuclear weapons? Different perspectives on national security* (pp. 360–381). New York: Oxford University Press.

Wunderlich, C., Hellmann, A., Müller, D., Reuter, J., & Schmidt, H-J. (2013). Non-aligned Reformers and Revolutionaries: Egypt, South Africa, Iran, and North Korea. In H. Müller & C. Wunderlich, 246–295.

Wunderlich, A. (2014). A "rogue" gone norm entrepreneurial? Iran within the nuclear nonproliferation regime. In W. Wagner, W. Werner, & M. Onderco (Eds.), *Deviance in international relations: "Rogue states" and international security* (pp. 83–104). Basingstoke: Palgrave Macmillan.

Wunderlich, C. (2008). *Vom Weltgewissen zum Mitläufer ohne Profil? Schwedens wertorientierte Außenpolitik im Anpassungsdruck an europäische Positionen – Nukleare Rüstungskontrollpolitik 1985–2005*. Wissenschaftliche Hausarbeit für das Lehramt an Gymnasien eingereicht dem Amt für Lehrerbildung. Frankfurt a. M. Unpublished Manuscript.

Wunderlich, C. (2013). Theoretical approaches in the study of norms. In H. Müller & C. Wunderlich (Eds.), *Norm dynamics in multilateral arms control, interests, conflicts, and justice* (pp. 20–47). Athens, GA: University of Georgia Press.

Youde, J., & Slagter, T. (2013). Creating "good international citizens", middle powers and domestic political institutions. *Seton Hall Journal of Diplomacy and International Relations, 14*(2), 123–133.

Chapter 9
Conclusion: Revisiting Norm Entrepreneurship

The aim of the present study was to broaden the analytical scope of existing norm studies. To date, key analytical concepts such as the concept of norm entrepreneurship have been applied in a selective manner, mainly to actors promoting Western liberal norms. Proponents of alternative normative visions are mostly considered as addressees of (new) prohibitionary norms or stigmatized as norm-deviating "rogue states." Whether these actors seek to promote the norms that they deem (more) appropriate, that is whether they act as norm entrepreneurs, is only rarely the focus of analysis. In this study I seek to address these theoretical shortcomings by counterintuitively applying the concept of norm entrepreneurship to state actors that are known for their normative deviance. The central question that I seek to answer with this study is: Can alleged "rogue states" be norm entrepreneurs?

To answer this question, in the theoretical part of the study I systematically explored how liberal-constructivist norm scholars have so far used the concept both empirically and theoretically. Based on the literature review, I developed an operationalization of the concept in order to apply it empirically to the case of the Islamic Republic of Iran, which has been labeled a "rogue state," especially by the USA, since its inception in 1979. Usually, the "rogue state" label is used to designate norm breakers. Therefore, based on the literature on "norm challengers" and "rogue states," I developed two alternative explanations that could be applied to explain Iran's behavior, assuming that Iran was either trying to undermine (AE1) or subsidize existing norms with counter-norms (AE2).

In order to probe the plausibility of the assumption that "rogue states" can act as norm entrepreneurs and for testing the alternative explanations, I turned to the field of the control of weapons of mass destruction. In fact, an analysis of Iranian arms control diplomacy revealed that Iran, in line with its historically rooted cultural self-image, has not only been exceptionally committed, but has taken a considerable norm entrepreneurial role in two of three selected cases. The country has been strongly engaged in establishing and strengthening effective protection and assistance measures for victims of chemical weapons: Article X of the CWC bears all the hallmarks

C. Wunderlich, *Rogue States as Norm Entrepreneurs*,
Norm Research in International Relations,
https://doi.org/10.1007/978-3-030-27990-5_9

of Iran's position. Iran maintained its outstanding commitment even after the formal institutionalization of the regime: On the initiative of Iran, a support network for victims of chemical weapons was established in 2011. Tehran's advocacy for a right to the full access to the fuel cycle, including uranium enrichment, also meets the criteria of norm entrepreneurship. Although Iran was not directly involved in establishing the norm of technology cooperation, the country has vehemently promoted what it perceives to be the "correct" interpretation and implementation of Article IV of the NPT and has tried to anchor its interpretation in the discourse.

In both cases, Iran acted as norm entrepreneur. Accordingly, alternative explanations can be rejected which either perceive "rogue states" as norm breakers only and exclude norm advocacy originating from these states (AE1) or which concede them to respond to global norms by promoting subsidiary counter-norms at best (AE2). It is true that Iran's commitment to a right to uranium enrichment comes close to the assumption formulated in AE2: After all, Iran's advocacy aims to counter what the country perceives to be a misinterpretation of the norm of technology cooperation that severely limits Iran's autonomy, i.e., the development of indigenous fuel cycle capabilities. But if judged by the level of activities undertaken to support its normative claim, Iran's behavior clearly exceeds purely reactive measures and thus qualifies as norm entrepreneurship.

The situation is different with regard to its commitment to nuclear disarmament. Tehran is undoubtedly committed to strengthening this norm, yet the norm-promoting activities only meet the criteria of weak norm entrepreneurship. On the one hand, a number of disarmament friendly non-aligned countries share this advocacy and show a similar level of activity (Wunderlich et al. 2013). On the other hand, other states show much stronger proactivism, e.g., South Africa or Sweden. Obviously, it seems necessary to conceptually distinguish different forms of norm entrepreneurship from weak to moderate to strong.

This insight is also confirmed by the comparison with the prototypical norm entrepreneur Sweden and the equally prototypical "rogue state" of North Korea, and it also sheds light on some further specifics of Iranian norm entrepreneurship.

Despite some similarities, Iranian norm advocacy differs from that of Sweden in terms of scope and the stratesgies used. Within the NPT, Iran prefers the norm of nuclear disarmament and technology cooperation over non-proliferation, thus blocking the strengthening of export control measures. Sweden, by contrast, is committed to strengthening all three pillars of the NPT. Stockholm uses strategies typical of good international citizens: It seeks active cooperation with like-minded states and civil society, prefers compromise-based and persuasive strategies, often acts as a mediator between opposing positions, and consistently shows its willingness to deviate from its own positions if this proves conducive to consensual solutions. Iran, on the other hand, focuses more on confrontational strategies and pursues its own objectives far more rigidly. So while Sweden and Iran's commitment is partly based on similar motives, the perception of discriminating structures and the feeling of being treated unfairly are more pronounced in Iran. This dissatisfaction leads Iran to resort to diplomatic blackmail strategies and destructive tactics, even if this behavior could risk the failure of negotiations. Sweden sees itself primarily in the role of a norm reformer feeling obliged to improve the current normative order within existing structures. Therefore, the country relies on consensus-oriented mediation strategies. Iran, by contrast, is maneuvering between reform-oriented and revolutionary norm entrepreneurship aimed at overcoming the prevailing order.

In contrast to North Korea, however, Tehran can in some instances be considered a classic norm entrepreneur. It claims an active role in shaping the current normative order, while for North Korea, reforming the current order seems not to be of concern: It argues in a predominantly self-referential manner, consistently acts reactively and refuses to play by the rules of the system.

The finding that "rogue states" can be norm entrepreneurs has consequences for theorizing about norms and practical implications for dealing with supposed deviants to the existing normative order. The next section discusses insights into the concept of norm entrepreneurship and for IR norms research more broadly. Specssifically, I suggest that a distinction be made between weak, moderate, and strong forms of norm entrepreneurship, depending on the scope of proactivism. My empirical findings also indicate that it might be apt to distinguish between reformist and revolutionary norm entrepreneurship, depending on how the respective norm entrepreneur and its normative objectives relate to the prevailing normative order (maintenance, overthrow, or subversion). Thereafter, I discuss the practical implications that follow from the finding that supposed "rogue states" can be norm entrepreneurs, and I will do so by focusing on how to deal with Iran. I will conclude this study with some remarks on the scope of my argument, and I will outline avenues for further research.

9.1 Conceptual Specification

That the concept of norm entrepreneurship can be applied to the alleged "rogue state" of Iran demonstrates that the narrow focus of liberal-constructivist norm studies on Western liberal norm entrepreneurs is untenable—a fact that has already been suggested by critical constructivist accounts on bottom-up processes of norm diffusion (see Chap. 4). Obviously, the universe of possible norm entrepreneurs is broader than suggested by existing empirical studies. Yet the fact that even "rogue states," i.e., designated norm breakers, can act as norm makers does not render the concept obsolete.

Rather, my findings confirm and supplement a series of more recent works that have been geared toward overcoming analytical limitations of established norm studies by including unorthodox actors in the spectrum of norm entrepreneurs, e.g., by investigating Islamic norm advocacy (Adamson 2005; Bettiza and Dionigi 2014). In contrast to these studies, my empirical analysis rests on a thorough operationalization of the concept of norm entrepreneurship. The analytical framework developed here might be a useful tool for future studies in order to ensure that the concept is no longer applied in an arbitrary manner. If the catalog of criteria were to become the default tool to identify and verify norm entrepreneurship, more generalizable insights could be drawn from (a systematic comparison of) the norm advocacy of various sorts of actors (states, civil society actors, international organizations, etc.).

My study has also demonstrated that it would be worthwhile for norm scholars to further expand the spectrum of norm entrepreneurs to non-Western, unorthodox actors, thereby abandoning the hitherto Eurocentric perspective of norm research. Poststructuralists and critical norm scholars have drawn our attention to the inherent power dimension of norms, which has so far only insufficiently been taken into account (Epstein 2012a: 136; Towns 2012; Widmaier and Park 2012: 131; Adler-Nissen 2014). While norms often constrain power by setting (new) standards of appropriateness, they can at the same time also consolidate power, since norms claim universal validity and form intersubjective expectations that stabilize social behavior. A limited focus on "feel-good" norm entrepreneurship risks neglecting this very dimension of power that is inherent to norms. And it also runs the risk of helping to maintain existing power structures. Studying norm entrepreneurship of a less feel-good sort (see also Checkel 2012: 3) seems advisable not only from a theoretical point of view, it also opens up interesting avenues for further theorizing regarding the scope-conditions of norm advocacy. Analyzing non-Western actors and even supposed norm breakers under the prism of norm entrepreneurship would make it possible to assess to what extent their behavior differs from mere resistance to the current normative order. Contestation thus comes to the fore as the *modus vivendi* of norm entrepreneurship and complements the focus on norm diffusion via genuine persuasion that has dominated empirical norm studies for long.

The findings obtained in this study expand previous knowledge on the concept of norm entrepreneurship in several aspects, which will be elaborated in the following sections. While some insights rather add to or supplement existing studies, I will also introduce a conceptual distinction between two types of norm entrepreneurs which might further specify our understanding of the concept and its underlying mechanisms.

9.1.1 "Only" Commitment or Fully Fledged Norm Entrepreneurship?

As has been mentioned earlier, the norm entrepreneurship shown by Iran varies in the individual cases: The country played a prominent role in establishing and strengthening the respective norms in the areas of peaceful uses/right to uranium enrichment and protection of chemical weapons victims. With regard to the norm of nuclear disarmament, Iran's commitment meets the criteria of norm entrepreneurship only to a limited extent.

In all cases, Iran was one of the first, but not the "only" norm-promoting actor: Other states also advocated the development of effective protection measures in the context of the CWC (e.g., Pakistan; Kenyon and Mashhadi 2007). The view that the right to the peaceful uses of nuclear energy also includes enrichment and reprocessing technologies is shared by a number of other states. Some of them acted as norm advocates long before Iran took up the issue, and they actively sought to anchor their norm interpretation in the treaty text when the NPT was negotiated (e.g., Brazil, Mexico, Romania; Shaker 1980: 293–299). After the NPT had entered into force, Western nuclear energy users such as Belgium, Germany, Japan, and Switzerland were particularly concerned that a restrictive reading of Article IV could adversely affect their competitiveness in nuclear trade. In the 1970s and 1980s, Germany, in particular, called for equal access to enrichment and reprocessing technologies for non-nuclear weapon states (Fey et al. 2014: 470–479). Today, other non-aligned states are advocating the right to full access to the fuel cycle alongside Iran.

Yet in both cases analyzed, while Iran was not the only norm advocate, its commitment clearly exceeds that of other actors in strength and consistency. In both cases under discussion, Iran's norm entrepreneurship can be described as "strong": It meets all criteria identified in Sect. 5.2.1 and meets the definition of proactive behavior established by Becker et al. (2008: 820). Iran consistently and continuously advocates the right to enrichment and protection of chemical weapons victims, both over time and across various forums and among various heads of government.

By contrast, its disarmament activities are merely a weak form of norm entrepreneurship: It is true that Iranian diplomats continuously and consistently demand the proper implementation and strengthening of the disarmament norm. Besides this rhetorical commitment, however, Iran only actively supports a small number of initiatives in this field and particularly falls behind other states when it comes to collaborative efforts with civil society. In fact, the extent of proactivism has to be evaluated in relation to the activism of other states: In the field of nuclear disarmament advocacy, a number of other actors clearly exceed the level of proactivism shown by Iran, e.g., Sweden or Ireland. Within Iran's primary group of reference, the NAM, some states are at least as committed to nuclear disarmament, if not even more (e.g., Egypt; Brazil; Indonesia; South Africa; Mexico). An example of a moderate norm entrepreneur in the field is Canada, whose disproportional commitment to nuclear disarmament-related measures is sometimes hampered by alliance considerations (Becker et al. 2008: 840).

While it seems quite logical to distinguish between different degrees of norm entrepreneurship displayed by actors, one aspect needs further discussion: Does the fact that Iran was not the only norm entrepreneur in the analyzed cases weaken its norm advocacy? It is true that most empirical studies on norm advocacy focus on single actors—particularly when it comes to investigating state norm entrepreneurship (among many Björkdahl 2002). Yet this should not distort the finding that usually more than one actor is involved in establishing or strengthening norms. In their seminal study, Finnemore and Sikkink (1998) identify transnational networks of state and non-state actors engaging for a common cause as prototypical norm advocates. While many scholars have adopted this notion and in their empirical analyses focus on the collaborative efforts of these actors, insufficient attention is being paid to the fact that in one particular policy field, different actors—state and civil society, Western and non-Western—can act as norm entrepreneurs independently of each other. Norm construction and diffusion processes need not be initiated by "one" norm entrepreneur (or one TAN), but should be understood as complex processes in which several actors are involved, and at times even compete against each other or try to sabotage their rivals' aims (Bob 2012). Actors might engage in modifying or maintaining a somehow challenged norm even without having been previously involved in its construction (see also Acharya 2013: 468–469). Unpacking the peculiarities of the different types of norm entrepreneurs would be an interesting and potentially fruitful endeavor. A systematic comparison of various types of norm advocates might also indicate what kind of factors render certain types of actors (state, non-state, substate, international organizations, etc.) more or less likely to engage in norm entrepreneurship and it might also allow interesting insights as to the conditions for success or failure of norm advocacy.

9.1.2 Multiple Roles and Contexts of Norm Entrepreneurship

A comparison between Iran and Sweden shows that norm entrepreneurs can become active in different phases of the norm cycle and play different roles simultaneously (see also Hamilton 2008: 40; Müller 2013: 353). With regard to assistance and support for chemical weapons victims, Iran was not only one of the main drivers of norm construction, but was also significantly involved in specifying, strengthening and further institutionalizing the norm. With respect to the norm of peaceful uses of nuclear energy, Iran predominantly acted as the guardian of what Tehran perceived to be the original meaning of the norm and therefore sought to institutionalize and anchor this interpretation into the discourse.[1] In the case of nuclear disarmament, Iran also acts as guardian of the norm. At the same time, in some aspects of its behavior, Iran demonstrates its opposition to the global normative order, thereby challenging core norms, e.g., supporting terrorist groups, drawing on anti-American and anti-Zionist sentiment and violating human rights norms at home. Apparently, norm entrepreneurship in selected policy fields and norm-deviating behavior in others can go hand in hand.

Sweden, which in this study served as a contrasting case of a prototypical norm entrepreneur, also displayed multiple roles in various policy fields, such as norm initiator, keeper, and entrepreneur. It would be interesting for future studies to investigate in which phase of the dynamic evolution of norms which role comes to the fore, as well as whether certain norm entrepreneurs are more inclined to take over certain roles over others.

The findings of this work—limited to the field of arms control—point to the influence of various contextual factors. For example, for Iran, the fact that the country had itself been affected by CW use played a key role in the decision to advocate for

[1] Iran pursues discursive anchoring by constantly activating its interpretation of norms in the discourse, i.e., the debates of the respective disarmament forums. In addition, Iran seeks to institutionalize its norm interpretation, for example by anchoring it into politically binding final documents of the NPT Review Conferences. UN Security Council Resolution 2231, which while not referring to it in wording, implicitly confirms the right to uranium enrichment, constitutes an example of a legally binding anchoring of Iran's norm interpretation.

effective assistance and protection measures against these weapons in the context of the CWC, and to call for a strengthening of these measures when the negotiated norms seemed to be insufficient in terms of their scope. The existence of field-specific expertise and the availability of resources (knowledge, material and human resources, reputation) also increase the likelihood that states might participate in processes of norm construction or strengthening. The respective normative context also influences whether and to what extent an actor can act as a norm entrepreneur by providing windows of opportunity (Wunderlich 2013: 30–1). However, these contextual factors are by no means deterministic. Whether a state acts as a norm entrepreneur ultimately also depends on national interests, personal priorities, or preferences of relevant decision-makers as well as on the identity of the country or actor in question.

The example of Sweden illustrates that the political culture and traditions that arise from a country's self-image influence whether and how a country engages as a norm advocate. Its disarmament activism was shaped by various outstanding personalities calling for a world free of weapons of mass destruction, such as Olof Palme or Alva Myrdal. Sweden's identity as a disarmament activist has earned it a reputation and entrusted the country with a certain "moral authority." This in turn positively affected the inclination of the international community (as well as norm scholars) to grant norm entrepreneurial status to Sweden.

Overall, the findings of this study demonstrate the role of ideological and domestic political factors influencing state norm entrepreneurship (see also Becker et al. 2008; Hanson 2012; Becker et al. 2013; Müller 2013). For Iran, the policy of exporting the revolution forms a central component of the country's political identity leading to an inclination to proactively diffuse its own normative ideas globally—a perfect breeding ground for norm entrepreneurship. By contrast, North Korea's Juche ideology is turned inwards; a fact that might explain the lack of North Korean norm entrepreneurship. The impact of domestic political factors on a country's norm entrepreneurial profile (Hanson 2012: 76; Müller 2013: 359) can also be seen in shifts in meaning or loss of activity that go hand in hand with changes in government: Sweden's norm entrepreneurship declined heavily with the shift of government in the 1990s and late 2000s.

Against this background, it is particularly surprising that the analyzed cases of Iranian norm entrepreneurship were not affected by changes in government. The advocacy for a right to uranium enrichment and the demand for nuclear disarmament were upheld by various political leaders and even transcended regime types. Ultimately, the continuity of state-based norm entrepreneurship (at least in [semi-]democracies) also depends on the respective electorate. Again, Sweden is a case in point: The decline in disarmament proactivism was met with fierce opposition by civil society activists, who called on their government not to "sell" old traditions. Civil society also plays a stronger role in Iran than one might expect with regard to the semi-democratic system of government: This is obvious in the case of Iranian advocacy for the protection of chemical weapons victims. Iran's civil society continued to support its government's vehement and persistent commitment to a right to uranium enrichment, despite the economic plight Iran suffered as a result of nuclear sanctions.

9.1.3 Genuine Advocacy Versus Interest-Based Rhetorical Action

The latter point leads to another question that is subject to frequent discussion among norm scholars: The motivation for norm entrepreneurship (see Sect. 2.5). In purely analytical terms, scholars contrast interest-based with norm-driven motifs. In practice, however, the pursuit of interests and norm-based behavior is not mutually exclusive and actors usually act according to a mixture of both (Klotz 1995: 13; Müller 2004). Norms and interests are inseparably interwoven—a norm-based justification for action can result from genuine moral conviction and at the same time serve the pursuit of vested interest.

As discussed in Chap. 2.5, norm scholars nevertheless tend to portray norm entrepreneurs primarily as altruistic "do-gooders" driven by purely normative motives while neglecting the strategic aspects of their behavior as an explanatory factor (for exceptions, see Björkdahl 2002; Ingebritsen 2002; Bob 2012). By contrast, alleged "rogue states" are generally conceived as strategic actors who follow norms for purely instrumental reasons and as rhetorical covers for veiled interests at best in order to improve their position in the international system or to divert attention from own normative transgressions (e.g., Thränert 2003; Pirseyedi 2013). During my research, I was more than once confronted with such views on Iranian norm advocacy (an exception being the case of protection for victims of chemical weapons), especially in interviews with representatives of Western countries.

Some authors claim norm entrepreneurship to be genuine only in such cases in which norm-driven behavior runs counter to the pursuit of national interests (e.g., Goertz and Diehl 1992). This view conflicts not only with my view that norms and interests are in a dialectical relationship to each other. It is also disproved by my findings, which show that state-based norm entrepreneurship is always caught between national interests and normative motives.

At times, national interests prevented Iranian norm entrepreneurship in some cases. For instance, Iran abandoned its advocacy for a nuclear weapon-free zone in the Middle East when its partner Egypt announced its readiness to recognize Israel (see Chap. 7.3). Even the "strongest" case of Iranian norm entrepreneurship analyzed for this study, the advocacy for assistance and protection for victims of chemical weapons depict elements of norm opportunism when national interests are affected. This is underscored by Iran's unconditional backing of the Syrian government, notwithstanding its use of chemical weapons. It is with such political decisions that Iran reinforces doubts about the credibility and authenticity of its norm entrepreneurship. However, the case study on Sweden reveals a biased treatment when it comes to supposed "good international citizens" and normative outsiders to the international community: For prototypical, Western liberal norm entrepreneurs, a norm-based motivation seems to be the default option, while interest-based reasons for action receive less attention. For example, the norm advocacy of countries such as Canada, Germany, or Sweden in the control of weapons of mass destruction at times collides with their interest-based roles, e.g., within NATO or as arms exporters that set their activism clear limits.

It is also undeniable that Iran's advocacy for a right to uranium enrichment or nuclear disarmament also follows an interest-based rationale: First, advocacy in these cases matches ideological traditions and can therefore be used to level domestic conflicts for a common national cause ("nuclear rights"); second both normative endeavors are well received within the non-aligned countries and could be interpreted as a strategy to expand Iran's position within the group. Third, the norm advocacy could be interpreted as a way of prestige advertising and as a means of distracting attention from Iran's own normative defiance. Iran's advocacy of a right to uranium enrichment is probably the case which is most strongly related to the pursuit of material interests. At the same time, the advocacy is most strongly justified with perceptions of injustice and linked to the pursuit of the common good. And the advocacy also had disadvantages for Iran, since norm entrepreneurship is dependent on the allocation of resources. Particularly in the case of the right to uranium enrichment, norm advocacy inflicted massive costs on Iran: By insisting on and further developing indigenous enrichment capabilities, Iran not only maneuvered itself more and more into the role of an outsider of the international community, but also provoked a war that it could not have won. In addition, the sanctions imposed by the West caused immense damage to the Iranian economy. That Teheran was willing to bear these consequences can hardly be framed as the pursuit of national interests as conventionally understood.

Instead of assessing the authenticity of norm entrepreneurship by searching for interest-free motives, it seems more promising to evaluate a second criterion mentioned in the literature, namely the consistency of engagement. In all three cases, a high degree of continuity and consistency in word and deed could be observed across various forums and contexts as well as over time. This applies not only to the commitment itself, but also to the normative framings that were used. In particular, in all three cases, Iran referred to injustice frames: In its own understanding, Iran's advocacy for the construction or strengthening of norms also serves a broader objective, i.e., to overcome unjust structures and to create global justice. The literature on social movements has already emphasized the importance of injustice frames for the success of campaigns (Gamson 1992; Busby 2007). While much of this literature focuses on the strategic aspects of framing, recent research has shown that perceptions of (in-)justice are deeply rooted in the identities and beliefs of actors and that they should therefore be regarded as authentic (Müller and Wunderlich 2013; Müller 2013: 362). Various studies have pointed to the importance of justice as the driving force behind conflicting and cooperative behavior (Welch 1993; Albin 2001; Müller and Wunderlich 2013). Social psychological findings indicate that for many actors, justice takes on the status of "sacred value" (Atran and Axelrod 2008; Dehghani et al. 2010). Therefore, they are often unwilling to trade perceived claims to justice even if they are offered material incentives. Various authors also interpret the vehemence with which Iran adhered to its nuclear program, which entailed considerable costs for both its reputation and its economy, with reference to perceptions of injustice (Dehghani et al. 2010; Wunderlich et al. 2013; Wright and Sadjadpour 2014).

In this sense, Iran's consistent reference to injustice frames could also be seen as an indicator of the authenticity of Iran's norm entrepreneurship. At the same time, its credibility as a norm entrepreneur in the nuclear non-proliferation regime is at the least called into question by the contradiction between the demand for nuclear disarmament and the establishment of its own nuclear program. And injustice frames also serve Iran for blocking normative progress in other fields. The fact that Iran grounds its advocacy in the fight against injustice might actually compensate for its lack of moral integrity. Future research projects could further investigate how the attribution of moral authority (which is often seen as a characteristic of norm entrepreneurs; seminal Finnemore and Sikkink 1998: 898), and thus the success or failure of norm entrepreneurship, relate to (in-)justice framings used by the actors in question.

9.1.4 Reformist and Revolutionary Norm Entrepreneurship

The description of norm entrepreneurs as agents of social and normative change (Finnemore 1996: 5; Risse and Sikkink 1999: 5) indicates that they usually adopt an oppositional attitude to the current normative order, sometimes even expressly distance themselves from it and/or demand a more or less radical modification—in extreme cases even a departure from it. Consequently, norm entrepreneurship not only manifests in the construction, further development and stabilization of a normative order, but also in (active) resistance to it—a fact that has not yet been sufficiently reflected in norms research. Norm entrepreneurs should therefore be conceptualized not only as change agents, but above all as agents of contestation, who are characterized in particular by adopting an oppositional attitude to the current normative order, articulating dissatisfaction with it and formulating more or less radical alternatives to solving perceived grievances. Based on the findings of my study, I therefore propose a conceptual distinction between reformist and revolutionary norm entrepreneurs depending on their attitude vis-à-vis the prevailing normative order. Before the two types are discussed in detail, it seems appropriate to refer to a distinction between norm entrepreneurs and norm antipreneurs, a concept that has been introduced by Bloomfield (2016). Bloomfield defines norm antipreneurs as actors who seek to prevent the construction or diffusion of new norms (e.g., the R2P) by pushing competing foundational norms (such as sovereignty). Other authors have used the concept for actors who deliberately misinterpret emerging norms in order to sabotage them (Carpenter 2014). As such, antipreneurs are conceptualized in opposition to norm entrepreneurs, resisting the latter's claim that there is a normative problem in need of regulation or actively undermining the proposed norm candidate. Table 9.1 illustrates the distinction between norm entrepreneurs and antipreneurs.[2]

[2]These patterns of behavior represent ideal types that can hardly be found in pure form in reality. As already discussed, an actor can assume different roles simultaneously in relation to different norms or across policy fields.

Table 9.1 Distinction between norm entrepreneurs and norm antipreneurs

Role type	Pattern of behavior	Description
Norm antipreneur	Resistance to (emerging) norms	Actors who reject emerging norms and actively seek to prevent their diffusion by sabotaging or undermining them
Norm entrepreneur	Norm advocacy	Actors who are committed to a particular idea/norm which they deem to represent appropriate normative alternatives for improving the current normative order. Several norm entrepreneurial roles may be distinguished, depending on the phase of norm dynamics in which actors become active: *Norm initiators*: Actors who are committed to the construction of "new" standards of appropriateness *Norm keepers*: Actors who are committed to maintaining and strengthening existing norms *Norm enforcers*: Actors who are actively involved in processes of norm implementation (such as monitoring and further institutionalization) and who seek to ensure that contested norms do not lose validity, i.e., by upholding their meaning in the discourse or sanctioning norm-compliant behavior

Turning to the findings of my study, the comparison between the good international citizen Sweden and the norm advocacy of Iran suggests that the concept of norm entrepreneurship can be further differentiated in order to better capture its nuances. Obviously, norm advocacy is not only shown by "progressive" reformers working toward the steady evolution of normative structures. Actors who challenge the ruling normative order and seek to overthrow it or to lead it back to its "original" meaning can also act as (revolutionary) norm entrepreneurs. Table 9.2 presents a brief description and comparison of both types of norm entrepreneurs:

Reformist norm entrepreneurs are embedded in existing normative structures and hold an affirmative attitude toward the prevailing order. Within the international community, they are recognized as reputable actors who are granted participatory rights. Their advocacy is geared toward adapting the established order to changed external conditions. Normally, the change initiated by norm reformers is gradual and manifests itself in rather subtle shifts in meaning (Wunderlich et al. 2013: 246; Wunderlich

Table 9.2 Differences between reformist and revolutionary norm entrepreneurship

	Reformist norm entrepreneurship	Revolutionary norm entrepreneurship
Position within the ruling order	– Integrated – Recognized as a political actor	– Included/excluded/non-conformist – Not or only partially recognized as political actor
Overarching goal	Modification of the ruling order in the sense of adaption or a return of degenerated norm interpretations to originally intended meanings	Undermining the existing order with the aim of overthrowing the old one and establishing a new, alternative order that is clearly distinct from the established system
Direction of action	– Progressive, geared toward a more effective system, or – Restorative, in the direction of originally intended normative meanings	– Subversive, with the aim of undermining or overthrowing the ruling order
Means/strategies	– Recourse to prevailing "rules of the game" – Focus on persuasion strategies through the power of the better argument; less blaming than naming and shaming – Tendency to offer intermediary services to mediate between conflicting positions – Cooperation with a broad group of like-minded actors (states and civil society)	– Rejection or subversion of the "rules of the game" – Focus on countermeasures aimed at undermining the current order (e.g., counter-framing, norm transgressions, blaming, diplomatic blackmail strategies, etc.) – Willingness to rely on destructive and dissuasive strategies at the risk of damaging the prevailing order – Less cooperation with civil society
Modus operandi	– Willing to compromise, rather constructive	– Driven by an "absolute ethic" and therefore inclined to pursue radical policies; rather intransigent

2014: 89). However, the desired changes can also be large-scale with the objective to further differentiate existing norms in order to increase their effectiveness. Moreover, reformist norm entrepreneurship can also aim to return supposedly "degenerated" normative meanings to originally intended purposes.

In their actions, norm reformers resort to the "rules of the game." While aiming for an adaptation of existing norms, they have no interest in overthrowing the normative order as such. That is why they mainly use "affirmative" persuasion strategies. Although they clearly criticize perceived grievance, they are cautious when it comes to using aggressive naming, shaming, and blaming strategies, but instead tend to seek to mediate between conflicting positions. The organizational platforms that they select for their norm-promoting activities are entrenched within the normative status quo. Usually, norm reformers work together with a broad group of like-minded actors, both states and civil society. Their strategies are characterized by a compromise orientation, i.e., they are quite willing to forego maximum demands in favor of effective and sustainable solutions. In sum, my conceptualization of norm reformers largely corresponds to the list of criteria derived from the literature on norm entrepreneurship and as such embodies the prototype norm entrepreneur as described in mainstream norm studies.

In contrast to reformist norm entrepreneurs, *norm revolutionaries* generally do not locate themselves within the ruling order or are only insufficiently integrated into it.[3] They express their dissatisfaction with existing normative structures by strong and active resistance. In their view, a reform of current structures is insufficient as a means of solving existing problems. Instead, revolutionary norm entrepreneurs intend to dissolve the ruling normative order and establish a new one, including new or alternative norms. Revolutionary norm entrepreneurship might take the form of open rejection of the current rules of the system, for norm revolutionaries regard the status quo as unfair or discriminatory. Revolutionary norm entrepreneurs can also act subversively if they use the prevailing rules, but in the long term aim to undermine or overthrow the current system.[4]

Norm revolutionaries therefore prefer to resort to measures that are directed against current norms, e.g., they try to counteract the argumentative framings of norm keepers or bearers of the current order; they undermine negotiations through unsustainable accusations and aggressive blaming and shaming; and last but not least, they use diplomatic blackmail strategies or destructive tactics. They make particular use of the counter-strategies identified by Bob (2012; see also Sect. 4.1 of this work): In order to strengthen their position, they try above all to discredit their opponents and to question the legitimacy of the current normative order. They see norm transgressions as an effective means of demonstrating the inadequacy of the current order and as a means of undermining it.

Norm revolutionaries tend to work less closely with international civil society and—if at all—are more likely to seek cooperation with a selective group of like-minded actors. In pursuing their normative goals, they are less accommodating and resemble the type of the proselytizing "moral entrepreneur" according to Howard Becker, who can be regarded as a precursor of the prototypical norm entrepreneur.

[3]In a similar way, Christopher Daase and Nicole Deitelhoff distinguish oppositional and dissident forms of resistance. Both formulate political alternatives, but differ in whether they accept the ruling order and its participatory rules, as in the case of opposition, or whether they reject or deliberately exceed these rules, as in the case of dissidence (Daase and Deitelhoff 2014).

[4]Mahoney and Thelen (2010) use a similar distinction. In their explanation of institutional change, they distinguish between different types of actors (so-called "change agents") according to whether they basically want to preserve the existing institutions and adhere to the applicable rules. They differentiate between "insurrectionaries," "parasitic and mutualistic symbionts," "subversives" and "opportunists." However, since the present study was not about the explanation of institutional change, it does not make use of this distinction.

Driven by "absolute ethics," these actors regard their task as being a mission to restore justice and believe they are fighting for the only "true" cause (Becker 1963: 148).

Reformist norm entrepreneurs differ from the mere norm challengers or norm antipreneurs discussed in research on norm localization and contestation insofar as their actions are not purely reactive. Antipreneurs are understood as being actors opposed to attempts by prototypical norm entrepreneurs to establish or promote (predominantly Western liberal) norms because they perceive them to violate their interests (Prantl and Nakano 2011; Carpenter 2014; Bloomfield 2016) or endanger their autonomy (Acharya 2009, 2013). By contrast, revolutionary norm entrepreneurs not only react to other actors' efforts; they actively work to establish or promote new norms or normative meanings. Since the normative visions that are propagated by norm revolutionaries fundamentally differ from the prevailing normative order, their participatory rights in and access to decision-making processes are considerably curtailed or fully denied by the bearers of the ruling order. Therefore for norm revolutionaries, the overthrow of existing normative structures remains the only viable option for the promotion of their normative vision.

This distinction can be illustrated by the empirical cases analyzed in this study. Sweden corresponds to the image of a norm reformer in the field of multilateral arms control, whose aim is to change the nuclear non-proliferation regime within the current structures in order to strengthen it in terms of effectiveness. In her seminal study on conflict prevention, Annika Björkdahl similarly understands Sweden "as a reformist gradually reforming the normative context, rather than a radicalist transforming the existing normative framework" (Björkdahl 2002: 50). However, especially in the early years of Swedish disarmament commitment, its advocacy aimed at far more than gradual changes: Stockholm's goal was to level the difference between nuclear weapon states and non-nuclear weapon states. Although its activism went far beyond existing regime structures, the goal was not its overthrow, but a strengthening of the ruling order. In its behavior, Sweden is keeping in line with the rules of the system. And it was not least the Swedish commitment that prevented the frustration of some non-aligned non-nuclear weapon states with the inappropriate implementation of regime norms from turning into more radical, subversive opposition.

With regard to Iranian norm entrepreneurship, the picture is less clear-cut. Partly, Iran assumes the role of a reformist norm entrepreneur. This is particularly evident in the protection of victims of chemical weapons: Tehran acted within the current structures, and its commitment was geared toward their correction. Iran's weak norm entrepreneurship in nuclear disarmament and its fight for a right to uranium enrichment also display predominantly reformist elements. With regard to the case of the right to the peaceful uses of nuclear energy, Iran's reform efforts were less intended to adapt existing structures to external circumstances. Instead, the country propagates a norm interpretation which, in its view, reflects the originally intended meaning, but has been unlawfully restricted since the NPT was established (Wunderlich et al. 2013: 272; Wunderlich 2014: 95). In none of the analyzed cases has Iran attempted to overturn the current normative order in the respective policy field.

Elements of revolutionary norm entrepreneurship can be found above all in the confrontational strategies, the aggressive rhetoric, and the norm transgressions. Despite this, Iran's behavior has been and still is deeply entrenched within the normative order of the non-proliferation regime and the CWC. Its norm entrepreneurship is not aimed at overthrowing these regimes and establishing alternative orders, but rather at reforming them in the sense of the favored norm interpretations. In practice, however, this sometimes leads to Iran blocking progress: For example, in line with the NAM position, Tehran is vehemently opposed to strict export control measures since the country sees this as an illegitimate narrowing of its claims based on Article IV. Also, the persistent adherence to its own nuclear program has challenged the stability of the non-proliferation regime for years.

Evidently, the different types of norm entrepreneurship identified in this study are not mutually exclusive, but are to be understood as a continuum: Obviously, Iran's behavior in multilateral arms control is characterized by a more or less revolutionary attitude. Despite all revolutionary rhetoric and confrontational strategies, Iran is committed to the further development and strengthening of regime norms. At the same time, dissatisfaction with the current structures, which are perceived as unjust and discriminatory, prevents Tehran from making progress and lead it to embarking on revolutionary norm entrepreneurship.

The proposed conceptual distinction between reformist and revolutionary norm entrepreneurs complements research on norm contestation and further broadens the theoretical and conceptual toolbox of norms research. The distinction would not only pay tribute to the diversity of norm dynamics, it also allows disaggregating the complex process of norm dynamics further by identifying and describing more clearly the actors involved in the shaping and contestation of the normative world order. Of course, further studies are needed to prove and evaluate the analytical benefits that would come with the proposed distinction. For example, it would be interesting to examine to what extent the norm entrepreneurs considered in the literature so far correspond to the image of a norm reformer. It has already been mentioned that both types of norm entrepreneurship constitute ideal types and are to be understood as two poles on a spectrum of possible norm entrepreneurial roles. Presumably, the majority of norm advocacy and contestation that we see today does not constitute revolutionary norm entrepreneurship per se—in most cases, actors contest some of the norms (or their interpretations) in a given policy field rather than seeking to overthrow the entire normative order. Yet assessing to what extent an actor displays elements of revolutionary norm entrepreneurship instead of mere destructiveness might prove helpful when considering strategies of how to respond to the actor in question. Perhaps most importantly, including revolutionary norm entrepreneurs into their empirical focus allows norms researchers to transcend their bias on Western liberal do-gooders and theorize as to what extent contestation is a central tool/element of norm advocacy.

9.2 The Practical Consequences of Dealing with Alleged "Rogue States"

The results of this study suggest that "rogue states" can also be norm entrepreneurs and thus call into question the common perception of these states, both in the literature and in (USA) politics, as mere norm breakers and challengers of international norms. My findings thus confirm critical work on the "rogue states" concept, according to which the label is a social construct foremost used for strategic purposes (Herring 2000; de Graaff and van Apeldoorn 2011; Wagner et al. 2014; Wunderlich 2017). Alleged "rogue states" are only constructed through the act of labeling and do not exist independently of it. Ultimately, the concept has to be seen as an expression of the definitional power of a few hegemonic states, for whom it serves primarily to maintain the current Western liberal world order (Nincic 2005; Derrida 2006: 95; Geis and Wunderlich 2014; Kustermans 2014). In this way, the "rogue states" concept functions as an instrument for delegitimizing deviating normative visions and denying the bearers of these concepts agency. Being stigmatized as norm breaking "rogue states" is equivalent to being turned into outsiders of the international community—Daniel Jacobi, Gunther Hellmann, and Christian Weber therefore call terms such as "rogue state" as "discursive weapon" (Jacobi et al. 2014: 105). The labeling actors neither recognize the alternative normative visions as legitimate, nor do they grant the "villains" participatory rights. They stylize the challengers of the current order as "enemies" and brand them above all as a threat to world peace and international security.

It is with this respect that Müller (2014) discusses the "rogue states" concept in analogy to the concept of securitization as a form of "evilization." In the "rogue" of today, he sees a successor to Kant's "unjust enemy", whom the USA—bearer of the current liberal world order—has identified as an illiberal opponent and "evil" force in order to justify the use of extraordinary measures in dealing with these states.

Geis and Wunderlich (2014: 468) point to negative political consequences arising from the use of the "rogue states" concept: By labeling a state as a "rogue state," the labeling actor is already initiating a confrontation course that includes recourse to the preemptive use of military force and blocks possible alternative options for action. Such stigmatization may also lead to an escalation spiral of mutual demonization (Beeman 2005; Senn 2009).

The findings of this study furthermore warn against understanding "rogue states" as mere objects of hegemonic intervention. Instead, they should be perceived and analyzed as rational, norm-driven actors. Even if they act against established norms (such as human rights norms at home) in some policy fields, "rogue states" are in a position to change norms within the established normative structures, making use of classical strategies of norm entrepreneurs. Obviously, norm socialization literature is wrong in assuming that the reintegration of supposed "rogue states" into the international community is extremely unlikely, since being outsiders to the international community, they have no incentives to adhere to international standards of appropriateness (e.g., Flockhart 2004: 367). Or at least this assumption needs to be qualified.

Another conjecture, namely that "rogue states" have a low overall interaction capacity (e.g., Ogilvie-White 2007; Litwak 2012: 187), also cannot be maintained in the case of Iran. It is true that the country was excluded from certain contexts of cooperation by the international sanctions regime and the punitive measures associated with the alleged violations of norms. Nevertheless, it played an active role in the analyzed arms control regimes over the entire period of investigation and in some cases even acted as norm entrepreneur.

On the basis of these findings and the criticism that has been elaborated in Chap. 3, it seems apt to entirely abandon the "rogue state" concept. It neither has analytical benefits, nor has it generated the desired political effects. Geis and Wunderlich (2014) suggest using the term "rogue" for self-reflective purposes at best: Instead of applying the term selectively to certain states, they suggest that it should be used consistently for those states that have committed certain (previously defined) acts of deviance (see also Chomsky 2000: 1; Litwak 2000: 54; Thompson 2002; Derrida 2006: 113). For the authors of future studies, this requires a self-reflective insight that "roguishness" is inherent in every actor (Geis and Wunderlich 2014: 470). Violations of norms should therefore not per se lead to the exclusion of alleged "rogue states" from the international community (Thompson 2002: 4). This consequence is also suggested by insights of sociological research about deviant behavior, which warn against the difficulties of wanting to determine deviance on the basis of objective criteria: What the current normative order exactly looks like, and which moral imperatives follow from the mostly vague and ambiguous norms, is controversial even in national or local contexts (an insight that is also promoted by critical constructivist scholarship on norm contestation, see Wiener 2014). This applies all the more to the global level. Instead of confrontational policies, constructive policies that aim at revising hostile relationship patterns are needed in dealing with norm-deviating actors (Malici 2009: 50; Malici and Walker 2014: 146–147).

From the finding that "rogue states" can be norm entrepreneurs, it follows that on closer inspection the alleged "black sheep" turn out to be a "sheep in wolf's clothing"—at least in certain policy fields—that can be (re-)integrated into processes of norm diffusion. It is true that all states designated as "rogue states" are to various extents contesting the current normative order. In practice, however, the results of this study show that Iran in particular has a desire for integration and a political will to shape matters. Studies on norm acceptance by rebel groups (Jo and Bryant 2013; Herr 2015) have demonstrated that the longing for recognition can lead actors to adopt international norms. The purpose of this study was not to explain under which circumstances "rogue states" are prepared to accept international norms. Nevertheless, the findings suggest that the desire for recognition played a central role in Iran's (arms control) policies: Iran's commitment is to a great extent driven by the longing to overcome unfair global structures through promoting alternative norms or normative meanings. Norm scholars have indicated on several occasions that norm acceptance and the binding force of norms is higher the more inclusive the process of norm construction is considered to be (e.g., Acharya 2013: 468). Recognizing the norm entrepreneurial potential even of supposed "rogue states" is therefore both analytically and politically important, because it assigns ownership to these actors.

If the international community perceives their normative visions of order as being potentially worthy of recognition and discussion, there are also opportunities for integrating them into norm negotiation and deliberation processes. Only an international community that takes the plurality of normative positions seriously and tries to foster integrative solutions will be able to develop joint, future-oriented solutions to common problems. Such deliberation processes need to allow room for contradiction and contestation. Admittedly, this presupposes overcoming discriminatory practices and double standards in dealing with a plurality of actors.

Especially in the case of actors such as Iran, who seem to be torn between their role as reformist and revolutionary norm entrepreneurs, a strategy that seeks to integrate their commitment seems more promising than to exclude or confront them. Cooperation and the recognition of alternative normative concepts of order can possibly contribute to a strengthening of the reformist elements in the policies of these states, reversing revolutionary strategies and thus reducing their threat potential. This is even more so because their behavior is not solely driven by material interests and security considerations, but also by perceptions of injustice and the desire for recognition. Moreover, the role of an outcast attributed to "rogue states" is not necessarily a consequence of their alleged misconduct alone. It may also be the cause for hardened positions, as the case of North Korea illustrates.

It has to be noted, however, that the recognition and inclusion of alternative notions of order, which I have called for, do not imply that all kinds of norms (interpretations) propagated by these states should be accepted and adopted by mutual agreement. The fact that an actor acts as a norm entrepreneur in one or more policy fields does not mean that it assumes a role as a norm entrepreneur overall. This is illustrated, for example, by the downside of Swedish arms exports practices that are often insufficiently taken into account. Ultimately, Iran's credibility as a norm entrepreneur and its moral authority will be under discussion as long as Tehran has not unequivocally dispelled doubts about the peaceful nature of its nuclear program, continues to support terrorist organizations, and maintains its aggressive rhetoric toward Israel and America and human rights violations toward its domestic population.

I will end this section by illustrating these considerations with reference to the case of Iran: I have argued that Iran's normative claims are basically just as valid as those of other states and therefore must be taken seriously.

That Iran partly acts as norm entrepreneur and is involved in the construction and further development of norms has some political potential. In order to take advantage of these possibilities, the international community should acknowledge that Tehran is seeking to actively shape the normative order. In cases of convergence of interests, this insight can serve to appeal to Iran's norm entrepreneurial potential and to involve the country in norm-setting processes. This would not only be of benefit for substantial reasons, but it could also prevent Iran from falling into old patterns of hindering deliberation processes by means of offensive criticism and strategic maneuvering. The moderate political style of Iranian President Rouhani and the nuclear agreement reached in July 2015, through which Iran has expressed its willingness to dispel doubts about its military options, have created the necessary conditions for this. In fact, the current situation holds a particular opportunity to appeal to Iran's role as a norm entrepreneur: With the USA having withdrawn from the Iran nuclear deal in May 2018, the remaining EU3+2 have expressed their commitment to keeping the deal alive and to ensuring that Iran remains within the accord. An inclusive approach seems more necessary than ever. The Joint Comprehensive Plan of Action was proof that the nuclear non-proliferation regime is capable of dealing with challenges. The deal could be reached not only due to the sanctions regime imposed upon Iran, but also because all negotiating parties were prepared to take the normative claims of their opponents (in the case of Iran, the right to uranium enrichment) seriously.

A central finding of norm research is that states that refer to their rhetoric and practice to norms can be obliged to conform to them. After all, a state's reputation within the international community is (also) assessed on the basis of whether words are followed by deeds. Recognizing Iran's potential as a norm entrepreneur therefore offers an opportunity to gauge the country against its own normative standards.

9.3 Avenues for Further Research

The study has demonstrated that it may be fruitful to apply the concept of norm entrepreneurship to cases that have not been considered to date. The counterintuitive assumption that "rogue states," i.e., alleged norm breakers, can commit themselves to norm promotion holds innovative potential both theoretically and for practical purposes. Nevertheless, the question arises to what extent the findings presented here can be generalized. That the transferability of the concept could be proven by applying it to an extreme case suggests that it can also be applied to other unorthodox and previously unconsidered types of actors. Yet this assumption remains to be confirmed in future studies.

Moreover, the study focused on one policy field only. It would therefore be interesting to investigate whether the alleged "rogue state" of Iran is acting as a norm entrepreneur in other policy fields as well. It would be particularly interesting to focus on "softer" policy fields in which norm entrepreneurship does not directly affect national interests—e.g., protection of the environment.

At the same time, the comparison with North Korea shows that not every ("rogue") state acts as a norm entrepreneur. In order to be able to arrive at further qualifications, it would be interesting to analyze whether the behavior of some of the other states designated as "rogues" by the USA qualifies as norm entrepreneur. Such an analysis could answer the question under which circumstances these states act as mere norm destroyers and when they act as reformist or revolutionary norm entrepreneurs respectively. Recent work on deviance (most recently Smetana 2019; Wagner et al. 2014) and dissidence (Daase and Deitelhoff 2014) as well as on the "dynamics of dissent" (see the special issue edited by Stimmer and Wisken 2019) in IR present interesting connecting factors. For example, Jacobi et al. (2014) analyze the foreign policy of dissident states (including alleged "rogue states") from the perspective of whether these actors distance themselves from the current normative order ("isolation"), seek to overthrow it ("revolution") or aim at "antihegemonic integration".

I have argued that differentiating between reformist and revolutionary norm entrepreneurship holds particular analytical value and could improve the understanding of complex processes of norm dynamics and the actors involved. However, further studies are needed to confirm and further differentiate the analytical benefits of such a distinction. It would be helpful if the catalog of criteria developed in this work were used to identify (and verify) supposed norm entrepreneurs in order to prevent the concept in question from degenerating into an inconsistent collective term for a large number of actors with above-average commitment. Subsequently, it would have to be examined to what extent the norm entrepreneurs previously considered in the literature correspond to the image of the norm reformer. My findings also indicate that norm entrepreneurship can manifest itself in various forms. However, the exact differences between weak, moderate, and strong norm entrepreneurship were not a central concern of this study and should therefore be specified in further comparative studies using the catalog of criteria developed here.

Moreover, norm researchers could analyze other previously unconsidered types of actors by drawing on the catalog of criteria developed here, especially those that distinguish themselves from the current international system or are excluded from it.[5] A variety of interesting actors is conceivable here, including rising powers such as China, Brazil, or India or other challengers of the current order such as Russia, which are perceived as being dissatisfied with the current order, particularly by power transition theorists (Organski 1958; Tammen et al. 2000). In recent years, non-state actors have come to the fore as challengers of the normative order, including groups of organized crime and terrorist networks such as al-Qaeda and Daesh. If it emerges that some of these actors can be described as norm entrepreneurs, it would have to be clarified whether their behavior corresponds to the mode of reformist or revolutionary norm entrepreneurship.

Such a broadening of perspectives could help to link the literature on norm entrepreneurship and norm contestation/resistance more closely by more clearly identifying the differences between the respective types of actors (and the transitions between them). While initial attempts to broaden the range of possible norm entrepreneurs to include non-liberal/illiberal or unorthodox norm advocates are being made, these efforts so far lack conceptual precision. Only if the identification of norm entrepreneurship were to rest on the same analytical framework would a comparison of prototypical and unorthodox actors gain analytical value. Broadening the array of norm entrepreneurs to include actors from the global South and illiberal norm advocates is a much-needed step to further mitigate "tendencies of West-centrism and elitism in norm diffusion scholarship" (Dunford 2016: 163).

This in turn would make it possible to gain more generalizable insights about the nature of norm advocacy. A comparison between unorthodox and prototypical norm entrepreneurs may reveal insights into which characteristics are actually of a defining nature for the concept and which are only concomitant. Possibly, such accompanying characteristics are decisive for the success or failure of norm entrepreneurship or have

---

[5] In addition, countries of the global South or "failed states" have so far not sufficiently been considered as state norm entrepreneurs.

an effect on the phase in which norm entrepreneurship occurs. Is moral authority an accompanying characteristic, explaining success, or is it the strategies used or the credibility attributed to actors from outside?

From my findings, further interesting questions arise, e.g., whether and under what conditions reformist entrepreneurship can change into revolutionary norm entrepreneurship. This in turn raises the question of how to deal with norm revolutionaries without risking them breaking completely with the existing order. Under what conditions do revolutionary norm entrepreneurs leave their subversive path toward a more reformist course? Are revolutionary norm entrepreneurs possibly more inclined to use violence to achieve their goals? It would also be relevant for research to examine what conditions have to be met in order for norm entrepreneurship to remain peaceful (see also Checkel 2012). Answers to these questions would also be of practical use in dealing with challengers to the current system. In this context, the question of the relationship between norm entrepreneurship and the willingness to use violence is particularly interesting, because it raises the issue of the limits of the concept of norm entrepreneurs: Does resorting to violence disqualify an actor from being labeled a norm entrepreneur?

My findings also provide a starting point for responding to Charlotte Epstein's (2012b: 144) call for a research program on the diffusion and socialization of less desirable norms. My work shows that a dichotomous juxtaposition of "good" (Western liberal) and "bad" (alternative) norms is not tenable. Instead, norms are desirable per se from the perspective of the respective norm advocates (Finnemore and Sikkink 1998: 892). Consequently, norm researchers must acknowledge and tolerate that the concepts they shape can also be applied to actors whose normative visions contradict their own ideas. As a corollary, the subjects of inquiry should comprise the dissemination and strengthening of all sorts of norms: those that are considered "progressive" from a Western liberal perspective, but also their normative counterparts and what in their view may constitute "less appropriate" standards of behavior.

As the opening quotation of this study emphasizes, it is indispensable for a comprehensive understanding of norm dynamics not only to grasp the norm entrepreneurship of "do-gooders" such as Mother Theresa or Gandhi. The devastating normative visions of such actors as Hitler, Osama bin Laden, or terrorist groups from an analytical perspective also constitute attempts to universalize their own normative visions and standards of appropriateness.[6]

Of course, this is not meant to justify these attitudes. Demanding a certain analytical openness does not mean that researchers should give up their normativity. Each researcher is free to disclose his or her own normative attitude and in this way take a position on their subject of analysis.[7]

[6]One could object that, according to the criteria for norm entrepreneurship, there must always be a common good orientation. However, what constitutes the common good is in itself a highly subjective question and up to the perspective of the respective norm entrepreneur.

[7]Some authors argue that scholars should adopt an explicit normative attitude to ethical and moral questions. For example, Price (2008), calls on his colleagues to be transparent on what they understand by "morally desirable progress" and provide normative recommendations for action based on their research findings. Above all, he calls on them to disclose their evaluation criteria (Price

This outlook on avenues for further research has shown that the application of the concept of norm entrepreneurship to unorthodox actors and the distinction between reformist and revolutionary norm entrepreneurs raise follow-up questions. The answers to these questions might help clarify whether there may be "sheep in wolf's clothing" behind alleged "black sheep" who, despite all resistant rhetoric, selectively act as norm entrepreneurs. Ultimately, norm entrepreneurship is a political undertaking whose complexity far exceeds the altruistic motivation that has long been assumed to be the sole driving force behind the concept in the past.

References

Acharya, A. (2009). *Whose ideas matter? Agency and power in Asian regionalism*. Ithaca, NY: Cornell University Library.

Acharya, A. (2013). The R2P and norm diffusion. Towards a framework of norm circulation. *Global Responsibility to Protect, 5*(4), 466–479.

Adamson, F. (2005). Global liberalism versus political Islam: Competing ideological frameworks in international politics. *International Studies Review, 7*(4), 547–569.

Adler-Nissen, R. (2014). Stigma management in international relations: Transgressive identities, norms, and order in international society. *International Organization, 68*(1), 143–176.

Albin, C. (2001). *Justice and fairness in international negotiation*. Cambridge: Cambridge University Press.

Atran, S., & Axelrod, R. (2008). In theory: Reframing sacred values. *Negotiation Journal, 24*(3), 221–246.

Becker, H. (1963). *The outsiders. Studies in the sociology of deviance*. New York, NY: The Free Press.

Becker, U., Müller, H., & Wisotzki, S. (2008). Democracy and nuclear arms control—Destiny or ambiguity? *Security Studies, 17*(4), 810–854.

Becker-Jakob, U., Hofmann, G., Müller, H., & Wunderlich, C. (2013). Good international citizens: Canada, Germany and Sweden. In H. Müller & C. Wunderlich (Eds.), Norm dynamics in multilateral arms control, interests, conflicts, and justice (pp. 207–245). Athens, GA: University of Georgia Press.

Beeman, W. O. (2005). *The "Great Satan" vs. the "Mad Mullahs": How the United States and Iran demonize each other*. Chicago, IL: University of Chicago Press.

Bettiza, G., & Dionigi, F. (2014). *Beyond constructivism's liberal bias: Islamic norm entrepreneurs in a post-secular world society*. EUI Working Paper MWP 2014/10. http://cadmus.eui.eu/bitstream/handle/1814/31692/MWP_WP_Bettiza_Dionigi_2014_10.pdf?sequence=1. Accessed April 28, 2017.

Björkdahl, A. (2002). *From idea to norm: Promoting conflict prevention*. Lund: Lund University.

Bloomfield, A. (2016). Norm antipreneurs and theorizing resistance to normative change. *Review of International Studies, 42*(2), 310–333.

Bob, C. (2012). *The global right wing and the clash of world politics*. New York, NY: Cambridge University Press.

Busby, J. (2007). Bono Made Jesse Helms cry: Jubilee 2000, debt relief, and moral action in international politics. *International Studies Quarterly, 51*(2), 247–275.

2008: 3, 49). I take the view that norm entrepreneurship that serves to be supported stops where the implementation of the propagated norms can only be achieved through massive bloodshed. Such actors in my opinion forfeit any moral authority and thus legitimacy.

Carpenter, C. (2014). *"Norm Antipreneurship" and Russia's [Reported] use of autonomous weapons*. Resource Document. Duck of Minerva. http://duckofminerva.com/2014/04/norm-antipreneurship-and-russian-use-of-autonomous-weapons.html. Accessed April 28, 2017.

Checkel, J. (2012). Norm entrepreneurship—Theoretical and methodological challenges. Memo prepared for a workshop on *"The Evolution of International Norms and 'Norm Entrepreneurship": The Council of Europe in Comparative Perspective*. Oxford: Wolfson College, Oxford University.

Chomsky, N. (2000). *Rogue states: The rule of force in world affairs*. Cambridge, MA: South End Press.

Daase, C., & Deitelhoff, N. (2014). *Reconstructing global rule by analyzing resistance* (Internationale Dissidenz Working Paper 1/2014). Resource Document. Internationale Dissidenz Working Paper. http://dissidenz.net/wp-content/uploads/2013/03/wp1–2014-daase-deitelhoff-en.pdf. Accessed April 28, 2017.

De Graaff, N., & van Apeldoorn, B. (2011). Varieties of US post-cold war imperialism: Anatomy of a failed hegemonic project and the future of US geopolitics. *Critical Sociology, 37*(4), 403–427.

Dehghani, M., Atran, S., Iliev, R., Sachdeva, S., Medin, D., & Ginges, J. (2010). Sacred values and conflict over Iran's nuclear program. *Judgment and Decision Making, 5*(7), 540–546.

Derrida, J. (2006). *Schurken. Zwei Essays über die Vernunft*. Frankfurt am Main: Suhrkamp.

Dunford, R. (2016). Peasant activism and the rise of food sovereignty: Decolonising and democratising norm diffusion? *European Journal of International Relations, 23*(1), 145–167.

Epstein, C. (2012a). Stop telling us how to behave: Socialization or infantilization? *International Studies Perspectives, 13*(2), 135–145.

Epstein, C. (2012b). Symposium: Interrogating the use of norms in international relations. An introduction. *International Studies Perspectives, 13*(2), 121–122.

Fey, M., Melamud, A., & Müller, H. (2014). The role of justice in compliance behavior. Germany's early membership in the nuclear non-proliferation regime. *International Negotiations, 19*(3), 459–486.

Finnemore, M. (1996). *National interests in international society*. Ithaca, NY: Cornell University Press.

Finnemore, M., & Sikkink, K. (1998). International norm dynamics and political change. *International Organization, 52*(4), 887–917.

Flockhart, T. (2004). "Masters and Novices": Socialization and social learning through the NATO Parliamentary Assembly. *International Relations, 18*(3), 361–380.

Gamson, W. (1992). The social psychology of collective action. In A. Morris, & C. Mc Clurg Mueller (Ed.), *Frontiers in social movement theory* (pp. 3–76). New Haven, CT: Yale University Press.

Geis, A., & Wunderlich, C. (2014). The good, the bad, and the ugly. Comparing the notions of "rogue" and "evil" in international politics. *International Politics, 51*(4), 458–474.

Goertz, G., & Diehl, P. (1992). Toward a theory of international norms: Some conceptual and measurement issues. *The Journal of Conflict Resolution, 36*(4), 634–664.

Hamilton, D. (2008). *The United States: A normative power?* Working Document 291/2008. Centre for European Policy Studies CEPS. http://aei.pitt.edu/9320/2/9320.pdf. Accessed April 28, 2017.

Hanson, M. (2012). Advocating the elimination of nuclear weapons: The role of key individual and coalition states. In T. Ogilvie-White & D. Santoro (Eds.), *Slaying the nuclear dragon. Disarmament dynamics in the twenty-first century* (pp. 56–84). Athens, GA: University of Georgia Press.

Herr, S. (2015). Nichtstaatliche Gewaltakteure und das Humanitäre Völkerrecht. SPLM/A und LTTE im Vergleich, Studien der Hessischen Stiftung Friedens- und Konfliktforschung (Bd.29), Baden-Baden: Nomos.

Herring, Eric. (2000). Rogue rage: Can we prevent mass destruction? *Journal of Strategic Studies, 23*(1), 188–212.

Ingebritsen, C. (2002). Norm entrepreneurs: Scandinavia's role in world politics. *Cooperation and Conflict, 37*(1), 11–23.

Jacobi, D., Weber, C., & Hellmann, G. (2014). Dissident foreign policy and the (re-)production of international orders. In W. Wagner, W. Werner, & M. Onderco (Eds.), *Deviance in international relations: "Rogue states" and international security* (pp. 106–131). Basingstoke: Palgrave Macmillan.

Jo, H., & Bryant, K. (2013). Taming of the warlords: Commitment and compliance. In T. Risse, S. Ropp, & K. Sikkink (Eds.), *The persistent power of human rights: From commitment to compliance* (pp. 239–258). New York, NY: Cambridge University Press.

Kenyon, I., & Mashhadi, H. (2007). Helping those threatened or attacked: Article X. In I. Kenyon & D. Feakes (Eds.), *The creation of the organisation for the prohibition of chemical weapons: A case study in the birth of an intergovernmental organisation.*

Klotz, A. (1995). *Norms in international relations: The struggle against Apartheid*. Ithaca, NY: Cornell University Press.

Kustermans, J. (2014). "Roguery" and citizenship. In W. Wagner, W. Werner, & M. Onderco (Eds.), *Deviance in international relations: "Rogue states" and international security* (pp. 15–35). Basingstoke: Palgrave Macmillan.

Litwak, R. (2000). *Rogue states and U.S. foreign policy: Containment after the cold war.* Washington, DC: Woodrow Wilson Center Press with Johns Hopkins University Press.

Litwak, R. (2012). *Outlier states: American strategies to change, contain, or engage regimes*. Washington, DC: Woodrow Wilson Center Press with Johns Hopkins University Press.

Mahoney, J., & Thelen, K. (2010). *Explaining institutional change: Ambiguity, agency and power*. New York: Cambridge University Press.

Malici, A. (2009). Rogue states: Enemies of our own making? *Psicología Política, 39,* 39–54.

Malici, A., & Walker, S. G. (2014). Role theory and "rogue states". In W. Wagner, W. Werner, & M. Onderco (Eds.), *Deviance in international relations: "Rogue states" and international security* (pp. 132–151). Basingstoke: Palgrave Macmillan.

Müller, H. (2004). Arguing, bargaining and all that. Communicative action, rationalist theory and the logic of appropriateness in international relations. *European Journal of International Relations, 10*(3), 395–435.

Müller, H. (2013). Conclusion: Agency is central. In H. Müller & C. Wunderlich (Eds.), *Norm dynamics in multilateral arms control, interests, conflicts, and justice* (pp. 337–366). Athens, GA: University of Georgia Press.

Müller, H. (2014). Evilization in liberal discourse. From Kant's "unjust enemy" to today's "rogue state". *International Politics, 51*(4), 475–491.

Müller, H., & Wunderlich, C. (2013). *Norm dynamics in multilateral arms control, interests, conflicts, and justice*. Athens, GA: University of Georgia Press.

Nincic, M. (2005). *Renegade regimes: Confronting deviant behavior in world politics*. New York, NY: Columbia University Press.

Ogilvie-White, T. (2007). International responses to Iranian Nuclear Defiance: The non-aligned movement and the issue of non-compliance. *European Journal of International Law, 18*(3), 453–476.

Organski, A. F. K. (1958). *World politics*. New York: Knopf.

Pirseyedi, B. (2013). *Arms Control and Iranian Foreign Policy: Diplomacy of Discontent*. New York, NY: Routledge.

Prantl, J., & Nakano, R. (2011). Global norm diffusion in East Asia: How China and Japan implement the responsibility to protect. *International Relations, 25*(2), 204–223.

Price, R. (2008). Moral limit and possibility in world politics. In R. Price (Ed.), *Moral limit and possibility in world politics* (pp. 1–52). Cambridge: Cambridge University Press.

Risse, T., & Sikkink, K. (1999). The socialization of international human rights norms into domestic practices: Introduction. In T. Risse, S. C. Ropp & K. Sikkink (Eds.), *The power of human rights: From commitment to compliance* (pp. 1–38). Cambridge: Cambridge University Press.

Senn, M. (2009). *Wolves in the woods: The rogue state concept from a constructivist perspective*. Baden-Baden: Nomos.

Shaker, M. I. (1980). *The nuclear non-proliferation treaty: Origin and implementation 1959–1979* (vol. 1–3). London.

Smetana, M. (2019). *Nuclear deviance stigma politics and the rules of the nonproliferation game*. Basingstoke: Palgrave Macmillan.

Smetana, M. (2020). *Nuclear deviance stigma politics and the rules of the nonproliferation game.* Basingstoke: Palgrave Macmillan (forthcoming).

Stimmer, A., & Wisken, L. (2019). The dynamics of dissent: When actions are louder than words. *International Affairs, 9583*, 515–533.

Tammen, R., Kugler, J., Lemke, D., Stamm, A. C., Abdollahian, M., Alsharabati, C., et al. (2000). *Power transitions: Strategies for the 21st century*. New York: Seven Bridges Press.

Thompson, J. (2002). *Is there such a thing as a rogue state?* Working Paper, 2002(8). Centre for Applied Philosophy and Public Ethics.

Thränert, O. (2003). *Der Iran und die Verbreitung von ABC-Waffen*. Berlin: SWP-Studie.

Towns, A. (2012). Norms and social hierarchies: Understanding international policy diffusion "from Below". *International Organization, 66*(2), 179–209.

Wagner, W., Werner, W., & Onderco, M. (Eds.). (2014). *Deviance in international relations: "Rogue States" and international security*. Basingstoke: Palgrave Macmillan.

Welch, D. (1993). *Justice and the genesis of war*. Cambridge: Cambridge University Press.

Widmaier, W., & Park, S. (2012). Differences beyond theory. Structural, strategic, and sentimental approaches to normative change. *International Studies Perspectives, 13*(2), 123–134.

Wiener, A. (2014). *A theory of contestation*. Berlin/Heidelberg: Springer Briefs in Political Science.

Wright, N., & Sadjadpour, K. (2014). What neuroscience can teach us about making a deal with Iran. *The Atlantic*. http://www.theatlantic.com/international/archive/2014/01/the-neuroscience-guide-to-negotiations-with-iran/282963/. Accessed April 28, 2017.

Wunderlich, C. (2013). Theoretical approaches in the study of norms. In H. Müller & C. Wunderlich (Eds.), *Norm dynamics in multilateral arms control: Interests, conflicts, and justice* (pp. 20-47). Athens, GA: University of Georgia Press.

Wunderlich, C. (2014). A "Rogue" gone norm entrepreneurial? Iran within the nuclear nonproliferation regime. In W. Wagner, W. Werner, & M. Onderco (Eds.), *Deviance in international relations: "Rogue states" and international security* (pp. 83–104). Basingstoke: Palgrave Macmillan.

Wunderlich, C. (2017). Delegitimisation à la Carte: The "rogue state" label as a means of stabilising order in the nuclear non-proliferation regime. In S. Gertheiss, S. Herr, K. Wolf, & C. Wunderlich (Eds.), *Resistance and change in world politics: International dissidence* (pp. 143–189). Cham: Palgrave Macmillan.

Wunderlich, C., Hellmann, A., Müller, D., Reuter, J., & Schmidt, H.-J. (2013). Non-aligned reformers and revolutionaries. Egypt, South Africa, Iran, and North Korea. In H. Müller & C. Wunderlich (Eds.), *Norm dynamics in multilateral arms control, interests, conflicts, and justice* (pp. 246–295). Athens, GA: University of Georgia Press.

MIX
Papier aus verantwortungsvollen Quellen
Paper from responsible sources
FSC® C105338

If you have any concerns about our products,
you can contact us on
ProductSafety@springernature.com

In case Publisher is established outside the EU,
the EU authorized representative is:
Springer Nature Customer Service Center GmbH
Europaplatz 3, 69115 Heidelberg, Germany

Printed by Libri Plureos GmbH
in Hamburg, Germany